NAGASAKI

NAGASAKI

LIFE

AFTER

NUCLEAR

WAR

SUSAN SOUTHARD

VIKING

VIKING

An imprint of Penguin Random House LLC
375 Hudson Street
New York, New York 10014
penguin.com

ISBN 978-0-670-02562-6

Printed in the United States of America
1   3   5   7   9   10   8   6   4   2

Set in Sabon LT Std
Designed by Alissa Rose Theodor

For hibakusha *in Nagasaki, Hiroshima, and across the world*

For my parents, Gary and Sue

For Eva—and generations beyond

CONTENTS

JAPAN TODAY

EAST ASIA, 1945

Lake Baikal

USSR

Sakhalin

MONGOLIA

Manchuria
(Manchukuo)

Kuril Islands

Beijing

KOREA

Seoul

Sea of Japan

JAPAN

Tokyo

CHINA

Shanghai

Nagasaki

Korea Strait

Pacific Ocean

Taipei

Ryukyu Islands

Hong Kong

TAIWAN

VIETNAM

Hainan

Philippines

RUSSIA

Hokkaido

Sapporo

Sea of Japan

Fukushima

Honshu

SOUTH
KOREA

Tokyo

Lake Biwa

Kyoto

Nagoya

Hiroshima

Osaka

Yokohama

Tsushima

Korea Strait

Sasebo

Gotō
Islands

Shikoku

Nagasaki

Kitakyushu
(formerly Kokura)

Kagoshima

Kyushu

Pacific Ocean

0 Miles   300

0 Kilometers   300

© 2015 Jeffrey L. Ward

NAGASAKI 1945: Scope of Atomic Bomb Damage

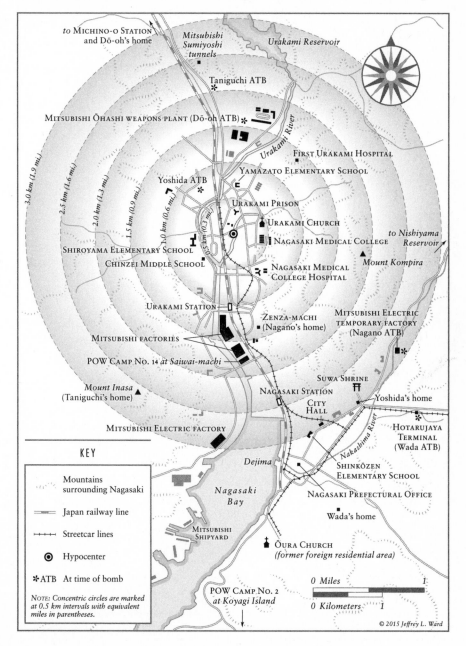

to MICHINO-O STATION and Dō-oh's home

Mitsubishi Sumiyoshi tunnels

Urakami Reservoir

Taniguchi ATB

MITSUBISHI ŌHASHI WEAPONS PLANT (Dō-oh ATB)

FIRST URAKAMI HOSPITAL

YAMAZATO ELEMENTARY SCHOOL

Yoshida ATB

URAKAMI PRISON

3.0 km (1.9 mi.)
2.5 km (1.6 mi.)
2.0 km (1.3 mi.)
1.5 km (0.9 mi.)
1.0 km (0.6 mi.)
0.5 km (0.3 mi.)

URAKAMI CHURCH

NAGASAKI MEDICAL COLLEGE

to Nishiyama Reservoir

SHIROYAMA ELEMENTARY SCHOOL

CHINZEI MIDDLE SCHOOL

NAGASAKI MEDICAL COLLEGE HOSPITAL

Mount Kompira

URAKAMI STATION

ZENZA-MACHI (Nagano's home)

MITSUBISHI ELECTRIC TEMPORARY FACTORY (Nagano ATB)

MITSUBISHI FACTORIES

POW CAMP NO. 14 at Saiwai-machi

SUWA SHRINE

Mount Inasa (Taniguchi's home)

NAGASAKI STATION

CITY HALL

Yoshida's home

MITSUBISHI ELECTRIC FACTORY

Urakami River
Nakashima River

HOTARUJAYA TERMINAL (Wada ATB)

KEY

Dejima

SHINKŌZEN ELEMENTARY SCHOOL

⋰ Mountains surrounding Nagasaki

Nagasaki Bay

NAGASAKI PREFECTURAL OFFICE

Wada's home

═ Japan railway line

+++ Streetcar lines

◉ Hypocenter

MITSUBISHI SHIPYARD

ŌURA CHURCH (former foreign residential area)

✳ATB At time of bomb

NOTE: Concentric circles are marked at 0.5 km intervals with equivalent miles in parentheses.

POW CAMP NO. 2 at Kōyagi Island

0 Miles 1

0 Kilometers 1

© 2015 Jeffrey L. Ward

PREFACE

In the summer of 1986, I received a last-minute call asking me to step in as a substitute interpreter for Taniguchi Sumiteru, a fifty-seven-year-old survivor of the 1945 Nagasaki atomic bombing. Taniguchi was in Washington, D.C., as part of a speaking tour in the United States. I had just met him the night before when I attended one of his talks. Over the next two days, I spent more than twenty hours with Taniguchi, listening to and interpreting his story in public presentations and private conversations.

Years earlier I had lived in Yokohama, just south of Tokyo, as an international scholarship student. At sixteen, I was placed with a traditional Japanese family and attended an all-girls high school in the neighboring city of Kamakura, Japan's ancient capital. Nearly everything was foreign to me, including the language—and I had little knowledge of the Pacific War and the atomic bombings that had taken place thirty years earlier. Later that year, after my language skills and integration into Japanese life had improved, I traveled to Nagasaki for the first time during my high school's senior class trip to southern Japan. Inside the Nagasaki Atomic Bomb Museum, I stood arm in arm with friends who had embraced me as their own, staring at photographs of burned adults and children and the crushed and melted household items on display. In one of the glass cases, a helmet still had the charred flesh of a person's scalp stuck inside.

The memory of Nagasaki stayed with me into adulthood. And yet, as I listened to Taniguchi speak in a dimly lit church hall near downtown D.C., I realized how ignorant I still was of the history of the Pacific War, the development of the atomic bombs, and the human consequences of their use.

Taniguchi was sharply dressed in a gray suit, a white dress shirt, and a deep purple and navy striped tie. On his left lapel he wore a pin—a white origami crane set against a red background. His thick black hair was combed neatly to the side. Small—maybe five foot six—and noticeably thin, he told his story quietly, the syllables toppling one upon another: At 11:02 a.m. on August 9, 1945, sixteen-year-old Taniguchi was on his bicycle delivering mail in the northwestern section of the city when a plutonium bomb fell from the sky and exploded over a Nagasaki neighborhood of about thirty thousand residents. "In the flash of the explosion," he said, his voice trembling, "I was blown off the bicycle from behind and slapped down against the ground. The earth seemed to shiver like an earthquake." Although he was over a mile away, the extraordinary heat of the bomb torched Taniguchi's back. After a few moments, he lifted his head to see that the children who had been playing near him were dead.

As he spoke, Taniguchi held up a photograph of himself taken five months after the blast during his protracted stay at a hospital north of Nagasaki. In the photograph he is lying on his stomach, emaciated. Down one arm and from neck to buttocks where his back would be, there is no skin or flesh, only exposed muscle and tissue, raw and red. As Taniguchi finished his speech, he made eye contact with his audience for the first time. "Let there be no more Nagasakis," he appealed. "I call on you to work together to build a world free of nuclear weapons."

After his presentation, I drove Taniguchi to the small house outside of D.C. where he was staying. We sat on the front porch; the light from the front hallway allowed us to see each other only in shadow. I plied Taniguchi with questions about the bombing and the weeks, months, and years that followed. He handed me a small stack of photos that resembled mug shots—medical photos, I presumed—full-body back, front, and side views. They showed Taniguchi, perhaps in his forties, naked except for his traditional Japanese undergarment. His entire back was a mass of rubbery keloid scars. Near the center of his chest, deep indentations still remained where his skin and flesh had rotted, the result of lying on his stomach for nearly four years. It was a time, he told me, when the pain was so excruciating that every day he had begged the nurses to let him die. I asked Taniguchi which memories from his life were most important to him. "Just that I lived," he said. "That I have lived this long. I have sadness and struggle that goes with being alive, but I went to the very last edge of life, so I feel joy in the fact that I'm here, now."

By the time Taniguchi left Washington, I longed to more fully under-stand what it took for him and others to live day by day in the face of acute physical pain, psychological trauma, and a personal history split in half by nuclear war. What kinds of radiation-related injuries did they experience, and what did survival look like in the days, months, and years that followed the attack? And how was it that I, who had lived in Japan and had been educated in excellent public high schools and uni-versities in the United States, had no specific knowledge about the survi-vors of the atomic bombings? Why do most Americans know little or nothing about the victims' experiences beneath the atomic clouds or in the years since 1945?

———

As single weapons, the atomic bombs used against Japan were unmatched in their explosive force, intense heat, and ability to cause instantaneous mass death. Radiation doses larger than any human had ever received penetrated the bodies of people and animals, causing cellular changes that led to death, disease, and life-altering medical conditions. More than 200,000 men, women, and children died from the Hiroshima and Naga-saki attacks—either at the time of the bombings or over the next five months from their wounds or acute radiation exposure. In the years that followed, tens of thousands more suffered from injury and radiation-related diseases. An estimated 192,000 *hibakusha* (atomic bomb–affected people—pronounced *hee-bakh-sha*) are still alive today. The youngest, exposed in utero to the bombs' radiation, will turn seventy in August 2015.

Many critically acclaimed books have addressed the United States' decision to use the bomb, but few have featured the eyewitness accounts of atomic bomb survivors. Those that have, such as John Hersey's *Hiro-shima* and several collections of *hibakusha* testimonies, focus almost exclusively on the immediate aftermath of the bombings; stories detail-ing the brutal long-term physical, emotional, and social manifestations of nuclear survival have rarely been told. As the second city bombed, Nagasaki is even less known than Hiroshima, which quickly became the global symbol of the atomic bombings of Japan. The invisibility of Na-gasaki is so extreme that "the bomb" is often expressed as a singular event for both cities, without regard for the fact that the two atomic bombings were separated by time, geography, and the need for distinct analysis of military necessity.

Many Americans' perceptions of the atomic bombings are infused with inaccurate assumptions—in large part because the grave effects of whole-body radiation exposure were categorically denied by high-level U.S. officials. For years after the attacks, news accounts, photographs, scientific research, and personal testimonies of nuclear survival were both censored in Japan by U.S. occupation forces and restricted in the United States by government request. U.S. officials also constructed and promoted an effective but skewed narrative defending the decision to drop the bombs on Hiroshima and Nagasaki. Most Americans, relieved that the war was over, easily accepted the government's simplified message that the bombings had ended the war and saved a quarter of a million, half a million, or a million American lives. With wartime propaganda in both nations depicting the enemy as subhuman, and with Americans' fury over Pearl Harbor, Japan's mistreatment and killings of Allied POWs, and its slaughter of civilians across Asia, a common American response to the atomic bombings was that "the Japanese deserved what they got." All of these factors have limited Americans' public inquiry into and understanding of the true impact on the people—nearly all civilians—who experienced the world's first wartime use of atomic bombs.

Compelled by a greater understanding of these historical influences and ongoing questions about the survivors' personal experiences, I traveled to Nagasaki numerous times over a period of eight years. I conducted multiple extended interviews with Taniguchi and four other *hibakusha*—Dō-oh Mineko, Nagano Etsuko, Wada Kōichi, and Yoshida Katsuji—all of whom were teenagers at the time of the bombing. They and their families also provided me with extensive supporting materials, including personal essays, correspondence, medical records, and photographs. The stories of these five survivors, both epic and intimate, create the primary narrative strands of this book, documenting the seventy-year impact of nuclear war on them, their families, and their communities.

I also interviewed twelve other *hibakusha,* some of whom had never told their stories to anyone outside of their immediate families. I met with Nagasaki atomic bomb specialists, including historians, physicians, psychologists, social workers, educators, and staff researchers at atomic bomb museums, hospitals, research centers, libraries, and survivor organizations. I also studied the written testimonies of more than three hundred Nagasaki survivors as well as privately printed documents, collections, government sources, and thousands of archival photographs of Nagasaki before and after the bombing.

Hibakusha history is a complex and multidimensional story, and there are few straight lines in the survivors' lives. In order to create a semblance of order for their chaotic postnuclear years and the sometimes disparate aspects of their stories, I have arranged the book into nine chronological and thematic chapters, covering 1945 to the present. As the lives of the five *hibakusha* unfold, I document the bombings' larger medical and societal effects, including little-known details of physical injuries and disfiguration, acute and late radiation-related illnesses, extreme isolation during many years of hospitalization and home care, and the numerous challenges *hibakusha* encountered as they tried to redefine normalcy after nuclear war. In the face of societal discrimination and fears of genetic effects on their children, each decided whether to hide or reveal their identities as *hibakusha*, if and when to marry or have children, and whether they would break their silence and talk about their experiences with their families, friends, employers, or the public. Their stories are set against the backdrop of U.S.-Japan relations before, during, and after the war, and are intertwined with the political, social, and economic transformations in postwar Japan, scientific information about the effects of radiation, and evidence of U.S. policies of censorship and denial that continue to affect public opinion and create barriers to understanding. Except for Taniguchi, whom I met when he was in his fifties, I've known these *hibakusha* from their midseventies into their eighties. They provide a rare view of the memories and perspectives of aging adults whose early lives were permanently interrupted by a nuclear bomb.

——

There were many challenges in taking on this project, not the least of which was trying to write about nuclear annihilation and terror at a scale that defies imagination. My approach was to stay with the survivors' individual experiences and perspectives as much as possible to keep the story real and imaginable, while offering context for clarification and understanding of larger social, political, and medical issues. In any

historical account that incorporates personal narrative, there are com-
plications due to the inherent limitations and unreliability of memory,
especially traumatic memory. I countered this by cross-checking survivors' accounts against support documentation to verify or expand on
their memories of events, places, and people. Further, I am an American,
of another culture and generation than the subjects of this book, and I
wanted to prevent potential manipulation or appropriation of the survivors' stories, even more so because they were people who, no matter
what the rationale, had already been violated by my country. My answer
to this challenge was to use the survivors' own words and images to relay
their experiences as accurately as possible, and to draw on the clearest
scientific, medical, political, military, and historical analyses I could find
to place the survivors' experiences into the larger framework of the various histories in which they played a part.

When I talk with Americans about this book, some of the first questions I am asked relate to the necessity and morality of the U.S. decision
to use the atomic bombs on Japan. Many people hold unequivocal opin-
ions that fall on either side of these issues. One of the critical (and difficult) questions to ask is how we as Americans defined then—and define
now—just action, the cost of victory, and our criteria for committing to
and accepting the mass killing or wounding of civilians of a nation we
consider our enemy. Numerous scholars have analyzed and continue to
debate U.S. motivations to use the atomic bombs and the relative impact
of the multifaceted events leading up to Japan's capitulation, including
the atomic bombings. Their work has provided valuable political and
military context for the Nagasaki story and provoked questions about
the accepted narrative of the bombs' military necessity, especially regarding the need for the second atomic bomb. They do not offer easy
conclusions.

In answering queries about the necessity of the bombings, I redirect
people to the stories of those who experienced them, without which
discussions of the military, moral, and existential questions about the
Hiroshima and Nagasaki attacks are incomplete. At the very least, if we
choose to take and defend actions that cause great harm to civilians
during war, I believe we must also be willing to look at the impact of
those actions. *Hibakusha*—the only people in history who have lived
through a nuclear attack and its aftermath—are at the end of their lives,

and they hold in their memories stirring evidence of the devastating long-term effects of nuclear war.

———

The large majority of *hibakusha* do not speak about their atomic bomb experiences, even within their own families. Their memories are too excruciating, and traditional Japanese culture—particularly for those born in the early twentieth century—does not promote public disclosure of personal, family, or societal struggles. Further, the risk of discrimination against *hibakusha* exists even today. Many survivors still keep their identity hidden to avoid being perceived as "different"—or worse, seeing their children or grandchildren denied employment or marriage because of a parent's or grandparent's *hibakusha* status.

A select few—including Taniguchi, Dō-oh, Nagano, Wada, and Yoshida—felt compelled to speak openly about their experiences, even though doing so required them to relive the horrors of their childhoods and young adulthoods. On behalf of those who died before their voices could be heard, these five *hibakusha* devoted much of their adult lives to eliminating ignorance about the realities of nuclear war and petitioning nuclear nations to reduce or eliminate their weapons stockpiles. They are trying, at all costs, to prevent worse nuclear horrors from taking place in the future.

As we approach the seventieth anniversary of the second and last atomic bomb attack in history, it is my hope that this book will unveil these neglected stories to a larger audience and help shape the course of public discussion and debate over one of the most controversial wartime acts in history. The stories of those who were beneath the mushroom clouds can transform our generalized perceptions of nuclear war into visceral human experience. "Now, to be A-bombed," Nagasaki poet Oyama Takami wrote, "[there] is nothing really abstract in that."

Susan Southard
July 2015

A NOTE ON JAPANESE NAMES AND TERMS

I have retained the order in which Japanese express their names—that is, surname first, followed by the given name. For example, Taniguchi Sumiteru's surname is Taniguchi, so this is the name I use for him. In cases where survivors' spouses are part of the story, I have deviated from this policy by using the spouses' first names in order to differentiate them from their husbands or wives. The use of first names in this way would not be typical in Japan. Also, Nagano Etsuko's maiden name is Kanazawa Etsuko. Because Nagano was her name at the time she told me her story, and for narrative cohesiveness, I refer to her as Nagano throughout the book, including the periods in her life before she got married.

Japanese words are italicized except those that are now integrated into the English language. I have used macrons over Japanese vowels to indicate they have a long sound, except when the Japanese name or term is commonly used in English without the macrons, or when Japanese authors do not use macrons in their names or book titles.

NAGASAKI

PROLOGUE

Off the eastern coast of the Asian continent, five hundred miles from Shanghai and less than two hundred miles south of the Korean Peninsula, a long, narrow bay carves deeply into the western coast of Kyushu—Japan's southernmost main island. At the head of this bay lies Nagasaki, acclaimed in Japan for its natural coastal beauty and for being the nation's earliest Westernized city. In the four hundred years leading up to World War II, Nagasaki was unmatched in Japan for its exposure to European cultures, a result of the extensive amount of trade that took place at its port.

Prior to the late 1500s, Nagasaki was a secluded, loosely bound feudal village of farmers and fishermen, almost completely isolated from Japan's industrial and commercial center in Kyoto. In 1571, however, Portuguese ships exploring the region made their way into Nagasaki's harbor. As word spread about its prime location on Japan's western coast with proximity to numerous Asian nations, more and more European and Chinese merchant ships arrived carrying never-before-seen guns, tobacco, clocks, fabrics, and spices. Within decades, Nagasaki grew to a city of fifteen thousand and became both the center for Japan's foreign trade and the vanguard of the nation's early modernization. The Europeans also introduced Christianity to Japan, and for a time Nagasaki was not only the country's hub for Catholic missionary outreach but also the most diverse city in the region—where Portuguese, Spanish, British, Dutch, Chinese, and Japanese residents attended Buddhist, Shinto, and Catholic services at temples, shrines, and churches.

1

By the late 1500s, however, the powerful feudal lord Toyotomi Hideyoshi, who was taking control of southern and western Japan and would later help unify the entire nation, became increasingly fearful that such deep infiltration of Christian ideology into Japanese society would result in political upheaval and an ultimate loss of power. In a preemptive strike, Hideyoshi initiated a brutal anti-Christian campaign. Churches were destroyed, and thousands of Christians were expelled, imprisoned, or executed. In Nagasaki, twenty-six foreign and Japanese missionaries and their converts were publicly crucified. Numerous Buddhist temples and Shinto shrines—including the city's renowned Suwa Shrine—were built to reinvigorate traditional religious practices and to provide a means by which people who did not participate in them could be identified and persecuted. Japanese Christians fought back, leading to violent conflicts between Christians and non-Christians throughout the region. By 1635, the Tokugawa shogunate severed trade ties with Portugal and other Christian nations and imposed a long period of national isolation. Japanese citizens were prohibited from leaving the country, and foreigners were forbidden to enter.

Except in Nagasaki. As a means to preserve a portion of the economic benefits provided by foreign commerce, Japan's rulers allowed Nagasaki to continue trade with China and the Netherlands—the latter in part because the Dutch had promised not to engage in Christian activities. For more than two centuries, Nagasaki served as Japan's sole window to the outside world. With Chinese and Dutch ships arriving at their port, the people of Nagasaki were continually introduced to Asian and European arts, architecture, science, and literature.

In the early to mid-1800s, Russia, France, Britain, and the United States began pressuring Japan to reverse its seclusion policies; in 1853, U.S. commodore Matthew Perry's armed entry into Tokyo Bay forced Japan to formally acquiesce to Western demands and reopen the country to international trade and diplomatic relations. As this small island nation began its quest for political, economic, and military parity with the West, the next sixty years were defined by rapid industrialization, political transformation, and expansion of the Japanese Empire. Japan became a centralized political state for the first time, with its formerly titular emperor now strategically positioned at its head to strengthen the government's authority over the newly unified nation. Rising Japanese leaders launched Japan's first conscript army, established a national education system, and pushed for democratic reforms—including religious freedom, women's rights, and universal suffrage. Over time, however, Shinto was sanctioned as the state religion and politicized to manipulate Shinto's myths and traditions in order to promote concepts of Japanese racial exceptionalism and mandatory obedience to the emperor.

In an effort to achieve military and economic security, Japan emulated Western nations' colonization of East Asian countries by waging short wars with Russia and China, seizing much-needed coal, iron, rubber, and other resources not available in its mountainous terrain. By the early twentieth century, Japan had colonized Formosa (Taiwan), gained territory in Manchuria and Russia's northern islands, and annexed the entire Korean Peninsula, suppressing Korean language and culture. During World War I, Japan provided ships and military supplies to the Allies. When the war ended, Japan emerged as Asia's first world leader, signified by its acceptance as one of the Big Five at the postwar peace conference at Versailles.

Nagasaki thrived. Its port expanded to accommodate increased international trade, and in 1855, a naval training institute was established, a precursor to the Imperial Japanese Navy. Two years later, the precursor to Nagasaki Medical College opened, the first school in Japan to educate physicians in Western medicine. The city dissolved its rules that had earlier confined Dutch and Chinese residents to tiny enclaves near the harbor, so that they, as well as Nagasaki's British, French, Russian, and American residents, were free to live anywhere in the city. By the early 1900s, dams and reservoirs were built to secure an ample water supply, and an expanded railroad system and national road improved accessibility into and out of the city. Nagasaki had also fortified its emergency defense armaments in the event of an invasion, most particularly by Russia. In the fourteen years between 1889 and 1903, Nagasaki's population nearly tripled from 55,000 to 150,000, making the city Japan's seventh largest. After eleven generations of families practicing their faith in secret, thousands of Nagasaki Catholics came out of hiding. Numerous Catholic, Episcopal, and Presbyterian churches—as well as Japan's first synagogue and a Masonic lodge—sprang up throughout the city. By the early 1920s, workers and volunteer parishioners had

completed Urakami Church, the largest Catholic church in the Far East.
With the establishment of the massive Mitsubishi Shipyard and Machinery Works, shipbuilding surpassed trade as the city's dominant industry,
and Nagasaki became the third-largest shipbuilding city in the world.

Nagasaki Harbor and environs, ca. 1920. The Nishinaka-machi Catholic Church can be
seen in the foreground. (*Topical Press Agency/Hulton Archive/Getty Images*)

In 1926, during the period between the two world wars, twenty-five-
year-old Hirohito Michinomiya was crowned emperor of Japan. Following the ancient tradition of assigning an era name (*nengo*) to each new
emperor's reign, the time of Hirohito's rule was christened the Shōwa era
(the era of enlightened peace). The first twenty years of Hirohito's reign,
however, were anything but peaceful. The emperor's relationship to

Japan's military aggression remains a contested issue among historians, but it is inarguable that during his regime, the Japanese military carved out for itself a unique, nearly autocratic leadership role with power to control national policy. To minimize public dissent over Japan's forced acquisition of neighboring countries' resources and labor, ultranationalistic leaders introduced the concept of *kokutai*—defined as Japan's national essence under the supreme guidance of a divine emperor. Patriotism was redefined as compulsory and unconditional loyalty to both emperor and state.

Japanese citizens began living under oppressive policies that restricted free speech and individual rights. Adults and children were required to free themselves of Western concepts such as democracy and individualism, and abide by *kōdō* (the Imperial Way), by which they were duty-bound to pursue "moral excellence" as defined by the state. They were taught that because of the benevolent leadership of their godlike emperor, Japan was uniquely positioned to use its superior morality and power to unify and lead all of Asia and the entire world. Japan's Home Ministry and other government departments established special police forces charged with monitoring the activities of civilians and military personnel who questioned or opposed national policy, a crime punishable by up to ten years in prison.

The Japanese military began new campaigns to expand the nation's empire across Asia. The army invaded Manchuria, where it had maintained a presence since its victory over Russia in 1905, and subsequently colonized the region. The League of Nations protested this action, and in 1933, Japan withdrew as a member, hostile to this criticism and to perceived disdain from the United States and other Western nations over its quest for equal military, political, and social standing. Four years later, Japan invaded China to increase its access to natural resources needed both for domestic industrial production and its continued military actions in Asia. As the Japanese Imperial Army Air Forces implemented a massive strategic bombing campaign, Japanese army commanders and soldiers tore through Shanghai, Nanjing, and other Chinese cities, slaughtering, mutilating, or torturing millions of Chinese soldiers and civilians. In 1940, Japan invaded French Indochina and signed a military pact with Germany and Italy to secure the cooperation of the Axis powers in its bid to extend its military, political, and economic boundaries.

At home, the military government tightened its control. All political parties were dissolved, and the Imperial Rule Assistance Association was established—a national communication system that reached every Japanese citizen. In prefectures, cities, townships, and villages across the country, every neighborhood was divided into groups of five to ten households known as *tonarigumi,* which held mandatory monthly meetings to disseminate information from Tokyo, promote solidarity, and unify around the rigid ideals of *kokutai* and *kōdō.* In their schools and neighborhood association meetings, adults and children were required to chant slogans such as "One hundred million [people], one mind" and "Abolish desire until victory."

After years of advancing and holding positions in vast regions of China and the Indochina Peninsula, by 1941, Japan's financial and military resources had worn thin. International protest embargoes led by the United States worsened the country's situation by cutting off essential supplies of petroleum, aviation gasoline, and scrap metals. From Japan's perspective, it had two options, neither of which offered potential for anything but the ultimate demise of its empire. The first was to end the embargo by complying with U.S. demands for Japan's withdrawal from China and Indochina—an unthinkable choice in the context of Japan's political, economic, and military ambitions for Asian dominance and economic independence from the United States. The second: to seize British, Dutch, French, and U.S. colonies in Southeast Asia and take possession of the region's vast oil, rubber, and mineral resources—which would inevitably trigger a war of retaliation with these countries, most particularly the United States.

Japan chose the latter course—and made the additional decision to preempt any U.S. military response by attacking the United States first. On December 8, 1941 (Japan time), amid heightened economic and military upheaval, high-level political debate, and the government's ever-increasing bellicose fervor that gave no value to individual life except in service to the nation, Japan attacked Pearl Harbor, a U.S. naval station in Hawaii. A war between Japan and the United States and its allies had begun—a war that quickly spread throughout the entire western Pacific and ultimately led to the destruction of nearly every Japanese city.

Even as late as the summer of 1945, Nagasaki was, in large part, spared.

CHAPTER 1

CONVERGENCE

Before the sun rose on August 9, 1945, eighteen-year-old Wada Kōichi slipped on his black wool uniform and visored cap, closed the wooden sliding door behind him, and left his grandparents' house in the Maruyama district of Nagasaki, a half mile inland from the bay. Through narrow, darkened streets, he walked his familiar route through the old city, two miles to the north and east to Hotarujaya Terminal to begin his six a.m. shift as a streetcar operator.

Even in the faint light of daybreak, the city looked largely green. Set into trees and foliage, wooden houses were clustered in small neighborhoods called *machi*. Verdant, low mountains hugged the city in a near circle around the bay. As he walked, Wada passed permanently closed streetside markets, reminding him once again of his persistent hunger. Throughout Japan, fruits and vegetables were scarce, meat was no longer available, and fish was rarely obtainable. Rice, tightly rationed for years, was down to approximately two cups per person per month. To offset hunger, most families planted sweet potatoes in the small gardens behind their houses. That morning, enveloped in fog and near darkness, principals and teachers across the city were already at their schools fertilizing, weeding, and harvesting the potatoes and small number of vegetables they'd planted in every patch of ground they could find. "I thought constantly about food," Wada remembered, "and wondered when the day would come when I would be able to eat until I was full."

Arriving at Hotarujaya Terminal, Wada pressed his signature seal

7

into ink, stamped the work log to document his presence, and stood in line with his friends and coworkers to receive a brake handle and the number of the streetcar he would drive that day. More than eighteen months earlier, the Japanese government had assigned him to this job, and now he served as a leader of the mobilized students working there. Wada walked over to the depot, stepped up into his designated streetcar, and attached the brake. Another young worker boarded as well to collect fares and distribute tickets. Short but strong, Wada stood at the helm and steered his streetcar out of the terminal toward the first stop on his daily route, Shianbashi—Reflection Bridge—very close to his home, where he had started out that morning.

Wada Kōichi (at bottom left, wearing glasses), age seventeen, with other student workers at the Nagasaki Streetcar Company, October 1944. The ribbons on two of the students' jackets meant that these boys would soon be sent to war. Both died in the Philippines. (*Courtesy of Wada Kōichi*)

Surrounded by mountains on three sides, Nagasaki is built along the banks of a long, narrow bay and the two rivers that flow into it. The smaller Nakashima River curves southwestward toward the port through a valley where the city's oldest neighborhoods and government offices have existed for centuries. The Urakami River flows north to south through the

Urakami Valley, a narrow fertile region filled with rice paddies and farm-
land until it was incorporated into the city in 1920. Near the harbor, Mount
Inasa, Nagasaki's largest peak, overlooks both valleys, the shipyards that
line the bay, and the residential districts south of the Nakashima Valley.
To the far south and west, the blue of the ocean and sky stretches to the
end of sight.

In 1945, Nagasaki's streets were not yet paved, and buildings rarely
rose higher than three stories. Streetcars serving Nagasaki's 240,000
people wound through the city on tracks, their wires connected to cables strung between electrical poles lining the roads. Churches stood
throughout the city, the bell towers of Urakami Church rising higher
than the rest. Numerous steel and armament factories were situated to
the north and south of the main port, and two prisoner-of-war camps
operated within the city limits—one on Koyagi Island near the mouth of
Nagasaki Harbor, and the other just north of the port in an abandoned
spinning mill at the Mitsubishi Shipyard Saiwai-machi Plant.

As the sun broke over the horizon, Wada steered his car north past
Dejima, the former site of the Dutch trading post during Japan's two
hundred years of isolation. At eighteen, he was old enough to remember
a childhood before Japan was at war, when he had played with British,
Chinese, Russian, and American diplomats' children. "I thought they
were just like me," he remembered. "Sometimes I went to their homes,
and the American and British mothers made cakes. The Chinese families
made delicious buns. But the Russians gave me black bread"—he winced,
laughing—"that wasn't so good."

As a child, Wada lived with his parents, grandparents, and younger
sister. He and his father, a bank employee, often went to baseball games
at the local stadium; young Wada was thrilled whenever the Tokyo team
was in town so he could watch its star player, Russian Victor Starffin,
pitch at record speed. When he was five, his father purchased a radio, a
rare item in Nagasaki in the 1930s. There was no broadcast station in the
city, however, so his father mounted an antenna on top of a tall bamboo
pole to receive radio waves from Kumamoto. Weather and music programs aired sporadically throughout the day, but the specific broadcast
times for sports programs were published in the newspaper, so neighbors
arrived uninvited at Wada's house to listen to baseball and sumo wres-
tling. His parents weren't happy with the crowds, but Wada loved having

all the people packed inside his house. "The thing I remember most," he said, "is listening to the 1936 Berlin Olympics when a Nagasaki swimmer named Maehata Hideko swam the two-hundred-meter breaststroke. Everyone cheered and clapped when she won!"

When Wada was ten, his mother and newborn sibling died during childbirth. Two years later, his father died of tuberculosis, a disease that, due to lack of antibiotics and poor living conditions, killed an estimated 140,000 Japanese each year. "All he could do was rest," Wada remembered. "If there had been medicine, he might have lived." Wada's grandparents took over caring for him and his younger sister, but twelve-year-old Wada was overwhelmed: His parents were gone, his grandparents had little means, and Wada was too young to get a job. "Because I was a boy," he recalled, "I was not allowed to cry."

The deaths of Wada's parents coincided with Japan's invasion of China and the beginning of a long period of Japanese military aggression against other nations. Daily routines transformed for every Japanese citizen. New legislation pushed forward by militarist leaders allowed the government to control and utilize Japanese industry, media, and human labor to subsidize the war. In Nagasaki and across the country, munitions factories accelerated output. Gasoline and leather goods were rationed, and later public access to charcoal, eggs, rice, and potatoes was tightly regulated. Radio announcements—underscored by rousing wartime marches—celebrated Japan's battle victories and fed propaganda to the Japanese people about their country's supremacy and its innate destiny under the emperor to become both emancipator and guardian of all of Asia. To quash Japan's earlier support for democratic principles, the government introduced intense military indoctrination, social restrictions, and rigid mandates of personal behavior. Every household was required to display a portrait of the emperor and empress. Elementary schools were now called national citizens' schools. At school, children were trained to praise their country's military successes in China and were instructed to write letters of encouragement to soldiers. In Nagasaki, Chinese cultural festivals held in the city for centuries were canceled, and Nagasaki Station became the scene for enormous crowds cheering and waving flags as young soldiers were sent off to the front. Under tight security and hidden from public view, thousands of workers at the Mitsubishi Shipyard and Machinery Works built the seventy-thousand-ton *Musashi*—at the time, the largest battleship ever made.

Nagasaki Station, the hub for trains entering and leaving the city, ca. 1930. (*U.S. Army Institute of Pathology/Courtesy of Nagasaki Atomic Bomb Museum*)

In August 1941, the Japanese Ministry of Education released *Shinmin no michi* [The Way of Subjects], a manifesto that condemned the West's world domination throughout modern history and commanded the Japanese people to embrace a vision for a new world order ruled by Japan's benevolent emperor. The proclamation contextualized Japan's invasions of Manchuria and China as steps toward a world restored to peace based on Japanese nationalistic moral principles. Japanese citizens were pressed to purge themselves of "the evils of European and American thought," acquiesce to a systemized military state, and demonstrate absolute loyalty to the emperor by forgoing their individual needs and desires. Even as they felt the impact of the U.S.-led embargo of oil and other natural resources, many Japanese supported the government's refusal to withdraw from China, particularly because a withdrawal order from the prime minister would have likely resulted in his assassination.

But the Japanese people could not have imagined their country's next step. On December 8, 1941 (December 7 in the United States), Prime Minister Tōjō Hideki stunned the nation when he announced in a live radio address that Japan had attacked Pearl Harbor, initiating a war against the United States and its allies. "The key to victory lies in a 'faith in victory,'" he said. "For 2,600 years since it was founded, our Empire has never known a defeat. . . . Let us pledge ourselves that we will never stain our glorious history."

Fourteen-year-old Wada heard the announcement on his father's radio. As a child, when Japan was invading China, he had dreamed of enlisting as soon as he was eligible. Before her death, however, his mother had taught him that "Banzai!"—the Japanese battle cry in the name of the emperor—was wrong. Hearing the news of his country's attack on Pearl Harbor, he now "questioned a little whether Japan was truly fighting to save people in the world." At that time, protest was severely punished, so Wada kept his misgivings to himself. Meanwhile, Japanese soldiers battled farther into the Chinese interior and simultaneously raced into U.S., British, French, Australian, and Dutch-held territories in Southeast Asia, fighting against inevitable loss at the hands of a far more powerful enemy.

It was, in the words of historian John W. Dower, a "war without mercy," in which both Japan and the United States promoted racist, dehumanizing language about and perceptions of each other. In the United States, a *Time* magazine article reported that the "ordinary unreasoning Jap is ignorant. Perhaps he is human. Nothing . . . indicates it." Within this climate of racism and political fear-mongering, the U.S. government rounded up and interned an estimated 120,000 Japanese American citizens and "resident aliens" deemed high risks for espionage and sabotage. In Japan, American and British enemies were portrayed as terrifying demons, and everything "Western"—including literature, English classes, music, and political philosophy—was purged from Japanese education and society. In Nagasaki alone, an estimated twenty to thirty foreign monks, nuns, and priests were suspected as enemy spies and interned in a convent on the outskirts of the city. The indoctrination of Japanese soldiers intensified: Chanting the slogan "We'll never cease fire till our enemies cease to be!" they were trained to believe that the destiny of the empire depended on every battle. Military personnel were forbidden to surrender or become prisoners of war; they were ordered to kill themselves instead as an act of honor for their families and their nation and to avoid any trace of shame.

Day-to-day life became more and more austere and controlled, focused solely on compliance and economic survival. The government granted stowed enormous contracts for production of weapons and war supplies to Japan's *zaibatsu*—massive privately owned business conglomerates such as Mitsubishi and Mitsui—while most other commercial industries and family businesses were forced to redirect their labor and production to serve the vast needs of the Japanese military. Nagasaki men who lost their jobs because of government closures joined the factory labor teams of Mitsubishi's four major industries (shipbuilding, electrical machinery, munitions, and steel), which now employed an even larger percentage of the city's workforce. Consumer goods disappeared, and messages via radio, newsprint, teachers, and ever-present military personnel pummeled the Japanese people with refrains of "Luxury is the enemy!" and "Let's send even one more plane to the front!"

Over time, nearly every Japanese citizen was required to work for the war effort—an attempt to offset the extreme imbalances between Japan and the United States in both coal and steel production and the manufacturing of aircraft, tanks, and ammunition. Initially, the Japanese government ordered all men not serving in the military to manual labor, manufacturing, communications, and transportation jobs that in some way supported the government's mission. Eventually, young unmarried women, jailed convicts, and malnourished, weakened, and often lice-infected prisoners of war were similarly assigned. Married women were urged to bear as many children as possible to increase Japan's population. Korean and Chinese men, forcibly recruited from their homelands, toiled in Japanese mines and factories; in 1944, nearly sixty thousand Koreans and one thousand Chinese worked in and around Nagasaki, living in minimal barracks near their worksites and eating thin gruel three times a day. On the eighth day of every month—designated "Imperial Edict Day" to commemorate Japan's entry into the war—workers were sometimes given an extra *onigiri*—rice ball—to fuel their determination. To further boost Japan's domestic workforce, "education" was redefined to include labor service; at first, students fourteen and older were mandated to participate in part-time labor projects around food and coal production. By 1944, the national government ordered these students to cease their education and part-time labor, and work full-time for the war effort. Children over ten were mobilized into volunteer labor corps.

The Japanese people surrendered clothing, jewelry, every possible metal household item, and even gold teeth to help the government fund the war. Most of all, they sacrificed their fathers, sons, grandfathers, uncles, and brothers, sending them off to the front without protest, only to receive their ashes back in small wooden boxes. Publicly they could show no grief or remorse and had to passively accept their neighbors' congratulations for their son's or father's honorable death in service to the nation. Local branches of national women's organizations made care packages for soldiers overseas and *senninbari*—thousand-stitch belts— for new recruits leaving for war, a symbolic gesture to protect them from harm. Every family was required to belong to a *tonarigumi,* through which Japan's military police monitored not only public obedience and resistance but also every individual's private enthusiasm level or "treasonous" attitudes toward the war. Nagasaki alone had 273 *tonarigumi,* each with five to ten families. Those in the minority who expressed disbelief in the emperor's divinity, the government's political ambitions, or Japan's military aggression were imprisoned, tortured, and often killed. Even at work, disobedience to one's supervisor could result in extreme physical punishment.

Eventually, Wada's European and American friends were expelled from Nagasaki, and again he questioned the government's intentions. "I was told that America, England, and Holland were evil, but I wondered how that was possible when the families I knew had such nice parents." It was also clear to Wada that despite Japan's pronouncements of superiority, his life was getting worse. He had been ordered to withdraw from school to work for the war effort and was paid with a loaf of old bread at the end of each day; later as a streetcar driver, he earned only half of what the adult workers were paid. Wada's grandparents sold their kimonos and other precious items for a small percentage of their value. He was always hungry. When his older friends left for the war, he and everyone else knew they weren't likely to return, especially by 1945, when many recruits were "invited" into the kamikaze corps. "I thought something was wrong," Wada remembered. He later wished that he had spoken out publicly against the war. "But to tell you the truth, I was scared. I worried that I might be killed."

As his own draft age drew near, Wada faced a serious decision. Not only was he against the war, but he also knew that if he went away, his grandparents would have no one to support them. In an act of subversive resistance, he deliberately failed his pre-service physical examination. "I wore glasses at the time, which was not an automatic disqualifier," he said, "but at the examination, I pretended that I was nearly blind." Wada was dismissed from military service, but even with a medical justification, he was labeled an antiwar student and was verbally berated, slapped, and beaten, often by police officers. He survived by working overtime, allowing him to double his wages and better support his sister and grandparents, and he spent time with his friends whenever he could. "From the time I was very young, I was not one to give in," he explained. "I had to manage on my own. No matter how hard things got, no matter how difficult things were, there was always tomorrow. If tomorrow was hard, there was always the next day."

On the morning of August 9, Wada drove his streetcar north past Nagasaki Station into the Urakami Valley. Thick white smoke rose from the smokestacks of the Mitsubishi factories that lined both sides of the river. On either side of him, Wada could see thousands of tile-roofed houses huddled close together. More than 150 shops, pharmacies, tailors, and furniture stores were now closed or serving as ration stations. Staircases ascended into the hills, leading to more closed shops and houses with narrow balconies. Nagasaki Medical College and its affiliated hospital stood at the base of the eastern hills. Farther north, the redbrick Urakami Church with its twin bell towers overlooked the entire valley.

By eight a.m., Nagasaki's streetcars were packed with adults and children heading toward their assigned worksites. Those who couldn't fit into the jammed cars walked—often for more than an hour—to arrive on time for their shifts. Some skipped work to search the hillsides for edible plants and weeds—risking the punishment of having their names posted on a board at their worksite that would identify them as enemy collaborators. As Wada steered through the Urakami Valley, he received word of a streetcar derailment elsewhere in the city that caused him to change his usual route. He had no idea that this accident would save his life.

———

Earlier that morning, another Nagasaki teenager, Nagano Etsuko, awakened and joined her family in morning calisthenics. "Physical exercises guided by someone on the radio," she explained. "I really hated it! Even in the winter, my father made us throw open the windows and exercise." Despite his strictness, sixteen-year-old Nagano loved and respected her father, a small man who, at just over forty years old when the war began, had aged out of the draft and worked instead at Mitsubishi Electric. Nagano felt less warmly toward her mother. "She was a little bit self-centered," she recalled, "and she was always irritated with my siblings and me." Still, Nagano appreciated that her mother had taught herself how to make clothes. During the war when clothing was rationed and no fabric was available, her mother had taken her own kimonos, undone the stitching, and made dresses for Nagano and her younger sister, Kuniko. "My friends thought I was lucky."

Nagano's memories before the war centered on her family—her parents and three siblings—who lived in a single-family home in the Urakami Valley, just north of Nagasaki Station. "My older brother was kind-hearted," she said. "Because I'm his sister, it's strange for me to say this, but—he was handsome. My girlfriends would beg me to introduce them to him, and they'd come over to my house for no particular reason just so they could see him." Nagano thought her younger sister, Kuniko, was very pretty, with her huge eyes and fair skin, though the two girls often quarreled. Before the war, Nagano sometimes walked to the book rental store carrying her baby brother, Seiji (whom her family called Sei-chan), on her back. "I could stand and read, and my mother wouldn't say anything because I was babysitting." Their yard was filled with pomegranate, fig, mandarin orange, and loquat trees, and as Sei-chan grew older, he, Kuniko, and Nagano climbed them to pick the fruit and eat it. "Ah," Nagano sighed, "they were so delicious. We were *so* happy."

Nagano was eleven when the Pacific War started, and over the next two years, as she and her family faced increased challenges, she watched her city transform. By 1943, as the Allies began to push back Japanese advances in

Nagano Etsuko, age fifteen, ca. 1944. (*Courtesy of Nagano Etsuko*)

the Pacific and use bases in China to launch air strikes on Japan's main islands, Nagasaki officials implemented the city's first defense measures against possible Allied attacks. Ten sites—mostly schools and other public buildings—were chosen to serve as first-aid stations. During mandatory *tonarigumi* air raid drills, everyone dropped what they were doing—or rose from their sleep—to report to designated locations where attendance was taken. People of all ages practiced bucket relays and other firefighting exercises. Near City Hall and in the older sections of Nagasaki, entire city blocks were razed to create firebreaks and evacuation routes, forcing schools to relocate and countless families to move in with relatives or friends in the Urakami Valley or in areas outside the city. Every family was required to remove the wooden ceilings in their houses to help slow potential fires. Someone—usually a woman because most men were either drafted or working—had to be at home at all times to prevent the spread of fires in the event of an air attack.

Company employees and members of civilian defense corps dug underground air raid shelters beneath large factories, offices, city prefectural buildings, and schools. Others carved hundreds of primitive, tunnel-shaped shelters into the hillsides surrounding the city; some shelters could hold as many as a hundred people, though many leaked and puddled after every rain. Families were also required to dig shelters beneath their homes. "We lifted the *tatami* and dug a hole just big enough for all of us to squat inside," Nagano remembered. "We placed our valuables and food into oil drums and put them in the hole, then covered it with a door and put buckets of water on top to use in case of fire."

Neighborhood residents gather for a wartime fire drill beneath the *torii* gate leading to a shrine. After 1943, these mandatory drills were practiced monthly throughout the city as a defense against air raids. (*Courtesy of Nagasaki Foundation for the Promotion of Peace, Committee for Research of Photographs and Materials of the Atomic Bombing*)

Most mobilized students worked at railroad stations and in armament and shipbuilding plants situated on the bay and along the banks of the Urakami River. Nagano was assigned to the production line in a Mitsubishi airplane parts factory built inside a college gymnasium over the eastern hills from her Urakami Valley home. Every morning she rode a streetcar to the stop in front of Suwa Shrine, then walked three-quarters of a mile north to the factory. In mandated silence, she operated a lathe alongside adult employees. During her time off, there was virtually nothing to do. "Movies were not allowed," she remembered, "and restaurants were closed due to lack of food. To entertain ourselves, my friends and I took photographs of each other and swapped them back and forth. I was still a child, and I wasn't able to think very deeply about the war situation."

Nagasaki was bombed for the first time in late 1944, part of the first U.S. test raids of nighttime incendiary attacks on Japanese urban areas. Physical damages in the city were minor, but twenty-six people were injured and thirteen people died, becoming Nagasaki's first civilian deaths. By the end of that year, U.S. troops had claimed victories in Guam and the other Mariana Islands, providing them easier access to Japan's main islands and allowing the United States to intensify its targeted bombing attacks on Japanese military, industrial, and transportation sites. U.S. bombers flew over Nagasaki day and night en route to targets across Japan.

Nagasaki prepared itself for another attack. To fortify citywide defense measures, municipal leaders reinforced antiaircraft, searchlight, and radar brigades, repaired hillside shelters weakened by rainfall, kept water tanks full, and secured emergency telephone communication systems. In a multitiered firefighting strategy, thirty-seven teams totaling nearly 3,300 workers were deployed throughout the city to lead emergency fire brigades, each with its own pumper truck, and some with gasoline-run pumps as well. Civilian bucket brigades remained trained and ready. In the event of an attack, auxiliary police and fire units were prepared to direct pedestrian and vehicle traffic, support first-aid and epidemic prevention efforts, and oversee the disposal of the dead.

City and prefectural leaders selected additional sites for emergency relief stations, and more than 280 doctors and nurses were in place to execute the city's crisis relief plan—though some doctors were young, not-yet-fully-trained medical students who had received their degrees early to fill in for physicians drafted into the military. Concrete buildings in the city and surrounding villages served as emergency evacuation sites. Clothing, medicines, and large stores of rice, noodles, soy sauce, condensed milk, dried sardines, salt, corn, and soybeans were stockpiled inside Urakami Church and other buildings believed to be safe from attack. To hinder enemy vision of potential targets, the city implemented mandatory blackouts: Families were forbidden to use lights after dark, and factories operating overnight were ordered to cover their windows to eliminate any seepage of light. From inside their homes and air raid shelters, children listened to and glanced up at Allied planes overhead; some learned to identify each type of aircraft by the sound of its engines.

Heeding the national government's call to evacuate their children to rural areas outside the city, in late 1944, Nagano's parents sent Kuniko, thirteen, and Seiji, nine, to live with Nagano's grandparents in Kagoshima, at the southern tip of Kyushu. Nagano's older brother was drafted and sent outside the city for training, so Nagano, mandated to serve as a mobilized student worker, remained in Nagasaki with her parents. "Up until then, we were an ordinary family."

Her loneliness was unbearable, and in the spring of 1945, she begged her parents to let Kuniko and Sei-chan come home. After much discussion, her mother finally gave in and agreed to let Nagano go to Kagoshima to retrieve them, but she was adamant that Nagano could bring them home only if they *wanted* to come. Otherwise, Nagano could not bring them back.

Nagano eagerly agreed. She rode the train to Kagoshima alone, and when she got there, her brother and sister insisted that they had made good friends there and did not yet want to return home. When Nagano pressed them with different reasons they should come back, Kuniko and Seiji began to cry. "You shouldn't force them," Nagano's grandparents scolded her. But Nagano didn't listen. During Kuniko and Seiji's school break, she took them by train back to Nagasaki.

Four months later, on the morning of August 9, Nagano and her family completed their calisthenics. By this time, people across the city were awake, and everyone, including Nagano, was hungry. Mothers, grandmothers, and daughters scraped together meals out of acorns, sawdust, soybean grinds, potato stems, peanut shells, and pumpkin gruel, with protein sources from bugs, worms, rodent flesh, and snakes. One girl Nagano's age was so thin that her friends called her *Senko* (incense stick). Others fought lethargy resulting from a combination of malnutrition and lack of sleep.

A citywide air raid alarm wailed across loudspeakers and radios, prompting formulaic responses. Factories stopped production. Hospital staff carried their patients to their designated shelters. People across the city pulled on their air raid hoods, and parents yelled to their children to run for cover in the holes beneath their houses or in nearby air raid shelters. Thousands of people—including Nagano and her family—huddled in these dark, damp caves. Mothers, aunts, and eldest sisters stayed behind to fight anticipated fires in their homes.

After a long wait, the all-clear sounded. Nagano returned home and prepared herself for work. She had received a ration of new white running shoes, a rare treasure in the summer of 1945. But she wanted to protect them from becoming soiled, so she chose instead to wear *geta*—raised wooden sandals. The city was bright in the morning sun when she departed for work, leaving her mother and younger sister and brother behind.

———

Fifteen-year-old Dō-oh Mineko was, in her own words, a bit of a "wild child." Her boisterous energy and strong competitiveness worried her mother, who warned Dō-oh that the gods were watching her and would become angry if she didn't demonstrate more feminine behaviors. "But I couldn't see the gods, so I thought that maybe they didn't exist," Dō-oh explained. "In Japanese, we have a word *wanpaku* [impertinent]. That was me."

Dō-oh's family followed traditional Japanese gender roles, giving higher esteem and priority to men and boys. Her father, who had served in Manchuria, now worked as a high-level employee at Mitsubishi Shipyard. At home, he was a strict authoritarian who demanded absolute obedience from his children, including two hours of study a night. At dinner, he sat at a separate table in the front of the room, and even during the most dire wartime deprivation, he was given an extra serving of food. Dō-oh thought men were pretty lucky.

Her mother, in contrast, was gentle, patient, and obedient without complaint. Her elegant beauty was evident even during the war, when she wore no makeup and tied her hair back with a kerchief. Before strict rationing was implemented, she had sold fish to supplement the family income: Pulling a two-wheeled cart to the fish market, she would load up her purchases, return home, and repack the fish into two baskets. She then hung them from either end of a pole across her shoulders and walked from house to house peddling her merchandise. Dō-oh, the fourth of seven children, had inherited her mother's beauty—large almond eyes, smooth skin, and articulated round lips. In addition to helping look after her younger siblings, Dō-oh had two daily chores: hauling water from a nearby community well back to her house for dishes, baths, and laundry; and cleaning rice or other grains for family meals the next day. On winter nights, the tips of her fingers froze as she washed the rice, but Dō-oh persevered because of her father's strict policy: "No work, no food."

Dō-oh and her family lived on Mount Inasa, just west of Nagasaki's port. As a young girl, she had played hide-and-seek, jumped rope, and drawn chalk pictures on stones with her friends. At Inasa Elementary School, Dō-oh had a hundred percent attendance record and above-average grades. But Dō-oh was a tomboy, not the genteel young woman her parents and teachers would have wanted. She was captain of the dodgeball team, placed first or second in many of her school races on sports days, and even represented her school in a citywide running competition. At recess, she ignored the other girls and ran around the playground.

In December 1941, her country's attack on Pearl Harbor initiated numerous changes in Dō-oh's life. "All the students were gathered in the assembly room," she recalled. "We bowed to the emperor's photo, then the principal talked with us about Japan's alliance with Germany and Italy and told us that we were now at war with the United States and England. He said we needed to study hard and build physical strength. . . . The teachers' faces looked worried and tense." The following year, twelve-year-old Dō-oh and her family evacuated for safety farther inland to a rural area in the northwestern corner of the city. Dō-oh passed the admissions exam for Keiho Girls' High School, a two-hour walk from her home.

During her first year there, classes were held as usual, and after school, Dō-oh studied flower arranging, tea ceremony, koto, and Japanese archery. Gradually, however, students were required to plant potato sprouts on the school grounds during their physical education classes and after school, and Dō-oh's academic instruction became increasingly focused on militaristic indoctrination. She and her classmates recited the Imperial Rescript on Education, commanding total adoration and loyalty to the emperor and the nation under his rule. "Should emergency arise," one line read, "offer yourselves courageously to the State." Dō-oh, however, did not expect her country to lose. "We were taught that Japan was God's chosen country, and because of this, Japan would definitely win the war." Japanese soldiers had become an elite class, and Dō-oh and her young friends daydreamed of becoming their wives.

Dō-oh's oldest brother received a "red paper" in 1942, signifying his immediate military conscription. He was twenty-three. Like many new recruits, he prepared his last will and testament, sealing it in an envelope with fingernail and hair clippings as physical remembrances in the event of his death. On the day he left for war, Dō-oh's mother rose early and used food she had secretly stashed away for the occasion to make *ohagi*—sticky rice balls covered with sweetened adzuki beans. "Eat until your stomach is full," she told her son. Members of the *tonarigumi* arrived to bid him farewell; as they sang a patriotic song, Dō-oh's brother saluted and told the crowd that he would work hard for the sake of the country. Not long after, Dō-oh's second-oldest brother was also drafted. Two years later, her eldest brother died in a naval battle near Guam. Her father traveled by train to Sasebo, fifty miles north of Nagasaki, to collect his ashes—but the white box he received was empty, so Dō-oh's parents placed their son's fingernail and hair clippings inside the box in his memory. Her mother cried for months.

In 1944, fourteen-year-old Dō-oh was just starting to dream about her future when she was forced to leave school to work full-time for the war effort. With thousands of other students, she was assigned to the Mitsubishi Arms Factory Ōhashi Plant, where the aerial-launched torpedoes used in the Pearl Harbor attack had been manufactured. Dō-oh's job was to inspect the bolts of newly made torpedoes as they came off the assembly line. Once a month, students returned to their schools for "attendance day," where they were required to do military drills under the command of an officer. One of Dō-oh's only surviving photos was taken by a friend on one of these days. In order to look nice, Dō-oh had defied school rules and worn street clothes—a dark skirt and white cotton blouse—instead of her school uniform. "I was fashion-conscious." She shrugged. "I had my own image."

To "undermine the morale of the Japanese people," in early March 1945, the United States initiated an unrelenting firebombing campaign of Japanese cities. Over the next four months, enormous industrial and residential sections of Tokyo, Nagoya, Osaka, and nearly every major Japanese city burned to the ground, killing, wounding, and displacing vast civilian populations.

Nagasaki went into high alert, feverishly reinforcing its air raid defense systems, emergency stockpiles, and evacuation sites. Employees

Dō-oh Mineko, age fourteen, ca. 1944. (*Courtesy of Okada Ikuyo*)

and mobilized student workers moved large Mitsubishi machinery, precision instruments, and administrative departments to schools and underground shelters. Others blasted and dug six parallel, interconnected tunnels into a hillside in the northwest sector of the city. Inside the tunnels, Mitsubishi constructed a makeshift factory to continue its round-the-clock production of torpedo parts. Between mandated evictions for fire prevention purposes and voluntary evacuations of children, the elderly, and pregnant family members, an estimated fifty thousand people moved—either to the perceived-to-be-safer Urakami Valley, areas outside the city, or nearby islands. Elementary schools relocated their classes to shrines, private homes, and other temporary locations.

At Nagasaki Medical College, students now kept helmets and medical supplies near their desks. High school students and community volunteers formed emergency relief squads and carried kits containing hydrogen peroxide, iodine, bandages, scissors, aspirin, tissues, tweezers, and handkerchiefs. Every *tonarigumi* was equipped with a water tank, small manual pump, stretcher, and an appropriate number of ladders based on population. In addition to their required belowground shelters, every household was mandated to have at least two waterproof buckets, a shovel, a pickax, and fire-smothering equipment. In the event of a bomb attack, "we students were told to kneel down, bend over, and use thumbs to plug our ears and our fingers to cover our eyes," Dō-oh remembered, "to prevent our eardrums from getting damaged and our eyeballs from popping out. We practiced this over and over."

Nagasaki was bombed a second time in April 1945, leaving 129 dead. Occasionally, American planes approached the city, turned their engines off to avoid detection, and flew low over the shipyards, pelting them with machine-gun fire. Other Allied planes dropped leaflets warning of Nagasaki's destruction by fire and urging people to leave—though by Japanese law, citizens could not read or discuss the leaflets, and they faced arrest unless they immediately handed them over to the police. Day after day through the spring and early summer, however, no additional conventional or incendiary bombs fell on Nagasaki, even as other Japanese cities collapsed in flames. Rumors circulated—or perhaps they were hopeful speculations—that the Americans were treating Nagasaki differently because of its history of international trade, renowned beauty, Christian population, or the Allied POWs interned there.

That spring, news arrived that Japan's allies, Germany and Italy, had surrendered. By that time, however, many people's profound weariness overwhelmed any previous nationalistic fervor. Chronic hunger now outweighed fear of punishment for illegally fleeing Japan's cities. Tuberculosis claimed the lives of many babies and young adults, mortality rates spiked among children under seven suffering with diarrhea, and thousands were affected by beriberi, a serious condition resulting from malnutrition. Women and girls slept in their work clothes, and men and boys wore gaiters (protective leg coverings) around the clock to be ready for nightly air raid alarms. "We had no time to take a bath," one boy remembered, "so we had a hard time removing fleas and lice all over our bodies." Japan's diminishing raw materials and disabled transportation systems had resulted in sharp decreases in factory production levels, but adults and mobilized students were still required to work long shifts, if only to demolish buildings and dig shelters or sit silently and do no work at all. Schoolchildren collected pine sap in the woods to help make fuel for Japanese fighter planes. With nearly three million soldiers and civilians killed in battle or Allied bombings at home—more than 3 percent of Japan's population—the atmosphere in families and work communities was heavy as people waited for news of another soldier's death.

Even without accurate media reports, most people could now surmise the gravity of Japan's military losses in the Pacific and the devastating impact of Allied firebombing attacks, which by August had incinerated all or part of sixty-four Japanese cities. According to postwar surveys, by July 1945, public trust in the country's leaders had reached an all-time low, with two-thirds of the Japanese people certain that the nation's defeat was inevitable. "Even as kids we understood we were losing the war," a Nagasaki man recalled. "Any fool could see it. We needed everything. We didn't even have shoes. How could we win the war?"

Some Japanese Cabinet members had recognized as early as the spring of 1944 the urgency of their country's losses and its certain defeat. Right-wing promilitary Cabinet members, however, seemed ready to sacrifice their citizens in what they saw as their nation's ultimate battle. As Allied troops advanced toward Japan's main islands, these two factions heatedly deliberated over Japan's terms of surrender. Consensus, mandated by Japan's constitution, could not be achieved—and without it, the Japanese people could do nothing but brace for invasion.

The government redeployed its already-weakened troops from China and Manchuria to Kyushu and Honshu, Japan's largest home islands. In Nagasaki, officials set up heavy artillery in bunkers on nearby islands and ordered mines to be placed in the waters leading up to the bay. Workers at Mitsubishi Shipyard constructed several models of special attack boats, including an estimated six hundred *shinyō*—one-man ply-wood motorboats with bombs in the hull, designed to emerge from hidden coves on Nagasaki's coastline and surrounding islands and strike enemy ships after their mobilized student drivers had jumped into the sea. Approximately one hundred *kaiten*—individually manned suicide torpedoes launched from a submarine or ship—were also deployed.

While imperial portraits were removed from schools and government offices and hidden in locations outside the city, all men ages fifteen to sixty and women seventeen to forty were drafted into the National Volunteer Fighting Corps and emboldened to die "like shattered jewels" for their emperor—that is, to give their lives in battle or commit suicide rather than dishonor the emperor's name by surrendering. Every household had a bam-boo spear posted near the door, and Dō-oh, her classmates, and thousands of other students participated in combat training on how to use these spears to attack enemy soldiers, despite how ridiculous this seemed to those who understood that they would be shot before they could even get close.

In their house five miles inland, Dō-oh and her family were safe when, in late July and early August, Allied attacks bombarded Nagasaki three more times with over two hundred tons of conventional bombs. Parts of the Mitsubishi and Kawanami shipyards and dozens of houses were destroyed, and the Mitsubishi steelworks factory and Nagasaki Medical College suffered minor damages. More than two hundred people were killed, including a young family inside their home, twelve in an air raid shelter that collapsed, and thirty-two more who drowned when the wall of their air raid shelter cracked, causing water to flood in.

On the morning of August 9, Dō-oh put on her hated wartime attire—loose-fitting trousers, a long-sleeved work blouse, and split-toed heavy cloth footwear. Her blouse had a tag sewn into it providing her name, address, and blood type, and she wore an armband with the name of her school on it. Crisscrossed over her shoulders and chest were straps holding a first-aid kit and a padded cotton hood to protect her ears from loud explosions during an air raid, or—if soaked in water—from fire.

Dō-oh had not let go of her vision of a future after the war. "I loved fashion," she said. "That was my dream."

———

Unbeknownst to the people of Nagasaki, Japan, or the United States, in the months leading up to the morning of August 9, leaders of the United States, the USSR, and Japan played out a series of mostly covert political maneuvers and military operations to end the war and attain, from each nation's perspective, optimum postwar goals. In the early 1940s, the United States had established the Manhattan Project and hired world-renowned scientists to create the world's first atomic bomb. After years of top-secret development, the scientists were close to achieving their objective: to split the nucleus of an atom, manipulate and harness the forces that hold it together, and unleash an explosive power greater than any human had ever generated.

Vice President Harry S. Truman knew nothing about the development of the bomb prior to President Franklin Roosevelt's death in April 1945. Two weeks later, top military advisers briefed Truman about the Manhattan Project and told him that the first bombs would be ready for use on Japan by August. There were no consequential debates on whether to use the bomb at all or prohibit its use on noncombatant Japanese citizens. Top U.S. officials briefly discussed but ultimately vetoed proposals to issue an official warning to Japan or detonate a demonstration bomb over an uninhabited area to intimidate Japan into surrendering. Final plans were made to deliver the bombs as soon as they were ready.

That spring, a group of U.S. military personnel and scientists met to establish target criteria for the atomic bombings. The committee did not prioritize the military activity within potential target cities; instead, its two primary goals were "obtaining the greatest psychological effect against Japan," and making the attack "sufficiently spectacular" so that "the weapon [would] be internationally recognized when publicity on it is released." Specifications for target cities included their size (larger than three miles in diameter), location (within B-29 bombers' 1,500-mile maximum flight range from the U.S. airbase in the South Pacific), capacity for "being damaged effectively by a blast," and the existence of a war-related factory surrounded by workers' houses. For accuracy—particularly because of the $2 billion price tag of the bombs—predictable, clear weather was required for a visual sighting (versus radar) of the predetermined aiming point. To measure the effects of the bomb, Japanese cities already destroyed by incendiary bomb attacks could not be considered. From an original list of seventeen possible cities, the Target Committee narrowed the choices to four that met all or most of the criteria: Hiroshima, Kokura, Nagasaki, and Niigata. General Carl A. Spaatz, commander of the Strategic Air Forces in the Pacific, informed the War Department about one of Nagasaki's POW camps near the center of the city; ultimately, this information did not exclude Nagasaki as a priority target.

For Japan's part, Hirohito and Japanese foreign minister Tōgō Shigenori made tentative requests in June and July for the Soviets' assistance in surrender mediation. The United States knew of these communications, but because of Japan's simultaneous preparation for the invasion of Kyushu and its need for Cabinet consensus, U.S. analysts debated about how close Japanese leaders were to actually agreeing on surrender. Japan also sought guarantees of the USSR's continued neutrality—not knowing that the Soviets had already agreed to join the Allies against Japan and that Soviet entry into the war was now set for early August.

Allied leaders were preparing to convene in Potsdam, Germany, to deliberate over the division of postwar Germany and draft a unified demand for Japanese surrender when—in the predawn hours of July 16—the United States conducted its first nuclear weapon test, code-named Trinity, in the desert of Alamogordo, New Mexico. The detonation ignited a terrifying, massive fireball that melted sand into glass, warmed the faces of official witnesses ten miles away, released radioactive debris, and confirmed that an implosion-type plutonium device was feasible for use as a weapon against Japan. To maintain tight secrecy and appease local citizens' concerns, area media outlets cooperated with the U.S. Office of Censorship by releasing the story that the explosion was a "harmless accident in a remote ammunition dump."

Ten days later, the United States, Britain, and China issued the Potsdam Declaration, an ultimatum calling for Japan's unconditional surrender and demanding immediate disarmament, postwar occupation, prosecution of war criminals, and the end of Japan's imperial system. "The alternative for Japan," the declaration read, "is prompt and utter destruction." Some of Truman's advisers believed this message could hasten Japan's surrender and had advocated the inclusion of a clause guaranteeing Japan's retention of the emperor, but this idea was rejected for the final draft. The atomic bomb was not mentioned.

Unable to agree on a response to these conditions, the Japanese Cabinet announced its *mokusatsu* position—reported in the United States as "silent contempt," though the word can also be translated as "withholding comment" or "remaining in wise and masterly inactivity." But Japan's delay in responding to the Potsdam Declaration had no impact on the United States' decision to use its atomic bombs on Japan; that is, on the day before the declaration was issued, Truman had already ordered the bombing of Hiroshima—scheduled for early August "as soon as weather will permit." Less than two weeks later, at 8:15 a.m. on August 6, 1945, a uranium bomb nicknamed Little Boy detonated 1,900 feet above Hiroshima's Shima Hospital, decimating the city and its residents with an explosive force equal to sixteen thousand tons of TNT. One hundred and forty thousand people were killed that day or died from injuries by the end of the year.

"This is the greatest thing in history," Truman exclaimed when the news reached him on board the USS *Augusta* on his return from Germany. Later that day, Secretary of War Henry L. Stimson released a statement on behalf of the president, written prior to Potsdam, announcing the Hiroshima attack and introducing the atomic bomb to the American public. "We are now prepared to obliterate more rapidly and completely every productive enterprise the Japanese have above ground in any city," the statement read. "We shall destroy their docks, their factories, and their communications. Let there be no mistake; we shall completely destroy Japan's power to make war."

Again, no immediate response came from Tokyo. On the day of the bombing, Japanese officials had heard that Hiroshima had been hit by some kind of new bomb, and that night, the Domei News Agency had reported Truman's announcement about the atomic bomb used over Hiroshima. But it took two days for a team of thirty Japanese scientists and military specialists to get to Hiroshima to investigate the bombing, and it took several more days for them to scientifically confirm that the August 6 weapon was indeed an atomic bomb. Their official report would arrive in Tokyo on August 11.

The delivery of additional atomic bombs, however, did not depend on a reply from Tokyo or any further directive from President Truman. His original order was to use them on Japan "as ready"—and on August 8, two days after the Hiroshima attack, the second atomic bomb's assembly was complete.

News of the Hiroshima bombing reached Nagasaki on August 8, when a newspaper headline announced: "Enemy Drops New-Type Bomb on Hiroshima—Considerable Damage Done." Many in the city didn't see the story that day, but those who did were alarmed: By then, most people understood that the Japanese media drastically underplayed the impact of Allied attacks on Japanese cities, so they knew that the words "considerable damage" meant that something far worse had happened.

Some members of Nagasaki's medical community heard about the bombing from Nagasaki Medical College president Tsuno-o Susumu, who had passed through Hiroshima by train on his way home from Tokyo. As soon as he arrived in Nagasaki on August 8, he hurriedly gathered college faculty and staff to describe reports of "a great flash . . . violent blast . . . and fire." With extreme agitation, he told the group about the damages and burned bodies he had seen, and he warned them that Nagasaki's air raid shelters might not provide sufficient protection. Medical College officials decided to suspend classes starting on August 10. That evening, Nishioka Takejiro, chairman of the Nagasaki Shimbun Company, which published the city's newspaper, rushed into Nagasaki Prefecture governor Nagano Wakamatsu's office to similarly report his own eyewitness details of Hiroshima's damages, shocking the governor with descriptions of total devastation, death, and injuries unlike anyone had ever seen. Hoping there was still time to somehow protect Nagasaki, Governor Nagano called a meeting for the next morning with local police chiefs and administrators to formulate a citywide evacuation order.

As the night of August 8 came to a close, the world's first plutonium bomb lay waiting in a specially constructed concrete-lined pit next to the airstrip on Tinian Island—a tiny dot in the Northern Marianas chain, ten miles long and three miles wide, just north of Guam and southwest of Saipan in the vast western Pacific. Fat Man, they called the bomb, and at ten feet eight inches in length and five feet in diameter, and weighing 10,800 pounds, the name fit. At the bomb's core, a small amount of subcritical, enriched plutonium-239 was ringed by sixty-four timed high explosives that, when detonated, would compress the plutonium into a critical mass, triggering a nuclear explosion. The bomb's nose, sides, and tail were covered with the signatures and hometowns of ground and mission crew members, along with brief handwritten messages. "Here's to you!" wrote one soldier from Chicago.

By eleven p.m., the bomb had been hydraulically lifted and loaded into the womb of a specially modified B-29 named *Bockscar*. Members of the 509th Composite Group of the U.S. Army Air Forces, who had trained for more than a year to successfully deliver the nuclear bombs over their target cities, were making final preparations for the second atomic bomb mission. The crews of *Bockscar* and the two companion planes—tasked with visually recording the bombing and collecting scientific data at the time of the blast—gathered for a final briefing. At midnight, as they studied maps and aerial photographs of Kokura and Nagasaki, the mission's primary and secondary targets, the USSR declared war on Japan. One and a half million Soviet troops entered Japanese-occupied Manchuria on three fronts.

At nearly four a.m. (three a.m. Japan time), Major Charles Sweeney climbed into *Bockscar*'s pilot seat, started the engines, rolled the plane forward, and accelerated down the runway. Weighing more than seventy-seven tons, with thirteen crew members, seven thousand gallons of fuel, and the plutonium bomb, *Bockscar* barely lifted off the Tinian airfield and lumbered upward over the ocean. The two companion planes followed. With radio contact between them silenced to prevent detection, Sweeney and the men in all three planes settled in for their 1,500-mile flight through darkness to southern Japan.

The people of Nagasaki hardly slept that night. After eleven p.m., air raid alarms blared, and families across the city awakened and fled to the tiny shelters beneath their houses. Night-shift workers at factories, city services, and watchtowers took refuge in the nearest hillside shelters, and physicians, nurses, and medical personnel at Nagasaki's hospitals and clinics pulled themselves out of bed or left their work areas to carry patients down to basements for protection.

Sixteen-year-old Taniguchi Sumiteru was working the night shift at Michino-o Post Office, where he watched for fires and prepared, if needed, to evacuate records. Taniguchi was fourteen when he was mobilized to

Taniguchi Sumiteru in his post-office uniform, age fifteen, ca. 1944. (*Courtesy of Taniguchi Sumiteru*)

work for the postal service, and the extra income, though small, was vital to his family's survival. His mother had died in 1930 when he was a year old, and that year, his father had left to work as a train engineer in Japanese-held Manchuria, leaving Taniguchi and his older brother and sister to be raised by their grandparents. "My father came back in 1946,"

Taniguchi said, "so I didn't see him for sixteen years. I had one photo of him. He wrote letters and sent money home to help my grandparents."

As a young boy, Taniguchi had helped plant and harvest soybeans, potatoes, cucumbers, watermelons, and chrysanthemums on his grandparents' small plot of land halfway up Mount Inasa, which helped supplement their tiny rations of food during the war. He followed the rules—of his grandparents, his school, and his government. "I was a child then," he reflected. "I pretty much thought that whatever adults said was correct: that the war was good, that Japan—and only Japan—was good, and that the Koreans, Chinese, and Americans were bad. These weren't *my* thoughts," he clarified. "They're what the adults taught me. When I grew older, I understood that these were lies."

When he finished his shift in the early hours of August 9, Taniguchi lay down on a *tatami* mat on the post-office floor and fell asleep. He awoke in the morning with the expectation of several hours off until his next shift started at noon. Instead, a superior asked him to cover his morning route, so Taniguchi packed his assigned mail into his mailbag, attached the bag to his red bicycle, and headed out. Though he was sixteen, he was small and slight, and with his soft, round face, he looked closer to twelve. As he rode through the rural countryside, his feet barely reached the pedals.

By 9:45 a.m., *Bockscar* had crossed the Pacific, but as it approached Kokura on the northwest coast of Kyushu, it was now accompanied only by the mission's instrument plane; the third plane, equipped to film the atomic bombing, had mistakenly missed their planned rendezvous point. The operation's plans were thwarted again when the wind over the region changed, causing cloud cover and heavy smoke to blow in from the nearby city of Yawata, which was still burning from a U.S. firebombing attack the day before. The two U.S. pilots dodged antiaircraft fire from the ground and flak from approaching Japanese planes, but after three runs over Kokura, *Bockscar*'s crew still could not make a visual sighting of the city, so Sweeney turned his plane and directed it 150 miles southwest toward Nagasaki. It was 10:30 a.m.

At the same time, more than seven hundred miles north in Tokyo, an emergency meeting of Japan's "Big Six" Supreme Council for the

Direction of the War (Prime Minister Suzuki Kantarō, Foreign Minister Tōgō Shigenori, Navy Minister Yonai Mitsumasa, Army Minister Anami Korechika, Army Chief of Staff Umezu Yoshijirō, and Navy Chief of Staff Toyoda Soemu) convened to discuss the Soviet Union's surprise invasion of Manchuria and to try again to find agreement on Japan's surrender terms. The mood was somber. Even without yet knowing the scale of the Soviet attack, Japan's leaders knew that their troops could not effectively retaliate, and the Soviet declaration of war had ended any last hope of Japan's securing Soviet neutrality or its assistance in attaining better surrender terms. Prime Minister Suzuki had met Emperor Hirohito earlier that morning and received approval to advocate for acceptance of the Potsdam surrender terms. Grave concern over Japan's dire domestic situation and the Hiroshima bombing fortified the arguments of those pressing for immediate surrender.

Meanwhile, on the ground in Nagasaki, different levels of air raid alarms had continued to sound during the morning, and people had scurried to and from nearby shelters. Some were so exhausted and frustrated with the routine that they ignored the alarms and went on with whatever they were doing. Thirteen-year-old Yoshida Katsuji and six of his childhood friends had walked from their homes across the mountains into the Urakami Valley to the Nagasaki Prefecture Technical School, where Yoshida was a student in the shipbuilding course. When they tried to get into one of his school's air raid shelters, they found it was already filled to capacity with teachers and staff. Instead, they fled to a shelter in the woods and crouched inside.

"Us?" Yoshida said. "We thought Japan would win for sure. We had to endure until we won. That's how it was. Everyone wanted to fight in the war. We longed to. We were educated this way starting in elementary school. We were brainwashed, so we didn't think it was possible for us to lose." The emperor, he explained, "was considered a descendant of God. At school, there was a portrait of him. We would bow and pay our respects when we entered a room. That was the Japanese way." For more than a year, Yoshida's classes had been canceled; instead, he had dug air raid shelters, joined bucket brigades, made bamboo spears, and participated in drills to use them to fight the enemy.

When the alarm lifted on the morning of August 9, Yoshida and his

Yoshida Katsuji, age ten, ca. 1942.
(*Courtesy of Yoshida Naoji*)

friends—seven in all—were supposed to return directly to school, but they took their time coming down from the mountain as they tried to decide whether to skip their assigned duties and go swimming instead. They stopped for a drink of water at a roadside well in the hills bordering the western edge of the Urakami Valley.

By then it was eleven a.m. People throughout the city were back to their daily routines, hanging laundry, reading newspapers, weeding gardens, visiting sick family members, scouring the hills for food, lining up at ration stations, or chatting with neighbors. Twenty-four parishioners and two priests gathered inside Urakami Church for confession. One mother set some beans out to dry in preparation for cooking a special dish for the annual Catholic Feast of the Assumption on August 15. A child played near his family's front door. Of nine Nagasaki residents who had survived the Hiroshima bombing, some had already returned to Nagasaki, while others arrived in the city that morning by train. One man,

Northeastern section of the Urakami Valley, from the hills slightly south of where Yoshida stood just before the bomb detonated. In the foreground is a rice field, behind which a Japanese National Railways train can be seen traveling from north (*left*) to south (*right*). Urakami Church is visible in the back center of the photo. (*U.S. Army Institute of Pathology/ Courtesy of Nagasaki Atomic Bomb Museum*)

who had dug into the ruins of his Hiroshima home to find the bones of his wife, now walked through the streets of Nagasaki carrying a washbasin filled with her ashes to give to her parents.

Korean and Chinese workers, prisoners of war, and mobilized adults and students had returned to their work sites; some dug or repaired shelters, others piled sandbags against the windows of City Hall for protection against machine-gun fire. In the Mitsubishi sports field, bamboo spear drills in preparation for an invasion had just concluded. Classes had resumed at Nagasaki Medical College. Streetcars meandered through

the city. Hundreds of people injured in the air raids just over a week earlier continued to be treated in Nagasaki's hospitals, and at the tuberculosis hospital in the northern Urakami Valley, staff members served a late
breakfast to their patients. One doctor, trained in German, thought to
himself, *Im Westen nichts neues* (All quiet on the western front). In the
concrete-lined shelter near Suwa Shrine that served as the Nagasaki Prefecture Air Defense Headquarters, Governor Nagano had just begun his
meeting with Nagasaki police leaders about an evacuation plan. The sun
was hot, and the high-pitched, rhythmic song of cicadas vibrated throughout the city.

Six miles above, the two B-29s approached Nagasaki. Major Sweeney
and his crew could hardly believe what they saw: Nagasaki, too, was
invisible beneath high clouds. This presented a serious problem. Sweeney's orders were to drop the bomb only after visual sighting of the
aiming point—the center of the old city, east of Nagasaki Harbor. Now,
however, a visual sighting would likely require numerous passes over the
city, which was no longer possible due to fuel loss: Not only had a fuel
transfer pump failed before takeoff, rendering six hundred gallons of fuel
inaccessible, but more fuel than expected had been consumed waiting at
the rendezvous point and while circling over Kokura. *Bockscar* now had
only enough fuel to pass over Nagasaki once and still make it back for
an emergency landing at the American air base on Okinawa. Further,
Sweeney and his weaponeer, Navy commander Fred Ashworth, knew
that not using the bomb on Japan might require dumping it into the sea
to prevent a nuclear explosion upon landing. Against orders, they made
the split-second decision to drop the bomb by radar.

Air raid alarms did not sound in the city—presumably because Nagasaki's air raid defense personnel did not observe the planes in time
or did not recognize the immediate threat of only two planes flying at
such a high altitude. When antiaircraft soldiers on Mount Kompira
finally spotted the planes, they jumped into trenches to aim their weapons but didn't have time to fire; even if they had, their guns could not
have reached the U.S. planes. Several minutes earlier, some citizens had
heard a brief radio announcement that two B-29s had been seen flying
west over Shimabara Peninsula. When they heard the planes approaching, or saw them glistening high in the sky, they called out to warn
others and threw themselves into air raid shelters, onto the ground,

or beneath beds and desks inside houses, schools, and workplaces. A doctor just about to perform a pneumothorax procedure heard the distant sound of planes, pulled the needle out of his patient, and dived for cover. Most of Nagasaki's residents, however, had no warning.

By this time, the crews on both planes were wearing protective welders' glasses so dark that they could barely see their own hands. Captain Kermit Beahan, *Bockscar*'s bombardier, activated the tone signal that opened the bomb bay doors and indicated thirty seconds until release. Five seconds later, he noticed a hole in the clouds and made a visual identification of Nagasaki.

"I've got it! I've got it!" he yelled. He released the bomb. The instrument plane simultaneously discharged three parachutes, each attached to metal canisters containing cylindrical radiosondes to measure blast pressure and relay data back to the aircraft. Ten thousand pounds lighter, *Bockscar* lurched upward, the bomb bay doors closed, and Sweeney turned the plane an intense 155 degrees to the left to get away from the impending blast.

On the ground below, eighteen-year-old Wada had just arrived at Hotarujaya Terminal at the far eastern corner of the old city. The driver responsible for the accident that caused the earlier streetcar derailment was being severely scolded by the company chiefs. "I went to have a bite to eat," Wada remembered, "then sat down on a bench with my friends to discuss the cause of the accident."

Nagano was at work in the temporary Mitsubishi factory in Katafuchimachi, on the other side of the mountains from her family's home.

Taniguchi was delivering mail, riding his bicycle through the hills of a residential area in the northwestern corner of the city.

Sixteen-year-old Dō-oh was back at her workstation inside the Mitsubishi weapons factory, inspecting torpedoes and eagerly awaiting her lunch break.

On the side of a road on the western side of the Urakami River, Yoshida was lowering a bucket into the well when he looked up and, like others across the city, noticed parachutes high in the sky, descending through a crack in the clouds.

"*Rakka-san*, they were called back then," he remembered. Descending umbrellas. "I just thought that they were regular parachutes—that maybe soldiers were coming down."

"Hey, look! Something's falling!" he called out to his friends. They all looked up, putting their hands to their foreheads to block the sun so they could see.

"The parachutes floated down, *saaatto*," he said. Quietly, with no sound.

CHAPTER 2

FLASHPOINT

The five-ton plutonium bomb plunged toward the city at 614 miles per hour. Forty-seven seconds later, a powerful implosion forced its plutonium core to compress from the size of a grapefruit to the size of a tennis ball, generating a nearly instantaneous chain reaction of nuclear fission. With colossal force and energy, the bomb detonated a third of a mile above the Urakami Valley and its thirty thousand residents and workers, a mile and a half north of the intended target. At 11:02 a.m., a superbrilliant flash lit up the sky—visible from as far away as Ōmura Naval Hospital more than ten miles over the mountains—followed by a thunderous explosion equal to the power of twenty-one thousand tons of TNT. The entire city convulsed.

At its burst point, the center of the explosion reached temperatures higher than at the center of the sun, and the velocity of its shock wave exceeded the speed of sound. A tenth of a millisecond later, all of the materials that had made up the bomb converted into an ionized gas, and electromagnetic waves were released into the air. The thermal heat of the bomb ignited a fireball with an internal temperature of over 540,000 degrees Fahrenheit. Within one second, the blazing fireball expanded from 52 feet to its maximum size of 750 feet in diameter. Within three seconds, the ground below reached an estimated 5,400 to 7,200 degrees Fahrenheit. Directly beneath the bomb, infrared heat rays instantly carbonized human and animal flesh and vaporized internal organs.

As the atomic cloud billowed two miles overhead and eclipsed the sun, the bomb's vertical blast pressure crushed much of the Urakami Valley. Horizontal blast winds tore through the region at two and a half times the speed of a category five hurricane, pulverizing buildings, trees, plants, animals, and thousands of men, women, and children. In every direction, people were blown out of their shelters, houses, factories, schools, and hospital beds; catapulted against walls; or flattened beneath collapsed buildings. Those working in the fields, riding streetcars, and standing in line at city ration stations were blown off their feet or hit by plummeting debris and pressed to the scalding earth. An iron bridge moved twenty-eight inches downstream. As their buildings began to implode, patients and staff jumped out of the windows of Nagasaki Medical College Hospital, and mobilized high school girls leaped from the third story of Shiroyama Elementary School, a half mile from the blast.

The blazing heat melted iron and other metals, scorched bricks and concrete buildings, ignited clothing, disintegrated vegetation, and caused severe and fatal flash burns on people's exposed faces and bodies. A mile from the detonation, the blast force caused nine-inch brick walls to crack, and glass fragments bulleted into people's arms, legs, backs, and faces, often puncturing their muscles and organs. Two miles away, thousands of people suffering flesh burns from the extreme heat lay trapped beneath partially demolished buildings. At distances up to five miles, wood and glass splinters pierced through people's clothing and ripped into their flesh. Windows shattered as far as eleven miles away. Larger doses of radiation than any human had ever received penetrated deeply into the bodies of people and animals. The ascending fireball suctioned massive amounts of thick dust and debris into its churning stem. A deafening roar erupted as buildings throughout the city shuddered and crashed to the ground.

"It all happened in an instant," Yoshida remembered. He had barely seen the blinding light half a mile away before a powerful force hit him on his right side and hurled him into the air. "The heat was so intense that I curled up like *surume* [dried grilled squid]." In what felt like dreamlike slow motion, Yoshida was blown backward 130 feet across a field, a road, and an irrigation channel, then plunged to the ground, landing on his back in a rice paddy flooded with shallow water.

Inside the Mitsubishi Ōhashi weapons factory, Dō-oh had been wiping perspiration from her face and concentrating on her work when *PAAAAAHTTO!*—an enormous blue-white flash of light burst into the building, followed by an earsplitting explosion. Thinking a torpedo had detonated inside the Mitsubishi plant, Dō-oh threw herself onto the ground and covered her head with her arms just as the factory came crashing down on top of her.

In his short-sleeved shirt, trousers, gaiters, and cap, Taniguchi had been riding his bicycle through the hills in the northwest corner of the valley when a sudden burning wind rushed toward him from behind, propelling him into the air and slamming him facedown on the road. "The earth was shaking so hard that I hung on as hard as I could so I wouldn't get blown away again."

Nagano was standing inside the school gymnasium–turned–airplane parts factory, protected to some degree by distance and the wooded mountains that stood between her and the bomb. "A light flashed—*pi-KAAAAH!*" she remembered. Nagano, too, thought a bomb had hit her building. She fell to the ground, covering her ears and eyes with her thumbs and fingers according to her training as windows crashed in all around her. She could hear pieces of tin and broken roof tiles swirling and colliding in the air outside.

Two miles southeast of the blast, Wada was sitting in the lounge of Hotarujaya Terminal with other drivers, discussing the earlier derailment. He saw the train cables flash. "The whole city of Nagasaki was— the light was indescribable—an unbelievably massive light lit up the whole city." A violent explosion rocked the station. Wada and his friends dived for cover under tables and other furniture. In the next instant, he felt like he was floating in the air before being slapped down on the floor. Something heavy landed on his back, and he fell unconscious.

Beneath the still-rising mushroom cloud, a huge portion of Nagasaki had vanished. Tens of thousands throughout the city were dead or injured. On the floor of Hotarujaya Terminal, Wada lay beneath a fallen beam. Nagano was curled up on the floor of the airplane parts factory, her mouth filled with glass slivers and choking dust. Dō-oh lay injured in the wreckage of the collapsed Mitsubishi factory, engulfed in smoke. Yoshida was lying in a muddy rice paddy, barely conscious, his body and face brutally scorched. Taniguchi clung to the searing pavement near his mangled bicycle, not yet realizing that his back was burned off. He lifted his eyes just long enough to see a young child "swept away like a fleck of dust."

Sixty seconds had passed.

The atomic cloud, rising more than forty thousand feet over Nagasaki. (*Courtesy of U.S. National Archives*)

———

The enormous, undulating cloud ascended seven miles above the city. From the sky, *Bockscar*'s copilot Lieutenant Frederick Olivi described it as "a huge, boiling caldron." William L. Laurence, the official journalist for the Manhattan Project who had witnessed the bombing from the instrument plane, likened the burgeoning cloud to "a living thing, a new species of being, born right before our incredulous eyes." Captain Beahan remembered it "bubbling and flashing orange, red and green . . . like a picture of hell."

Outside the city, many people who saw the flash of light and heard the deafening explosion rushed out of their homes and stared in wonder at the nuclear cloud heaving upward over Nagasaki. A worker on an island in Ōmura Bay, several miles north of the blast, described it as "lurid-colored . . . curling like long tongues of fire in the sky." In Isahaya, five miles east of the city, a grandmother feared that "the sun would come falling down," and a young boy grabbed at ash and paper falling from the sky, only to realize that they were scraps of ration books belonging to residents in the Urakami Valley. From the top of Mount Tohakkei four miles southeast of Nagasaki, a man loading wood into his truck was "stunned speechless by the beauty of the spectacle" of the giant rising cloud exploding over and over again as it transformed from white to yellow to red. In neighborhoods at the edge of the city, people peered out of windows and stepped outside to see the atomic cloud rising above them, only to bolt back inside or to nearby shelters in anticipation of a second attack.

Inside the city, the bomb's deadly gale quieted, leaving Nagasaki enveloped in a dark, dust-filled haze. Nearest the hypocenter (the point on the ground above which the bomb exploded), almost everyone was incinerated, and those still alive were burned so badly they could not move. In areas beyond the hypocenter, surviving men, women, and children began extricating themselves from the wreckage and tentatively stood, in utter terror, for their first sight of the missing city. Twenty minutes after the explosion, particles of carbon ash and radioactive residue descended from the atmosphere and condensed into an oily black rain that fell over Nishiyama-machi, a neighborhood about two miles east over the mountains.

Nagano pulled herself up from the floor of the airplane parts factory and stood, quivering, rubbing debris from her eyes and spitting dust and glass fragments from her throat and mouth. Around her, adult and student workers lay cowering on the ground or rose to their feet, stunned and bewildered. Opening her eyes just a bit, Nagano sensed it was too dangerous to stay where she was. She ran outside and squeezed herself into a crowded mountain air raid shelter, where she crouched down and waited for another bomb to drop.

"The whole Urakami district has been destroyed!" one of the male workers called out to her. "Your house may have burned as well!" Nagano fled from the bomb shelter and ran toward the Urakami Valley. Outside, the neighborhood around the factory was almost pitch-dark and hauntingly still. Large trees had snapped in half, tombstones had fallen in a cemetery nearby, and streets were filled with broken roof tiles and glass. Small birds lay on the ground, twitching. Compared to what she had imagined, however, the damages around her seemed minimal, and Nagano—who could not see the Urakami Valley—half believed that her family might be safe after all.

She hurried through the streets to the southern end of Nishiyama-machi toward Nagasaki Station, over a mile to the east, pressing past partially collapsed wooden houses and people fleeing the blast area. As the road curved west, Nagano rushed by the 277-step stone staircase leading up to the seventeenth-century Suwa Shrine, still intact, and Katsu-yama Elementary School, just next to City Hall. Forty-five minutes later, Nagano finally passed the mountains that had stood between her and the expanse of atomic destruction. In front of her, the main building of Nagasaki Station had collapsed. But it was the view to her right that shocked her into finally realizing that the rumors she had heard about the Urakami Valley were true. Where the northern half of Nagasaki had existed only an hour before, a low heavy cloud of smoke and dust hovered over a vast plain of rubble. Nothing remained of the dozens of neighborhoods except tangled electrical wires and an occasional lone chimney. The huge factories that had lined the river near Nagasaki Station were crumpled into masses of steel frames and wooden beams, and the streetcar rails were, in one survivor's words, "curled up like strands of taffy." No trace of roads existed beneath miles of smoking wreckage. Blackened corpses covered the ground. Survivors were stumbling through the ruins moaning in pain, their skin hanging down like tattered cloth. Others raced away, shrieking, *Run! Escape!* A barefoot mother in shredded clothes ran through the wreckage screaming for her child. Most people, however, were silent. Many simply dropped dead where they stood.

Nagano's house was just over a half mile to the north and west, a ten-minute walk on any other day. She faced in that direction to scan the area, but there was nothing—no buildings, no trees, and no sign of life where she had last seen her mother and younger brother and sister. Her eyes searched frantically for a way home, but the flames spreading through the ruins prevented access from all directions. Paralyzed and confused, Nagano stood in front of Nagasaki Station, alone, with no idea what to do next.

———

The three-square-mile region obliterated by the bomb stretched just over a mile east to west and three miles north to south, from the top edge of the Urakami Valley to the bay, close to where Nagano stood. The affected area would have been significantly larger, as in Hiroshima, had not the blast, heat, and radiation been contained by the mountains surrounding the valley to the north, east, and west. The location of the bay, a mile and a half south of the hypocenter, also limited the extent of the bomb's destruction.

In both Hiroshima and Nagasaki, fatalities, injuries, and physical destruction from the bombs' blast, heat, and radiation are described in relation to distance from the atomic explosion, creating an imagined overlay of concentric circles radiating outward from the hypocenter. Within Nagasaki's first concentric circle—a half kilometer (three-tenths of a mile) in all directions from the blast—nearly all buildings were demolished, and bodies were disintegrated or burned beyond recognition. Mortality was estimated at over 90 percent.

Because the city and its infrastructure were destroyed and government investigations took place only after the war ended, records to account for every fatality could not be collected, but some of the tens of thousands of instantaneous deaths throughout the hypocenter area were later documented. Almost directly beneath the bomb, 43 people in an underground air raid shelter and 134 staff members and prisoners at the Urakami Branch of Nagasaki Prison suffered fatal burns and injuries, including more than 40 Chinese and Koreans. To the east, 314 physicians and medical students died in the auditorium of Nagasaki Medical College, and an estimated 200 patients were killed in the hospital next door. Farther north, 2 Catholic priests and 24 parishioners waiting for confession died beneath the imploded Urakami Church. Just west of the hypocenter, 52 mobilized students and teachers were fatally injured at Shiroyama Elementary School, and an estimated 1,400 children enrolled at the school perished in their homes and shelters throughout the neighborhood. Sixty-eight students and teachers were killed at Chinzei Middle School, less than a third of a mile southwest of the hypocenter. Inside the Urakami railway station, most of the 85 adult and youth employees died. To the south, well beyond this first radius of death, at least 4 Allied prisoners of war—3 Dutch and 1 British—were killed instantly at the Fukuoka POW Camp No. 14 at Saiwai-machi. Four more Dutch POWs died within two weeks. Out of the 9,000 Japanese military personnel throughout Nagasaki, 150 were killed.

Yoshida, Dō-oh, and Taniguchi were north of the explosion. The well where Yoshida had stood was in the second concentric circle, its outer boundary marking a radius of one kilometer (six-tenths of a mile) from the hypocenter. There the blast pressure tore off heads and limbs and caused eyes and internal organs to explode. The bomb's heat scalded the water in a nearby pond and caused terrible burns on the bodies of children playing by the shore. A woman who had covered her eyes from the flash lowered her hands to find that the skin of her face had melted into her palms. Most trees were downed or shattered. Thousands of people were crushed beneath toppled houses, factories, and schools, and thousands more suffered severe thermal burns. Roof tiles blistered in the heat.

Like everyone else in Nagasaki that day, Yoshida's immediate survival and degree of injury from burns and radiation depended entirely on his exact location, the direction he was facing in relation to the bomb, what he was wearing, and what buildings, walls, trees, or even rocks stood between him and the speeding force of the bomb's titanic power. Yoshida had been facing in the direction of the hypocenter only a half mile away in a rural region of the Urakami Valley, with very little to shield him from the bomb's blast force and heat. "I was hurled backward into a rice paddy, right? At some point I regained consciousness and could feel the coldness of the water. I stood up, and my body was covered in mud." The skin on his arm had peeled off and was hanging down from his fingertips, and he could feel that his chest and legs were burned, but Yoshida did not yet know the extent of his facial burns. "Blood was pouring out of my flesh," he said. Like thousands of others, he went into shock. "I know it sounds strange, but I felt absolutely no pain. I even forgot to cry."

The blast had thrown Yoshida and his friends in different directions, but all six survived, albeit with serious burns and wounds. After some time, they found one another and slowly made their way to a small tributary of the Urakami River, where they rinsed the mud off their bodies and lay down together in the grass, hoping that someone would find them. One of Yoshida's friends handed him a broken piece of mirror, and when Yoshida looked at his reflection, he could not comprehend what he saw. "All I can say is that I didn't recognize my own face."

Hundreds of field-workers and others staggered by, moaning and crying. Some were missing body parts, and others were so badly burned that even though they were naked, Yoshida couldn't tell if they were men or women. He saw one person whose eyeballs hung down his face, the sockets empty. Everyone begged for water, and some died while drinking from the stream. During the war, Yoshida's teachers had incorrectly warned their students that drinking water while injured would cause excessive bleeding and death—so Yoshida held out all day with no water to ease his extreme dehydration.

A group of wailing mothers coming down from the mountains shook Yoshida and his friends out of their dazed state and awakened them to their own physical pain and terror. "We were only thirteen years old," he recalled, "and when we heard these mothers crying, we started sobbing too, even louder than they were." The boys rose to their feet and followed the women down the slopes toward the city. At the Urakami River, however, Yoshida wavered. Clutched by pervasive heat and choking dust, he saw people on the ground with severed limbs and heads split open, their brains oozing out. Other bodies were completely carbonized—"turned into charcoal," he remembered. The river, to which people had fled for relief from the heat and intense thirst, had become a mass grave—*because they drank the water,* Yoshida thought. Corpses bobbed in the river, now red with blood.

Yoshida began to feel his face and body swell. He looked down to see leeches from the rice paddy stuck to his bare legs. He and his friends stumbled back to the small stream where they had come from, removed the leeches from their bodies, and placed uncharred leaves over their raw flesh. In an attempt to escape the heat of the sun, the seven boys burrowed into the tall grass against the riverbank. Pain shot through Yoshida's body, and by this time, his face was so swollen that he couldn't see.

"Hang in there, okay?" the boys whispered to one another. "Gotta keep going—do our best to stay alive!"

Dō-oh was injured three-quarters of a mile from the hypocenter—within the third concentric circle. There, blistered clay roof tiles later indicated exposure to heat over 3,000 degrees Fahrenheit, and the death rate was estimated at 50 percent. When the Mitsubishi Ōhashi plant collapsed on top of Dō-oh and thousands of others, some people were thrown so far that when they regained consciousness, they were in a different part of the factory. In Dō-oh's area, nearly everyone lay dead beneath an avalanche of heavy equipment, steel beams, concrete walls, and metal columns.

Section of the destroyed interior of the Mitsubishi Arms Factory Ōhashi Plant, where Dō-oh Mineko worked, October 1945. (*Photograph by Hayashi Shigeo/Courtesy of Nagasaki Atomic Bomb Museum*)

The crushed room was utterly quiet. After a few moments, Dō-oh opened her eyes to find herself lying on the factory floor covered with huge pieces of debris. She extricated herself and stood up to get her bearings, but thick smoke and dust barred visibility in every direction. "The silence scared me. No one else was there." In the intense heat, with flames darting up around her, Dō-oh searched for the exit but could not see it anywhere. "I didn't know what to do!" she said. "I knew if I stayed there, I would die. I panicked and searched for the door again. *I have to escape!* I thought. *I have to escape! If I don't escape, I will burn and die!*"

Finally, she spotted an older man staggering in the shadows, his shirt and pants smoldering. She moved toward him as fast as she could, tripping over asbestos roofing, broken iron framing, crisscrossed wooden beams, and unidentified blackened objects she later discovered were the bodies of her coworkers. When she reached the old man, Dō-oh followed him through the smoky remains of the factory, past countless people trapped and moaning beneath the wreckage, to the outside where she thought she would be safe.

But the city as she had known it no longer existed. All around, thick layers of splintered glass, metal dust, and twisted wire covered the ground, along with scorched corpses staring upward or facing down as though sleeping. Hundreds of men and women who had climbed out of the factory rubble staggered across the grounds, half-naked, their blistered skin falling off their bodies; many held their arms stretched out in front of them—probably, one survivor guessed, to keep the skin that had peeled off their arms and hands from dragging on the ground. "They all looked gray," one woman remembered. "No, not even gray; they were simply colorless, dusty figures with two blank holes for eyes, a stubby nose, and another hole for a mouth." A mother cradled her headless infant and wailed.

Dō-oh stumbled toward the main road, where she met two of her classmates emerging from nearby factory buildings. The girls were startled when they saw Dō-oh's injuries, but Dō-oh was in such shock that she didn't register the meaning of their expressions. The three girls joined hands and agreed to escape to the hills together. Within moments, Dō-oh felt too weak to go on. She squatted on the ground outside the factory gates. "Don't worry about me," she assured her friends, urging them to keep going. "I'll meet up with you soon." As they left for safety, the girls encouraged Dō-oh not to give up and told her they'd be waiting for her.

Dō-oh rested in the rubble, but she was too scared to stay where she was, so she forced herself up and walked in the direction of a Buddhist temple, then made her way down an embankment to some railroad tracks. She had no strength to climb up the other side. She paused and looked up again, then grabbed the exposed roots of a fallen tree on the ridge above her. Holding on with all her strength, Dō-oh pulled herself up the steep incline. On top of the embankment, she collapsed on the ground surrounded by dozens of other wounded people.

It was here that Dō-oh finally realized the gravity of her injuries: The whole left side of her body was badly burned, a bone was sticking out of her right arm at the elbow, hundreds of glass splinters had penetrated most of her body, and blood was streaming down her neck. Too dazed to cry, she reached back to the base of her head and felt a wide and deep horizontal gash stretching from one ear to the other, filled with shards of glass and wood. "Daddy!" she cried. "Please come! Please help me!" As she lay on the embankment, a plane flew over at very low altitude—so close, Dō-oh remembered, that she could see the pilot. Panicked at the idea of possible machine-gun fire, she crawled to a fallen tree and squeezed her body under one of its limbs as the plane flew over a second time. Nearly invisible, desperately thirsty, and surrounded by disfigured strangers— some silent and others crying out for their loved ones—Dō-oh felt completely alone.

Slightly over a mile from the hypocenter, Taniguchi had been riding his bicycle in a rural area surrounded by rice paddies and vegetable fields, in the direct path of the bomb's unyielding force. He lay on his stomach in the road and waited for the earth to stop shaking. After some time, he raised his head. The bodies of children who had been playing by the road lay scorched all around him. Petrified that he, too, would die there, Taniguchi willed himself to stay alive. *I can't die now, I can't die now,* he told himself. *I refuse to die.*

He heaved himself up. All the houses around him were destroyed. Flames spurted from the ruins. Near him, a woman lay in agony, her hair burned off and her face terribly swollen. Taniguchi glanced over at his crushed bicycle. His postal bag was open and mail had scattered all around. Bewildered, he wandered along the road, collecting the letters and stuffing them into his pockets—and for the first time he noticed his injuries. His right hand was seared black. From his fingertips to his shoulder, the skin on his left arm had melted and was hanging in shreds. His left leg, too, was badly burned. Taniguchi felt something strange and slippery on his back, so he reached around to find that his shirt was gone—and when he pulled his hand back, his fingers were covered with charred, melted skin, black and slimy, like grease. "I did not feel any pain, and there was not a single drop of blood."

Leaving his bicycle and mailbag behind, Taniguchi dragged himself forward, as though sleepwalking, to search for help. Up the road, he passed the women's dorm of the Mitsubishi factory, where people squirmed in pain on the ground, their hair singed and their bodies and faces burned and swollen. A short distance farther, he made his way into one of Mitsubishi's Sumiyoshi mountain tunnels and fumbled through a dark, narrow passageway packed with injured factory workers. Taniguchi collapsed onto a worktable. A woman offered him a bit of water, apologizing that there wasn't more because the city's waterlines had been destroyed. She cut off the skin dangling from Taniguchi's arm, and since all the medicines stored in the tunnel were already used up, she applied machine oil to try to soothe the raw, dust-filled flesh of his back.

Fear of a second attack spread through the tunnel. As everyone clambered to escape to the hills, Taniguchi tried to hoist himself off the table, but his legs couldn't support him. Several men carried him outside to the top of a hill where they laid him down on his stomach surrounded by injured people begging for water, crying out for help, and muttering their names and addresses in the hope that someone would tell their families where and how they had died. By then it was past noon. Half-conscious and unable to move, Taniguchi lay facedown in that spot for the rest of the day, the flesh of his back and arms unprotected from the lingering heat of the nuclear blast and the intense sun bearing down through the atomic haze.

———

Until the night before, when he had first heard reports of the Hiroshima bombing, Nagasaki prefectural governor Nagano Wakamatsu's lack of understanding about the nature of atomic weapons had allowed him reasonable confidence in Nagasaki's wartime rescue preparedness. Nagasaki

Medical College served as the principal site for emergency medical care, supported by eighteen hospitals and medical clinics throughout the city that could provide outpatient care for 1,240 people. If needed, the faculty and staff of Nagasaki Medical College and its hospital could provide extra care, and its student body could offer additional basic first-aid support. Large stores of medicine and supplies had been stowed for safekeeping in concrete-reinforced warehouses. In reality, however, even if the governor had been given more information and preparation time, neither Nagasaki nor any city in the world had the capacity to build rescue and relief operations adequate for a nuclear attack.

When the bomb detonated, the governor had just convened his emergency evacuation planning meeting inside the concrete-lined air raid shelter that served as the Nagasaki Prefecture Air Defense Headquarters, situated southeast of the Urakami Valley on the other side of the mountains. After hearing immediate accounts from area workers that several parachutes had descended, followed by a brilliant flash of light and a tremendous explosion, the governor believed that "new-type" bombs like the one reportedly dropped on Hiroshima had been used on Nagasaki as well. When he ran outside to investigate, however, he saw that houses in the immediate neighborhood near Suwa Shrine were undamaged except for windows shattered by the explosion. He turned to the south and scanned the Nakashima Valley and city center, seeing nothing that fit the descriptions he had heard of a completely annihilated Hiroshima. Details from various Nagasaki police stations reported minimal damage and no serious injuries. Based on these early observations and descriptions of damages, the governor concluded that—unlike Hiroshima—the new-type bombs dropped on Nagasaki had caused only fires, and that the atomic cloud he could see rising and expanding above Mount Kompira was only intense smoke. Within minutes, he dispatched telegrams to key officials in Kyushu and western Japan stating that the bombs were smaller versions of those used on Hiroshima and that his city's structural damages and casualties were minimal.

But the governor soon realized that the early police reports he had received had come only from Nagasaki's outlying areas; no reports had come in yet from the northern sections of the city. "Telephone lines were dead," he later explained, "and we had no idea that thousands of people, including the police, had been killed or injured in the Urakami area." It would be nearly an hour after the bombing when he first learned, with great anguish, that almost none of the city's emergency medical services had survived the nuclear attack: The Medical College and its hospital were destroyed, and a large number of its staff and students were dead. A majority of the city's other hospitals, clinics, and designated relief stations and their personnel, mostly located within a half mile of the hypocenter, were also gone. Too late for evacuation measures, the governor ordered the mobilization of doctors and nurses in the old city to provide aid to victims—but even they were mostly helpless because nearly all medicines had been destroyed in the blast. Few treatment options remained beyond water, pumpkin juice, sesame oil, machine oil, Mercurochrome (an antiseptic), zinc oxide cream, and an occasional tin of petroleum jelly. Mothers applied cooking oil to their children's burns, and some boys removed their bleached cotton loincloths to use as bandages.

Wada was among the first civilians to support the city's search and rescue efforts. Initially knocked unconscious when Hotarujaya Terminal collapsed, when he regained his senses, Wada found himself lying face-down beneath large wooden beams and debris. He called out for help, and eventually several students found him and pulled him out of the wreckage. Wada had suffered minor cuts and injuries but was otherwise unharmed. As he sat in the partially collapsed station house, a little girl about five years old wandered in and sat down in front of him, crying. Her forehead was raw with burns and her face and body were covered in blood. "[Her] eyes were so big," Wada recalled. "She never said a single word."

Still weakened and scared, he hoisted the girl onto his back and carried her outside the station toward a neighborhood clinic. "It was still around noon," Wada remembered, "but the atomic cloud blocked the sun, so it was dark like night." Nothing around him was the same as before. Every house was damaged. People escaping the hypocenter region walked past him in silence, but they were so badly wounded that "they didn't look like humans." When he got to the relief station, it was already jammed with people, so Wada took a wet rag and wiped the girl's face and body as best he could. In time, a doctor applied *akachin* (Mercurochrome) and gauze bandages to her forehead and asked Wada to take the girl to a nearby elementary school being used as an emergency shelter. Wada lifted her on his back again and took her to the school's athletic field, already overflow-ing with injured and burned people. "I had no choice but to lay her down there," he said. He went back to the field a few days later, and the girl was no longer there. Wada guessed that she had died.

In the early afternoon, he made his way back to Hotarujaya Ter-minal, where injured drivers and other employees of the streetcar com-pany had begun to gather. News arrived of the total destruction of the Urakami area, prompting Wada, as the student leader, to take an imme-diate roll call. Of sixty student workers, twelve were missing. Wada sent the girls home immediately and told them to escape with their families as far away as possible, then he and a group of male students set out in search of their friends. He kept thinking about three of the drivers who were heading into the Urakami Valley just before eleven a.m., including his best friend, Tanaka, and he tried to calculate their positions at the time of the bomb. Praying they were safe, he and his colleagues followed the streetcar lines to Nagasaki Station, but fires blocked them from going farther, so they turned back and joined the early relief efforts taking place all around them. As policemen assisted victims, civilian air raid wardens hurried through neighborhoods calling out to the injured, tell-ing them to go to the temporary relief stations being set up in elementary schools. Medical relief personnel worked side by side with citizen aid volunteers, trying to help the seemingly endless numbers of survivors without any knowledge of the kinds of burns they were treating or the weapon that had caused them. Wada and his friends used wooden doors to carry the injured to makeshift aid stations. Of those they tried to save, few lived.

By 12:30 p.m., most of the buildings near the hypocenter were burn-ing, including Nagasaki Medical College, and the numerous smaller fires that had erupted after the explosion had converged into a sea of flames. Everything in the Urakami Valley not initially destroyed by the atomic blast burned to the ground, and the fires quickly reached as far south as the Nagasaki Prefectural Government Building, the courthouse, and contiguous neighborhoods on the eastern side of the bay, all of which were gutted. In areas farther out, flammable objects such as trees and wooden houses that had absorbed the immense heat of the bomb spontaneously burst into flames. City officials could not comprehend the magnitude and speed of the conflagration. Beneath a dark, crimson sky, an early citizen firefighting crew set out toward the Urakami Valley along the railroad tracks to Yachiyo-machi, the southernmost neighborhood of the hypocenter area. Wearing helmets, gas masks, canteens over their shoulders, and daggers at their waists, the firemen were a stark visual contrast to the burned and naked bodies of those fleeing the scene. The power of the fires, however—along with the destruction of trucks and equipment and lack of water due to broken water mains and melted and damaged water pipes—prevented firefighters from containing the inferno. Able-bodied citizens raced to the edges of the blazes and created bucket brigades to extinguish the fires, but fanned by summer winds, the firestorm intensified. By early afternoon, the popping and hissing of encroaching flames terrorized survivors in almost every section of the city.

From Nagasaki Station, Nagano had pressed north along the melted railroad tracks parallel to the Urakami River, searching for a way around the fires to get to her home. "There were so many dead bodies on the ground, everywhere," she remembered. "Heads here, bodies there, and next to them, people barely alive crying, '*Tasukete kudasai!*' [Please help me!]" At every turn, fires stopped Nagano from moving closer to her neighborhood. As she crossed Inasa Bridge, by total coincidence she ran into her uncle, who was coming toward her. He and Nagano's father worked at the same Mitsubishi Electric factory near the shipyard. Before racing away to search for his family, her uncle urged Nagano to stay where she was because her father would be coming along soon. Nagano waited, straining in the direction of the Mitsubishi Electric plant to the south, desperate for a glimpse of her father among the throngs of people moving in both directions.

Suddenly, he appeared in front of her. Relieved beyond words, Nagano sobbed and hugged him. Time was critical, however, so they quickly returned to the western side of the Urakami River and maneuvered their way over broken utility poles and severed power lines toward the next bridge to the north. Across the river they could see the crushed Mitsubishi steelworks factory, its towering smokestacks bent at the middle by the force of the blast wind. Hordes of injured people passed them, heading south to flee the area, "their bodies burned and bloated," Nagano remembered, "naked except for patches of torn clothing stuck to their wounds." Some of them staggered toward Nagano and her father and grabbed at them, begging for help and for water. "It was so terrible for them. But—" Nagano choked as she recalled the scene: "*Dooooooooh suru koto mo dekinatta!* [We could do absolutely nothing for them!] At least if we had had a canteen with us, we could have given them sips of water! We apologized—we said we were sorry—that's all we could do. One after the other, people collapsed right in front of us and died."

The air smelled of smoke and death. As Yoshida had seen farther north, here, too, the riverbanks were piled high with dead bodies. Corpses floated just below the surface of the river, "like potatoes in a tub," one survivor remembered, some facedown and others sinking headfirst so only their feet were visible. When Nagano and her father approached the Yanagawa Bridge, they halted at the sight of a dead horse standing on all four legs, totally blackened, its head stretched upward. Nagano clung to her father's arm as they walked past it and crossed the bridge to get closer to their house—but fires continued to block every entrance to their neighborhood. After many attempts, they grudgingly turned around and crossed back to the west side of the river, where they came to an air raid shelter. They crawled inside and huddled together on the ground. There was nothing to do but wait.

———

By two p.m., the atomic cloud had drifted twenty-four miles east and now hung over Mount Kinugasa on the Shimabara Peninsula. In Nagasaki, as the firestorm spread and burned to death people trapped beneath fallen buildings, gunpowder ignited in the Mitsubishi Ōhashi factory, creating another explosion that reverberated throughout the valley. The four main thoroughfares into and out of the city were mobbed with dazed survivors wandering through the ruins, people trying to evacuate, and city workers racing to (unsuccessfully) restore power and water to the city. Desperate family members rushed to find their loved ones, bowing in reverence to the dead and injured people they passed or stepped over. From every direction, the ground in the hypocenter area was still too hot to enter, and people raced frantically in search of detours. Many waded through dead bodies to cross the Urakami River only to be stopped on the other side by a wall of heat.

Mothers and fathers searched for their children at schools, factories, and shelters throughout the area, but facial burns and swelling rendered people so unrecognizable that many parents could only identify their sons or daughters by reading the ID tags on their school uniforms. Fortunate families were overwhelmed with gratitude when a loved one returned. When one mother burst out shouting and crying with happiness when her daughter finally came home, a military policeman rebuked her loudly: "Such effeminate behavior has caused Japan to be defeated!"

Using still-functioning train cars, the first relief train had already left the Ōhashi area carrying injured people to medical facilities outside Nagasaki. Many victims died en route or soon after arrival. In the meantime, medical relief and firefighting teams poured into the city from surrounding townships. By late afternoon, regional navy officials had also dispatched medical teams from hospitals outside the city, though many were delayed in arriving due to recurrent air raid alarms in their regions and damaged roads into Nagasaki. Navy rescue workers entering the city by train from the north were shocked by the eerie scenes before them of people crawling toward the tracks, the annihilated city burning in the distance, and the horrific smell of burning flesh, food, and buildings. The men began loading people into the empty trains and sending them off to naval hospitals in Isahaya (sixteen miles northeast), Ōmura (twenty-two miles north), and Sasebo (fifty-six miles northwest), though these hospitals were not equipped to handle the simultaneous arrival of hundreds of severely burned and injured people. It was impossible to notify the patients' families about their locations, and many victims died alone before anyone knew where they were.

While Yoshida and his friends crouched against the embankment, the leaves they had placed over their open wounds dried and crumbled off their bodies, and with no buildings or trees left to provide shade, their raw flesh was exposed to the direct heat of the sun. "No words can describe how excruciating the pain was. I really thought I was going to die," he remembered. "The heat of the sun was more unbearable than the atomic bomb." When the sun finally fell behind the mountains to the west, the visceral relief the boys felt deluded them into thinking that at last they were saved.

But Yoshida's burned face continued to swell. At first he used his fingers to keep his eyes open, but within a few hours, the swelling was so severe he could no longer see. Whenever he heard someone passing by, he called out, pleading with them for information about his neighborhood near Suwa Shrine. "Is it damaged?" he cried. "Are the people there okay?" Wounded victims called back to him that the whole city was destroyed. Yoshida faded into unconsciousness.

"Mineko! Mineko!" Dō-oh's father called out for her. When she didn't return home after the bombing, he had set out to find her, searching the areas around the Mitsubishi Ōhashi factory and moving as close as he could to the hypocenter. At the embankment where Dō-oh was hiding under the limb of a fallen tree, the faces of people lying on the ground were so swollen that he was unsure he would be able to recognize her even if she was there. Still, he called out her name. By then, however, Dō-oh, still bleeding, had fallen into semiconsciousness and couldn't hear her father's cries. He returned home to find out what she had been wearing that day, then left again, this time with the hope of identifying his daughter by her clothes.

Some time later, Dō-oh regained momentary consciousness and peered up from beneath the tree to see one of her classmates, who told her that her father had been there looking for her. Panicked that she would still be too hidden for her father to find her, she tried to stand up. But she couldn't move. Eventually Dō-oh mumbled loudly enough to catch the attention of a young man passing by, and she asked him to carry her to a grassy area closer to the road. He placed her in a line of dead bodies and injured people, some of whom were moaning in pain. Another stranger covered her with mosquito netting.

Pain shot through Dō-oh's body, and she longed for water to relieve her intensely dry throat. "Anything, even muddy water would have been fine." Shivering, she reached up to touch her wound a second time, and the slimy gash was so deep that her fingers went in all the way up to the first knuckle. Again, Dō-oh drifted into unconsciousness. This time she hallucinated, seeing images of herself walking barefoot along an endless path between rice paddies with vast fields of bright rape blossoms all around. Yellow and white butterflies flew over the meadows. "It was a world where no one goes," she recalled, "an extremely lonely, isolated world." In the dream, she sat on a rock. In the distance, an old man in a white kimono beckoned her close to him. As she tried to approach him, another voice awakened her with a small whisper: *"Don't sleep! Don't sleep!"* It was God's voice, the creator's voice, Dō-oh later believed, calling her back from the edge of death.

Dō-oh's father returned to the embankment and again searched among the bodies for any recognizable scrap of clothing. He called out Dō-oh's name over and over. This time she heard him. Summoning every fragment of energy, Dō-oh whispered back—*"Yes!"*—in a voice just loud enough for him to hear. Her father and three others lifted her onto a broken wooden door and carried her two and half miles to the house of Dr. Miyajima Takeshi, a retired army physician who lived in Dō-oh's neighborhood in northwest Nagasaki, where the doctor and his family had begun providing treatment to victims fifteen minutes after the explosion. It was dark when Dō-oh's group arrived. The doctor's yard spilled over with injured and dying people lying on the ground—hoping, praying, and begging for help.

———

The sun set on Nagasaki at 7:12 p.m., eight hours after the atomic blast. Near the hypocenter, flames darted out of the rubble, and outlying neighborhoods were still ablaze. People lying on the ground were consumed by fire. At makeshift relief stations and safe zones, volunteers distributed rations for the first time that day—*onigiri*, crackers, canned meat, and dry biscuits with sesame seeds—prepared by volunteer women's groups outside Nagasaki and donated through their municipal governments. Workers used megaphones to announce the availability of food, but by then, most able-bodied people had fled. Scraps of burning documents and papers fluttered over the city. The Catholic orphanage and girls' schools in the northern Urakami Valley had already burned down, and sometime that night, the ruins of Urakami Church ignited, sending pillars of fire high into the night sky.

Darkness had forced most family members to stop searching for their loved ones, though some with lanterns pressed on. A young father found his wife behind their house; charred and covered with ashes, she was calling out the names of their children, who were never found. Some survivors retreated to pumpkin fields beyond the fires to sleep among the injured and dying. Others fought off their drowsiness, afraid they would die if they fell asleep. An eleven-year-old girl slept on the ground close to her mother, her sole surviving family member, only to wake up in the middle of the night to find her mother dead.

By midnight, relief trains had carried an estimated 3,500 injured people to cities and villages beyond Nagasaki, where countless more survivors had also arrived by foot or truck. Teams of medical staff and volunteers worked through the night to treat them, though their supplies quickly ran out.

In Nagasaki, tens of thousands of burned and injured men, women, and children remained trapped beneath collapsed buildings and heavy debris or lay wounded on hillsides, by the railroad tracks, or along the banks of the Urakami River. In what can only be explained as an unintentional error of timing in the Allies' ongoing psychological warfare initiative across Japan, U.S. B-29s flew over the city in the middle of the night and dropped thousands of leaflets that demanded that Japan end all military action and surrender. The leaflets warned the people of Nagasaki about a possible atomic bomb attack and urged them to evacuate immediately. Most survivors did not see the leaflets until the next day or later, but hearing these and other enemy planes overhead, those who could still move scrambled to hide themselves in mountaintop graveyards, under bridges, or inside overcrowded air raid shelters, where the stench of scorched flesh and blood, the mosquitoes, and the penetrating screams of the injured were unbearable. Across the sweltering city, the sounds of small explosions, fires crackling, and voices of adults and children searching for, comforting, or crying out for their loved ones created a haunting cacophony.

Near the well where he'd seen the parachutes falling through the clouds, Yoshida lay on the ground under the rising crescent moon, fading in and out of consciousness. His face was swollen like a balloon, his throat was so hot he thought it was burning, and he was shivering due to extreme loss of skin. One of his six friends, Tabuchi, who could still see out of one eye, left the group to try to make it in darkness over the mountains to their neighborhood in Nishiyama.

Nagano and her father hid inside the packed air raid shelter not far from Inasa Bridge. With no electricity, flashlights, or candles, they sat in pitch-blackness, terrified as they listened to a series of explosions outside. One by one, people died all around them, crying for water or mumbling their names and addresses.

On the veranda of his house, Dr. Miyajima treated Dō-oh before others because of the severity of her injuries, while dozens waited their turn. Working by candlelight and with no anesthesia, he removed hundreds of glass splinters embedded in her head and body. *"Stop! Stop!"* Dō-oh shrieked, thrashing in agony. Her parents and two other adults used all their weight to hold her arms and legs to the table. "If we stop treating you, you will die," someone told her. But Dō-oh didn't care, and she screamed over and over for the doctor to stop and let her die. The doctor persisted, and before morning, the rice bowl that lay near her head was filled with bloody glass slivers. Her head now wrapped in bandages, Dō-oh languished near death.

That night, Wada had walked through the darkened, smoldering streets east of Nagasaki Bay to his home in Maruyama-machi. His house was damaged but still intact. To his great relief, he found a note from his grandparents saying that they and his younger sister were alive and had fled to the suburb of Tagami. From the hillside behind his house, he watched the fires raging in the city center and the Urakami Valley to the north. Filled with apprehension about the fate of his friends, he returned to Hotarujaya Terminal, where he and his coworkers slept on the debris-laden station floor. Outside, refugees from neighboring districts continued to stream through streets lit by flames. Some brought nothing; others carried on their backs—or in handcarts—any possessions they could salvage.

Taniguchi's grandfather had walked all afternoon and evening through scorched neighborhoods searching for his grandson, getting as close as possible to the hypocenter. But his efforts yielded nothing. Exhausted and scared, the old man finally lay down to sleep in a field not more than a mile from where Taniguchi lay on a hillside surrounded by corpses. The sound of an approaching relief train echoed in the distance.

"The city was burning . . . ," Taniguchi remembered, "illuminating the sky like a midnight sun." A plane flew overhead and sprayed the area with machine-gun fire. Bullets hit a rock near Taniguchi's face and bounced into the bushes, but Taniguchi could do nothing to protect himself.

Later in the night, a drizzling rain fell. Lying facedown and unable to move, Taniguchi noticed some bamboo leaves hanging low to the ground just a few inches away. Desperately thirsty, he pulled his head up, stretched his neck out as far as he could, and strained to suck the raindrops off the leaves before setting his head down and waiting in darkness for someone to come.

CHAPTER 3

EMBERS

Approximately thirty minutes after the bomb detonated over the Urakami Valley, Japan's Supreme Council for the Direction of the War received its first news of the Nagasaki bombing, an abbreviated account of Governor Nagano's initial perceptions that damages and casualties were minimal. Council members had been in the middle of a heated debate over the Soviets' entry into the war the night before, the impact of the Hiroshima bombing, and the fate of their nation. Most particularly, they argued over whether and under what conditions to surrender and how to protect the emperor's postwar sovereignty. As Nagasaki burned, the announcement of Japan's second atomic bombing had no apparent impact on council members' deliberations, which proceeded without further mention of the Nagasaki attack.

Through the rest of the day, the Big Six remained deadlocked over surrender terms. Peace faction members Prime Minister Suzuki, Foreign Minister Tōgō, and Navy Minister Yonai argued for a single condition that would maintain the emperor as imperial leader of Japan, while Army Minister Anami, Army Chief of Staff Umezu, and Navy Chief of Staff Toyoda held out for three additional conditions—self-disarmament, Japanese control over war-crimes trials, and no U.S. occupation of the Japanese homeland. Eventually they were joined by the full Japanese Cabinet. Debates continued late into the night of the Nagasaki bombing, but no agreement could be reached.

Just after eleven p.m., the Big Six and four Cabinet members were summoned to the *obunko* annex, an underground complex next to the imperial library where the emperor and empress lived in the final years of the war. Inside, the Japanese leaders waited in a hot, dismal chamber until Emperor Hirohito entered at ten minutes before midnight. For the next two hours, each of the ministers stated his position on surrender terms before the emperor. When they were finished, Prime Minister Suzuki stood and asked Hirohito to make a decision on behalf of the nation. The emperor responded by sanctioning Japan's surrender with the sole condition that he remain in his position as imperial leader so that Japan could maintain *kokutai*—its national essence under the supreme guidance of a divine emperor. Within the hour, Hirohito's decision was ratified by the full Cabinet. Many of Japan's leaders wept out loud.

In the early morning hours of August 10, government workers rushed to draft the official surrender offer, and Japan's Foreign Ministry sent telegrams to U.S., British, Chinese, and Soviet leaders via officials in Switzerland and Sweden, initiating the first legitimate surrender negotiations between Japan and the Allied powers. Due to the slow process of diplomatic communications, however, the United States would not receive Japan's surrender offer for nearly fifteen hours.

Later that morning (Japan time), President Truman addressed the American people by radio to report on the Potsdam Conference. Most of the speech outlined a political and economic framework for postwar Europe. Truman mentioned the atomic bombing of Hiroshima only once, calling the city a military base chosen "because we wished in this first attack to avoid, insofar as possible, the killing of civilians." He also made a short statement about the United States' duty with regard to atomic weapons: "We must constitute ourselves trustees of this new force—to prevent its misuse, and to turn it into the channels of service to mankind," he said. "It is an awful responsibility which has come to us. We thank God that it has come to us, instead of to our enemies; and we pray that He may guide us to use it in His ways and for His purposes." Twenty-four hours had passed since the second atomic bombing, but nowhere in his address did Truman mention Nagasaki.

Once the United States received Japan's official surrender offer, Secretary of the Navy James Forrestal and Secretary of War Henry L. Stimson recommended halting all air and naval actions against Japan. Unsure that Japan and the Allies would come to an agreement on surrender terms, Truman rejected the proposal. For five more days, Allied and Japanese troops in the Pacific continued to fight, and U.S. Air Force B-29s carried out bombing raids over Japanese cities. Truman did agree to curtail U.S. plans for a third atomic bomb attack on Japan unless the outcome of surrender negotiations failed. Secretary of Commerce Henry Wallace noted that "[Truman] said the thought of wiping out another 100,000 people was too horrible. He didn't like the idea of killing, as he said, 'all those kids.'" Truman's statement contradicted the U.S. government's position that the atomic bombs were delivered on Japanese military targets.

———

Nagasaki mayor Okada Jukichi had spent the night of August 9 atop a hill on the eastern border of the Urakami Valley, waiting in a panic for the fires below to diminish. At three a.m. on August 10, he made his way down the hill. In darkness lit only by scattered embers, he stumbled through debris and bodies to the place where his house had stood the day before, just a few hundred feet from the hypocenter. The soles of Okada's shoes burned as he frantically combed through the hot ashes for his wife and children. Finding no trace of them, he hurried to the air raid shelter beneath his house to discover at least ten dead bodies, including those of his entire family. Simultaneously crazed and clearheaded, he proceeded to the next neighborhood over, where he identified the deceased family members of his deputy mayor.

Okada was one of the earliest witnesses to the still-smoldering hypocenter area, which had been totally unreachable the day before. Covered in soot, he ran across the low southeastern mountains bordering the Urakami Valley to the air raid shelter of the Nagasaki Prefecture Air Defense Headquarters near Suwa Shrine. The mayor reported what he had seen to Governor Nagano, estimating the death toll at fifty thousand people—far higher than Governor Nagano could have imagined. Stunned, the governor decided to request regular updates from police chiefs in each region of the city and to dispatch reports to Japan's home minister in Tokyo every half hour with updated damages and fatality estimates from what he still called the new-type bomb.

While Okada was searching for his family in the middle of the night, a three-man documentary crew—veteran war photographer Yamahata

Yōsuke, writer Higashi Jun, and painter Yamada Eiji—arrived at Michino-o Station, in the rural outskirts of Nagasaki two miles north of the hypocenter. The team, sent by Japan's News and Information Bureau—the government's military propaganda organization—had been given orders to record Nagasaki's damages for use in anti-U.S. propaganda campaigns. Due to Nagasaki's damaged tracks, Michino-o Station was as far south as the train could go.

After their eleven-hour journey, the men stepped off into the cool night air and began walking toward the city to report to the military police headquarters in southern Nagasaki. Their path took them along hillsides near where Taniguchi lay. From the top of a small mountain at Nagasaki's northern edge, the vast atomic plain lay before them, dotted by small fires still burning in the ruins. Layers of smoke wafted overhead.

"We made our first steps into this macabre domain," Higashi later wrote, "as though embarking on a journey into a different world." With only the light of the crescent moon and the scattered fires to help them see, the men reached the main prefectural road running north-south through the Urakami Valley, barely detectable beneath layers of ashen rubble. The air was hot. They stumbled over bodies and passed people lying on the ground begging for water. A mother, dazed and confused, held her dead child in her arms and whimpered for help. The men offered the victims kind and encouraging words, but there was little else they could do. Higashi, however, was aghast when he stepped on something "soft and spongy" and discovered that he was standing on the corpse of a horse—and he was terrified when a person suddenly surfaced from a hole in the ground and grabbed his leg, begging for help.

The men walked for two hours, past the areas where Yoshida lay on the ground and Nagano and her father huddled in a crowded air raid shelter. They finally reached the military police headquarters, damaged but still standing. After reporting in, the team walked to the hills to wait for the morning light.

The sun broke over the horizon at 5:42 a.m., barely penetrating the smoky haze that blanketed the city. In the dim light, the massive expanse of atomic destruction gradually became visible to Yamahata, his colleagues, and the thousands of people who emerged from air raid shelters or descended from the hills where they had hidden during the night. Those who could move wandered aimlessly through the remains of the city or stumbled and crawled to flee the devastated region. "Even their eyes were burned," Yamahata remembered. "The backs of the eyelids were red and swollen as though they had been turned inside out, and the edges of the eyes were yellow like the fat of chicken. Blinded, people groped their way forward with both hands extended in front of them." As the team began its journey north, past the flattened Nagasaki Station and into the barren Urakami Valley, Yamahata focused solely on his task to photograph what one survivor called a "monochromatic, soundless hell."

A muscular human thigh protruded from a disheveled mound of wreckage. A girl, perhaps eighteen, stood next to a skeleton on the ground and stared out into the vast destruction. An old woman dressed in a kimono crawled through the wreckage; a small figure against the backdrop of a crushed and mangled factory. Adults, children, and babies lay dead on the ground, their bodies scorched. Some of their mouths were open as if calling for help, others died with their arms extended, "grasping at the air," Higashi wrote, "a last expression of their extreme distress in the sea of fire." A boy, perhaps ten years old, carried his younger brother on his back, his face streaked with vertical lines of dried perspiration or tears. The smaller boy gripped his brother's arms and pressed his chin into his shoulder, his round face covered with blood and dirt as he peered into the camera.

Police and rescue teams from nearby towns and villages worked alongside civilian volunteers, using doors, wood scraps, and stretchers to carry the wounded from the bombed-out region. Emergency crews used hand tools to begin clearing small portions of the main north-south route through the city. Family members poured into and through the city from every direction and searched for anything, near or far, that could orient them in the atomic plain. Two men argued loudly over a woman's scorched body found between their houses, each claiming that she was his wife. Another man pulled his still-breathing pregnant wife from under the ruins of their house, but she died as he placed her on a wooden plank. A young girl found her mother's ring in the ashes but not her mother; another identified a corpse with no eyes as her mother based on a gold tooth in her mouth. A sixteen-year-old boy rushed into his neighborhood to the site of his former house and dug through the rubble to find the bodies of his older sister, grandfather, and uncle. He reached down to take a tortoiseshell clip from his sister's hair, a final keepsake. The scorched earth burned through the soles and tips of people's shoes, and their hands blistered from burrowing through the still-hot remains of their homes. A seven-year-old boy crouched on the ground, his tears dropping into the ashes of his brother and sister. "The places where the tears fell turned black," the boy remembered. "The sheet of ashes soon became dotted with black spots."

In the less-damaged areas of the old city and over the mountains from the Urakami Valley, people gathered in small groups to exchange stories about what had happened to them the day before, telling one another how overwhelmingly relieved they were when family members had come home, or how terrified they were of the fates of those still missing. Trying to understand what was still incomprehensible, a rumor circulated through the city that the bomb's intended target was the Urakami Branch of Nagasaki Prison, a few hundred yards from the hypocenter.

Though their home near Suwa Shrine was slightly damaged, Yoshida's parents and four siblings were all safe, but when Yoshida didn't return home, his mother and father were fraught with fear that their son had died. On the morning of August 10, however, the parents of Tabuchi—Yoshida's injured friend who had left the group the night before—suddenly arrived at their house to tell them that Tabuchi had made it in darkness out of the Urakami Valley and across the mountains to his home. Tabuchi's parents quickly reported that, at least until late the night before, Yoshida was still alive. Yoshida's parents rushed from their house to find him.

Earlier that morning, members of a relief team had placed Yoshida, partially conscious, on a wooden stretcher and carried him to a temporary relief station inside an air raid shelter. Someone bandaged his face and entire body and carried him to the dirt school yard of the gutted Nagasaki Commercial School, where hundreds of injured adults and children lay in rows. When they heard airplanes overhead, the volunteers fled to air raid shelters, leaving Yoshida feeling alone and vulnerable. The heat of the sun bore down on him, he remembered, "like a slow execution." Eventually, he fell unconscious.

Yoshida's mother and father made their way into the hypocenter area, stifling their shock and despair at the number of corpses to press on through the blistering ashes. They stopped only to douse their feet in trickles of water from broken pipes, a meager attempt to relieve the excruciating pain. When they reached the ruins of the school where Yoshida lay, rows and rows of burned, swollen, and bandaged bodies stretched out before them, each person as unrecognizable as the next, many groaning and calling out the names of their family members.

"My parents were *ira-ira* [desperate] to find me," Yoshida said. "They called out my name—'*Katsuji! Katsuji!*'—but the voices that called back to them all sounded the same. 'We will never be able to find him!' my mother told my father. 'If that's the case,' he answered, 'then we need to lean in close to their ears and say his name in a small voice.'" They leaned into dozens of victims and whispered Katsuji's name. When they finally came to Yoshida's burned body, they knew he was their son. They lifted him up, placed him into an *ubaguruma* (baby carriage), and pushed him nearly four and a half miles through the smoldering rubble and over the mountains to their home. Yoshida cried and mumbled deliriously, begging for water, moaning about how hot he felt, and muttering that he missed his *okaachan* (mommy). Along the way, he blacked out and didn't regain consciousness until mid-December, four months later.

By late morning, Yamahata, Higashi, and Yamada had moved north past the tangled steel wreckage of Mitsubishi factories that lined the Urakami River. Under the cloudless sky, Yamahata shot panoramic views of the flattened Urakami Valley. Blackened factory smokestacks stood tall and desolate, wreathed by smoke wafting upward from the smoldering debris. Most electrical poles and trees lay on the ground, snapped in pieces, though some remained standing at varying angles, their wires swooping down and dragging along the ground. A charred mother and infant lay dead next to each other on a damaged streetcar platform. Inside mangled streetcars, scorched bodies of passengers were seated as they had been at the moment of the blast. Men, women, and children still trapped beneath buildings or lying injured in the ruins moaned, wailed, and whimpered for help and water. Yamahata later reflected on his state of mind that day—what he considered to be unforgivable detachment in a situation of such extreme suffering—confessing that "perhaps it was just too much, too enormous to absorb."

Pathway through the ruins near the hypocenter on August 10, 1945, between one and two p.m. To the left, Yamada Eiji is sketching the scene before him. At center, the opening to an air raid shelter is visible, and in the distance are Mitsubishi factory smokestacks. On the hill to the far right stand the ruins of Chinzei Middle School. (*Photograph by Yamahata Yōsuke/Courtesy of Yamahata Shōgo*)

People in school and work uniforms walked or rode bicycles through layers of debris to get to their homes or family members' workplaces. They carried home the bodies of loved ones for temporary burial on their ashened property, or cremated them on top of wood scraps in desolate fields. Some headed toward the hills, barely visible through the smoky haze, carrying tied and knotted *furoshiki* (wrapping cloths) that held items they had been able to salvage. As they walked, some people stopped and stared at corpses on the ground, unable to move on. Others looked down or straight ahead, their faces blank, as if lost in a trance—in Japanese, this state was called *mugamuchū* (without self, as in a dream).

Before midday, Yamahata and his team reached Zenza-machi, three-quarters of a mile from the hypocenter, where Nagano's family had lived.

That morning, Nagano and her father had crawled out of their air raid shelter and stepped over corpses "and other people with stuff trickling from their noses" to get home. When they finally arrived, they froze in front of the site where their house had stood the day before. There was no trace of Nagano's mother, Kuniko, or Seiji. Nagano saw a blackened body in the ashes and ran to it, calling out, "*Okaasan! Okaasan!* [Mother! Mother!]" She was sobbing over the body when one of her childhood friends appeared.

"Eh-chan!" the girl called out to Nagano. "Yesterday I saw your brother Sei-chan! He's lying near an air raid shelter. I'm so sorry I couldn't help him."

Nagano and her father raced away, stumbling through the ruins to search one shelter after another. "*Sei-chan! Sei-chan!*" they called. Near the entrance to one shelter, a child's body lay on the ground, completely burned. His face was covered in blisters and swollen like a balloon, and his eyes were forced shut. Blood and bodily fluids oozed from places where skin had peeled off.

"We didn't want to think that he was my brother," Nagano said, crying. "But since his height was about the same, we went over to the body.

"'Are you Sei-chan?' we asked. He couldn't see us, but he nodded yes. And even though he nodded—it's terrible to say—we desperately hoped that maybe this was the wrong person, that Seiji might be in a better state than this. So we asked again: 'Are you *really* Sei-chan?' The boy nodded again—*yes.*"

A cloth nametag sewn onto the breast of the boy's ragged school uniform was still intact. *Zenza Elementary School, 4th grade. Kanazawa Seiji. 9 years old. Blood type B.* Nagano collapsed in grief. Her mind raced as she tried to comprehend what it had been like for him the day before, burned, alone, and scared. *What went on in his mind? How did he end up here at the air raid shelter, as badly burned as he was? Had he tried to stay alive until someone came to save him? Did he long for our mother?* "I mean, he was *only nine*," Nagano remembered. "I felt so sorry for him. I just couldn't stop crying."

Nagano's father decided to carry Seiji to one of the temporary relief stations in the area, but when he tried to pick up his son, the blistered skin on Seiji's legs peeled off in his father's hand. Nagano's father quickly pulled his hand back and rushed away, leaving Nagano alone with Seiji. "Sei-chan," she asked through her tears, "do you know where Mother and Kuniko are?" Seiji moved his head slightly. "Hold on! Hold on, okay?" Nagano pleaded. "Father will come back. . . ."

Nagano's father returned carrying a door-size wooden shutter, the kind used in Japanese houses to cover glass windows to block the rain. He and Nagano gently lifted Seiji onto the board and carried him away. At the relief station, hundreds of injured and burned people were lined up waiting for help. The three waited their turn beneath the blazing sun. With no trees for shade or clothing to cover Seiji, Nagano and her father stood next to each other to create a shadow over their brother and son. When Seiji's turn finally came, all the relief staff could do was cover his body with *chinkyū*, a thick, white zinc oxide oil for burns. "Even so," Nagano said, "we thanked the doctor many times." She thought that because Seiji had received treatment, he would survive.

Nagano and her father were carrying Seiji back toward the shelter when they were shocked to see Nagano's mother and younger sister, Kuniko, coming down from Mount Kompira. Her mother, frantic and exhausted, turned to Seiji and "lost it and cried like a crazy person," Nagano remembered, "clinging to his body and sobbing, *I'm sorry, Sei-chan! I'm sorry! Where were you? I'm sorry! I'm sorry!*"

When she finally caught her breath, Nagano's mother told them what had happened the morning before. Seiji had gone outside to try to catch dragonflies. After the overpowering flash of light, their house had collapsed on top of Nagano's mother and Kuniko. Nagano's mother had screamed for help, but no one came. After some time, she was able to push the wooden posts off her body and free herself; she then lifted a weight-bearing column and a sewing machine off Kuniko and pulled her out of the wreckage. Remarkably, neither had suffered serious injuries. Standing in the debris of their home, they looked around. The neighborhood was flattened in every direction, and deadly quiet. No human life was evident. Fires were flaring up all around them. Stumbling over the ruins of their house, Nagano's mother and sister ran in the direction of where Seiji had been, but he was nowhere in sight. The fires surged closer. Nagano's mother, desperately conflicted, felt she had no choice but to flee with Kuniko. They ran to the top of Mount Kompira and hid there through the day and night.

Together now, the family lifted the door on which Seiji lay and carried him through the rubble to the air raid shelter in their former neighborhood. Inside, the heat of the afternoon sun intensified. They huddled in silence, except for Nagano's mother, who couldn't stop moaning and crying.

Early that morning, Governor Nagano had crossed over the mountains to see for himself the barren corridor stretching the length of the Urakami Valley. The scenes before him were unimaginable and surreal. "It was . . . it was just so horrible and pathetic that I couldn't look."

According to Japan's Wartime Casualties Care Law, rescue and relief for civilian war victims were funded through the national treasury and implemented by the prefectural governments. This meant that Governor Nagano, as head of Nagasaki Prefecture, was responsible for organizing all immediate recovery efforts for Nagasaki, an impossible task not only because of the overwhelming numbers of victims but also because government agencies, hospitals, clinics, medical and food supplies, and communications systems were destroyed, and most of the city's trained medical staff had been killed or injured. For the tens of thousands who needed help, fewer than thirty active and retired physicians had survived, and capacity in hospitals throughout the city was reduced to 240 beds.

The city's chaotic rescue and relief efforts that day were supported by hundreds of local and prefectural soldiers, policemen, firemen, civil defense and government workers, teachers, neighborhood association leaders, and individual adults and children who carried out assigned or self-designated tasks. Teams were formed to rescue as many people as possible from beneath fallen buildings. One policeman found two hundred girls trapped under their collapsed school; nearly all died before relief workers could extricate them. Volunteer teams turned over blackened bodies in search of survivors, loaded the injured onto trucks for transport to relief stations, or carried the dead to cremation sites. Others began clearing roads and streetcar and railway tracks, worked to restore communications, or prepared and delivered tubs of *onigiri* and oversize buckets of water to relief stations in the ruins. In some locations, very little food was consumed, presumably because most people were too injured to get to the aid stations, or those who could had no appetite. Around some of the water buckets, people had collapsed onto the ground before or after finally having a sip.

Teams of doctors and nurses from a number of Kyushu cities and military bases had already arrived in Nagasaki, and on August 10, the prefecture's health division requested more emergency medical assistance from other nearby municipalities. In the meantime, able-bodied adults and children helped with medical relief in whatever way they could. Loosely organized teams of surviving physicians and nurses set up additional relief stations in the devastated areas, with no walls or roofs, and in previously designated schools in the old city that were only minimally damaged. Teenagers walked through the ruins with their wartime-mandated first-aid bags, providing superficial medical support to any survivor they could find. Everyone involved in medical relief was instructed to first transport or treat victims they deemed likely to survive, requiring them to make impossible and excruciating choices between helping people they thought might live and leaving others to die waiting for help.

Atop Motohara Hill, almost a mile from the hypocenter in the far northeast corner of the valley, First Urakami Hospital was the only medical institution in the Urakami Valley still standing, though it had been burned from the inside out. Before the war, the hospital building had been a Catholic seminary, but when foreign Catholics were expelled in 1941, a Japanese Franciscan order had established a seventy-bed hospital there to provide specialized care for tuberculosis patients. The hospital's current director was the diminutive twenty-nine-year-old physician Akizuki Tatsuichirō, a man who had lost two sisters to tuberculosis and was himself frail from chronic asthma as a child and tuberculosis as a young adult. Dr. Akizuki was the only non-Catholic among the priests, monks, and nurses who staffed the hospital.

Akizuki had been in the middle of treating a patient when the bomb's blast had shaken the entire hospital, causing books, equipment, and sections of the ceiling to rain down on the patients and staff. He had avoided serious injury by taking cover behind a bed. As the hospital roof began to burn, Dr. Akizuki and his staff had raced through the corridors and up and down the stairs of the three-story building, walking over shattered glass and pushing through large debris to carry out all seventy of their patients before the building ignited into flames.

The burned-out First Urakami Hospital for tuberculosis patients, where Dr. Akizuki Tatsuichirō worked, fall 1945. (*U.S. Strategic Bombing Survey/Courtesy of Nagasaki Foundation for the Promotion of Peace, Committee for Research of Photographs and Materials of the Atomic Bombing*)

Everyone was placed outside on the ground. By night, they were joined by injured and burned victims from surrounding neighborhoods. The air was filled with their agonized cries as Urakami Church burned in the distance.

The next morning, Dr. Akizuki's first impulse was to run away. Instead, as some of the nurses and kitchen staff prepared rice and soup on a makeshift stove, he cheerfully greeted his patients and the hundreds of people who had gathered on the hospital grounds. Later that morning, a member of his staff directed Akizuki to an underground tunnel where he had been secretly storing medicine for several days before the bombing. Akizuki was ecstatic to open two large wooden boxes filled with small amounts of gauze, bandages, and medicines—including painkillers, antiseptic lotions, and ointments.

Dr. Akizuki was known not only for his dedication but also his short temper—both of which he demonstrated that day. As he and his staff treated hundreds of patients, Akizuki alternately offered words of hope and consolation or harsh comments, snapping at people with less serious injuries to stop complaining. One man, Kinoshita, had suffered burns on his face, shoulders, and chest and was in such pain that he could barely breathe. Even as Dr. Akizuki applied pain-relief ointment to his burns, he knew that Kinoshita was unlikely to survive. Later that day, he visited Kinoshita, by that time near death, at his home where his family had carried him. The sun was beginning to set when he left their house and walked back toward the hospital. Behind him he could hear Kinoshita's family sobbing, crying out, "Jesus! Mary! Joseph!"

"I was so depressed in spirit," Akizuki remembered, "overcome by the grief and pain of human existence in this transient world, that I felt as if I were myself insensible, lifeless, like a ghost."

By early afternoon on August 10, Yamahata and his team had reached the hypocenter area. Where buildings and trees once stood, they saw a vast, leveled plain—as if, Higashi remembered, the area had been completely "wiped away . . . by the bold stroke of a colossal brush." A man whose flesh had been burned off his feet was running through the ruins. A bewildered woman carried a bucket holding the severed head of her young daughter. Numb and exhausted, Yamahata and his colleagues proceeded north, past the hills where Taniguchi still lay on his stomach, unable to move. When the men reached Michino-o Station, hundreds of people sat or lay on the ground, waiting to be loaded onto trains that would transport them to relief stations and hospitals outside the city. As each train departed, a chorus of agonizing moans echoed in its wake.

Ten hours after they had started their journey, the three men boarded a train and returned to Hakata. In all, Yamahata had taken 119 photographs. After developing them, he expected to submit them to his superiors at the News and Information Bureau. Japan was in such chaos, however, that the agency did not immediately request them, so Yamahata was able to hold on to them until after the war. "One blessing, among these unfortunate circumstances," he later said, "is that the resulting photographs were never used by the Japanese army . . . in one last misguided attempt to rouse popular support for the continuation of warfare."

Bomb victims near the Urakami Valley's main thoroughfare, just over a half mile from the hypocenter, on August 10, 1945. Rescue workers provided the futon on the ground from a damaged inn. (*Photograph by Yamahata Yōsuke/Courtesy of Yamahata Shōgo*)

The sun set on the first full day after the bombing. Some survivors were safe at home with their family members or in homes that strangers had opened to them. Countless more were missing, and their families could not sleep for worry. Across the Urakami Valley and in outlying areas, tens of thousands still lay in the ruins with mosquitoes swarming over them. Others lay body to body in air raid shelters or were packed against one another on the ground outside or on the floors inside darkened relief stations, where as soon as people stiffened and died, their bodies were carried away to be replaced by more tormented patients. Many had not eaten since the morning before.

Throughout the night, people listened with dread for the elongated hum of approaching enemy planes passing overhead. A man wandered through the ruins dampening the lips of survivors and applying oil and bandages to their wounds. At Dr. Akizuki's hospital, the families of two tuberculosis patients arrived to find their sons alive and carried them home. Dr. Akizuki curled up on the ground wrapped in a blanket, envious of a medical team from Ōmura that had left Nagasaki that night to return home. From the top of a mountain, a boy heard the sound of Korean people wailing, a cultural ritual for their grief.

Nagano and her family stayed awake all night, crouched together in the shelter next to Zenza Elementary School, gently coaxing Sei-chan to stay alive. Nagano found a broken water pipe outside and used her hands to scoop water and carry it to her brother—but Seiji was too injured even to sip it. "Even with the many coincidences—one after the other—that helped us that day, there was nothing else we could do for him," Nagano remembered. "We stayed together as a family for one night."

By the next morning, Sei-chan had died. Nagano's family carried him to a flattened, scorched patch of ground where about ten other bodies were lined up. "We brought pieces of half-burned wood and laid them on top of the body," Nagano said. "Before our own eyes—" She paused, still incredulous at what they had to do. "Before our own eyes, the four of us—my mother, my father, my younger sister, and me—we lit a fire beneath Sei-chan's body, our own flesh and blood." Nagano's mother found a rice bowl in the ruins and scooped Sei-chan's remains into it. "We had no cloth to wrap it in, no handkerchief to cover the top," Nagano said, "so she held the rice bowl with my brother's ashes close to her chest, one hand over the top, and stroked it, over and over, whispering my brother's name and apologizing to him. She never put his ashes down, even inside the air raid shelter. That's how it was for us. There are really no words for the sadness I felt."

———

Over the next five days, thousands of people walked to the homes, schools, and workplaces they guessed, or hoped, their children, parents, and siblings might have been at the time of the blast. Many used bridges and the ruins of Urakami Church and Nagasaki Medical College to try to gauge distance as they searched for the sites of their destroyed houses; in some cases, families identified their former homes by a cement sink, stove, or iron bathtub. The fact that many victims had been transported out of the city caused even more confusion for their families, who had no clue about where to look for them. Some people left handwritten notices on trees to explain who they were looking for and where to reach them if their loved one was found. Others searched inside darkened air raid shelters, striking matches and putting them close to the faces of the people on the ground. One man identified his wife's skull by the shape of the teeth. In a school yard, a ten-year-old girl searching for her mother heard the ticking of wristwatches as she passed mostly naked, engorged bodies. Many people could not help but think about their last moments with their loved ones—the boy whose older brother had asked to borrow his watch that morning, a wife handing her husband his hat before he left for work, a mother telling her children that she was preparing eggplant for their lunch. One mother kept her front door unlocked every night in case her son came home.

Still, some people found their family members alive, and friends grabbed one another and rejoiced when they crossed paths. One unconscious eighteen-year-old girl had been carried out of the city and left for dead in a pile of corpses. Two days later, an old woman passing by noticed her foot moving. The woman called some men over, and after determining that the girl was still alive, they transported her twenty-five miles to a hospital. She woke up the next morning to find her whole body bandaged and breathing tubes in her nose and mouth. She was able to later return to her family in Nagasaki. In another miraculous reunion, an injured young girl had been transported by train to a relief station in a town called Togitsu, where a man told her that he was going to Nagasaki and asked if he could tell anyone that she was there. "Please tell Araki Shizue, my father's younger sister, living at twenty-one Maruyamamachi, that Kyuma Hisako is here," the girl said. The next day, as she lay on the ground in the relief station, the girl heard a voice in the room say, "Where is Hisako?" It was her father, who had already cremated what he thought were his daughter's remains.

For two days, Taniguchi's grandfather had combed the ruins for his grandson. On the morning after the bombing, Taniguchi had awakened facedown on the hilltop in Sumiyoshi-machi where workers had placed him the day before. His back and arms were completely burned, but he still felt no pain. Raising his head, he glanced around to see corpses surrounding him. The area was completely silent.

Desperate for something to eat and drink, Taniguchi spotted a half-demolished farmhouse below him. He grabbed on to the branches of the bamboo tree beside him and tried to pull himself up, but he fell back and was stabbed in the thigh by a branch. Determined, Taniguchi wriggled his body out of the bushes and down the hill, found a container of water, gulped down nearly a half gallon, and crawled under a tree for shade. A rescue team passed, but Taniguchi was too weak to call out to them. They continued on—perhaps presuming he was dead.

Taniguchi spent another night alone in the hills, and on the morning of August 11, another rescue team passed by. One of the men nudged Taniguchi with his boot; although barely breathing, he was still alive. The men carried him on a wooden door to Michino-o Station, where he ate some rice, the first food he'd eaten in two days. Reaching into his pocket, Taniguchi pulled out some of the letters he had intended to deliver on the day of the bomb and handed them to the relief team, asking if they could take them to the post office.

That afternoon, Taniguchi was lying on his stomach, waiting for a train to come to evacuate him from the city, when his grandfather finally found him. They rode together to Isahaya, about sixteen miles outside Nagasaki. Inside Isahaya Elementary School, volunteers placed Taniguchi facedown on top of a straw mat on the wooden floor. With no medicines available to treat the gravity of his burns, Taniguchi lay in this position for nearly a week as the flesh on his back began to rot and fall away. It was here, Taniguchi remembered, that pain first surged through his body and his wounds began to bleed.

Wada had stayed in the razed city to help with rescue efforts and to search for his friend Tanaka and the other eleven student streetcar operators who had never been found. Numbed to the grotesque scenes before their eyes, Wada and his friends traced their colleagues' streetcar routes; eventually they found two of their bodies and carried them to their families' homes. In one derailed streetcar, they found an unidenti-fiable body of a driver whose hands still gripped the brake handle.

Seventeen-year-old Tanaka, however, could not be found. "He was a year younger than I was and extremely cheerful," Wada remembered. "We were very close, so he was the person I worried about the most." Late on the night of August 12, Wada was resting against a wall of the terminal when he looked up and saw Tanaka's mother standing next to him. She told Wada that her son had come home. Wada quickly ac-companied her back to Tanaka's house, about five minutes away. As they walked, Tanaka's mother told Wada where her son had been at the time of the bomb—about three-quarters of a mile from the hypocenter. He had been severely burned, she said, and it had taken him three days to get home, a walk that would have normally taken forty minutes. "I think in his heart he was trying to get back to his mother," Wada said. "Since Tanaka's father died in the war, he was the only child of a single mother."

It was dark inside the Tanakas' partially destroyed house. In the front entryway, what looked like a body was lying on a single *tatami* mat. Mrs. Tanaka gave Wada a candle, which he used to light his way toward the body. At closer glance, the figure didn't look human, and it wasn't until Wada was right next to the body that he recognized his friend's face.

Something was stuck on Tanaka's cheek. "Without even thinking," Wada said, "I started to reach out to wipe it away—then suddenly I pulled my hand back." Tanaka's eyeball was hanging out of its socket. His other eye was completely crushed, and his mouth was split open all the way to his ear.

"It was unbelievable to me that someone who looked like that could still be alive," Wada remembered. "Then Tanaka said something that made a huge impression on me. 'I didn't do anything,' he whispered, and then he stopped breathing. I took it to mean 'I didn't do anything wrong, so why do I have to die this way?'"

By that time, some of the other mobilized students had arrived. Ev-eryone stood around Tanaka's body, not knowing what to do next. Fi-nally, one boy suggested to Wada that they set up a funeral pyre and burn his body. "Now, it might have been the circumstances, or it might have been that everyone was in such deep shock, but nobody thought the idea was in the least bit strange," Wada remembered. They carried Tanaka's body outside to an area just below a reservoir, collected scraps of wood from destroyed houses nearby and piled them high, then lifted Tanaka's disfigured body on top of the wood.

No one could bring themselves to light the fire. Wada desperately did not want to do it, but as the student leader, he felt that it was up to him. He struck the match, touched the flame to Tanaka's body, then lit different sections of the woodpile. Starting small, the flames gradually spread and grew until Tanaka's body was engulfed. For nearly twelve hours, Wada and his friends stood ten feet away, watching until all of the body was burned. No one cried. "We were in a state beyond grief or pity," Wada recalled. "Actually, I couldn't tell you what kind of state we were in."

———

Change came quickly for the Allied POW survivors in Nagasaki's two camps, providing early hints at the transition that would soon come. Just a mile south of the hypocenter at the destroyed Fukuoka POW Camp No. 14, eight Allied prisoners ultimately died from the bombing, and an estimated forty more were injured. While camping out in the smoldering ruins, prisoners had cared for their wounded and constructed a temporary shelter with a tin roof to protect the seriously injured from the sun. On August 12, they were marched three hours through the destroyed city to the small village of Tomachi, two and a half miles south of Nagasaki on the eastern side of the bay, to the vacated barracks of a Mitsubishi factory. The facility had better beds, plenty of fresh water, and more bandages and medicine for the injured men. At Nagasaki's second POW camp at the Kawanami Shipyard in Nagasaki Bay, prisoners had continued their daily routines, including waking up to reveille, delousing, eating their small rations of rice, and marching to and from the shipyard to work. On August 13, however, they received a luxurious half can of brine-cured beef for dinner, and the camp commander announced that there would be no work for the next three days. Cut off from all contact with the outside world, the POWs at both camps couldn't figure out exactly what was going on, but with these improvements, they felt hopeful.

For the average person in Nagasaki, however, each day in the week after the bombing pulsated with relentless suffering, panic, and death. The streets were filled with people leaving the city out of fear of another bombing, to try to reach relatives outside Nagasaki, or to get to a hospital in another part of Kyushu. Some, like Dō-oh and Yoshida, lay severely injured, burned, and unconscious in their homes in the far corners of the city or in Nishiyama-machi, far from the hypocenter.

They were the fortunate ones, some would say—safe in their homes, surrounded by their families. In the gray, atomized Urakami Valley, thousands struggled to survive without housing or adequate food, water, sanitation, medicine, or any way to comprehend what had happened to them, their neighborhoods, and their city. Tiny, barefoot children squatted in the ruins and wandered through the debris and corpses, calling out for their mothers and fathers. One woman whose husband had died and who would soon lose her four daughters and four-year-old son, came to understand that when one of her children stopped asking for water, it meant that she or he had died. One family peeled cucumbers and placed the skins on their son's burned back, an unsuccessful attempt to ease his pain. A fourteen-year-old girl spread mud over her mother's burns, but when the mud dried, it cracked and caused more pain. Numerous women miscarried or gave birth to stillborn babies. Maggots crawled in people's eyes, mouths, noses, ears, and every open wound; those who were too injured to move their arms and hands tried to wriggle their bodies to get them off. Numb to the horror all around, people began cracking death jokes, saying how great it would be if the swollen faces of corpses—which looked a little like watermelons—actually *were* watermelons that they could eat.

Many lived in the dark holes beneath or behind their former homes. Others, like Nagano and her family, stayed in air raid shelters, soaked by constantly dripping water; one family of eight took turns sleeping on a single *tatami* mat, four on, four off. Some slept beneath scraps of wood or metal leaned against tree stumps like tents as primitive protection from the sun. It was hard for any of them to imagine how they would survive. Those who could walk scavenged the ruins for food and scoured the rubble of their homes for fragments of clothing and undergarments; melted glass shards; roof tiles, cooking utensils, and hand mirrors; partially burned *tatami* mats and bedding; and seared books, letters, and photos. Most got little or no sleep at night, surrounded by the crackling of cremation fires and the sounds of people crying, moaning, calling out for help, or mumbling nonsensically. Parents held the bodies or ashes of their dead children, whispering, *"Forgive me! Please forgive me!"*

Huge deliveries of food continued to arrive from areas outside the city—mostly tubs full of *onigiri,* which often spoiled in the summer heat before they could be distributed. Later, canned food—including beef and seaweed—was also delivered. Survivors who had reached the sites of their former homes dug up emergency provisions they had stashed underground during the war—including canned milk, diapers, rice, salt, seaweed, tea, dried tofu, dried squid, pickled plums, and matches. Neighbors shared food and cared for infants, children, and injured adults whom they had never met. Still, hunger was rampant. Some people chewed on raw potatoes they dug up in scorched vegetable patches.

Christian families buried their dead. "It was a lonely funeral," one woman said, remembering how she and her sister buried the ashes of their mother, "with just the two of us, huddled together and flattening ourselves on the ground every time a plane passed over." Day after day, Dr. Akizuki watched one of his neighbors walk to a hillside cemetery with a hoe over his shoulder to dig graves first for the man's father, then his five children, and then his mother, all who died one after the other.

In keeping with Japan's Buddhist tradition—and because of the overwhelming number of corpses—cremation fires continued to burn at all times of day and night, curls of smoke rising into the sky. Adults and children stared with hollowed eyes as the flesh of their loved ones dripped down into the flames, then placed the ashes in rice cracker cans, burned pots, scraps of cloth, or newspaper. Relief workers and Allied POWs carried the bodies of strangers to the fires and burned them, twenty or more at a time, hundreds each day—and still, thousands of corpses remained scattered in the ruins. A group of student workers poured gasoline over the bodies and conducted a mass cremation of their friends who had been inside the Mitsubishi Electric division dormitories at the time of the bombing. Families of missing people scooped ashes or picked up a single bone from cremation sites near their loved ones' former homes or work sites to have something to hold on to.

A grim, pervasive smell penetrated the city. An emergency relief physician likened the sickening stench of burned flesh to "the smell of scorched chicken meat." Others described layers of stench—from bloated bodies in the river, people and animals lying dead in the ruins, the strong odor of medical ointments applied to people's burns, survivors' unbathed bodies in the hot summer with no breeze, and urine and excrement from tens of thousands who were too injured to move. "We couldn't eat," Nagano remembered. "Even though we received rations of *onigiri*, for a long time we couldn't eat them because of the smells all around us."

By August 14, five days after the bombing, 2,500 volunteers and military staff members joined Nagasaki's nearly 3,000 emergency personnel—including police, fire department, civil defense, and rescue teams; Mitsubishi crews; and student workers—to help stabilize city operations. Electricity was restored to all neighborhoods except those completely annihilated by the bomb, though the city maintained a nighttime blackout as a defensive measure against additional attacks. Workers scrambled to repair the thousands of breaks in the main lines and residential feeder lines to restore water access. Although the station house itself was destroyed, the tracks at Nagasaki Station were restored enough to allow train service all the way into and out of the city. Using only rakes, shovels, and their hands to push the debris aside, workers cleared the long stretch of the main north-south road, creating the only usable road in the Urakami Valley. The resumption of streetcar service within the city would take much longer.

Ongoing medical support remained an urgent problem. Only about three hundred relief workers were dedicated solely to medical care in Nagasaki's two working hospitals, the Japanese Red Cross clinic, and the twenty-six other emergency relief stations throughout the city. One Nagasaki school was designated an infectious disease "hospital" for the many people being diagnosed with dysentery, a huge concern among medical professionals and city leaders because of its highly contagious nature. An estimated ten hospitals and more than fifty temporary triage sites outside the city—and even outside Nagasaki Prefecture—took in an estimated ten thousand to twelve thousand victims, large numbers of whom died after arrival. Volunteers made their way to these and other distant hospitals to bring back small batches of gauze, bandages, painkillers, antiseptic and disinfectant lotions, sesame oil, zinc oxide powder, and iodine tincture.

One of the largest relief stations was set up in Shinkōzen Elementary School, a three-story concrete building with shattered windows and other minor damages, situated south of Nagasaki Station and east of the bay, 1.8 miles from the hypocenter. As the news spread that doctors were available there, hundreds gathered outside the school hoping to receive help. Inside, every classroom on every floor was full: four rows per classroom, fifteen people per row, the feet of those in one row touching the heads of those in the next. Each room was enveloped in the smell of burned flesh, urine, feces, and patients' vomit. Maggots hatched in every open wound. Volunteers carried seawater from Nagasaki Bay, boiled it in large oil drums, and sprinkled it over patients using watering cans. Three classrooms on the first floor were set up as operating rooms. Dr. Miake Kenji from the Sasebo Naval Hospital conducted surgeries in one of the rooms. "Most of the patients had suffered terrible burns all over their bodies," he recalled. "Many had limbs missing or entrails hanging out. We performed amputations and stump formations and sewed up bellies, but all of the people who came across the operating tables died without even being identified." The bodies of the dead were carried out and burned so quickly that no one could keep count or record their names.

At First Urakami Hospital, Dr. Akizuki and his staff found a desk and chair inside the burned-out building, moved it to the hospital yard, and draped a large cloth over bamboo poles to serve as a makeshift examination room. Each morning began as the one before: Firefighters and volunteers carried more injured into the area and placed them wherever they could find space, then heaved away the bodies of people who had died overnight for cremation. Hospital patients with milder cases of tuberculosis joined in the relief efforts, but the small medical team's workload never ended.

Among those who lay on the ground waiting for help were some twenty or more young nuns from an orphanage run by the Convent of the Holy Cross and a large number of male students from Nagasaki Medical College. At eleven a.m. and five p.m., nurses distributed boiled rice, soup made from pumpkins or seaweed, and slices of boiled squash to over two hundred people. The outside well had been destroyed, so staff rationed the water from a smaller well inside the hospital. As families came to claim their relatives, more people appeared begging for help. New supplies arrived sporadically. Trapped and completely unprotected from what they thought was another attack, patients screamed and moaned every time enemy planes flew over the city. Many of the injured were members of Urakami Church; they prayed constantly, uttering in hushed voices, "Hail, Mary" or "Jesus, Mary, Joseph, please pray for us." One little boy was baptized before he died. Mostly, hundreds of people lay on the ground with dazed expressions that asked, "What is to become of us?"

Like Dō-oh's doctor had done on the night of the bombing, Dr. Akizuki used pincers to painstakingly extract deeply embedded glass fragments and a sterilized needle and thread to stich wounds. Whenever supplies allowed, he applied oil, zinc oxide ointment, Mercurochrome, iodine, and bandages to massive burns and injuries. But each patient took time, and for every patient he treated, two hundred more were calling out to him for help. From the moment he awoke until the time he collapsed for a few hours' sleep, Akizuki felt overwhelmed, depressed, and helpless. He silently cursed the war, the Japanese government that had caused so much suffering, and the United States for dropping the bomb.

On the evening of August 11, someone gave Dr. Akizuki a copy of the *Asahi Shimbun,* and for the first time since the bombing, he glanced through the newspaper and briefly reconnected to the outside world. By candlelight, he read an article issued by the Ministry of Home Affairs that ostensibly informed readers about the "new-type bomb" and about how to protect themselves in the event of such an attack. The article suggested that people find an air raid shelter with a roof, or if that wasn't possible, wrap themselves in a blanket or layers of clothes, and turn off anything at home that could cause a fire.

Akizuki's head spun. Unaware that the Japanese media was prohibited from announcing the true effects of the bombs, he could barely contain his rage. "What was the use of a blanket or some clothing when everything would be burnt or charred in the brilliant heat of thousands of degrees centigrade?" he thought. "What opportunity did we have to go outside after putting out our kitchen fires when, in an instant, tens of thousands of homes became tinder-dry and burst into flames?" But there were hundreds of patients waiting for him, so Dr. Akizuki set down the newspaper and returned to the yard to treat them while one of his

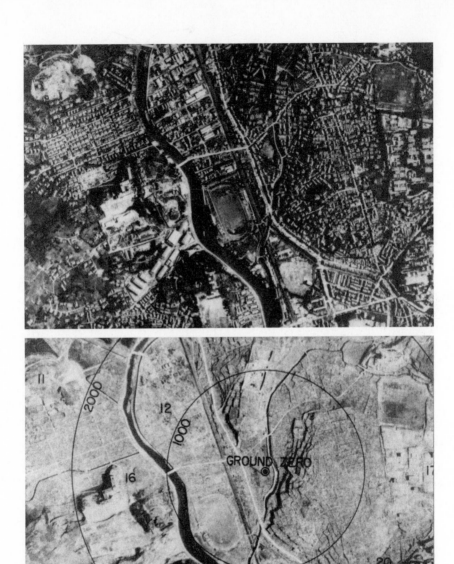

Aerial views of the Urakami Valley taken on August 7, 1945, by U.S. Army Air Forces two days before the bombing (*above*), and three days after the bombing on August 12, 1945 (*below*). The Urakami River runs through both photos from north to south (*top to bottom*). At center is the Mitsubishi Athletic Field. In the bottom photo, 16 is Shiroyama Elementary School; 17 (*far right*) is the Nagasaki Medical College; 18 is Chinzei Middle School; and 20 (*bottom right*) is the Nagasaki Medical College Hospital. (*U.S. Strategic Bombing Survey/ Courtesy of Nagasaki Atomic Bomb Museum*)

tuberculosis patients held up a candle for him to see. At eleven p.m. the next night, his hands stiff from long hours of extractions and medical care, Akizuki stopped his work, lay down on the ground, pulled a blanket over his head, and cried.

———

The end of the war would not come without more delays and major resistance in Tokyo. Although the emperor had made the decision to surrender on the evening of August 9—fourteen hours after the bombing—tension between military and peace factions intensified in the days that followed, complicating the Japanese Cabinet's required unanimous backing of its nation's capitulation.

On August 12, the Cabinet met to discuss the United States' response to Japan's surrender offer. To satisfy Japan's foremost concern, U.S. secretary of state James Byrnes had drafted purposefully ambiguous language about the future of the emperor's role, while carefully maintaining the perception that the United States was remaining steadfast in its commitment to unconditional surrender. But two key sections of the U.S. response would cause continued upheaval at the highest level of the Japanese government and postpone Japan's final surrender. The first stated that "from the moment of surrender the authority of the Emperor and the Japanese Government to rule the state shall be subject to the Supreme Commander of the Allied powers." The second asserted that "the ultimate form of the Government of Japan shall, in accordance with the Potsdam Declaration, be established by the freely expressed will of the Japanese people."

Conservative Japanese Cabinet members and military leaders fervently sought to reject the U.S. conditions because they did not adequately protect the emperor's role as sovereign ruler; these men feared that the U.S. surrender terms threatened *kokutai* and that Japan could be destroyed for good. They held out hope that the emperor would reverse his decision and allow the Japanese military to fight—even at the risk of its own destruction—for Japan's existence as an independent nation ruled by the emperor. In fact, some junior military officers—having concluded that the emperor had been manipulated into surrender and that capitulation would desecrate his dignity and turn Japan into a slave nation—were already plotting coups to topple the national government.

Other Cabinet members found the U.S. counteroffer acceptable and argued that the Cabinet should follow the emperor's August 9 surrender decision without question. They believed that Japan as a nation could be totally destroyed if it stayed in the war, and that the country had at least some chance of survival if it surrendered. After hours of debate, the Cabinet was still deadlocked, and heated arguments extended into the evening of August 12 and through the next day.

On the morning of August 14, the emperor gathered his Cabinet ministers in the imperial underground shelter. Again, he broke the stalemate and announced his decision to accept the Allies' terms of surrender, stating that he believed Japan's *kokutai* would not be lost under Allied occupation and that he could not bear to see his people suffer any longer. The emperor requested that every Cabinet member "bow to my wishes and accept the Allied reply forthwith." Again, the ministers clung to one another and sobbed. By eleven p.m. that night, the emperor and Cabinet had signed the final surrender papers, and an imperial rescript was prepared for the emperor to record for radio broadcast to the nation the next day. To maintain order, Army Minister Anami called for the military's complete support of the emperor's decision. Attempts by low-ranking officers to take over the palace and block the emperor's surrender announcement ultimately failed.

In the meantime, the war had raged on. Russian troops had continued to push back Japanese soldiers in Manchuria and on Sakhalin Island north of Japan. Allied planes had delivered more conventional and incendiary bombs on military, industrial, and key urban areas on Japan's main islands. Before President Truman received Tokyo's response, he ordered additional attacks on Japan. On August 14, just as Washington received word of Japan's acceptance of the Allied terms, Truman's orders were implemented: Approximately 740 B-29s dropped bombs on specific targets, and an estimated 160 more delivered over 12 million pounds of demolition and incendiary bombs on multiple urban areas, causing the deaths of thousands more Japanese.

At seven p.m. on August 14 in Washington (eight a.m. Japan time on August 15), President Truman held a press conference to announce the end of the war. The room was packed with White House correspondents and current and former Cabinet members. Two million people jammed New York City's Times Square, and millions of others crowded into city centers across the country to celebrate the long-awaited conclusion to the nearly four-year global war that had claimed fifty to seventy million lives across the world. All Allied armed forces were ordered to suspend their military operations against Japan.

The people in Japan, however, did not yet know that their country had surrendered. At 7:21 a.m. that morning, Tateno Morio at NHK Radio made a special announcement directed to all Japanese citizens, telling them that at noon that day, the emperor would broadcast a special rescript. Outside the emperor's close circle of family and government leaders, no citizen had ever heard the emperor's voice, and from house to house across the country, word spread that the emperor would address the nation. Rumors grew about what he would say: Some thought he would announce Japan's surrender, but many believed that he would rally the nation for greater support of the war and ask his subjects to be prepared to give their own lives for Japan's honor.

At noon, millions of people in neighborhoods across Japan huddled around single radios to hear the emperor's prerecorded announcement. At army headquarters, hundreds of officers stood at attention in their dress uniforms. Japanese soldiers at military bases throughout the Pacific waited by their radios for the news. The emperor himself listened on an old RCA radio in his underground shelter in Tokyo.

Japan's national anthem, "Kimigayo," played over the airwaves, then the emperor's quiet, stilted voice could be heard. Static splintered his words, and much of the ornamental language he used was difficult to comprehend. Some listeners remembered hearing the word *chin*—a term reserved only for the emperor's use—confirming for them that they were indeed hearing the emperor's voice. In his extended address, the emperor justified the attack on Pearl Harbor and referred to the United States' use of "a new and most cruel bomb." Without using the word "defeat," he stated only that "the war situation has developed not necessarily to Japan's advantage." The emperor portrayed Japan's surrender decision as a heroic and humane act—to prevent not only the "ultimate collapse and obliteration of the Japanese nation," but also the "total extinction of human civilization." He implored the Japanese people to "suffer what is insufferable" with "sincerity and integrity."

Reactions across Japan were swift, profound, and complex. Army officers in Tokyo wept. Others in the city and across the country cheered. A small group of people knelt in front of the imperial palace, bowing in respect to their emperor. Prime Minister Suzuki resigned. High-level officials frantically burned files that might incriminate them in war trials, and they destroyed or disbursed huge stores of food and supplies they had secretly and often illegally amassed for personal benefit. Soldiers at the Western Army Headquarters in Fukuoka blindfolded, handcuffed, and executed seventeen Allied POWs. Some Japanese officers would not concede that the war was over and rallied their men to join together to annihilate the enemy, but their emotional stirrings did not manifest into large-scale action. By August 17, the Imperial Japanese Army and Navy had ceased all military actions except in some remote locations where the message of surrender had not yet been received.

Approximately 350 military personnel, including Army Minister Anami, expressed their sense of personal accountability for Japan's defeat by committing *seppuku,* a ritual suicide by disembowelment using a short sword to slash one's abdomen, formerly part of the samurai Bushido code of honor. Nearly 200 more officers and soldiers, and a few civilians, would kill themselves by October 1948.

Many citizens throughout the country, however, did not fully understand what the emperor had said and relied on radio announcers and special editions of newspapers to summarize and explain the emperor's address in lay language. Surrender was an act previously forbidden to soldiers and considered traitorous for civilians even to think about—and when people realized that this was what the emperor had announced they clung to one another or collapsed to the ground, overwhelmed with conflicting emotions. They felt grief-stricken that their nation had lost the war, anguished about the extreme number of men sacrificed, and relieved that their suffering would end. They were also angry and confused at having been continuously lied to by their government, and many felt lost without the indoctrinated "divine" purpose that had united them for so many years. Thousands of families also felt grateful that their military sons and fathers would come home alive and hoped that they would not choose suicide over surrender as they'd been trained to do.

In Nagasaki, countless survivors remember exactly where they were when the surrender was announced. Many Catholics were observing the Feast of the Assumption of the Blessed Virgin Mary, honoring her death and ascension into heaven. A mother searching for her daughter in Shiroyama-machi listened to the emperor's broadcast in the shade of a house that had survived the bombing. When the surrender announcement ended, she stood silently and stared blankly at the vast nothingness all around, then started out again to find her child. One man had just gathered scraps of wood to cremate his wife's body. Three of his young children had died in the bombing, and he had found his injured wife on a *tatami* mat in the middle of a field, the corpse of their infant son next to her. In the days that followed, as his wife had become weaker, she had begged him to suck the milk from her engorged breasts to relieve her pain. On the afternoon of August 15, as the man stood next to the makeshift funeral pyre and watched his wife's body burn, he could hear the slow strains of the national anthem coming from a radio inside a house nearby. Outside Nagasaki, a fifteen-year-old girl sat in a hospital waiting room holding a still-warm urn filled with the ashes of her younger sister when an agitated military officer shouted, "Japan surrendered! We are defeated!"

Dr. Shirabe Raisuke, a professor of surgery at Nagasaki Medical College, was walking along a road when he first heard from local residents that the war had ended. Later that day, his badly injured older son, Seiichi, told Dr. Shirabe how much he detested the war, a sentiment that could never have been expressed before.

Dr. Akizuki had no radio, but he cried when he heard the news, not because his country had surrendered, but because the end of the war had come too late.

Taniguchi, Yoshida, and Dō-oh knew nothing of the surrender that day. Wada listened on his father's radio inside his damaged home. Although he couldn't understand everything the emperor said, he was deeply relieved that Japan would finally have peace. Nagano's experience most closely mirrored the reactions of many Nagasaki survivors. She and her parents were inside the air raid shelter when word of the emperor's announcement spread through the city, from one person to the next. "Everyone who had survived was crying and hugging each other," Nagano remembered. "'Why?' we asked. 'After everything we did to try to win the war! What purpose did it serve? So many people died. So many homes have burned down. *What will we do now? What will we do? What will we do?*'"

CHAPTER 4

EXPOSED

From the day after Japan surrendered, rumors circulated across the country that American troops would soon land on Japan's shores. Thousands of Japanese fled inland from coastal regions in fear of their enemy's mistreatment of civilians. City officials in Nagasaki urged women to leave the city, and some nurses were released from duty so they could get away. Many families packed their valuables and as much food as they could carry, then escaped to the mountains.

Dō-oh's parents agreed that their family should retreat to the hills, but since Dō-oh was too injured to join them, they decided that her father would stay behind to care for her. Her mother hastily packed *onigiri,* canteens of water, and a few changes of clothes for herself and her three youngest children. Before their departure, she and Dō-oh's father lifted Dō-oh, lying on a futon on top of a stretcher, high above their heads and placed her between the ceiling and roof of their house. At night she could see her father below, lit by candlelight. Whenever he was out of sight, though, she felt terribly alone and terrified about what might happen next. She remained hidden in the rafters until her mother and siblings returned three days later, when the panic began to subside.

U.S. soldiers did not arrive that week, but for Dō-oh, the unimaginable future she had feared was suddenly realized a few weeks later when she began to suffer a series of new and unexplainable symptoms: high fever, diarrhea, hair loss, inflammation of her gums, and mysterious purple spots all over her injured body. Dr. Miyajima, the retired military doctor who had treated Dō-oh since the bombing, told her parents that she would live only a few more days. He suggested that they "feed her well and let her go."

Dō-oh's parents would have liked to give their daughter rice, but they had none. Instead, they gave her tiny sweet potatoes they had planted near their house. Dō-oh's mouth was inflamed, so her mother steamed and mashed the potatoes and placed small bites into the deepest part of her daughter's mouth, gently encouraging her to eat. Dō-oh later learned that since there were no crematoria left in her area, her father had collected firewood and saved some kerosene to burn her body.

Isolated in her house, Dō-oh had no idea that within a week after the bombing, thousands of others across Nagasaki and the surrounding region had begun to experience various combinations of symptoms similar to her own—high fever, dizziness, loss of appetite, nausea, headaches, diarrhea, bloody stools, nosebleeds, whole-body weakness, and fatigue. Their hair fell out in large clumps, their burns and wounds secreted extreme amounts of pus, and their gums swelled, became infected, and bled. Like Dō-oh, they developed purple spots on their bodies—"at first about the size of a pinprick," one doctor recalled, "but growing within a few days to the size of a grain of rice or a pea." The spots were signs of hemorrhaging beneath the skin; they also appeared at medicinal injection sites, which became infected and did not heal. Infections in other parts of the body were rampant, too, including the large intestine, esophagus, bronchial passages, lungs, and uterus. Within a few days of the appearance of their initial symptoms, many people lost consciousness, mumbled deliriously, and died in extreme pain; others languished for weeks before either dying or slowly recovering. Even those who had suffered no external injuries fell sick and died. Some relief workers and victims' family members who had come into the hypocenter area after the bombing also suffered serious illnesses.

Fear gripped the city. As the pattern of symptoms, illness, and death became clear, some people pulled on their hair every morning to see if their time had come. Believing the illness was contagious, many families turned away relatives and guests who were staying with them after the bombing, and some farmers outside Nagasaki refused food to hungry refugees from the city.

Family around a cremation fire, mid-September 1945, three-quarters of a mile from the hypocenter. (*Photograph by Matsumoto Eiichi*/Asahi Shimbun *via Getty Images*)

At first, Dr. Akizuki and other physicians suspected dysentery, cholera, or possibly some form of liver disease. Others believed the illness was due to poisonous gas released by the bomb. By August 15, however, when Japanese scientists had confirmed that an atomic bomb had been dropped on Nagasaki, physicians deduced that what appeared to be an epidemic killing their city was somehow related to radiation contamination. This discovery was helpful in ruling out contagious diseases and other conditions, but it did nothing to minimize the mystifying, confusing, and terrifying truth about the invisible power of the bomb. People died *korokoro-korokoro*—one after another. Dr. Akizuki likened the situation to the Black Death pandemic that devastated Europe in the 1300s. Observing the cremations taking place in his hospital yard, he wondered if his body, too, might soon be burned. "Life or death was a matter of chance, of fate, and the dividing line between the man being cremated and the doctor cremating him was slight."

A second wave of radiation illnesses and deaths swept through the city in late August and early September. Dr. Akizuki and his whole staff came down with nausea, diarrhea, and fatigue, which, he remembered, "made me feel as if I had been beaten all over my body."

Dr. Shirabe Raisuke, the professor of surgery at Nagasaki Medical College, became sick as he was simultaneously grieving the death of his older son, Seiichi, and searching for the remains of his younger son, Kōji, a medical student who had been in class at the time of the bombing and never came home. Shirabe's initial fatigue was so intense he could barely function, but in this condition, he, his wife, and three daughters walked to the ruins of the college to look once again for Kōji's ashes. Dr. Shirabe was tall, with dark skin and deep-set eyes that still could not comprehend the scenes of the college's ruin. "Several hundred crows were flying in the sky overhead," he remembered, "scouring the ground below for the flesh of the dead." As Shirabe and his family picked through the debris, the doctor's youngest daughter found a fragment of blue wool trousers that provided the final confirmation of his son's death: Sewn into a belt loop was the name of Dr. Shirabe's nephew, a reminder that before leaving Nagasaki for the war, his nephew had given the pants to Kōji. Disconsolate, Shirabe and his family gathered ashes from the area where his son had died and carried them home.

A few days later, Dr. Shirabe collapsed. Small purple spots covered his body like those he had seen on his patients before they died. For weeks, he was so frail he could barely turn his head, and his days and nights were filled with anxiety over the future of his family. One day, however, a medical student came to visit and offered Dr. Shirabe a drink of nontoxic ethyl alcohol mixed with sugar water. Shirabe resisted at first but then took a few sips. "This tasted wonderful in my mouth," he recalled, "and I drank a whole glassful. My body warmed up, and I found that I could talk without getting tired." He began drinking small amounts of wine at meals, and though he couldn't say for sure that this was the reason for his recovery, he began to feel stronger, and the purple spots began to fade.

Still weak, consumed with grief over his sons' deaths, and concerned about the future of the Medical College, Dr. Shirabe resumed treating others suffering from injury and radiation illness. Later that fall, at the invitation of a joint team of U.S. and Japanese researchers, he directed a detailed survey of more than eight thousand people's atomic bomb injuries and deaths. Working under extreme conditions at Shinkōzen and in the surrounding community, he and his team of fifty medical students and ten physicians from Nagasaki Medical College and Kawatana Kyosai Hospital spent months conducting interviews and examinations to catalog injuries, illnesses, and mortality rates relating to various factors, including distance from the hypocenter, shielding, access to medical care, evacuation, gender, and extent of multiple types of injuries.

In early September, Nagasaki Prefecture issued a public notice—possibly linked to an (inaccurate) assessment by an American chemist reported in U.S. newspapers—stating that the atomic bomb had contributed a "devastating effect on all living organisms" in the Urakami Valley and that no trees or plants would grow there for seventy years. Nagasaki officials recommended that everyone living in the Urakami Valley relocate. Families with the means to escape had already evacuated in the immediate aftermath of the bomb, but those who remained now faced what they thought was the impending demise of their city. At the same time, torrential storms deluged the city with over twelve inches of rain, flooding the Urakami Valley and washing away the air raid shelters and makeshift shacks where an estimated seven hundred families still lived in the ruins.

Once the city dried out, families reconstructed tiny primitive huts, slept on the floors of train stations, or lived in burned-out train cars. Relief support had faded from the now-demilitarized Japanese armed forces, and emergency food and provisions provided by the Nagasaki Prefectural Government were difficult to access due to still-impassable roads, a dysfunctional streetcar system, and the inability of many victims to get to distribution sites because of injury and illness. Except for the Allied POWs in Nagasaki who were now receiving U.S. parachute drops of provisions and medical supplies, no one in the city had enough to eat. Nagasaki's municipal water system was still in disrepair, so many people walked long distances to access working wells. An eight-year-old boy drank the water from a vase of flowers set at a gravesite. Two young girls

Atomic wasteland at Yamazato-machi, along the road leading from the hypocenter (*right*) to Urakami Church (*at left beyond photograph*), October 1945. (*Photograph by Hayashi Shigeo/Courtesy of Nagasaki Atomic Bomb Museum*)

retrieved water each day by crossing a school playground-turned-crematorium covered with ashes and fragments of human bone. Some people washed their clothes in the river as unclaimed decomposing corpses floated by.

The second wave of radiation illnesses and deaths continued through early October. Wada, too, became ill, one of many who suffered radiation-related symptoms after spending significant time in the Urakami Valley and the hypocenter area as he searched for his missing colleagues, cremated bodies, and hauled rocks and debris from the streetcar tracks. Blood appeared in Wada's urine and excrement, and he started losing his hair. "Back then we didn't have shampoo; we had only soap. I wondered if my hair loss was because of that, so I started washing my hair with only water. But my hair kept falling out. Eventually I became bald."

At the few hospitals providing care, some patients were given medication to help stop internal bleeding and to relieve pain. But this was rare. In the place of nearly nonexistent medicines, physicians and family caregivers devised their own remedies. Doctors treated patients with blood transfusions, rations of fresh liver to boost white blood cell production, and large doses of glucose and vitamins B, C, and K. Dr. Akizuki, long interested in therapeutic nutrition, required his staff and patients to follow a high-salt, no-sugar diet to support the health of blood cells—a regimen to which he attributed his own and many of his staff's recovery. Dr. Shirabe promoted the drinking of sake. In rural areas outside the city, doctors recommended that their patients soak in mineral hot springs. Mothers and grandmothers treating family members at home served them a raw egg each morning and brewed bitter teas from mulberry leaves, cuttlefish, and Chinese herbs. Wada's grandmother insisted he drink *kakinoha* (persimmon leaf) tea. "It tasted pretty bad," he admitted, "but I was told over and over that if I didn't drink it, I wouldn't get well—so I grit my teeth and drank it every day." For caregivers, holding a dying child's hand, touching a patient's back or forehead, or speaking a few kind words was often all that could be done.

Those who did not fall ill lived in constant anxiety, haunted by the question of when their turn would come. From Dr. Akizuki's perspective on top of Motohara Hill, death carved a clear geographical path: The first people who suffered and died from radiation-related illness were living inside the Josei Girls' High School air raid shelter at the bottom of the hill. The illness then climbed the hill, killing people in relative order according to their distance from the atomic blast. When the next tier of people grew sick, they were carried to Akizuki's burned-out hospital by their neighbors who lived farther up the hill—and the distance between the homes of the sick and his hospital became shorter and shorter. "The Maekawa family, the Matsuokas, and then the Yamaguchis were attacked by radiation sickness," Akizuki remembered. "I named this widening advance of the disease the 'concentric circles of death.'" He watched as his neighbor, Mr. Yamaguchi, lost thirteen family members from atomic bomb sickness. After each death, Mr. Yamaguchi carried the body to the cemetery, dug the grave, and called for the priest. After each ceremony, he returned home to care for the remaining family members, all of whom had fallen ill. "They are dying, one by one," he told Dr. Akizuki. "Who will send for the priest when I am dying? Who will dig my grave when I am gone?"

Doctors were frantic to understand and stop the mysterious disease that was ravaging the city, but they had little means to conduct research. At the fully equipped Ōmura Naval Hospital north of the city, however, Shiotsuki Masao, a twenty-five-year-old doctor in training, took on the immense project of performing autopsies on as many dead bodies as possible from the piles of corpses waiting each day for transport to a burial or cremation site.

The hospital had taken in 758 victims on the night of the bombing three weeks earlier. A hundred had died before morning, and over a thousand more had arrived in the days that followed—mostly factory workers, students, and housewives transported out of Nagasaki by relief workers. The hospital's small two-story buildings had overflowed with patients—sometimes forty to a room—and Dr. Shiotsuki didn't sleep for three days and nights as he tried to treat the complex burns, injuries, and lacerations that had penetrated his patients' internal organs, none of which had been part of his training. Once the symptoms of radiation disease began, the rate of death increased so rapidly that at times all he could do was go from one dead patient to another to provide official confirmation of their deaths. Early on, when patients did not yet understand that hair loss was one of the first signs of probable and imminent death, Dr. Shiotsuki gently placed his hand on their heads where patches of hair still remained. "Loss of hair often accompanies burns," he falsely reassured them. "It should stop in a few days." It was, in his judgment, the most humane care he could give to patients who didn't know they would soon die.

Dr. Shiotsuki began his investigations as early as August 13, even before he knew the nature of the bomb or had any hint that radiation exposure was causing these mysterious symptoms. He started by photographing, X-raying, and documenting in detailed written reports the course of his patients' conditions, treatment methods provided, and their ultimate recovery or death. Observing his patients dying from whole-body

Ōmura Naval Hospital, the region's only remaining advanced medical facility after the bombing, twenty-two miles (by road) north of Nagasaki, where a large number of atomic bomb victims were evacuated. A young hospital physician, Shiotsuki Masao, conducted some of the earliest autopsies of atomic bomb victims here in an effort to understand their deaths. (*U.S. Army Institute of Pathology/Courtesy of Nagasaki Atomic Bomb Museum*)

radiation exposure, he noted: "There is no conspicuous damage to the heart or the circulatory system, but as the end approaches, the blood pressure plummets. Because of high fever or general weakening perhaps, a pneumonia-like condition is apt to occur. During this period, the body temperature continues to rise. In the final stages, the patient registers the highest temperature; then suddenly it falls and the patient dies. Some patients suffer severe vision disabilities and some receive brain damage. Victims who did not experience brain damage suffered no clouding of consciousness. In fact, in spite of their high fevers, most of them were extremely calm and lucid."

For Dr. Shiotsuki, however, external observations alone seemed inadequate. To surmount his feelings of despair and helplessness, he became fixated on the idea of conducting autopsies in order to observe and document the internal damages to his patients' bodies. As a new doctor, Shiotsuki felt that he was too inexperienced to understand everything he would see, but he fervently hoped that both his autopsy specimens and written records would provide more qualified doctors valuable information for later analysis.

The Ōmura Naval Hospital had no autopsy room, so Shiotsuki and a male orderly named Iyonaga Yasumasa set up a working space in a small shack on the hospital grounds that was used as a mortuary. "The room was hot and stuffy," Shiotsuki remembered. "Under a dim light covered by a shade, we would lift a corpse onto the table made of coffins, say a prayer, then wield the scalpel. What horrific damage had been done to the tissue! As I made those incisions, how many times did I stifle a gasp or let out a sigh. Everywhere the veins had been torn to shreds, and the blood had seeped everywhere."

Many of Shiotsuki's postmortem examinations shared common findings, including hemorrhaging of the lungs and kidneys, and blood clots on the outer membranes of the intestines, spleen, and kidneys. He also observed hemorrhaging in the brain, white spots on the large intestine, and ruptures in the liver, spleen, and lungs. Blood tests revealed that patients' white blood cell counts were lower than normal by 90 percent or more, their red blood cell counts were half of normal levels, and hemoglobin was significantly diminished.

"No one knew when those mysterious symptoms would suddenly appear and drag another victim to the abyss," Dr. Shiotsuki wrote. When he himself became ill, his tests showed a white blood cell count 50 percent lower than normal—the result, he believed, of his ongoing contact with radiation-exposed people. He treated himself with glucose and vitamin injections, continued working, and recovered within ten days, which he attributed to his stamina and early care. As he and Iyonaga examined more and more bodies, they placed the patients' irradiated organs in jars of formaldehyde on the floor, then found a tiny, unused storage room where they stacked more jars. When a senior hospital official deemed Dr. Shiotsuki's research unnecessary in the face of Japan's mortifying defeat, Shiotsuki began hiding the specimen jars between the wood paneling and the outside wall of the mortuary hut. "To the inexperienced eye," he explained, "these organs were merely grotesque lumps of flesh. But for us they were eloquent testimony to a horrible tragedy."

Dr. Shiotsuki was discharged from the navy in mid-September and ordered to return home to Tokyo. He was gravely concerned about the preservation of the specimen jars, which he imagined would be destroyed upon his departure. Sending them to Tokyo was not an option because Japan's shipping offices were in too great a disarray to guarantee their safe arrival. His only choice was to carry home as many specimen jars as he could. He had planned to pack as much food as possible to survive since much of Tokyo had been burned to the ground. Instead, Shiotsuki wrapped specimen jars in newspaper, sacks, and clothing and placed them into his baggage. After seeing his patients for the last time, he slung his duffel bag of specimens onto his back, lifted more bags holding his personal belongings and additional specimens, and left for home.

Shiotsuki's train out of Ōmura Station was crowded, filled mostly with discharged Japanese soldiers. He was fortunate to get a seat, but within a few hours, a passing soldier lost his balance and stepped on his duffel bag. Formaldehyde began leaking onto the floor of the train, creating a pungent smell. People's eyes began burning. When some of the passengers became agitated, Shiotsuki explained what had happened, apologized for the smell, and asked for their forbearance. But the commotion grew. Soldiers demanded that he throw the bag out the window. Shiotsuki sat quietly, his head bowed, anxious to protect his research. Suddenly, a commander with whom Shiotsuki had spoken earlier stood up and bellowed, "What do you think is preserved in that formaldehyde? The guts of the people who died in the special bombing at Nagasaki, that's what. The doctor is continuing his research in order to pray for the repose of those victims. The smell will soon go away, so just put up with it until it does." Everyone grew quiet, and Shiotsuki continued on his journey without further incident.

He traveled for two days and nights before reaching Tokyo. Once home, he opened the duffel bag to see that only one jar had broken. Two days later, he repacked the bag and set off for Tōhoku University, where he had received his medical degree. There, he divided the specimens between the departments of pathology and surgery, "with the prayer," he later wrote, "that these medical data might prove useful for the peace of the human race." For the first time since the bombing, he felt, at last, that the war had ended.

————

Before the atomic bombs were dropped, U.S. scientists conducted no studies on the potential effects of high-dose, whole-body radiation exposure, nor did they investigate or develop potential treatments for the medical conditions that would ensue. The absence of such studies was not due to lack of awareness of the dangers of radiation to the body. In the 1920s, the International X-Ray and Radium Protection Committee had issued the world's first safety standards both for professionals working with radioactive substances and for patients receiving X-rays or new cancer radiation therapies to specific areas of their bodies. By the 1940s, the risks of small doses of radiation to human organs, tissue, and cells had been explored by scientists worldwide. During the development of the bombs, too, U.S. scientists knew the dangers of radiation exposure, evidenced by the Manhattan Project's precise handling, hygiene, ventilation, and radioactive monitoring procedures at its sites. To some degree, U.S. scientists and military leaders also understood the dangers of the radiation released at the time of the bombs' explosions. In a May 1945 memo, for example, Dr. J. Robert Oppenheimer, scientific director of the Manhattan Project, stated: "During the detonation, radiations are emitted which (unless personnel are shielded) are expected to be injurious within a radius of a mile and lethal within a radius of about six-tenths of a mile."

However, as the bombs were developed and subsequently used on Hiroshima and Nagasaki, serious consideration was not given to the people whose entire bodies would in a single instant be exposed to massive, not-yet-calculable doses of radiation. "The chief effort at Los Alamos was devoted to the design and fabrication of a successful atomic bomb," wrote physician and radiologist Stafford Warren, chief of the Medical Section of the Manhattan Project. "Scientists and engineers engaged in this effort were, understandably, so immersed in their own problems that it was difficult to persuade any of them even to speculate on what the aftereffects of the detonation might be. Their concern was whether any one of their several designs for the bomb would actually detonate, and, if the detonation did occur, how massive it would be." Time was also a factor; once scientists had successfully tested the plutonium bomb in the New Mexico desert, they had only three weeks to finalize preparations for the Hiroshima bombing, leaving little time to study the radiation effects of the test blast. Without empirical evidence, no one knew how far or low to the ground the bombs' radioactive waves would travel, or the extent of their destruction on the internal organs of tens of thousands of Japanese civilians.

Instead, scientists and military leaders had made presumptions. They deduced that as the blast force and heat of the bombs inflicted mass destruction and death, most of the radiation released at the time of the explosion would be captured by the rising atomic cloud. Accordingly, the pilots of the planes involved in the Hiroshima and Nagasaki bombings were trained to get away from the blast areas in less than a minute in order to avoid unsafe proximity to the radioactive clouds. U.S. scientists also assumed that anyone who might be exposed to fatal radiation levels (which had not yet been empirically determined) would be killed by the blast before the effects of radiation exposure manifested in their bodies.

Even less understood was the human impact of *residual* radiation—nuclear fallout from the atomic clouds (which some scientists anticipated) and lingering radiation through absorption by the soil and debris (which few scientists expected due to the height of the bombs' detonation points). Manhattan Project director General Leslie Groves demonstrated conflicting assessments of the bombs' potential residual radiation levels by declaring before the bombings that U.S. troops could safely have moved into the targeted cities within thirty minutes of the attacks. However, in the days between the atomic bombings and American occupation troops' arrival in Hiroshima and Nagasaki, the general ordered U.S. research teams into both cities to measure radiation levels to ensure that his assumption of no danger was, in fact, true.

U.S. scientists' and military leaders' lack of knowledge and grossly miscalculated assumptions, combined with their desire to safeguard the United States' reputation, led to passionate repudiation of Japanese claims of radiation effects on the people of Nagasaki and Hiroshima in the weeks and months after the bombing. In late August, when U.S. and worldwide media outlets picked up stories from the Japanese press about the mysterious and deadly radiation-related illnesses, General Groves promptly dismissed the reports as pure propaganda, unsubstantiated by U.S. scientific studies. Coming out of a war in which both sides used the media to propagate negative portrayals of their enemy, it may have been reasonable for Groves to assume that the Japanese would exaggerate reports of suffering in Hiroshima and Nagasaki. In this case, however, the reports were true—and Groves neglected to say that Japanese claims of radiation illness and death were unsubstantiated by U.S. scientific studies only because those studies had not been conducted.

Even privately, Groves did not waver. In a late August telephone conversation with the director of clinical services at Oak Ridge Hospital in Tennessee, one of the Manhattan Project's secret sites, Groves asserted his belief that Japanese reports of radiation illness were a play for sympathy and that the rising death tolls in Hiroshima and Nagasaki were the result of rescue workers finding more dead bodies in the weeks after the bombings. Neither his public nor his private opinion seemed to change when, on August 21, 1945, physicist Harry Daghlian became exposed to high levels of radiation during an accident while handling plutonium at Los Alamos. Daghlian experienced severe and agonizing radiation-related symptoms similar to those of the survivors of Hiroshima and Nagasaki. He died twenty-five days later.

In late August and early September, Groves and other U.S. officials tried to quash public discussion on radiation effects—and its inherent challenge to the United States' morality in using the bombs—with deflective claims about the lawfulness of the bombs' use and their decisive role in ending the war. Groves also shifted focus to the scientific development of the bombs and emphasized Japan's wartime atrocities. "The atomic bomb is not an inhuman weapon," he stated in the *New York Times*. "I think our best answer to anyone who doubts this is that we did not start the war, and if they don't like the way we ended it, to remember who started it."

The disconnect between what was happening on the ground in Nagasaki and Hiroshima and what was being reported in the United States further intensified after the formal surrender ceremony on September 2 aboard the USS *Missouri,* anchored in Tokyo Bay. The Japanese media, free at last from Japan's oppressive wartime censorship, was initially told that General Douglas MacArthur—the newly appointed Supreme Commander for the Allied Powers (SCAP) and head of the U.S. occupation in Japan—was a fervent advocate of freedom of the press. But as soon as MacArthur arrived in Japan, Japanese journalists and media organizations were required to abide by strict mandates, particularly regarding what they could not report—which ultimately included any details of the radiation effects in Nagasaki and Hiroshima. Two of Japan's major media organizations were briefly suspended for breaching these guidelines in early September—the first, by criticizing the barbaric nature of the atomic bombs and suggesting that without them, Japan might have won the war; the second, by publishing a statement by a leading politician who called the atomic bombs a violation of international law and a war crime.

On September 18, General MacArthur issued an occupation press code, ending any final hope of press freedom in postwar Japan. Planned by U.S. officials prior to the end of the war, the comprehensive and exacting list of rules mandated that all Japanese news reports must be "truthful"—defined as containing no hint of editorial commentary, no "false or destructive criticism of the Allied Powers," and no grievance against U.S. occupation forces. Major Japanese newspapers and other publications were placed under *pre*-censorship rules, requiring them to deliver originals of all articles and publications to the occupation censorship office for approval and return before they were printed. Japanese books, textbooks, films, and mail going into and out of the country were closely scrutinized and controlled. Moreover, no one could mention that censorship existed. As a consequence, all media coverage about the atomic bombings and their radiation effects suddenly stopped—and journalists could not say why.

Foreign reporters in Japan were also highly restricted, allowed to operate only after applying for and being granted SCAP accreditation. They were required to submit all reports to occupation censors for approval before their release. In an effort to maintain control over the atomic bomb story, the U.S. War Department sponsored one official, tightly regulated press junket to Hiroshima and Nagasaki in mid-September, after which foreign journalists were limited to escorted trips to POW camps in northern parts of the country.

Two reporters—one from the United States and one from Australia—managed to secretly make their way to Nagasaki and Hiroshima and report on what they saw. The *Chicago Tribune*'s George Weller saw his chance in early September, when the occupation press office offered a sanctioned press junket to southern Japan to view an airstrip being used to refuel U.S. planes traveling between Japan and Guam. After landing in a tiny town at the southern tip of Kyushu, Weller dodged his escort and found his way to a train station. Twenty-four hours and numerous local trains later, he reached the outskirts of Nagasaki. Posing as a U.S. colonel, Weller demanded to be taken to Nagasaki's military headquarters, where a Japanese general believed his story and immediately provided him lodging, food, a vehicle, and two *kempeitai* (military police) daily to hand-carry his dispatches to Tokyo.

Over the next few weeks, Weller walked through the ruins of the city and witnessed firsthand the devastating effects of radiation on people's bodies, which he referred to as Disease X. He spoke with Nagasaki physicians and heard their best analyses of the effects of radiation on the different organs of the body. He also met with POWs in the two Nagasaki camps, who plied him with questions regarding sports, world news, and Frank Sinatra. Every night, Weller typed his stories by lamplight, addressed the package to "Chief Censor, American Headquarters, Tokyo," and handed them to the two military officers for delivery to Tokyo.

He never received a response. Years later, Weller found out that MacArthur's censors, who could not have been happy with him for defying their rules, had rejected all of his reports. Three weeks after arriving in Nagasaki, Weller left on a U.S. hospital ship transporting POWs to Guam. He carried with him carbon copies of every page he had written, though these dispatches would become misplaced, lost to history for sixty years.

Australian journalist Wilfred Burchett, too, eluded MacArthur's barriers to southern Japan. Just before the U.S. War Department's press junket for U.S. journalists, Burchett made his way to Hiroshima and became the first foreign journalist to witness the obliterated city. Burchett's first dispatch included graphic details of radiation-related illness and death—information that Groves had already adamantly denied. With the help of a Japanese and another Australian journalist, Burchett's story evaded U.S. censors in Tokyo and was sent by Morse code directly to London. The piece was distributed worldwide and appeared on the front page of Britain's *Daily Express.*

U.S. officials were outraged. When Burchett returned to Tokyo on September 7, he attended a press conference led by General Thomas Farrell— Groves's deputy commanding general and chief of field operations of the Manhattan Project. Farrell was in Japan to confirm the safety of U.S. occupation troops about to enter Hiroshima and Nagasaki. According to Burchett, during the press conference Farrell adamantly refuted Burchett's charges of radiation poisoning and insisted that what Burchett saw were injuries and burns from the bomb's blast and heat. In a fierce public exchange, Burchett retorted that he had observed evidence of radiation effects, including fish that were dying when they entered a stream in the outskirts of the city. Farrell countered: "I'm afraid you've fallen victim to Japanese propaganda."

Over the next week, General Farrell led a preliminary Manhattan Project investigation team to Hiroshima and Nagasaki. Contrary to some Japanese officials' assessments, the U.S. scientists confirmed that although radiation levels were higher than normal at both cities' hypocenter areas and in regions where black rain had fallen, the levels were low enough to be safe for U.S. occupation troops. The scientists stayed on to conduct further research, and additional teams from the U.S. Army, Navy, and Strategic Bombing Survey arrived in Nagasaki and Hiroshima to document the effects of the bomb's blast, heat, and radiation as a means to support American nuclear weapons development and bolster U.S. civil defense measures against a potential atomic bomb attack. The outcomes of these studies were classified and barred from release.

Many Japanese scientists who were conducting their own investigations in Nagasaki and Hiroshima initially offered and were later mandated to hand over their research to U.S. scientists. In some cases, they were ordered to give up their autonomy and work under the authority of a U.S. team. Some Japanese researchers, including Dr. Shirabe, were able to quietly continue their studies on atom bomb illnesses and mortality rates, though they could not publish their findings until after the occupation ended. In a policy of unmitigated appropriation, U.S. investigators seized bomb victims' medical records, autopsy specimens, blood samples, and tissue biopsies from both cities and shipped them to the United States for further analysis.

American military police also arrested a Nippon Eiga-sha (Japanese Film Company) crew as it was documenting Nagasaki's destruction and the impact of radiation exposure on survivors. All of the crew's footage of both Nagasaki and Hiroshima was confiscated, but when the U.S. teams recognized the black-and-white film's unparalleled value—impossible to duplicate "until another atomic bomb is released under combat conditions"—they ordered the Japanese filmmakers to complete their filming and edit the footage for submission to the United States. Pentagon officials screened the film in 1946 and denied its public release.

General Farrell's reports to General Groves and numerous U.S. studies confirmed that horrific radiation illnesses and deaths were caused by initial radiation exposure from the bombings, but when Farrell returned to the United States, he, along with Groves and others, persisted in minimizing the illnesses and deaths from both initial and residual radiation exposure. "The Japanese claim that people died from radiations [sic]," Groves said in a *New York Times* article. "If this is true, the number was very small."

To prove his point that residual radiation levels were safe in Nagasaki and Hiroshima, Groves invited a group of reporters to witness ongoing readings of low radiation levels at the Trinity test bomb site in Alamogordo, New Mexico. In a strange contradiction, however, the journalists entering the site were required to put on white canvas coverings over their shoes "to make certain that some of the radioactive material still present in the ground might not stick to our soles," one of them wrote. Without addressing this inconsistency, Groves again justified the bombings, telling the journalists, "While many people were killed, many lives were saved, particularly American lives."

A September 15 confidential memo from the U.S. War Department to American media outlets provided a final blow to open reporting on the bombs' radiation effects. The memo requested that all reports about the atomic bombs—particularly reports that included scientific or technical details—be approved by the War Department prior to publication in order to protect the military secrecy of the bomb. Typical of the era, U.S. media organizations complied almost uniformly, printing the government's press releases as they were written, with little question or opposition.

In combination with censorship of the Japanese media, most reports about the human impact of the bombs were effectively suspended in both Japan and the United States. Later that year, General Groves testified before the U.S. Senate that death from high-dose radiation exposure is "without undue suffering" and "a very pleasant way to die."

———

Nagano's younger sister, Kuniko, died from radiation toxicity on September 10. She was thirteen years old.

After the emperor's August 15 surrender proclamation, Nagano's father had decided to evacuate his family to the small village of Obama, his hometown on the Shimabara Peninsula. The next morning, Nagano, Kuniko, and their parents had left their air raid shelter, pressed through the destroyed Urakami Valley, and exited the city. Nagano's mother held the rice bowl with Sei-chan's ashes close to her chest. On unpaved roads, they had walked in silence twenty-one miles to the east along the edge of Tachibana Bay, then south for another fourteen miles to the village of Obama. "We may have slept," Nagano said, "but I don't remember. It was such a wretched time that there were no words to be spoken."

A distant great-aunt of Nagano's father had taken them in. As the family settled into their new residence, Kuniko was still so terrified of another atomic bombing that every time an airplane flew overhead, she hid under the bedcovers, shivering and crying—inconsolable even as Nagano and her family reassured her that the war was over and no more bombs would be dropped.

In early September, just as horror stories were arriving from Nagasaki about illness and death from the bomb's radiation, Kuniko became ill with the telltale symptoms. Nagano was consumed with grief and confusion. "After the bomb, she seemed *fine*," she said. "During the whole time we were walking to Obama, she didn't complain *even once*—she didn't say she was tired or *anything*—so I never thought for a moment, even in my wildest imagination, that she would die. But then she completely lost her hair, her gums bled, and big purple spots appeared on her body. She got a fever, vomited blood, had blood in her stool, and she was in so much pain.

"I begged God to save her," Nagano remembered. "I prayed to let me die in her place. But she died anyway. She writhed in agony for a week, and then she died."

Nagano blamed herself for Sei-chan's and Kuniko's deaths. "I had done a horrible thing," she said. "They didn't want to come home from my grandparents' house earlier that year, but I brought them home anyway. I *really* wanted to die," she remembered, unable to control her tears. "I *still* think I should have died instead of them."

When Kuniko died, Nagano's older brother came home from the Ōmura army base where he had been stationed, and her grandparents traveled to Obama from southern Kyushu—a family gathering that hadn't been possible when Sei-chan died. Her parents bought a *kotsutsubo* (ceramic urn) for Kuniko's ashes and a second one for Sei-chan's, finally giving him a dignified

Nagano with her family, early 1945, prior to her older brother's departure for military service. *From left to right:* Nagano's mother, Nagano's older brother (*standing in back*), Seiji, Nagano's father, Nagano, and Kuniko. (*Courtesy of Nagano Etsuko*)

resting place. Her mother was hospitalized with radiation-related symptoms but recovered within a month. For years, Nagano could not comprehend or accept the selective nature of radiation exposure: Kuniko had died an agonizing death, while her mother—"who was in the *same* house at the *same* time as my sister"—lived for fifty more years.

Nagano's father returned to Nagasaki to resume his job at the Mitsubishi Electric factory south of the harbor. He lived in a single men's dormitory and went back to see his family once a month when he received his small paycheck. Nagano's mother cried every day and barely spoke to Nagano. At seventeen, Nagano had lost her siblings, her home, and now her mother. As she began her new life in Obama, she struggled to survive in what felt like an endless state of emotional isolation.

———

Autumn arrived in Nagasaki, bringing cooler days and nights. After early teams of American soldiers swept Nagasaki Bay for underwater mines dropped by the United States in the final year of the war, U.S. military ships arrived in Nagasaki in mid-September to evacuate Allied prisoners of war. POWs poured into the city from camps across Kyushu. "It was an eerie experience travelling down the Nagasaki valley," an Australian soldier remembered. "Not a sound. No birds. Not even a lizard. Just brown, treeless soil like cocoa, no grass, and twisted girderwork."

The POWs were processed at the port in assembly-line fashion: first coffee and doughnuts, then showers, delousing, and brief medical inspections. Those who were seriously injured, malnourished, or ill with tuberculosis, infections, ulcers, or other conditions were carried out to the *Sanctuary* and the *Haven,* two fully equipped hospital ships anchored in Nagasaki Bay. Everyone else received new underwear, socks, fatigues, and toiletry supplies. The men had their first full meal in months or years—fried chicken, spaghetti, corn bread, and cake—and danced with nurses to a band playing "Two O'Clock Jump." After a movie, they slept in beds lined up on the ships' decks. Within two weeks, over nine thousand POWs, along with many foreign monks, priests, nuns, and missionaries who had been interned on Kyushu, sailed out of Nagasaki harbor to Allied-held ports across Asia, where they transferred to ships and planes that carried them to their home countries across the globe.

On September 23, U.S. occupation troops arrived in Nagasaki Bay. The marines on board were dressed in full combat gear, including bayonets and guns, to meet possible Japanese resistance. As their ships lumbered closer to land, the men were overwhelmed by the putrid smell of the city. They passed abandoned Japanese ships in the harbor and could see the tangled steel skeleton of a Mitsubishi factory. Rudi Bohlmann, a soldier from South Dakota, recalled the young orphaned boys who helped moor the ships to the docks and devoured the apples and oranges the soldiers dropped down to them. "They were just starved to death and had sores," he remembered. "Eyes were all mattered and running, their ears sort of dripping with matter. The sides of their mouth was all festered [*sic*]."

The victors met no opposition as they landed on their former enemy's shores. The first U.S. troops to disembark divided into small groups and left in jeeps and trucks every hour for short tours of the city. They were stunned and rendered speechless by the grisly scenes before them, brought on by a single bomb. The Urakami Valley had vanished from existence, corpses were burning on cremation pyres, skulls and bones were piled on the ground, and people were walking through the ruins with beleaguered and empty expressions—"going nowhere, it seems," remembered Keith Lynch, a sailor from Nebraska. "Just walking." In a letter to his parents the next day, he wrote that he saw "a sight I hope my children, if I am so fortunate, will never have to see, hear of, or ever think of. It was horrible and when you get to thinking, unbelievable. . . . Such a thing as I saw yesterday cannot be described in words. You have to see it and I hope no one ever has to see such a thing again."

The people of Nagasaki were shattered by death, illness, and the practical needs of survival, leaving little room for resistance or even anger toward the soldiers their government had called the "American devils." Many heeded official warnings to stay out of sight and avoid contact with the American soldiers, but even on the day the troops arrived, some stood at the sides of roads and pathways through the ruins and quietly watched as the Americans passed by. Over the weeks and months to come, some even dared to hope that their lives would now improve.

The occupation troops did not turn out to be violent and cruel as the Japanese people had been indoctrinated to believe. Before their arrival, many soldiers had been briefed in Japanese courtesy, as well as geography, culture, and basic language skills. Children, in particular, were enamored with the American soldiers, who played hopscotch and catch with them, and offered them chewing gum, chocolate, and milk, exotic treats that were otherwise unattainable in the months after the war's end. It was common to hear children speak to the troops with simple English words like "hello," "thank you," "good morning," and "please"—and their happy and safe interactions with the American soldiers quickly softened the worries of many adults. In turn, some U.S. soldiers took Japanese lessons from Nagasaki children and walked around the city greeting people with simple words like *ohayō* (good morning). A young deaf Japanese man was able to communicate with some of the soldiers using simple sign language. "I will never forget the destruction caused by the atomic bomb," he remembered, "but I have no grudge against those soldiers. They were kind and good."

Of the more than 450,000 occupation troops that would enter Japan, approximately 27,000 from the 6th U.S. Army were assigned to Nagasaki. Their first step was to "secure the surrender"—that is, "to establish control of the area, ensure compliance with surrender terms, and demilitarize the Japanese war machine." They set up command posts in the

Customs House on Dejima Wharf and other locations east and west of the harbor. Others established a division hospital and billets close by and maintained additional occupation facilities throughout the city. Next, they seized Nagasaki military installations, weapons inventories, communications equipment, and building supplies, all of which were destroyed, used for occupation operations, or turned over to the Japanese Home Ministry for governmental reuse. U.S. troops replaced Japanese military guards and became the policing authority across the region.

Not everyone in Nagasaki was happy with the U.S. occupiers. Dr. Akizuki mourned the loss of his country's sovereignty and felt that Japan had "finally become one of the United States of America." Others, angry

The lower Urakami Valley, looking north, fall 1945. From left, across the top, are the ruins of the Mitsubishi Mori-machi factory. (*Photograph by Joe O'Donnell*/Japan 1945, *Vanderbilt University Press, 2005*)

and embittered about the atomic bombing, found it hard to accept soldiers from their former enemy nation that had delivered the bomb. "The universal horror experienced by those living in the atom-bombed areas could not be shaken off by even the promise of peace," fifteen-year-old Hattori Michie remembered. "We knew war is appalling and has few rules, but what the enemy did to our innocent civilians on a mass scale we felt to be outside the purview of a civilized nation's warfare."

A small number of soldiers committed minor cultural infractions, such as wearing shoes while inside a *tatami* room. Other actions, however, were extremely offensive, including evicting Japanese residents from their Western-style homes in southern Nagasaki for use as private

homes for American officers, and taking over other buildings as well for occupation offices and barracks. Another conspicuous act of insensitivity came that winter when two well-fed and healthy units of the 2nd Marine Division pitted themselves against each other in a New Year's Day football game. At a time when Nagasaki students and teachers found it almost unbearable to study and work in school buildings where so many of their friends and colleagues had died, occupation leaders chose "Atomic Athletic Field No. 2" for the game—the athletic field of a former Nagasaki high school now designated for occupation troops' use. It was here, five months earlier, that hundreds of adults and children had been laid in rows, wounded and dying. Yoshida was among them; his parents had found him here on the day after the bombing, his face scorched and his eyes swollen shut. To prepare for the event, U.S. soldiers used scrap wood to construct goalposts and bleachers. On game day, spurred on by a marine band, thousands of occupation troops gathered to watch the teams battle for victory. Fragments of glass from the school's shattered windows still covered the field, so tackling was replaced by a two-hand touch. The Americans called the game the Atom Bowl.

Perhaps the Americans' most egregious activities took place in the Urakami Valley. Although General Groves and others had repeatedly denied that dangerous residual radiation was present in Nagasaki, the hypocenter area was cordoned off and U.S. troops were ordered not to enter the area. What that meant, however, was that "everybody and his brother headed directly for ground zero," one soldier remembered. Looting for atomic keepsakes was strictly forbidden and punishable by court-martial, but some soldiers rifled through the ruins for anything they could find that they could bring home as war trophies. Moreover, when American troops built an airstrip in the northwest corner of the valley—nicknamed Atomic Field—they used bulldozers to clear the ruins, crushing human bones scattered in the debris. "There were still many dead under the rubbish," fifteen-year-old Uchida Tsukasa remembered. "Despite that, the Americans drove their bulldozers very fast, treating the bones of the dead just the same as sand or soil. They carried the soil to lower places and used it to broaden roads there." Hayashi Shigeo, a prodigious photographer dispatched by Tokyo's Ministry of Education, was threatened at gunpoint by a U.S. military police officer when he tried to take a photograph of an American bulldozer dropping victims' bodies into a ditch. In both incidents, people who lived in the area, and those whose family members' bones were buried in the debris, could only stand by, outraged and helpless.

No one, however, begrudged the American government—along with the International Red Cross and American Red Cross organizations—for providing desperately needed medical support to Nagasaki's hospitals and clinics. To help stabilize the nation, prevent civil unrest, and protect U.S. troops, one of the occupation's goals was to curb widespread illness and death from the communicable diseases that were rampant across the country. In Nagasaki, this meant restoring the system of collecting night soil (human feces) using two occupation trucks and a group of forty Japanese workers. Doctors received deliveries of penicillin and other medications otherwise not available in Japan, allowing them to not only treat patients with infectious diseases such as dysentery, smallpox, and typhoid fever but also prescribe antibiotics for survivors with compromised immune systems and infections connected to radiation-related conditions. Under the leadership of Captain Herbert Horne, in charge of occupation medical services in Nagasaki, the temporary hospital inside Shinkōzen Elementary School was designated the official hospital for atomic bomb victims under the affiliation of Nagasaki Medical College. Dr. Shirabe was appointed the hospital's director. To help with Nagasaki's crushingly scant medical services, Horne also oversaw the opening of a 103-bed hospital and outpatient clinic in an undamaged Japanese army hospital, furnished with beds, equipment, and supplies salvaged from the ruins of Nagasaki Medical College and brought in from Ōmura National Hospital (formerly Ōmura Naval Hospital). Within the first two weeks of operation in late 1945, an estimated eight hundred patients were treated.

The Wartime Casualties Care Law that had provided financial and physical support to Japanese civilians injured in the war expired in October, forcing every Nagasaki family to pay for their own medical expenses. Consequently, many people suffering from radiation illness and extreme injury—including Dō-oh, Yoshida, and Taniguchi—were cared for at home without any medication or time frame for recovery. Dō-oh had pulled back from the edge of death, and every day her father and other family members or neighbors carried her on a stretcher to Dr. Miyajima's home, where he continued treating her even after he closed the temporary relief station at his house. But Dō-oh was still bald and her wounds were not healing. Day after day, she lay secluded in a room in her family's home except when her parents came in to care for her. Mornings were particularly hard; when her father removed the gauze from the three-inch gash in her arm, the skin peeled off with it. He regularly reset the broken bone in her arm so it wouldn't heal in the wrong position.

Yoshida's mother cared for him day and night as he lay unconscious, enveloped in the smells of his own decaying flesh and the burning bodies being cremated at the temple next door. His mother laid out a futon in the family's *tatami* room and placed newspapers and a kind of waxed paper on top of it to protect the bedding from the pus constantly oozing out of the burns on her son's face and body. Yoshida lay on top

U.S. occupation troops level the atomic ruins, fall 1945. (*Photograph by Tomishige Yasuo*/Asahi Shimbun *via Getty Images*)

The Urakami Valley, looking south, fall 1945. The cleared area at the lower right is the airstrip built by U.S. occupation forces, nicknamed "Atomic Field." (*Photograph by Joe O'Donnell*/Japan 1945, *Vanderbilt University Press, 2005*)

of that, and his mother hung mosquito netting to protect him from flies. Even with her caution, however, flies landed on her while she was outside the netting, and she inadvertently carried the flies to her son when she tended to him. The flies laid eggs all over Yoshida's burned body. His mother tried removing them with chopsticks, but the eggs were too small, so she heated a pair of scissors and scraped out the eggs and the maggots that were crawling in his wounds. Even though he was unconscious, his mother remembered that Yoshida would scream out in pain. "It's because of my mother that I am alive," Yoshida said. "She never slept, and any food she had she gave to me. My face was so badly burned that I couldn't open my mouth, so my mother used a chopstick to feed me. '*Kuu, kuu*,' she said softly, to encourage me to eat."

Sometime in the early winter after Shinkōzen was officially taken over by Nagasaki Medical College, Yoshida was brought there in a medical rescue vehicle. Despite U.S. donations, medicines and supplies were scarce inside the partially destroyed school. Helmets were used to carry water to patients lying close together on *tatami* mats on the floor. Medical staff and volunteers flushed patients' wounds with salt water—hauling it not from Nagasaki Bay, which they feared was contaminated by radioactivity and decomposing bodies, but from another bay on the other side of the mountains west of the city. Before and after the war, bedside care in Japan was provided by family members who attended to basic needs such as food, tea, and heavier blankets as the weather demanded. Every day, Yoshida's mother or father sat beside him, watching as dead bodies were carried out of the hospital, terrified that their son, too, would die.

Taniguchi was already at Shinkōzen. In the weeks after the bombing, he had been shuffled from one relief station to another in villages outside Nagasaki, but all doctors could do was apply oil mixed with ashes on his massive burns. In early September, his grandfather and others had transported Taniguchi in a three-wheeled wooden cart over more than six miles of unpaved roads to Shinkōzen. For the first time since the bombing, he had received bedding—a futon on top of a *tatami* mat—and a slightly elevated level of medical care. He was given blood transfusions, penicillin injections, raw cow liver, and persimmon tea, but none of these made a substantial impact on his healing.

Sergeant Joe O'Donnell, a young American marine photographer, arrived at Shinkōzen on September 15 and documented Taniguchi's whole-body burns. O'Donnell was in Nagasaki as part of a seven-month tour of Japan to photograph the impact of U.S. bombings, and he spent weeks wandering the streets. Every roll of black-and-white film that he snapped for the Marine Corps was sent to Pearl Harbor to be developed and then forwarded to Washington; he also carried a second camera to capture images he wanted to keep for himself, developing them in a makeshift darkroom he set up in his barracks.

At Shinkōzen, Taniguchi was lying on his side as O'Donnell photo-

Classroom inside the temporary relief hospital at Shinkōzen Elementary School, partially damaged in the bombing. Patients lay on the floor on top of futons and mats, and volunteer medical personnel from outside the city joined surviving Nagasaki physicians and nurses to treat them. (*Photograph by Ogawa Torahiko/Courtesy of Nagasaki Atomic Bomb Museum*)

graphed his emaciated body and the still-acute burns on his back, buttocks, and part of his left arm. "I waved the flies away with a handkerchief," O'Donnell remembered, "then carefully brushed out the maggots, careful not to touch the boy's skin with my hand. The smell made me sick and my heart ached for his suffering, particularly because he was so young. I decided then that I would not take other pictures of burned victims unless ordered to do so." His photograph of Taniguchi was one of three hundred personal images he developed in Nagasaki and hid from U.S. officials in order to safely carry them out of Japan.

Six weeks later, doctors decided to transfer Taniguchi to Ōmura National Hospital, twenty-two miles (by road) north of the city. His nurses at Shinkōzen had constantly soaked up the pus and decayed flesh that pooled around his body each day, but when they lifted Taniguchi off his *tatami* mat, both the mat and wooden floor beneath it had rotted, leaving a black hole about twenty inches in diameter where he had lain. Taniguchi's chest was covered with holes caused by infected bedsores that he had developed from lying on his stomach for so long. It was

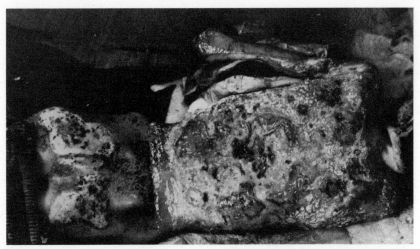

The severely burned back of Taniguchi Sumiteru, Shinkōzen relief hospital, September 15, 1945. (*Photograph by Joe O'Donnell*/Japan 1945, *Vanderbilt University Press, 2005*)

almost three months after the bombing when he arrived at Ōmura and finally received the best medical care available in the area. Yoshida was transferred to the same hospital that December, where he regained consciousness. He lay on a bed next to Taniguchi, though they would not meet until years later.

In the three months following the bombing, reconstruction efforts were slow, even with occupation support, in part because deaths and evacuations had reduced Nagasaki's population to 140,000, nearly half of its prebomb figure. Radiation-related illnesses and deaths had dropped off, but cremation pyres still burned for the bodies found beneath crushed buildings and layers of rubble. Many who remained in the city were either too maimed or ill to support the city's rebuilding efforts, and after years of wartime hardship and loss, countless other survivors were overpowered by *kyodatsu*—a condition of profound hopelessness, despair, and exhaustion. More than twenty thousand residential and industrial buildings in the city had been totally or partially destroyed, the city's administrative functions and infrastructure were not yet operational, and food was still scarce, resulting in widespread malnutrition.

Still, even in these early days, Nagasaki had begun to rebuild. That

Workers prepare to tile the roof of a temporary housing unit in the Urakami Valley, 1946. Visible behind the new houses are the steel skeletons of Mitsubishi factories. The ruins of Fuchi Elementary School stand on the hillside to the right. (*Photograph by Yamahata Yōsuke/ Courtesy of Yamahata Shogo*)

fall, electricity was slowly restored to homes that had withstood the blast, and even some families living in huts eventually received access to electricity and a single lightbulb. The long dirt roads through the Urakami Valley were cleared, the debris raked and shoveled to the sides of the roads like snow. Construction began on 332 emergency housing units on the east side of the Urakami River, just north of where Nagano had lived. Groups of survivors created grassroots associations to coordinate ongoing relief efforts for others.

The most severely damaged schools could not hold classes inside their skeletal buildings, but in early October, small teams of surviving administrators and teachers organized groups of as few as fifteen students and held rudimentary classes in stairwells and school yards surrounded by ashes and bones. Some were able to resume classes inside functional school buildings or local temples. In one case, elementary school students and teachers made room for their classes by moving torpedoes out of a building formerly used as a temporary weapons factory.

The return to school was a stabilizing activity, though not necessarily a happy one. Countless students had lost one or both parents, and some came to class with their bald heads covered with pieces of cloth. "They seemed to spend their school life cheering one another up," one teacher remembered. Some colleges reopened as well, but there were no textbooks and little food, and as the weather cooled, students wrapped themselves in blankets to study. Schools began the process of creating registries to account for their deceased students and teachers; at Yamazato Elementary School alone, twenty-six of thirty teachers and administrators had been killed, and more than a thousand children had died. The registry at Dō-oh's school listed her as deceased, an easy error because no one at the school had seen her since the day of the bomb.

Communities, families, and sole survivors honored their dead and prayed for their souls. In the fall of 1945, Urakami Church held an outdoor Mass for the approximately 8,500 Christian victims of the bomb. "The relatives of the dead people stood in rows holding white crosses, eight thousand crosses," remembered Nagai Kayano, a young girl who had lost her mother in the bombing. Her father, Dr. Nagai Takashi, a Nagasaki radiologist and devout Catholic, spoke at the ceremony and pronounced his deeply held beliefs that it was God's providence that carried the bomb to Nagasaki so that Japan's largest Christian community could sacrifice themselves to end the war. On a smaller scale, on October 9, the two-month anniversary of the bombing, teachers and students at a Catholic girls' high school held a memorial service in the school yard for the more than two hundred in their school community who had died.

Barrels were placed at intersections in the Urakami Valley for the collection of ashes and bones. A young girl and her siblings "fished" for human bones in the river and buried them under a tree. A mother collected gold buttons from a school uniform similar to her son's, as well as a fragment of a school cap and some bones from the ruins of his school,

Ruins of Urakami Church, ca. 1947. At center are the remains of the front inner wall and
one of the two fallen bell tower domes. (*Photograph by Ishida Hisashi/Courtesy of Nagasaki
Atomic Bomb Museum*)

and held a simple funeral for him—though whenever she heard foot-
steps, she longed to turn around and see that he had, in fact, returned
home. Whenever Wada passed by a cremation pyre or a newly uncovered
body, he placed his hands together and said a silent prayer.

A celebratory moment for the city came on November 25, when the
Nagasaki Streetcar Company resumed limited service. "I was so happy!"
Wada remembered. "Seven cars returned to service, and I drove the
fourth. When the streetcars started moving, children and adults were
running beside us shouting with excitement." When fishermen and farmers didn't have money, they offered Wada fish or vegetables instead.

"*Everyone* was so happy," Wada said. "At that time, I was so proud of my job. I really felt at peace again."

———

It would take five years for the city of Nagasaki to accomplish the nearly impossible task of counting the number of dead and injured from the atomic bombing. Officials lacked accurate population figures from before the bombing because older adults and young children had been evacuated, soldiers had been conscripted, and there was a lack of documentation for the thousands of Koreans, Chinese, and other Asian workers brought to Japan against their will. Tens of thousands of people, too, had left or returned to the city after the attack. Also, because no one had adequate knowledge of the effects of high-dose radiation exposure, an incalculable number of early radiation deaths may have been attributed to other conditions and not reported as related to the bombing.

Still, after an arduous process to determine figures as reliably as possible, the final numbers were complete. Because thousands died in the months immediately following the bombing, casualty estimates were determined through December 31, 1945:

Number of people killed: 73,884
Number of people injured: 74,909
Number of people (not killed or injured) impacted by death or injury of family members, destruction of their homes and communities, and job loss: 120,820

A new name was coined for the people of Nagasaki and Hiroshima: *hibakusha* (atomic bomb–affected people). The term referred to everyone directly affected by the bombings, including those who died in the blast and fires or later from injury or radiation illnesses, those who survived their injuries or radiation illnesses, and those who entered the cities in the weeks after the bombings. It was a word that, like the bombings themselves, would remain an integral part of survivors' private and public identities for the rest of their lives.

CHAPTER 5

TIME SUSPENDED

In January 1946, eleven U.S. military filmmakers and photographers arrived in Nagasaki. They came as part of the U.S. Strategic Bombing Survey (USSBS), assessing the effectiveness of the United States' conventional and nuclear bomb attacks on Japan as a means to support the "future development of the United States armed forces." In the fall of 1945, over a thousand USSBS military and civilian experts had traveled throughout Japan and its previously occupied territories to review surviving Japanese records, document the destruction from U.S. bombing strikes, and interview thousands of former Japanese military leaders, government officials, and civilians. In a second round of investigations in selected Japanese cities, a small USSBS team came to Nagasaki to further document the city's destruction.

They entered the city by train from the north, climbing over lush green mountains before descending into the leveled Urakami Valley. Not much had changed in the six months since the bombing. To their left, the Americans saw the vast expanse of atomic destruction and debris. In the distance, they glimpsed the wreckages of Urakami Church and Nagasaki Medical College at the edge of Nagasaki's eastern mountains. On their right, they passed the crushed Shiroyama Elementary School and the tangled webs of steel and mangled equipment of the Mitsubishi factories along the river. Their train came to a stop at a single shack serving as Nagasaki Station.

For weeks, the camera crew recorded Nagasaki's material damages.

"Nothing and no one had prepared me for the devastation I met there," Army Air Forces 2nd Lieutenant Herbert Sussan remembered. "The quietness of it all . . . it was like an enormous graveyard." Sussan's director, 1st Lieutenant Daniel McGovern, recalled bone fragments and hundreds of children's skulls scattered near cremation sites. The camera crew recorded survivors' physical suffering as they lay infirm in relief stations, hospitals, and crude huts constructed in the ruins. Some *hibakusha* died on camera during the filming. Others stared blankly, slowly turning their faces and bodies to reveal their whole-body burns and hardened, protruding keloid scars.

On January 31, the USSBS team arrived at the rural Ōmura National Hospital north of Nagasaki, where approximately four hundred burned and injured survivors languished inside small barracks-like buildings. Entering one of the patients' rooms, they saw Taniguchi lying on a bed low to the ground. Taniguchi had just turned seventeen, but with his tiny skeletal figure and shorn scalp, he looked much younger.

Now in his sixth month lying prostrate, Taniguchi was coping not only with relentless pain from burns that would not heal, but also with chronic diarrhea, minimal appetite, a weak pulse, and periodic fevers. Bedsores on his chest, left cheek, and right knee festered. His red blood cell count was half the normal level. Hospital staff administered penicillin compresses and boric acid ointment to his back, and gave him blood infusions, injections of vitamin C, vitamin B, and glucose from grapes. "The doctors were clueless about how to treat me," Taniguchi reflected.

As the crew set up their lights for filming, Taniguchi's breath was shallow, his pulse raced, and pus oozed from the burns on his back and arms. "I shuddered when the lights were turned on to film him," Sussan recalled, fearing the pain that the heat of the lights would cause on Taniguchi's burned flesh. But Taniguchi remembered that the warmth from the lights felt good as he lay there, always cold in his unheated hospital room with only a thin wooden wall to block the bitter winter chill.

The filmmakers captured three minutes of silent color footage of Taniguchi lying naked on the bed while three doctors in white coats ministered to his burns. At the start, the camera focuses on Taniguchi's back: From shoulders to waist, his raw, bloodred tissue glistens under the lights. The flesh of his emaciated left arm is salmon-colored and translucent. Exposed burns and blisters cover both his buttocks. Using foot-long tweezers, the doctors peel off a thin layer of gauze soaked in blood and pus and gently dab the excreting areas with swabs of cotton. With no skin or scabbing, nothing protects Taniguchi from the torment of even their grazing touch.

The camera shifts to the other side of his body. His face is visible now, propped up by his chin digging into the bed. Taniguchi's eyes are closed, and for a moment his face is calm. His torso barely expands and contracts with quick, shallow breaths—*in-out-pause, in-out-pause*. As the doctors place a fresh layer of thin gauze across his back, Taniguchi furrows his brow and bares his teeth in a silent growl of unbearable pain. A second later, his muscles relax and his calm expression returns—until his face twists in pain again.

The frames flutter to a stop as the camera is turned off and the American team moves on. Several months later, all of the reels of the estimated ninety thousand feet of USSBS Pacific Survey film, including the footage of Taniguchi, were locked into trunks and shipped to the United States, where they were classified and withheld from public view for more than twenty-five years.

———

For two years after the bombing, hundreds of thousands of people moved into and out of Nagasaki. Civilian families who had been forcibly moved to Manchuria to support Japan's military efforts came home—many underfed and sick with scabies or tuberculosis—only to find their homes burned and their families dead, injured, or struggling with the effects of whole-body radiation exposure. Thousands of Japanese military personnel and POWs also returned from locations across the Pacific, some carrying rations of rice and other food, to find no surviving relatives.

Thousands left Nagasaki as well, mostly non-Japanese. Forced laborers from Korea, China, Formosa, and other Asian countries were finally repatriated. As the occupation consolidated its operations throughout Japan, U.S. soldiers converged on the port city before boarding ships for home. Having completed Nagasaki's demilitarization efforts, approximately twenty thousand men from the 2nd Marine Division who had been stationed there had also departed by early 1946, leaving the 10th Marines in Nagasaki to oversee routine surveillance, reconnaissance, and the disposal of Japan's war supplies.

More *hibakusha* evacuated, too, often walking for days and weeks in search of a less penurious life in the countryside or on outlying islands. Some found solace away from the devastation and death; for others, living with distant relatives whose lives were still intact was too painful to bear, and many chose to return to Nagasaki, where they were surrounded by survivors who shared their suffering. Homeless *hibakusha* subsisted in flimsy shacks and slept on earthen floors or *tatami* mats found in the debris. Fourteen or fifteen people often lived in a single room with no furnishings. Running water was still not available, so survivors hauled springwater from the mountains and collected rainwater to boil and drink. Without toilets, people dug holes in the ground outside their shanties and covered them with wooden boards. Without bathtubs, they heated water in large oil drums and bathed standing up. To battle the winter winds, families wore as many layers of donated clothing and blankets as they could, huddling beneath umbrellas around wood-burning hibachi to protect themselves against the rain, sleet, and snow that fell through their makeshift roofs. In pitch-dark nights, survivors walking through the ruins cut their feet on glass shards, old nails, and slivers of wood and broken tile.

Aging men and women living alone, with no one to depend on or any way to provide for themselves, became known as the orphaned elderly. Uchida Tsukasa, sixteen years old at the time of the bombing, recalled the moment when an older homeless woman suddenly appeared in the doorway of his family's hut. His mother invited her to stay with them. "One day," Uchida remembered, "the old woman gathered charcoal from the ruins behind our house and began to make a fire in a clay stove. Looking at it closely, I was astonished to see that the charcoal contained charred fragments of human bones. We were literally living in a graveyard. My mother said that it was some kind of message, and she looked after the old woman until the very end of her life."

The city's social services were not yet operational, and many children with no surviving family members were forced to live on the streets. Monks at the Catholic monastery Seibo no Kishi took in more than a hundred orphans, and other organizations, including Dr. Akizuki's First Urakami Hospital, offered them free medical care. Relief workers sometimes adopted unidentified babies. But many girls with nowhere to go turned to prostitution to survive, and for months and even years, orphaned boys wandered the region alone or in pairs, living in train sta-

Woman and child living in the ruins near the edge of the hypocenter area, ca. 1946. They slept beneath the unwalled temporary structure, center, and cooked on an improvised outdoor stove. (*U.S. Marine Corps/Courtesy of Nagasaki Foundation for the Promotion of Peace, Committee for Research of Photographs and Materials of the Atomic Bombing*)

tions and under bridges, panhandling, stealing, and scouring for food as they were bounced back and forth from one location to the next by railroad authorities and local police who considered them a nuisance.

Expectant mothers gave birth in the atomic ruins without the help of a doctor or midwife, terrified of the rumors that their babies might die or be born deformed after being exposed to radiation inside their wombs. Death rates were, in fact, high for intrauterine-exposed infants: 43 percent of pregnancies in which the fetus was exposed within a quarter mile from the hypocenter ended in spontaneous abortion, stillbirth, or infant death. Many babies who survived birth were significantly underweight. With only thin rice gruel or other scraps they could find, their mothers, too, struggled to stay alive. An eighteen-year-old woman—three months pregnant when she was exposed just over a half mile from the hypocenter—had subsequently experienced a high fever, vomiting, bleeding gums, purple spots, and numbness in her back and hands. Just as she began to recover at the end of 1945, during her eighth month of pregnancy, she noticed that her baby was no longer growing in her belly. On a cold, snowy day several weeks later, with no water break, she suddenly went into labor and gave birth to a baby boy, his skin severely dry and creased. Some new mothers, unable to produce milk, quickly depleted their limited supplies of rationed milk and begged other mothers to share their breast milk. They did not know it yet, but the survival of their in utero–exposed infants marked the beginning of new lives for their families, with even greater hardships to come as their children's physical and mental disabilities would unfold.

Dō-oh and Nagano had homes, families, and just enough financial means to survive the immediate postwar crisis. In their own ways, however, both remained trapped by the impact of the bomb on their lives. Dō-oh's father still applied cooking oil and recycled gauze bandages to the gash at the back of her head, the burns on her arms and legs, and the deep lesions from glass fragments that had pierced her body. Each week, her parents, family members, and friends carried her to Dr. Miyajima's house for the limited medical care he could provide.

Their perseverance paid off. In the spring of 1946, Dō-oh's radiation illness subsided, some of her wounds began to heal, and she was able to stand, walk, go to the bathroom, wash her face, and use chopsticks on her own. But when she moved in certain ways, the glass slivers lodged in her back and arms caused intense pain. Most critically, the burned patches of her face were still raw and inflamed, and her hair would not grow back. Dō-oh stayed hidden in her house, too ashamed to allow anyone but her closest family to see her marred face and bald head.

In the village of Obama on the nearby Shimabara Peninsula, Nagano lived with her mother in a tiny one-room structure they had built on the grounds of her elderly great-aunt's house. Her older brother moved away for a job in another prefecture, and while her father worked in Nagasaki and came home when he could, Nagano worked at a salt factory during the day and helped at home on the evenings and weekends.

She and her mother got by with her own and her father's meager wages and through her parents' strategic efforts. At first, her father brought back the food they had stored in the underground bomb shelter next to their former house; later, he hauled back their *goemonburo* (cast-iron bathtub), which had survived the fires because it had been set in concrete and filled with water. A personal bathtub was a rare treasure in Japan, and Nagano's parents decided to use the public baths and trade their *goemonburo* for four straw bags of rice and the same amount of barley, giving them sufficient food staples for months. Her mother sold small amounts of the grains to buy fish and sometimes vegetables. Relatives in the area also gave them food, so they always had enough to eat. For safekeeping during the war, Nagano's mother had given their family's remaining kimonos to an acquaintance outside of Nagasaki, which she reclaimed and sold to pay for clothing.

"Every day, I watched my mother cry," Nagano remembered. "But she never said to me, 'Sei-chan and Kuniko died because you brought them back to Nagasaki.' If she had said that, I could have told her that I was sorry. I could have told her that I had never imagined an atomic bomb." But Nagano's mother never said a word about it. Nagano desperately wanted to approach her but had the impression that her mother wouldn't accept anything she said. She was further devastated to learn that her mother complained about her to other women in the neighborhood, telling them that Nagano wasn't a loyal child. "I felt so sad when I heard this," Nagano said. "It's like she had told them, *'Etsuko killed them. Etsuko killed Seiji and Kuniko.'* The neighbors glared at me with very cold eyes. The women told me that I was a terrible child for making my mother cry. It was unbearable for me."

Nagano wanted to move out and thought maybe she could stay with one of her friends who lived in another prefecture. But her mother strongly opposed the idea and told Nagano that if she left, she would be cutting off her relationship with her parents. "Because she said it like that, I didn't go," Nagano recalled. "With things as they were, I felt it was my fate to take care of my parents. I thought that nothing I did could change my destiny, so I gave up and accepted the situation. Looking back, I think that my mother would have been lonely if I had gone. Even though she complained a lot, I think she felt safe when I was there. But the air that flowed between us was incredibly cold."

Both in Nagasaki and across Japan, economic stability did not come for many years, and except for wealthy business barons who had amassed enormous profits during the war, most families faced unrestrained financial distress. Wholesale prices in Japan climbed over 500 percent in 1946, with inexorable increases over the next three years. Extreme hunger and malnutrition were exacerbated by poor harvests, dysfunctional distribution systems, internal corruption, and the postwar termination of food imports from countries Japan had invaded in its quest for resources. Thousands of Japanese starved to death. Even occupation supplies of antibiotics could not curb the many communicable diseases—already prevalent during the war—that ravaged the country. Over 650,000 cases of cholera, smallpox, scarlet fever, epidemic meningitis, polio, and other infectious diseases were reported; of these, nearly 100,000 people died. Every year until 1951, an additional 100,000 people died from tuberculosis. In Nagasaki, one tuberculosis patient remembered being treated only with vitamins and bed rest.

Fortunate *hibakusha* like Nagano's father had been able to keep their jobs at the Mitsubishi Shipyard and other industrial sites still standing after the bombing. Another Mitsubishi plant was transformed to manufacture cast-iron pots, providing jobs for some of the factory's former employees. Some *hibakusha* found work as teachers or medical support staff.

But a huge segment of Nagasaki's industrial capacity lay in ruins. Two major utility plants and a railway factory had been destroyed, and numerous sites that had produced munitions, steel, electrical machinery, and ships for Mitsubishi's four major companies were no longer functional. Material and financial assets for innumerable businesses and individuals, as well as records documenting their existence, were completely destroyed. Some businesses beyond the reach of the atomic bomb were able to keep their doors open, but even employers who were less impacted by the bombing found it almost impossible to operate effectively within virtually nonexistent economic, social, communications, and transportation infrastructures.

Thousands could find only part-time jobs with paltry wages in meat or bread shops or as janitors or day laborers in the limited number of operating factories, government offices, and businesses. Some *hibakusha* worked without pay in exchange for food, or left Nagasaki to search for jobs elsewhere. Countless more were too weak or too ill to work, and others stayed home to care for critically ill family members. To help provide for his family, Dō-oh's father went into the mountains every day to cut down trees, then hauled the wood back into the city to sell it for small sums. As prices for everyday items continued to soar, few could afford to provide even the most basic needs for themselves and their families. Many wore *waraji*—thin straw sandals—even in the rain and snow, and one survivor remembered sharing one pair of shoes with her brothers and sisters. In another family, six children who lost both parents and three of their siblings lived off the minimal earnings of their eldest brother, who was only sixteen.

Wada's postwar income could not support his sister and grandparents, so they supplemented his income with the savings his father had accrued from his job at a local bank before his death years earlier. Like Nagano's mother, Wada's grandparents traded many of their family's belongings to farmers for rice and vegetables. "Back then, we called it *take no seikatsu* [a bamboo shoot life]. When you eat bamboo, you have to peel off the outer skins and eat the small shoots. That's what it was like for us—we had to peel off our clothes and sell our possessions in order to survive. The only ones who weren't hungry were the unethical people in positions of power and particularly clever people who hoarded food during the war. Regular, ethical people couldn't do that. We never ate enough to feel full.

"I was unethical, too," Wada confessed. "One day when I was working on the train, someone gave me *onigiri*. I quickly ate half of it. To tell you the truth, I wanted to eat the whole thing. Then I thought about my grandparents—my grandfather was seventy-one and couldn't work anymore. When I thought about them, I stopped eating and saved the other half. When I brought it home, they were very happy. But I *did* eat half, which I shouldn't have done." On another occasion, Wada stole potatoes from agricultural fields and ate them raw. "I had to eat *something*," he said. "There were people who died from hunger because they were honest and couldn't bring themselves to do these kinds of things. I wasn't able to do that."

Wada quickly credited the United States for the food staples it provided to Nagasaki, part of its effort to prevent both disease and civil unrest in postwar Japan. Additionally, for six years after the war, the Licensed Agencies for Relief in Asia (LARA), a coalition of thirteen U.S. relief agencies, shipped food, clothing, and other provisions to Japan. "LARA was like UNESCO or UNICEF today," Wada explained, referring to the essential food staples LARA distributed to schools and families, including powdered milk, pineapple juice, bread, and canned goods. LARA also provided clothing, combs and brushes, soap, and toothpaste. "They saved a lot of children. It isn't widely known now that America did this for us. Of course the atomic bombs were wrong," Wada said, "but at the time, many *hibakusha* who hated America for dropping the bombs didn't know that the food they were eating came from America."

Still, U.S. support could not eradicate hunger or stabilize the Japanese economy. In 1946 alone, the price of rationed rice tripled, and fish, soy sauce, miso, and bread remained under strict distribution controls. Open-air black markets flourished across the country. Near the Shianbashi Bridge at the entrance to the older part of Nagasaki, throngs of hungry citizens swarmed around tents made of cardboard boxes and wooden-plank floors, where hawkers peddled rice, fish, vegetables, sweet cakes, and hand-rolled cigarettes. They also sold used clothing, occasionally taken from dead bodies, and scrap metal and wood from the wreckage of abandoned homes. Customers with any means at all scraped together the money to pay the vendors' high prices in order to supplement government rations and help their families survive. Shunned as failures for Japan's defeat and with no aid from the drained Japanese government, war veterans, many missing limbs, gathered in small groups nearby and begged for money by playing the accordion and singing wartime military songs.

Hibakusha without homes or jobs staved off hunger by planting vegetables, beans, and peanuts behind their huts and sifting through American soldiers' garbage for discarded food—scraping the sides of cans for remnants of meat and sipping leftover drops from empty pineapple juice cans. Many families ventured into the mountains to scour for firewood and edible weeds and tried to satiate their hunger by eating wild grass, roots, orange peels, pumpkin leaves, and grasshoppers. One *hibakusha* remembers her family being so hungry that they ate dog meat.

The city's physical recovery came in small steps. Despite earlier reports that plants and trees would not grow back for seventy years, some vegetation reappeared in the spring of 1946—although abnormalities and malformations were observed for three or four more years. That summer, gas service was restored to almost eight hundred households, and Mitsubishi Shipyard completed construction on the *Daiichi Nisshin Maru,* its first vessel since the atomic bombing. Rebuilding of the older sections of Nagasaki continued as construction of more rudimentary municipal housing units for *hibakusha* and veterans began at the periphery of the hypocenter area, each with a small kitchen and toilet. Parishioners cleared away the ruins of Urakami Church, leaving only parts of the facade, and held Mass in a damaged room inside Dr. Akizuki's First Urakami Hospital. Eventually they built a small wooden temporary chapel next to the damaged southern entrance to the church, but they lacked sufficient funds to build a roof, so services were held beneath the open sky. Nagasaki Medical College began offering classes at Shinkōzen and hospitals in the region. Near the center of the city, a new movie theater was built to present Hollywood films.

Schools across the city slowly began reopening at their original sites, though many children could not attend because of injury, illness, hunger, or the need to care for family members. A quarter mile west of the hypocenter, a limited number of classes resumed in Shiroyama Elementary School's partially crushed three-story concrete building, where fifty-two mobilized students and teachers had died at the time of the bombing. Classroom walls were still warped and buckled, and one teacher remembered that both faculty and students lost their focus as they gazed through broken windows at the huge sweep of atomic wasteland.

At Yamazato Elementary School, situated on a bared hillside a half mile north of the hypocenter, weeds sprouted up in the heaps of charred wood, tangled wires, and slabs of smashed concrete. The enormous U-shaped building had been internally gutted, so the classrooms and corridors had no walls to divide them, and rooms in the deep interior of the building had no light. Children who had been evacuated before

Later reconstruction efforts in the Urakami Valley, taken from a balcony of the ruins of the Nagasaki Medical College Hospital, ca. 1948. (*Photograph by Tomishige Yasuo*/Asahi Shimbun *via Getty Images*)

the bombing had returned to Nagasaki and rejoined their classmates, many of whom still suffered from hair loss, bleeding gums, and chronic weakness. During inclement weather, classes ended early and students walked home already soaked from the rain and wind that had swept through the building.

In March 1946, both Yamazato and Shiroyama elementary schools held modest graduation ceremonies for their sixth-grade students, bringing to a symbolic close the first seven months of postbomb life. At Yamazato, fewer than three hundred of sixteen hundred students had survived. Seventy-five students made up the graduating class, sixty-one of whom had directly experienced the bombing. A small vase with a solitary flower decorated the stark room, and the short commemoration ended with the students singing songs of gratitude and farewell, interrupted by the sobbing of both children and teachers. At Shiroyama—which had formerly graduated more than three hundred students every year—only fourteen sixth graders graduated. Thirty students, five teachers, and three parents attended the observances. In his address, the vice principal praised the students for their hard work in overcoming the immense challenges after the atomic bombing, and teachers and students wept as he offered prayers for the souls of their schoolmates, teachers, and relatives who had died in the attack, and good wishes to the graduating students for their futures.

In July, the United States' highly publicized tests of its first postwar nuclear bombs took place in a remote region of the South Pacific, a site that would become one of two U.S. testing grounds in the decades to follow. Two weeks later, on the hot summer morning of August 9, 1946, grieving *hibakusha* gathered in the rubble at the hypocenter to observe the first anniversary of the atomic bombing of their city. Simple ceremonies also took place in the ruins of Nagasaki Medical College, near the destroyed Mitsubishi factories along the river, and at Suwa Shrine near Yoshida's family home.

A year after the bombing, tens of thousands of survivors remained severely injured and ill from radiation exposure. Others, like Wada, had significantly recovered. Following his grandmother's bidding, he had continued to drink her persimmon tea each day. Eventually his gums had stopped bleeding, and he no longer observed blood in his urine. Still, overall weakness caused him to miss work sometimes—and his hair would not grow back. "I was nineteen years old, and I was embarrassed," he said. At times he thought it might be better to die than live through any more hardships.

But Wada was not one to give in, a characteristic he attributed to having lost his parents at a young age and feeling responsible for his family's well-being. Wearing a wool cap his grandmother knitted for him, he sat behind the steering wheel of the streetcar, maneuvering through the city—from Hotarujaya Terminal past the gutted Nagasaki Prefectural Office to the collapsed Nagasaki Station, then north along the river into the barren Urakami corridor. He came to see that compared with that of so many others, his suffering had been minimal. Sometime around the first anniversary of the attack, Wada made up his mind to do everything he could to forget this period of his life and never speak about the atomic bombing again.

———

Under General MacArthur's leadership, by the end of 1945, U.S. occupation personnel had demobilized the Japanese military, removed
promilitary ultranationalists from positions in the Japanese government,
abolished Shinto as the state religion and vehicle for nationalistic propaganda, and established a massive American oversight structure to monitor
all operations of the Japanese government. In what was perhaps Mac-
Arthur's most controversial occupation policy, Emperor Hirohito was retained as the head of state, contradicting the Allied nations' "unconditional
surrender" terms and countering many U.S. and Allied leaders' calls for
the emperor's prosecution as a war criminal. MacArthur believed that
removing the emperor from his position as the symbol of Japan's culture
and history would destabilize social order, trigger rebellion, and hinder
the goals of the occupation, and his insistence on preserving the emperor
prevailed. Over the next few years, Hirohito had no choice but to allow
occupation leaders to transform his relationship to the Japanese people—
from adulated deity who had inspired passionate loyalty during Japan's
holy war to pacifist human figurehead who represented "the symbol of the
State and unity of the People."

MacArthur's next step was to realize the United States' agenda, both
visionary and patriarchal, to metamorphose Japan into a new, egalitarian
nation. In what historian John Dower called a "revolution from above,"
the occupation's widespread political, economic, and social reforms
echoed Japan's individual and civil rights movements in the 1920s before
the right-wing military extremists rose to power. Economic restructur-
ing included the dismantling of the *zaibatsu*—large industrial and bank-
ing conglomerates that had dominated Japan's economy before and
during the war. Land reforms required the minority of large farm owners, who owned 90 percent of Japan's agricultural acreage, to sell all but
a small portion of their holdings to their tenants. New trade union laws
gave workers the right to organize, bargain collectively, and strike.
Within four years, an estimated 56 percent of Japanese workers were
union members.

Japan's education system also underwent massive reforms. The "imperial" label was removed from the names of elite universities, and the
emperor's portrait was removed from schools, government offices, and

public buildings. Teachers, who only six months earlier had been required to train Japanese children to die for the emperor, were now asked to embrace democratic and pacifist ideologies, and their new curriculum instructed students to reflect on the failure of the Japanese people to think critically about and resist the nationalistic military movement that had ultimately led to Japan's defeat. Coeducation was instituted in public schools, and new laws provided equal education for women. Newly issued textbooks endorsed Western concepts of individuality, rational thinking, and social equality.

At the same time, MacArthur and his team practiced secretive and oppressive policies that contradicted the democratic values they claimed to promote. An early example was Japan's new constitution, which MacArthur presented to the Japanese public in March 1946 as a document brought forth by the will and desire of the Japanese people. In reality, however, members of the occupation's Government Section had secretly drafted the new constitution over the course of a single week; the will—or even the knowledge—of the Japanese people played no part in Japan's adoption of its new parliamentary democracy, and Japanese government leaders provided only minor revisions after the fact. In an odd contradiction, the new constitution established many human rights and equalities for the Japanese people, but the country's social and economic reforms, individual freedoms, and its new democracy itself were, in effect, forced on Japan by an occupying nation.

Contradicting the new constitution's guarantee of freedom of expression and explicit wording that "no censorship shall be maintained," the occupation's Civil Censorship Detachment (CCD) continued to carry out broad media restrictions. Staffed by more than 8,700 American and Japanese personnel in Tokyo and in regional offices in northern and southern Japan, the CCD monitored radio and television broadcasts, films, personal mail, and telephone and telegraph communications. From 1945 to 1949, when it suspended its operations, the department examined an estimated 15 million pages of print media from 16,500 newspapers, 13,000 periodicals and bulletins, and 45,000 books and pamphlets, plus innumerable photographs, political advertisements, and other documents. Banned topics covered not only the more obvious subjects, such as emperor worship and militaristic fervor, but also any direct or perceived criticism of the United States, its allies, or the occupation government, including the physical damages, death tolls, and injuries caused by U.S. firebombings of Japanese cities.

Across the country, movie theaters could only show films approved by the CCD after stringent review; among other criteria, any challenges to the provisions of the Potsdam Declaration, the terms for Japanese surrender, or the announced objectives of the Allied occupation were forbidden. Documentaries about historical events were required to be "truthful," as defined by occupation authorities. Other subjects barred from media coverage included "overplaying" starvation across the country; black-market activities; the differences in living standards between occupation forces and Japanese citizens; and fraternization between U.S. servicemen and Japanese women and the biracial children born from these encounters. References to U.S. atomic bomb tests in the South Pacific were highly restricted. The Japanese people were prohibited from traveling overseas or communicating with anyone beyond Japan's borders, limiting their knowledge of world affairs to occupation-approved reports from U.S. or Allied media sources. As before, no reports about or even allusions to censorship policies were tolerated, so most Japanese knew nothing of those policies' existence.

No specific censorship rules related directly to the Nagasaki and Hiroshima atomic bombings, but the CCD eliminated most statements about the nuclear attacks in print and broadcast journalism, literature, films, and textbooks. Public comments that justified the U.S. use of the bombs or argued for their inevitability were sometimes permitted, but subjects that continued to be censored included technical details about the bombs' blast, heat, and radiation; the extent of physical destruction in the two cities; death and casualty counts; personal testimonies of atomic bomb survivors; and any photographs, film footage, or reportage of survivors' suffering from atomic bomb injuries and radiation effects. Even phrases such as "Many innocent people were killed in Hiroshima and Nagasaki" were banned. Nagasaki named its annual commemoration of the bombing the Memorial Day for the Restoration of Peace, calling it a "culture festival" to appease U.S. officials, who believed these services were Japanese propaganda tools that indirectly called for U.S. atonement and hindered U.S. efforts to promote Japanese war guilt.

Some *hibakusha* writings slipped by occupation staff and were published locally in Hiroshima and Nagasaki, but numerous books written by survivors were blocked from publication, including a small book by fourteen-year-old Ishida Masako, *Masako taorezu* [Masako Did Not Die], which described in vivid detail her memories of the Nagasaki bombing. The CCD felt the book was historically significant but banned it over the concern that it would "tear open war scars and rekindle animosity" toward the United States and tacitly indict the Nagasaki atomic bombing as a crime against humanity.

Also banned was Dr. Nagai's 1947 *Nagasaki no kane* (*The Bells of Nagasaki*), a personal account of the days and months immediately following the bombing in which Nagai offered unique perspectives as a physician, a man himself afflicted with radiation disease, and a Catholic—including his belief that Nagasaki had been chosen "to expiate the sins committed by humanity in the Second World War." Although his message reinforced the concepts of Japanese war guilt and repentance actively promoted by occupation officials, *The Bells of Nagasaki* was not permitted to be published for reasons similar to those that led to the banning of Ishida Masako's book. After numerous appeals, Nagai's book was finally approved for publication two years later, with the stipulation that it include an extended appendix, written by U.S. military officials, that provided a graphic written and photographic account of Japanese soldiers' complete destruction of Manila in 1945—including the torture, mutilation, rape, starvation, and burning of innocent women and children. Ironically, the inclusion of this appendix resulted in the juxtaposition of the U.S. atomic bombings with Japanese atrocities in the Philippines, which could have been easily construed as a statement of their moral equivalence.

CCD policies also impeded the efforts of hundreds of Japanese scientists and physicians racing to comprehend the nature of survivors' numerous radiation-related conditions and develop effective treatment methods. Scientists were already required to obtain permission to conduct studies on the effects of the atomic bombings. Further, on the basis of maintaining "public tranquility" in Japan and protecting the United States' exclusive knowledge about the bombs, all Japanese research findings had to be translated into English and submitted to censorship offices, where they were evaluated for clearance or shipped to the United States for additional review, with little hope of being returned. In either case, permission to publish was rarely given.

Numerous atomic bomb–related scientific reports were also blocked from publication in Japan, including the former Tokyo Imperial University's extensive early postbomb studies and Dr. Shirabe's meticulous 1945 study of the medical conditions of eight thousand Nagasaki *hibakusha*. Censorship actions were so pervasive, and the editors of medical journals were so afraid that their publications would be shut down if rules were broken, that the number of published atomic bomb–related scientific reports diminished to three each year in 1948 and 1949. Japanese scientists and physicians eager to support *hibakusha* health and recovery were further impeded by the United States' 1945 confiscation of early Japanese research teams' blood samples, specimens, photographs, questionnaires, and clinical records from victim autopsies and survivor examinations. Researchers' and survivors' grievances over this violation were later aggravated when they discovered that the United States claimed sole use of these body parts—taken without their consent—for military studies to help defend U.S. civilians against nuclear attack. Even after the CCD closed in 1949, research studies on atomic bomb–related topics were banned from discussion at Japanese medical conferences until 1951.

Prior to a postwar presentation at a university in Tokyo, Dr. Shiotsuki Masao, the physician who had painstakingly conducted and preserved *hibakusha* autopsy specimens at Ōmura Naval Hospital, received a note of warning. It read, "Please be careful what you say. There is a detective here from the Motofuji police station." Shiotsuki, who by then was working in a different field of medical research and had no knowledge of the censorship imposed on Japan's physicians and scientists, was dumbfounded. It would be years before he and others fully understood the U.S. policies that had constrained public dialogue of the atomic bombs, restricted doctors' efforts to improve treatment methodologies, blocked *hibakusha* themselves from understanding their persistent illnesses, and kept survivors' suffering almost completely concealed from public view.

In the United States, while the terrifying truth about Japan's nuclear cataclysm continued to be obscured from American citizens, top U.S. military and government leaders conducted a new, hard-hitting media campaign to justify the use of the bombs and promote public support for nuclear weapons development. In what social activist A. J. Muste called "a demonstration of . . . the logic of atrocity," the campaign's message was delivered through a new round of official denials of the impact of large-dose radiation exposure on *hibakusha,* combined with decisive statements that the bombs were an absolute military necessity that saved innumerable American lives and ended the war. Officials also deflected opposition to the bombs' use by making repeated statements that fueled U.S. wartime hatred and racism against Japan and built the foundation for justifying the bombings as righteous and deserving acts against a savage enemy. It is a matter of conjecture whether these efforts were needed to influence Americans' sentiments; in the immediate postwar years, most Americans—even those who felt disquieted by the enormity of harm the bombs had caused—supported the use of the bombs for reasons that included hatred of Japan's brutality during the war, pervasive anti-Japanese racism, and huge relief that the war was over.

Even so, in order to prevent potential questions about the necessity and morality of the bombs and abate disapproval of the nation's burgeoning nuclear weapons program, U.S. officials continued to limit American media access to Nagasaki and Hiroshima. With few exceptions, news stories out of the atomic-bombed cities were abstract and impersonal, focusing on the rebuilding of the cities, healing and rebirth out of the atomic ashes, and potential reconciliation with the United States that—according to American journalists—many atomic bomb victims desired. Reporters typically referenced the atomic bombings in the context of government calls for heightened civil defense policies, appeals for international control of atomic energy, or praise of U.S. scientific ingenuity and achievement. Photographs of the mushroom clouds became the iconic images of the atomic bombings, with no representation of the hundreds of thousands who died and suffered beneath them.

Mainstream journalists rarely challenged the government's perspectives. In early 1946, however, a small number of articles in the national press criticized the U.S. nuclear weapons program and examined the ethical dilemmas of the U.S. decision to use the bombs. These articles sparked a heated national debate. No formal opposition movement came together, but that summer new editorials and commentaries disapproving the bombs' use on Japan, combined with an increased number of articles and books that explored the *hibakusha* experience, fostered new dialogues about the ethics of the Hiroshima and Nagasaki bombings.

Public engagement with the *hibakusha* experience swelled in August, when, in a single issue, the *New Yorker* published John Hersey's new work, *Hiroshima,* a sixty-eight-page account of the Hiroshima atomic bombing through the eyes of six survivors. Hersey, a former war correspondent and Pulitzer Prize–winning fiction writer who had spent three weeks in Hiroshima in the spring of 1946, wrote a vivid nonfiction narrative that captured readers' imaginations, helping them to see Hiroshima as a real place and empathize with *hibakusha* as real people with families, homes, and jobs. *Hiroshima*'s graphic descriptions of instantaneous death, human anguish, and the mysterious symptoms from radiation exposure evoked powerful emotional responses across the United States. The issue sold out at shops and newsstands, requests for reprints multiplied, and approximately fifty American newspapers republished the story in serial form. Albert Einstein ordered a thousand copies. The Book-of-the-Month Club distributed hundreds of thousands of copies free to its subscribers because, in the words of club president Harry Scherman, "We find it hard to conceive of anything being written that could be of more importance at this moment to the human race." ABC Radio broadcast the entire text of *Hiroshima* in half-hour segments over four weeks. Letters, telegraphs, and postcards—most of which expressed approval of the story—poured into the *New Yorker* offices. By the end of October, Alfred A. Knopf had published *Hiroshima* in book form, and within six months, over a million copies were sold around the world. In Japan, however, the book was prohibited from publication for another three years over concerns that Hersey's depictions might invite perceptions that the bombs were "unduly cruel."

Immediately following the publication of Hersey's article, statements by two influential figures that challenged U.S. justifications for using the bombs ignited further controversy. At a mid-September press conference about other naval matters, Admiral William F. Halsey, commander of the Third Fleet, was quoted as saying that the bombings were a mistake because at the time they were dropped, Japan was on the verge of surrender. Two days later, a scathing essay in the *Saturday Review* by renowned journalist Norman Cousins presented readers with a series of pressing questions to blast open some of the unspoken realities of the atomic bombings and the implications of U.S. nuclear weapons development. "Do we know, for example, that many thousands of human beings in Japan will die of cancer during the next few years because of radioactivity released by the bomb?" Cousins asked. "Do we know that the atomic bomb is in reality a death ray, and that the damage by blast and fire may be secondary to the damage caused by radiological assault upon human tissue?"

Apologists for the atomic bombings fought back. Nervous that negative views of their decision to use the bombs might intensify public perceptions of the atomic attacks as immoral or even criminal, concerned that such sentiments would damage postwar international relations and threaten U.S. nuclear development, and eager to defend genuine beliefs that the bombs were necessary, government and military officials hurriedly strategized ways to prevent what they considered "a distortion of history." Their plan: to effectively argue the necessity of the bombs and suppress objections to their use. In the words of Supreme Court justice Felix Frankfurter, a longtime friend of former secretary of war Henry L. Stimson, their intention was to silence the opposition's "sloppy sentimentality."

Their efforts worked. Two articles by prominent government officials published in late 1946 and early 1947 offered intelligent and persuasive "behind-the-scenes" perspectives on the decision to use the bombs that effectively quelled civic dissent and directed focus away from personal stories of people who had experienced the bombs. The first article was authored by Karl T. Compton, president of the Massachusetts Institute of Technology and a respected physicist who had helped develop the atomic bombs. In the December 1946 issue of the *Atlantic Monthly,* Compton compared the death toll and damages in Hiroshima and Nagasaki with those from the Tokyo firebombing raids. Without mentioning the radiation effects and ongoing suffering caused by the atomic bombs, he provided casualty estimates for a land invasion of Japan had the war dragged on, claiming that the atomic bombs had prevented the loss of "hundreds of thousands—perhaps several millions—of lives, both American and Japanese." By most historical accounts, these figures are far higher than those estimated by the U.S. military prior to the bombings. Compton concluded that using the bombs was the only rational decision that U.S. leaders could make, and that the delivery of the two bombs one after the other and the emperor's decision to surrender less than a day after the Nagasaki bombing were evidence that the atomic bombs ended the war. In a short letter published in a later edition of the *Atlantic Monthly,* President Truman validated Compton's perspectives, describing his article as "a fair analysis of the situation."

Compton's *Atlantic Monthly* commentary set the stage for an extended article by former secretary of war Stimson, published in *Harper's Magazine* in February 1947, which Secretary of State James Byrnes hoped would "stop some of the idle talk" by those who opposed the use of the bombs. Though a team of military and political leaders contributed to Stimson's final draft, it was Stimson himself who provided the rank, respect, and reasoned communication style to successfully shut down almost all public criticism of the bombs.

With clarity and unquestionable authority, Stimson told American readers that during the war, the U.S. atomic bomb policy had been a simple one: "to spare no effort" in securing the earliest possible development of an atomic bomb in order to shorten the war, minimize destruction, and save American lives. Like Compton, however, Stimson omitted many critical facts that would have given American readers a more thorough grasp of the numerous and complex factors involved in choosing to use atomic weapons on Japan: He failed to include key officials' prebomb debates over modifying the "unconditional surrender" restriction that he himself had recognized as a possible key to bringing Japan to an earlier surrender. He explained that the Potsdam Declaration had provided adequate warning to Japan but did not clarify that the declaration's wording made no reference to nuclear weapons. He justified the two cities' death tolls by comparing them to an estimate of more than a million American lives saved by avoiding a costly invasion—without mentioning the impact of the Soviet Union's entry into the war, which would have caused Japan to fight on two fronts, altered Allied invasion strategies, and possibly ended the war prior to Allied forces landing on Japan's main islands. In claiming that Hiroshima and Nagasaki were military targets, Stimson obscured the obvious fact that the atomic bombs did not discriminate between military and civilian locations and personnel as they obliterated the two cities.

Ultimately, Stimson claimed that the decision to use the bombs was "the least abhorrent" option that resulted in exactly what military and government officials intended: Japan's surrender without a U.S. and Allied invasion of Japan's main islands. By the article's conclusion, Stimson had shifted readers' moral focus to the United States' obligation to retain international control over nuclear technology, weapons development, and testing to prevent other countries from producing or using atomic weapons. Nuclear weapons in U.S. hands, he maintained, would keep the United States and the world safe.

It would be decades before historians gained access to the internal memos and documents of Stimson and his team of contributors that would reveal the careful construction of the secretary of war's arguments and the number of misstatements and omissions they contained. In the meantime, in the months following its publication, the *Harper's* article was reprinted in its entirety by numerous newspapers and magazines across the country and quoted at length by dozens more. By virtue of his authority and careful reasoning, Stimson had created a singular atomic bomb narrative with such moral certitude that it superseded all others and became deeply ingrained as the truth in American perception and memory: *The atomic bombings ended the war and saved a million American lives.*

The U.S. government's campaign to justify the bombs and mute opposition had done its job. Media reports on the survivors' lives—and the empathy they evoked—virtually ceased. Even with the popularity of Hersey's book, the combined impact of occupation censorship and U.S. justification and denial diminished Americans' ability to grasp both the colossal scope of damages and death in Nagasaki and Hiroshima and the unpredictable and odious aftereffects of radiation exposure. Referring to atomic bomb dissenters, McGeorge Bundy—a behind-the-scenes contributor to Stimson's article and coauthor of Stimson's autobiography— remarked, "I think we deserve some sort of medal for reducing these particular chatterers to silence."

———

Shrouded in silence, *hibakusha* entered a new stage of long-term atomic bomb survival. At Ōmura National Hospital, the bedsores on Taniguchi's chest did not heal and were so deep that portions of his ribs and pulsing heart were visible. "Lying on my stomach with my chest wounds pressed down into the bed—the pain was excruciating," he said. New sores continued to develop on Taniguchi's lower left jaw, his knees, and both sides of his body near his hips—anywhere his body made contact with the bed. Powerless to move anything except his neck and right arm, Taniguchi lay drenched in pus secreted from these wounds and the swollen and festering burns on his back, arms, and legs. He was constantly enveloped in the smell of decomposing flesh that pooled around his body. Taniguchi's red blood cell count remained dangerously low, his pulse was strained, and he frequently experienced fevers that spiked to perilously high levels. When he was able to eat, he was forced to do so while lying on his stomach. Food often became stuck in his throat, and on at least one occasion he choked and stopped breathing. Sometime in 1946, his father returned after sixteen years in Manchuria. In Taniguchi's hospital room, father and son met for the first time since Taniguchi was an infant. Except to confirm that it happened, Taniguchi barely spoke of this moment. After their visit, his father moved to Osaka, where Taniguchi's sister and brother lived.

Every morning, the doctors and nurses whispered among themselves, amazed that he had survived another day. But in the daze of constant pain, all Taniguchi could think about was dying. He cried every time he heard the instrument cart approaching, and when the nurses removed the gauze from his back, he screamed in pain and begged the nurses to let him die. "Kill me, kill me," he cried, over and over again. "Please let me die." Again and again, his family members visited, then gathered at his grandmother's house on the slopes of Mount Inasa to plan his funeral. "No one thought I would survive," he said. "I lingered on the verge of death but failed to die. . . . Somehow I was made to live."

His grandmother stayed home to manage the farm, so Taniguchi's grandfather stayed at his bedside to support the physicians' and nurses' round-the-clock care. They made short entries in his medical record each day. *Bedsores desiccated. Body temperature up and down. Low-grade anemia. Top layer of skin beginning to form in certain places, like islands. Weak and small pulse. Bones are visible through bedsore wounds. Secretions slightly increased. Appetite good. Blood in stool, four times.* They treated Taniguchi with regular doses of vitamins B and C, cod liver oil, and penicillin ointment, but there was little indication of any significant impact on his condition. Throughout the hot summer of 1946, Taniguchi lay beneath mosquito netting, but flies managed to find their way through the mesh and lay their eggs inside his wounds. Maggots crawled through his flesh, creating an incessant sensation that Taniguchi could not relieve. Three times he fell into a coma. Whenever he was conscious, Taniguchi felt an intense hatred for the war and fierce resentment toward all the parents who had done nothing to try to prevent it. Day after day, he stared at a tall persimmon tree visible outside the window in his room, nostalgic for his childhood and heavy with sadness that he might never feel happy again.

Yoshida lay faceup in the hospital bed next to Taniguchi. His father and grandmother had both died that year, so Yoshida's mother and sister took turns staying at his bedside. He was able to see now, but he couldn't turn onto his side or stomach because of the blackened burns on his face. Over time, the left side of his face and the lower left side of his body began to heal, but the right side of his face remained scabbed and infected. At some point, his burned right ear finally rotted and fell off, leaving only a small hole on the side of his head through which he could still hear.

Doctors performed three skin graft surgeries to the right side of his face. The first procedure came quickly: In early 1946, the surgeon had taken skin from his left thigh and attached it across his right cheek. "We thought it was going to work," Yoshida recalled, "but ultimately an infection grew beneath the new skin and then the transplanted skin fell off. When the infection healed, the right side of my face scabbed over, as hard as a cast. The same problems happened after the second surgery. I remember feeling like I was going crazy from the pain."

With only enough skin left for one more surgery, doctors tried again, and this time, his wounds did not become infected, the grafted skin remained attached, and Yoshida's face gradually healed as much as it could. For the rest of his life, however, he suffered from having no sweat glands on the right side of his face, a problem that particularly affected him during the summer when his face became overheated because he could not perspire to cool it down.

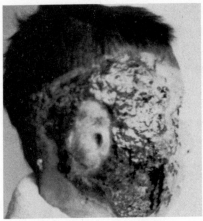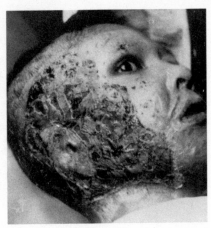

Yoshida Katsuji, age fourteen, before and after skin graft surgery. (*Courtesy of Yoshida Naoji*)

———

Norman Cousins's impassioned call that "the atomic bomb is in reality a death ray" and a "radiological assault on human tissue" not only reflected survivors' immediate postbomb hardships, but also foreshadowed a heavy stream of recurring atomic bomb–related diseases and deaths. After tens of thousands of survivors had endured—and in some cases recovered from—the initial effects of radiation exposure, many more became ill and died from radiation-related conditions that developed in the decade after the war. They faced repeated episodes of purple spots on their skin, internal bleeding, fevers, diarrhea, nausea, low blood pressure, hypersensitivity to cold, low blood cell counts, and weight loss due to an inability to hold down food—all indications of atomic bomb disease. Radiation toxicity also caused severe liver, endocrine, blood, and skin diseases; impairments of the central nervous system; premature aging; reproductive disorders leading to full or partial sterility, miscarriages, and stillbirths; gum diseases; vision problems; and ailments such as sharp pains and deep coughing that could not be linked to a specific diagnosis. The living cells in people's mouths were damaged, causing their teeth to fall out, leaving only rotting bone. Most commonly, survivors experienced violent and unpredictable dizzy spells, fainting, dramatic losses of consciousness, and a profound depletion of energy. From the survivors' perspective, the atomic bomb had burned their bodies from the inside out.

Although not caused by radiation exposure, thick, rubbery keloid scars developed on many *hibakusha* with moderate to severe burns on their faces, limbs, and across large areas of their bodies. This ungainly scar tissue—"like molten lava," one physician remembered—caused intense itching, stinging, and throbbing pain, and when it covered elbows, shoulders, or leg joints, mobility was limited or impossible. Some survivors with keloids on their faces could not open their mouths, constricting their ability to eat. Physicians' attempts to excise the keloids in order to perform skin grafts were thwarted because the scar tissue often grew back.

Many survivors suffered destabilizing physical and emotional exhaustion from chronic pain, loss, caring for family members with protracted injuries and diseases, and the financial burden of having to borrow money to cover the costs of medical care. Countless *hibakusha* felt isolated, ashamed of their physical disfigurement or their inability to feed and house their families. The sense of being internally contaminated led to constant fear of what the invisible and deadly radiation was doing inside their bodies.

In these early years, *hibakusha* also struggled with what psychologist Robert Jay Lifton called "the suddenness and totality of their death saturation." In Nagasaki, seventy-four thousand people had been killed indiscriminately, equaling nearly 70 percent of everyone living in the central Urakami Valley and over 40 percent of communities in adjacent townships. Guilt plagued many *hibakusha* who, in order to survive, had left a family member trapped beneath a building or engulfed in flames—or who had not been able to answer their loved ones' or strangers' cries for help, or give them a sip of water before they died. For years, identifiable corpses were still found in stairwells or the ruins of a home being cleared away. Though most people relinquished hope of ever finding their missing loved ones, some survivors never stopped searching and listening to daily radio programs dedicated to reuniting missing persons with their families. Some held memorial services without a body. One man who lost his wife and three children in the bombing could not set his eyes on other people's children without feeling overwhelmed with grief. Every day until the first anniversary of the bombing, he sat in front of his eldest daughter's ashes and asked himself why he had survived.

In their own ways, two American occupation officials strived to support Nagasaki's survivors' psychological recovery. The first, Lieutenant Colonel Victor Delnore, a decorated combat veteran, had taken over as commander of the Nagasaki Military Government Team (NMGT) in the fall of 1946 after the last of the 10th Marines regiment had left. Delnore directed a small administrative team that supervised activities to increase public safety, oversaw the training of Japanese police officers on subjects including democracy and Japan's new constitution, monitored labor conditions, and tracked the Japanese government and military leaders who had left or been forced out of their positions. Except for several serious crimes against Japanese citizens by U.S. soldiers, the period of civilian occupation under Delnore's direction passed with relatively minimal conflict between the Japanese and their American conquerors, and the overall relationship between the NMGT and Nagasaki's civilian government leaders and officials was both cooperative and respectful.

But Delnore saw his responsibilities as more than administrative. "I had to wake the people up to the fact that life was not over," he remembered. During his four years in Nagasaki, he frequently visited Shinkōzen, where he knelt down to speak with patients at eye level. He attended a special memorial service at which Buddhist monks consecrated the ashes of thousands of unidentified *hibakusha*. "I was deeply moved," he later wrote. "Whether it was the strangeness of the ceremony, the numerous mourning womenfolk, or the boxes of the ashes of the 10,000 unclaimed and unidentified victims of the atom bomb that were piled all around the altar, I'll never know." Delnore also supported survivors in telling their stories, exemplified by his letter to U.S. censors advocating for the publication of Ishida Masako's *Masako Taorezu*: "For us to properly realize the significance of the atomic bomb," he wrote, "to experience vicariously the feelings that so many thousands of Japanese people experienced, is desirable in these propitious times." Two years after his arrival, Delnore authorized the first public commemoration in Nagasaki for the third anniversary of the bombing.

Winfield Niblo, the NMGT's chief education officer, tried to offer *hibakusha* a sense of hope by introducing American square dancing as a wholesome mode of entertainment for the devastated city. Niblo, a former high school social studies teacher, football coach, and square-dancing caller from Denver, Colorado, had attended a dinner for Japanese athletics teachers from across the city at the home of the chief of physical education for Nagasaki Prefecture. After dinner, the teachers performed traditional Japanese folk dances, and Niblo in turn offered to teach them the Virginia reel. The teachers caught on quickly, and from there the idea took hold to train Japanese athletics instructors in American folk dances and offer classes in Nagasaki's schools. "*Hidari te!* [Allemande left!]" callers bellowed. "Swing your lady!"

Eventually, the phenomenon spread throughout Japan and was endorsed by occupation officials as a form of physical education that also promoted Western perceptions of healthy social interactions between men and women. By the early 1950s, the National Folk Dance Training Course had been established in Tokyo, and thousands of Japanese across the country were sashaying and do-si-do-ing to American folk tunes like "Little Brown Jug" and "Oh! Susanna." The Japanese Ministry of Education later asked Niblo to contribute to a textbook on the subject. "Dancing people are happy people," he wrote, "and America is happy that this bit of American culture can bring a portion of happiness to Japan."

Delnore's and Niblo's efforts notwithstanding, survivors' ways of coping with profound trauma and moving forward in their lives varied for each *hibakusha*. Some who had lost their entire families reminded themselves that if they didn't stay alive to look after their family's graves, no one else would. Some survivors directed their focus each day to their children or to others who were dependent on them as a way not to kill themselves. Others drank excessively to escape their exhaustion, loss, and shame. Obeying their religious tenet forbidding suicide, many Nagasaki Catholics had to find ways, in one survivor's words, to "just suck it up" and keep going.

But in the first years after the bombing, many *hibakusha* reached a point where they could no longer endure and saw no other option but to end their lives. In the woods behind Ōmura National Hospital, a young woman with severe facial burns hanged herself. A man caring for his younger brother at the Shinkōzen temporary relief hospital jumped from a high window to his death. A young husband and father, too ill to work, tried repeatedly to hang himself, and when his despairing wife called the police, he pleaded, "Let me die! I can't stand the agony of my life anymore!" A twenty-year-old girl who couldn't work because of crippling injuries to her legs tried to overdose on medication three times. A young boy, taunted in elementary school for the keloid scars on his feet and legs, swallowed poison, but his mother found him before he died. Another mother suffering burns over half her body and tormented over the loss of four sons threw herself from an upper-story window of the former Nagasaki Medical College Hospital. Even as late as 1952, a young man, despairing over the suicide of his best friend and his own inability to get a job because of his disfigurement, climbed a hill overlooking the city, cut his wrists, and lay down to die; he survived only because the sleeve of his shirt slowed the blood flow. In 1955, a nineteen-year-old girl who ten years earlier had lost her mother on the day of the bombing and had herself been afflicted with poor health ever since, walked to the railroad tracks, placed her sandals and umbrella next to the rails, and threw herself in front of a moving train.

Nagano experienced anguish and guilt so overpowering that she repeatedly considered ending her own life. "Really, there weren't any good days with my mother," she said, "and whenever I asked myself why my sister and brother had died, my sadness was so intense, it felt like someone had scraped out the inside of my chest. But no matter how sorry I felt, they didn't come back." She heard that her grandparents, too, blamed her, and when they died, the intensity of her guilt kept her from attending their funerals. She felt it would be better if she died, thinking suicide could be a way to apologize to her parents. "But if I died," she remembered, "I realized there would be no one to take care of my parents when they got older. When I thought about that, I realized that dying wasn't an option, either."

Dō-oh, too, came close to killing herself. Like countless other young women who were disfigured and sick with persistent radiation-related symptoms, she remained secreted inside her house, tormented by the scars on her face and her loss of hair. Her face broke out as if toxins were being released from her body. "It itched a lot, and fluid came out of the pimples," Dō-oh remembered. "It smelled awful, like rotten fish." She constantly stared at her face in the mirror, trying to find even the smallest improvement. But there was little change. Instead of hair, soft raggedy fuzz grew on her scalp, so thin and transparent that she looked almost bald, but even that would fall out—then grow in and fall out again. She had almost no understanding of what had happened to her or why she wasn't getting better. "My mother cried as she washed my face and head," Dō-oh recalled. "She felt sorry for me and made a black scarf—black to look more like hair. I spent my adolescence with my head wrapped in a scarf." When guests came to their house, Dō-oh hid behind a sliding door and wished she could die. Alone in her room, she quietly fumed. *Why me? Why do I have to stay so ugly—I didn't do anything!* "I still had a lot of dreams then," she remembered. "I wanted things to go back to how they'd been before."

One day when Dō-oh was alone in her house, she found a pink-colored bump the size of her thumb on the top of her head. "I was so tired from this long period of recuperation, and I felt so desperate, that it didn't matter anymore what happened to me," she recalled. "If I was going to have this kind of life, it didn't matter if I died." She picked up a pair of sewing scissors and cut the bump off her head. Blood poured from her scalp. When her family came home, they found her with a bloody towel wrapped around her head. Her parents reprimanded her harshly. "My mother cried," Dō-oh remembered. "She said she wished she had been injured instead of me so I wouldn't have to suffer. She took the scissors and knives from the kitchen and hid them."

When Dō-oh heard that the two friends she had escaped with on the day of the bomb had died, she began questioning why she had been allowed to live—particularly with such a "pitiful face." "I wondered what God wanted me to do with my life," she said. "That was my question. What had God given me this life for?"

Hibakusha who managed to live could only search for ways to endure the traumas they could not forget. Many schools held regular ceremonies to mourn the deaths of teachers and students who died on the day of the bombing and in the years that followed. Teachers at Shiroyama Elementary School held memorial services for their colleagues who had died instantly while weeding the vegetable gardens, as well as for the unidentified victims whose ashes they had buried on the school grounds. City and prefectural government officials worked with Mitsubishi to collect data on *hibakusha* who had died in the company's factories. The staff of Junshin Girls' High School compiled a complete list of the 214 teenage girls who had died in the blast or afterward from injuries and radiation-related illnesses. Later, the school disinterred and cremated the bodies of those students who had been buried in the public cemetery at Togitsu and gave a portion of the ashes to the girls' families, then buried the remaining ashes beneath a memorial built on the school grounds.

Personal commemorations often took place out of the reach of occupation censors. Even in the crudest of huts within the atomic wasteland, families managed to display the urns containing the ashes—or the presumed ashes—of their family members and pray every day for the repose of their souls. Hayashi Tsue, the mother of a girl who died at Shiroyama Elementary School on the day of the bombing, planted young cherry trees in the playground of the school in memory of her daughter and all the victims she had seen during her harrowing search for her child in the days after the attack. No saplings were available anywhere in the city, so a gardener transported them from another prefecture northeast of the city. As the trees grew, every spring Hayashi quietly observed the beauty of the trees, consoling herself by imagining that her daughter's soul had transformed into their blossoms.

In the privacy of their classrooms, Nagasaki teachers guided their students in writing about their postbomb lives, and under the direction of Dr. Nagai, their essays were later published in a collection called *Living Beneath the Atomic Cloud*. Tsujimoto Fujio, a fourth grader at Yamazato Elementary School who lost his parents and siblings in the attack, wrote about living with his sixty-year-old grandmother in a shanty constructed where his house used to be. Every morning, his grandmother attended Mass, then went to the banks of the Urakami River to search for shells, which she sold to help pay for their food. She was always holding her rosary, he wrote, always praying. She would tell him that all was fine, that everything was the will of God.

But Tsujimoto did not feel as hopeful as his grandmother. He longed for his former life, when his grandmother ran a food shop, his father was a well digger, and the family had plenty of money. "Please give me that life back . . . please," he begged in his essay. "I want my mother. I want my father. I want my brother. I want my sisters. . . ."

His mother had been cremated in young Tsujimoto's school yard. As he ran and played with his friends there, sometimes a sudden memory of that day filled him with longing, and when his schoolmates walked across the area where his mother's body had lain atop the funeral pyre and burned, he felt anger rise up in his body.

"I go to [that] spot . . . ," he wrote, "and touch the ground with my fingers. When you dig into the ground with a bamboo stick, flakes of black ash come out. If I stare at these, I can see my mother's face with my mind's eye."

CHAPTER 6

EMERGENCE

As years passed and Nagasaki's days and nights became further distanced from the detonation that forever split its history, *hibakusha* who had survived the chilling first years after the bombing pushed forward to reconstruct their city, their lives, and their identities. Contrast and contradiction defined everyday life. In the late 1940s, rationed food was more available than before, but still there was not enough. Some *hibakusha* found jobs to help stabilize a subsistence income for their families, even as unemployment and inflation continued to rise. Newly constructed housing provided shelter for some, but as late as 1950, less than 5 percent of survivors' housing applications could be met, and thousands still lived in shacks with dirt floors, surrounded by atomic ash and debris. Most startling, just as survivors were finally healing from their injuries, illnesses, and burns, new radiation-related illnesses began to appear, some of them fatal. For many, survival remained tenuous, and long-term planning was nearly impossible. With tremendous will, the help of their families and communities, and as much strength as their physical and emotional health would allow, the people of Nagasaki inched their way through their postnuclear existence, trying to regain some semblance of a recognizable world.

In late 1946, Taniguchi was able to move his lower legs. Still lying on his stomach, he bent his legs at the knee and moved them in random directions to stretch and strengthen his knee joints. Doctors continued to use gauze soaked in liquid penicillin to treat his back and left arm.

Scabs finally began to harden over small sections of these areas, and skin formed along the edges of his burns. The scorched patches of skin on his buttocks were nearly restored, and his blood cell counts had stabilized.

One day in early 1947, surrounded by his medical team, Taniguchi twisted his legs to the edge of his bed, lifted his torso, and sat up for the first time in seventeen months. Everyone applauded, thrilled that this moment—which none of them could have imagined even a year earlier—had actually come.

Taniguchi had never seen his burned back, and as he allowed himself to believe that he might recover, he decided to take a look. While he lay facedown, doctors brought in a large mirror to his bedside and held it at an angle near his head. Taniguchi lifted his chin and held it up for a brief moment, glancing into the mirror to see his back, arms, and legs covered with infected scar tissue and barely scabbed flesh. Overwhelmed with disappointment, he lowered his head to the bed. Everyone had told him that his wounds were getting better, and before that moment, he had visualized improvement far greater than what he saw.

Soon, Taniguchi was able to stand up for the first time since the bombing. Dizziness overcame him at first, and sharp pain coursed through his feet. After resting, he stood again—and with immense resolve and the aid of bamboo crutches, he took his first steps. "I had never been happier than on that day," he remembered. "I felt at that moment that I was resurrected."

The left side of Yoshida's face and body also healed significantly, and at last he, too, was able to walk. On his release date in January 1947, sixteen months after the bombing, hospital staff drove him to the Ōmura train station. When he walked into the small waiting room, Yoshida heard people gasp and whisper about his face; then the room went completely silent. Everyone stared. During his entire stay at the hospital, Yoshida had avoided catching even a glimpse of his own reflection, so while he and other patients had become accustomed to each other's burns and scars, he was totally unprepared for how people outside the hospital would react to his face. Yoshida lowered his head and walked to the corner of the room, where he crouched down, crying.

He hoped he would be left alone on the train, but at each stop, people stared as they got off and on. Keeping his head bowed, Yoshida wept as the train passed through one rural village after another, then over the mountains into Nagasaki. *Maybe the people in the city will be accustomed to seeing faces like mine,* he thought. But in Nagasaki, too, people gasped. "When I think back," he said, "I can't believe I went back to Nagasaki with that face."

For the next two years, Yoshida lived with his mother and four siblings. His mother helped him fill the gaps in his memory—of the day of the bombing, his unconscious months at home, and his first weeks at Ōmura Naval Hospital. He learned that each of the six friends he was with at the time of the bombing had died.

Twice a week, Yoshida went to a neighborhood clinic where a doctor applied ointment to the grafted skin on his face. In between visits, however, the salve hardened beneath the bandages, like a cast. "Every time I went back," he remembered, "the doctor told me to look out the window—and then he tore off the bandage. Blood poured out. It was *excruciating.*" His injuries prevented him from opening his mouth more than a tiny degree, making it difficult to eat. Yoshida also suffered unyielding pain in his side; he later discovered that at the time of the bombing, he had broken two ribs that had never been reset. Further, the scar tissue on his legs prohibited him from sitting cross-legged or in *seiza*—the formal Japanese way of kneeling and sitting back on the soles of one's feet, required for many occasions. The tissue beneath the skin of his right hand had been destroyed, and the skin that had healed over the wounds was so tight and dry that it split open every winter. His fingers were curled up almost in a fist, frozen in the position they were in at the moment of the atomic blast. In an attempt to straighten his fingers, Yoshida's doctor instructed him to fill a bucket with sand, turn his hand palm up, wedge the bucket handle between his curled fingers and palm, and then allow the weight of the bucket to pull the handle down and force his fingers to straighten. "*Itaaaaaaaaai* [it *hurt*]," he recalled, wincing. "It felt like my hand would break."

More than any other challenge, however, fifteen-year-old Yoshida's profound fear of people staring at his facial scars and disfigurement kept him hidden inside his house. He would not leave even to bathe at the public baths with his family, so his mother placed a metal washtub outside their house, out of sight of the neighbors, permitting her son to bathe in private. Even at home, a woman from the local neighborhood association stopped by to visit and gawked at his blackened face and the scars that covered his neck. Mortified, Yoshida told his mother he would rather die than live with injuries that evoked such horrible responses from people.

It was the need for a haircut that finally compelled Yoshida to leave his house. "By that time, my hair had gotten *bosa-bosa* [long and messy]," he remembered. But Yoshida was terrified to walk even the fifty yards from his house to the barbershop, so his mother asked the barber to come to their house on his day off to cut her son's hair. The barber offered instead that Yoshida could come to his shop early one morning before it opened.

As the barber cut Yoshida's hair, he asked Yoshida what had happened to him. Yoshida had just begun to tell his story when he was interrupted. *"Oops!"* The barber gasped. Yoshida looked up and was petrified to see in the mirror that a customer had walked into the shop. The man didn't see him, and for a moment Yoshida thought he was safe. He peeked into the mirror again, and this time the customer was staring at him. "Our eyes met in the mirror," Yoshida said. "The man looked away immediately. I don't know why, but at that moment I became very sad. Then I panicked. My haircut was almost done, but I couldn't wait." Yoshida raced out of the shop in tears. That night, the barber went to his house to finish cutting his hair, but Yoshida's shame could not be allayed, and for many months he again refused to leave his house.

On March 20, 1949—three years and seven months after the atomic bombing—Taniguchi was finally released from Ōmura National Hospital. Though he still struggled with persistent fevers, nausea, diarrhea, generalized weakness, and infections in his wounds, he had learned how to walk freely without assistance. Doctors had performed two surgeries to try to increase the mobility of his left elbow and the extension of his arm, but neither procedure was successful, so his elbow remained permanently bent, and he could not raise his arm above shoulder level. As his release date approached, Taniguchi felt extremely anxious—about his injuries that had not fully healed, about his ability to go back to work, and about how people would react when they saw his scars. "These thoughts filled me with sorrow and hatred toward war," he remembered. "Night after night before leaving the hospital, I went outside the ward and cried."

He was twenty years old and over a foot taller than when he had entered the hospital in 1945. On the day of his release, Taniguchi put on a borrowed blue suit, tied up his few personal items in a *furoshiki,* thanked his doctors and nurses, and bowed good-bye to hospital staff who gathered to wish him well. Like Yoshida, Taniguchi took the train from Ōmura, but because his injuries were mostly hidden, he did not suffer people's stares. Arriving at Nagasaki Station, Taniguchi walked to the ferry that took him across the bay to the base of Mount Inasa, and from there he climbed the steep slope to his grandparents' house, where they greeted him with a special meal of raw fish, soybeans, rice, and sake.

Within two weeks, he was welcomed back to work at the post office by supervisors and workers who had also survived the bombing. Taniguchi's new job was to deliver telegrams across the city, riding through Nagasaki on a new red bicycle. After an eight-hour workday, he ascended the mountain to his grandparents' house, where he collapsed with exhaustion.

As Taniguchi crisscrossed the city on his bike, he saw signs of Nagasaki's renewal. Telephone service was restored to prewar levels, and some retail shops in the city's older districts and in front of Nagasaki Station had reopened. Streetcars now moved north of the main station into the leveled atomic plain and beyond. With gradually increasing support from the national government, hundreds of public housing units now stood in the scorched fields bordering the hypocenter area. Administrators, teachers, students, and parents had rebuilt their local schools and furnished them with desks, chairs, cabinets, shoe racks, and bookshelves that, one teacher recalled, "gave off the fragrance of new wood." Donated tree saplings grew outside Yamazato Elementary School, where young students, many of them orphaned by the bomb, had carried away pieces of broken concrete and debris to plant vegetable and flower gardens. Every morning and evening, church bells sounded across the city.

The city held lotteries for new housing units, giving priority to *hibakusha* whose houses had burned down. Nagano's father had gone to every drawing until he finally won a single room in a four-unit row house on Heiwa Doori (Peace Street), built on top of a burned field in Shiroyamamachi. In 1948, Nagano and her parents finally returned to Nagasaki to their new 157-square-foot room, which included a tiny kitchen with an earthen floor and a wood-burning stove. Like most other people in the city, they walked to the public baths to bathe.

The year 1949 was a turning point for Nagasaki's recovery. Although the economy had not yet stabilized, skyrocketing inflation was finally subdued, and food shortages had eased. The National Diet—Japan's legislature—passed the Hiroshima Peace Memorial City Construction Law and the Nagasaki International Culture City Construction Law, legislation that proclaimed new public images for each city and provided additional funding for their rebuilding projects. Under strict occupation supervision, Nagasaki's docks were again open to foreign trade. That year, Victor Delnore left his post as Nagasaki Military Government Team director, leaving a minimal occupation presence in the city—part of General MacArthur's "progressive relaxation of controls" toward the eventual goal of full Japanese self-government. Most of the occupation's censorship policies ended, allowing publishers to gradually release popular literature and medical journals relating to the atomic bombings. Ishida Masako's and Nagai Takashi's books were published; Nagai's *Nagasaki no kane* (*The Bells of Nagasaki*) sold 110,000 copies in the first six months.

As the largest Christian community in the nation, Nagasaki was briefly propelled into world view when it hosted the massive opening celebration honoring Spanish missionary Saint Francis Xavier's arrival in Japan four hundred years earlier. To prepare for the ceremonies, the city underwent major beautification efforts. Nagasaki Station was restored, a main thoroughfare was widened, and a new park was built on a hill just east of the station where twenty-six Christian martyrs had been executed in 1597.

When Catholics and media representatives from across the nation and the world converged in the city on May 29, 1949, Nagasaki experienced the largest influx of outside visitors since rescue and research teams had arrived immediately after the bombing. Starting at Ōura Church in the south, three priests led a procession of children's choirs, a brass ensemble, several hundred nuns, and thousands of Japanese Catholics clutching rosaries in their hands. Tens of thousands more lined the streets and attended services led by Vatican representatives on the hill of the twenty-six martyrs and in the ruins of Urakami Church. When the ceremonies came to a close and international press coverage ended, Nagasaki and its citizens returned to relative obscurity and their tenacious efforts to endure and rebuild.

———

For many of the estimated ten thousand Catholic *hibakusha* in Nagasaki, physician and spiritual leader Nagai Takashi offered a message of destiny and sacrifice that fulfilled their existential confusion and gave spiritual significance to the devastation of their city, the loss of their loved ones, and their survival. Before the bombing, Nagai was already ill with leukemia from his years of radiological work, and in the spring of 1946, he had collapsed near Nagasaki Station and was restricted to bed rest thereafter. On a hillside overlooking the hypocenter area, members of the Urakami congregation used corrugated tin siding to construct a forty-three-square-foot hut for Dr. Nagai and his two young children. He named his tiny residence Nyōkōdō—an abbreviated term for "Love Thy Neighbor as Thyself House."

Nagai continued to interpret the Nagasaki bombing as a baptism—a means by which Japan and the world could purge itself of its sins and begin anew—and an act of providence, for which the people must give thanks for being chosen for such a high purpose. Carrying forward the city's nearly four-hundred-year history of Christian martyrdom, Nagai believed that the Urakami Valley was sacrificed for the peace that came to the world after Japan surrendered. He praised Catholic *hibakusha* for being faithful martyrs for God. "And as we walk in hunger and thirst, ridiculed, penalized, scourged, pouring with sweat and covered with blood," he wrote in *The Bells of Nagasaki*, "let us remember how Jesus Christ carried His cross to the hill of Calvary. He will give us courage." Nagai also publicly condemned the war and denounced Japan for its military aggression. "It is not the atomic bomb that gouged this huge hole in the Urakami basin," he wrote in a later book. "We dug it ourselves to the rhythm of military marches. . . . Who turned the beautiful city of Nagasaki into a heap of ashes? . . . We did. . . . It is we the people who busily made warships and torpedoes." He saw the atomic bombings as "anti-war vaccinations" and prayed that the Nagasaki bombing would serve as the last act of war in human history.

Confined to his bed, Dr. Nagai wrote fifteen books and numerous articles, becoming the best-known *hibakusha* writer during the occupation. He donated much of his proceeds to plant trees in Nagasaki, built a private library for impoverished *hibakusha* children, and supported the rebuilding of the city and Urakami Church. People across Japan hailed him as "the saint of Nagasaki" and considered him an unparalleled spiritual teacher. He received a commendation from the prime minister, was paid a rare visit by the emperor, and was named a national hero by the Japanese government for his contributions to Japan's postwar restoration and healing. The Vatican sent two papal messengers to Nagai's bedside, one of whom carried a gift of a rosary from Pope Pius XII. In 1950, *The Bells of Nagasaki* was made into a feature film—but only after occupation officials required filmmakers to eliminate all visual images of the atomic bombing except for two: a distant view of the atomic cloud rising above the city and a scene in which Dr. Nagai finds his wife's rosary in the ruins of their home. After a national release, the film's beloved title song became an unofficial theme song for Nagasaki. Although the Catholics in Nagasaki were a small percentage of the population, Nagai's writings strongly influenced the Japanese public's characterization that Nagasaki's response to the atomic bombing was prayerful and even passive—different from the national perception that Hiroshima survivors were activists willing to express public outrage.

Dr. Nagai died on May 1, 1951, at the age of forty-three. Twenty thousand people attended his funeral, packing the interior of Urakami Church and the rubbled fields all around. A close friend rang one of the church's famous bells, still temporarily mounted on a wooden platform outside the church. Several days later, huge crowds assembled again at Sakamoto International Cemetery, where Nagai was buried beside his wife, Midori, in the hills overlooking the Urakami Valley.

He left behind a generation of Nagasaki Catholics, many of whom believed, in the words of one survivor, that "God dropped the atomic bomb on Urakami as a test of love and forgiveness." Another said, "It was good that the bomb dropped on Urakami. If it had dropped on people without faith, they could not have borne the burden." Nagai also influenced the lives of non-Catholics: In 1978, thirty-three years after the bombing, a Japanese man told Catholic missionary Paul Glynn that Nagai's writing, which he had stumbled upon in a public library, had changed his life. The man had been enraged with Japan's leaders and his

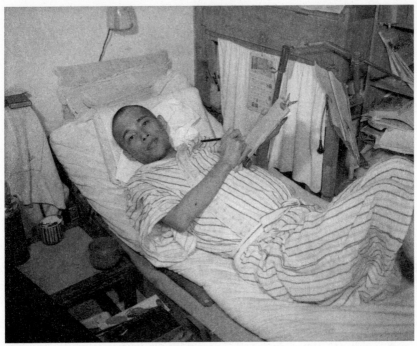

Dr. Nagai Takashi, ill with leukemia, inside his tiny hut built for him by members of the
Urakami Church congregation, August 1949. (*Bettmann/Corbis Images*)

wartime teachers who had brainwashed everyone into believing that Japan was a divine nation that could never be conquered, and he agonized
that perhaps "human effort and personal values were ultimately mean-
ingless." Nagai's writings persuaded him to convert to Christianity and
believe in a God "who is always good, even though it may not appear so
in the short term."

Nagai was not without his critics, however. Dr. Akizuki, a former student of Dr. Nagai's, adamantly opposed Nagai's views and believed that
his message—that the people of Nagasaki had served as sacrificial lambs
to God for the sake of peace—minimized and silenced the survivors'
suffering, provided a rationalization for the United States' use of the
bombs, and gave credence to the existence of nuclear weapons. Raised a
Buddhist, Akizuki had also explored the Bible and other sacred texts,
and he could not believe in a God whose will and divine plan allowed

the suffering he had witnessed after the atomic bombing. The barely five-foot-one doctor often challenged *hibakusha* nuns at his hospital about their beliefs. "Why is it that you have to suffer like this?" he demanded. "Why people like you, who've done nothing but good? It isn't right!" Unshaken, the Catholic sisters replied that they believed in providence, in the will of God. But Akizuki could not agree. He blamed the Americans for dropping the bomb and hated the Japanese government "who had willfully perpetuated this senseless war."

Still, Akizuki's perspectives on the bombing and its grim aftereffects did not offer him a deeper meaning that could help him cope with the surreal horror he had witnessed. After more than two years of caring for injured and irradiated survivors, he found himself physically and mentally depleted, and overwhelmed by a penetrating anxiety and a sense of emptiness. Standing at a hospital window overlooking the scorched atomic ruins, he decided to leave the city in order to reclaim a quiet life and cleanse himself of the grimy "victim of war" mentality that plagued him. "I protected this place by giving up everything," he thought, "but now it's time for me to go."

Before his departure, he visited his former mentor, Dr. Nagai. Inside Nyōkōdō, Akizuki sat on the *tatami* mat next to his friend, who lay on a futon, extremely pale and his stomach bloated as a result of the leukemia. Akizuki told Nagai that he felt his heart "was covered with weeds" and that he could no longer tolerate staying in Nagasaki. "I want to leave Urakami," he said. "I want to clean my mind."

In March 1948, thirty-two-year-old Akizuki placed a few items of clothing and some small possessions into a willow basket and left First Urakami Hospital. Boarding a train, he headed twenty-two miles northeast of the city to the rural village of Yue, where he had studied agriculture in high school. At the foot of Mount Taradake, he rented a single room inside a grilling shack behind a farm, where he planned to rest, write, and improve his health by following a diet of brown rice, seaweed, and sesame seed salt as an alternative to traditional medicines.

Akizuki's life was tranquil at first, enveloped in fresh air, sunlight, and the green of the mountain. He began his new diet, recorded its effects on his health, and wrote a thirty-page essay titled "A Week Covered with Blood," documenting both the horror of Nagasaki and the courageous work of his colleagues during the first seven days after the bombing. But his life took an unexpected—and unwanted—turn when the people of Yue discovered that a doctor lived in their midst. Every day, sick villagers arrived at his door, and despite his longing for rest, Akizuki could not turn them away. The stethoscope he had brought with him to monitor his own heart became an instrument for treating the local villagers, and he took the limited amounts of medicines he had brought with him and divided them into small doses for patients with colds or stomach pain.

In return, the villagers cared for Akizuki, felling trees, constructing a small house and clinic for him, and insisting—against Akizuki's protests—that he find a nice wife. Upon reflection, Miss Murai Sugako came to his mind, a young woman who had assisted him in a medical procedure at the moment of the bombing and had worked by his side ever since. Dr. Akizuki sensed that Sugako might understand his way of living, thinking, and searching for meaning.

He invited her to visit him in Yue, and as they stood together on top of the mountain with the Ariake Sea in the distance beyond, Sugako resolved to marry him. Following a tiny marriage ceremony in Nagasaki, they returned to Yue for a rustic reception the villagers held for them. Soon, after much anxiety over the impact of their radiation exposure on their unborn child, Sugako gave birth to a healthy baby girl.

During his five years in Yue, Akizuki had succeeded in improving his health, had written and published short works on the atomic bombing and alternative food therapies, married, and had a child. Still, he longed for the quiet life he had never achieved. They never had enough money to pay for even their basic living expenses, so Sugako attended to patients in their home clinic. They rarely had time to share a meal together. As Akizuki rode his bicycle on bumpy, muddy paths between rice fields to the homes of sick villagers, he grumbled to himself that he "hadn't come all the way to Yue to live like this."

Then in the spring of 1952, Dr. Akizuki's chronic asthma worsened and the tuberculosis he had experienced nine years earlier recurred. He felt he had no choice but to return to Nagasaki with his family. The First Urakami Hospital on Motohara Hill was now run by sisters of the order of Saint Francis, whose head offices were located in Springfield, Illinois. Renamed St. Francis Hospital, the rebuilt and newly equipped

Dr. Akizuki Tatsuichirō, age seventy-four, at St. Francis Hospital, ca. 1990. (*Courtesy of St. Francis Hospital*)

facility was again fulfilling its earlier purpose as a tuberculosis sanatorium. While receiving medical treatment, Akizuki resumed his work there.

In an unusual twist, Akizuki converted to Catholicism in 1953. His motivations remain somewhat unclear; he later hinted that he felt isolated as a Buddhist working at a Catholic hospital, surrounded by daily masses, hymns, and nuns who prayed for his conversion, and he said that he appreciated the profound support his Catholic friends and colleagues derived from their faith. He also admired their dedication, commitment, and self-sacrifice in almost single-handedly rebuilding the hospital—even before their own houses were reconstructed and while their family members lay sick and dying at home. After his conversion, however, Akizuki remained ambivalent toward his religion. "If this hell day came to me again, and the atomic bomb burned us up again," he said, "would Jesus Christ save us?"

As he searched for the deeper meaning of his survival and a potent way to support the healing of others, Dr. Akizuki came to believe in the immense power of personal story as a means for individual and social transformation. Over the next forty years, Dr. Akizuki forged a life of activism and became one of Nagasaki's leading advocates for *hibakusha* to articulate their atomic bomb experiences in writing and in oral presentations. His efforts offered survivors new ways to heal their psychological trauma while also heightening international understanding of the effects of nuclear war and furthering the cause of eliminating nuclear weapons arsenals across the globe. Akizuki wholeheartedly believed that had Dr. Nagai lived longer, his perspectives and teachings on the atomic bombing would have changed over time to include the unequivocal denunciation of nuclear war.

———

For countless *hibakusha,* trying to understand their new identities as atomic bomb survivors included coping with chronic health conditions and the inability to fully recover from their injuries, burns, and radiation-related conditions. Slow recovery was often a result of high doses of radiation that had destroyed regenerating cells and damaged their natural defense mechanisms. For many, postsurgery scars did not heal and developed infections. Large numbers of *hibakusha*—particularly those exposed within 1.25 miles of the hypocenter—also complained of various unclassifiable symptoms, including bouts of extreme dizziness, lack of mental energy, numbness, and incapacitating fatigue.

Numerous new health conditions also emerged. Cataracts, the clouding of the eyes' crystalline lenses, were so frequently diagnosed that for a time they were called atomic bomb cataracts, caused by radiation damage to cells on the back surface of the lens. Researchers later determined that the incidence and severity of survivors' cataracts correlated to their age and estimated radiation dose. Microcephaly—a condition defined by a significantly smaller-than-average head size in proportion to a child's body, reduced life expectancy, and decreased brain function—occurred in approximately 15 percent of children exposed to radiation in utero up to 1.25 miles from the hypocenter, a rate almost four times higher than for those not exposed. Other intrauterine-exposed infants were born with brain damage that resulted in mental retardation or other developmental disabilities. Many *hibakusha*—like Yoshida's father in 1946 and Nagano's father in 1948—died prematurely for unknown reasons or from conditions their families believed, but could not confirm, were caused by radiation exposure. Although the high mortality rate of their patients alarmed them, Nagasaki doctors remained cautious in attributing radiation exposure to survivors' unexplainable conditions and deaths until further studies were conducted.

Some diseases, however, were accurately ascribed to radiation toxicity, first by informal observation and later by documented research. After a period of latency, in 1947, physicians began observing increased rates of childhood and adult leukemia among *hibakusha*—and these rates swelled in the years that followed. Later studies confirmed disturbing figures: Depending on shielding, *hibakusha* exposed within three-quarters of a mile from the hypocenter were up to six times more likely to develop leukemia than those not exposed, and people exposed within a mile and a half of the hypocenter faced double the risk compared to those not exposed. At highest risk were children under ten within a mile at the time of the bombing, who developed leukemia at a rate eighteen times greater than the general population. Children ages ten to nineteen followed, with an incidence rate eight times higher than average. Autopsies continued to reveal the severe internal damages radiation had caused to survivors' bodies. One young man, twenty-eight years old and healthy at the time of the bombing, became more and more sick in the years after the war and was eventually diagnosed with leukemia. He died in 1950. In their autopsy report, doctors described the man's internal organs as "black and pulpy, like coal tar."

Other malignancies also escalated, including cancers of the stomach, esophagus, larynx, colon, lung, breast, thyroid, uterus, ovaries, bladder, and salivary glands. Later analysis of their medical records confirmed that *hibakusha* exposed to radiation within approximately three-quarters of a mile were 40 to 50 percent more likely to develop cancer than those not exposed. Physicians who knew the details of how these cancers manifested remained exasperated and furious with occupation censorship policies that had blocked them from speaking publicly about their cases. Grieving family members and friends felt intense bitterness and outrage. Fear of illness and death never ceased.

Brutal private and social stresses persisted as well. As with Nagano's painful emotional distance from her mother, many families remained shattered by blame and guilt. Children with visible injuries and hair loss were taunted by their uninjured schoolmates who called them "one-eyed devil," "chicken leg," "baldy," "monster," "atomic bomb," and *"tempura"*—the last referring to Japanese deep-fried shrimp and vegetables. Some microcephalic children were blocked from enrolling in elementary school or participating in school sports and extracurricular activities. Inaccurate rumors circulated that one could get atomic bomb illness by touching a survivor.

Even young children without physical injury or illness experienced ongoing distress. One day in her second-grade Japanese literature class, a Nagasaki teacher led her students in reading and discussing a popular story about five children growing up together with the loving care and support of their parents. A small girl raised her hand. "These children are really happy, aren't they?" she asked, her voice filled with melancholy. The teacher quickly remembered that the parents of this girl and many others in the class had died in the bombing, and she marveled that even she, who spent every day with them, could so easily forget the depth of their losses. During the lesson, some children would not look at the blackboard where the words "mother" and "father" were written. Others bit their lips, scribbled in their notebooks, or gazed blankly out the window.

Adolescents like Yoshida with visible disfigurements remained constantly vigilant of people's stares, looks of disgust, and degrading comments, and many rarely ventured from their homes. Yoshida credited his mother's love for keeping him going. She came to him one day and told him that she understood how he felt—more than he knew—and she asked him to listen to her for just a moment. "You *can't* stay inside the house your whole life," she told him. "I know you don't want to do it. I know it's sad for you. But do you think you could practice walking just around the neighborhood?"

"No!" Yoshida yelled at her. Eventually, however, he decided to take his mother's suggestion and go walking outside—first to the shrine, three houses away, where he thought he wouldn't run into many people. "The first day I walked a hundred yards," he remembered. "The next day, one hundred and fifty yards. A little bit farther each time." He avoided children because they stared at him without reserve. "I was too scary to look at, but they looked anyway." Yoshida was crushed when he said hello to a pretty girl and she started to cry. One day, as he walked toward a group of mothers, he saw their expressions of disgust and revulsion before they turned their faces away and walked past him. Yoshida started to cry, but he kept moving forward. *Keep calm,* he whispered to himself, tears streaming down his face. *Don't look back. Don't look back!*

For physically able survivors, returning to work played a major role in their recovery, but finding a full-time job was particularly difficult, in part because few were available, and also because employers repeatedly rejected *hibakusha* out of fear of survivors' current and future health issues. Many survivors resigned themselves to day labor as fishermen, farmhands, or construction workers. Even those without observable injuries began hiding their *hibakusha* status from current and prospective employers—and those with jobs did everything they could to keep them, showing up to work even when extremely ill.

For twenty-year-old Nagano, finding employment as a shop clerk allowed her to step out of her gripping loneliness at home. Later, she worked as an aide in the facilities department at Nagasaki Medical College. In the small wooden hut where staff designed the rebuilding of the college, Nagano made tea, did the filing, and helped with odd jobs.

Yoshida, now eighteen, felt so compelled to help support his family that he hazarded people's derisive looks to work as a part-time manual laborer at his neighbor's furnace shop. Eventually, he secured a full-time job in the warehouse of a small wholesale food company. During the first year, he was able to improve his abacus skills and study the kanji for each food item while staying out of public view. After that, Yoshida was assigned to work directly with customers. He tried to understand their feelings as they stared at him—*You can't make a good first impression without a good-looking face,* he told himself—but every day was unbearable. "I cursed the war and the atomic bomb," he said. "Why

Yoshida Katsuji, age nineteen, in wholesale food
company uniform, ca. 1950. (*Courtesy of Yoshida Naoji*)

did my face have to be burned? Why hadn't I been allowed a chance to
protect myself?"

———

Dō-oh was twenty and in her fifth year sequestered inside her house
when new hope finally appeared at her door. It was 1949, at the time of
year, she remembered, that "the persimmon fruits started to develop
color." Her injuries still hadn't fully healed, and her hair had not grown
back; short, soft fuzz still grew in periodically, then fell out again. "I felt
like giving up," Dō-oh remembered. "At about that time, an unfamiliar,
foreign car arrived and parked in front of our house.

"'I have come from the ABCC to take you there,' the person told us.

'Please cooperate with our research.' I got into the car believing that I would be healed by them." Driving away, Dō-oh stared out of the car window at the city she had not seen since the bombing. She had no idea of the underlying purposes of the medical examination she would undergo that day or the intense international dispute in which she would play a small part.

Three years earlier, the United States had seized on what it saw as a critical and unique opportunity to conduct long-range scientific and medical research on *hibakusha*—which an Army Medical Corps senior researcher on atomic bomb effects had believed "may not again be offered until another world war." To this end, President Truman had signed an order to establish the Atomic Bomb Casualty Commission (ABCC), charged with studying atomic bomb survivors to determine how radiation exposure affected their health. U.S. leaders projected that the ABCC's studies would offer the United States numerous military, scientific, and regulatory benefits—including greater understanding of the impact of nuclear weapons currently in development, support for civil defense planning for potential nuclear attacks on U.S. cities, and data for the reevaluation of international radiation dose limits for physicians, scientists, radiation workers, and patients. These goals inadvertently reflected how little, prior to the atomic bombings, U.S. scientists and military officials knew about the immediate or long-term impact of whole-body radiation, and they foretold how blatantly the ABCC would ignore the medical needs of the survivors. The choices the agency made in fulfilling its mission ignited a bitter, decades-long controversy between the ABCC and *hibakusha,* their physicians, and research scientists across Japan.

Tensions began early. On paper, the ABCC was established as a collaboration between the United States' National Research Council and Japan's National Institute of Health, but in practice the commission was predominantly funded and controlled by agencies of the U.S. government, and it operated inside a country under U.S. military occupation. After years of vitriolic wartime slurs by each country against the other, U.S. and Japanese scientists distrusted one another's professional integrity and feared the ABCC's research outcomes would be tainted by national bias: Americans were concerned that the Japanese would exaggerate radiation effects for political purposes, and the Japanese worried that the Americans would minimize radiation effects for their own political gain. Japanese doctors working at the ABCC appreciated the

United States' advanced scientific methodologies, but some felt disrespected by U.S. physicians' lack of confidence in their medical skills as well as their ability to evaluate research. One American ABCC doctor wrote: "Just the thought of what the Japanese would do if they had free unrestrained use of our data and what they might publish under the imprimatur of the ABCC gives me nightmares."

The imbalance of power at the ABCC was made worse by wage inequities between U.S. and Japanese physicians working there. The agency's longtime policy to designate only U.S. physicians and scientists as directors of each city's operations resulted in the majority of the ABCC's staff—Japanese doctors, nurses, and support personnel, including many who had survived the atomic bombs and endured extraordinary losses—having to work under U.S. authority. Extreme insult arose when the United States took full possession of all of the ABCC's research data, study outcomes, and specimens, in part to prevent other nations from gleaning technical information about the bombs that might advance their own nuclear weapons programs. Even Nagasaki and Hiroshima doctors treating *hibakusha* on a daily basis had no access to these critical findings that could have supported their diagnoses and care. Nagasaki physician Nishimori Issei reflected that "the ABCC's way of doing research seemed to us full of secrets. We Japanese doctors thought it went against common sense. A doctor who finds something new while conducting research is obligated to make it public for the benefit of all human beings."

In Nagasaki, the ABCC's first offices were set up over a fish market on the wharf, and patients were initially examined at the temporary hospital at Shinkōzen Elementary School. During the late 1940s into the early 1950s, thousands of survivors like Dō-oh heard a knock at their door and saw an ABCC jeep and staff person waiting outside to transport them to Shinkōzen. The ABCC had identified and located them by using the medical studies and informal surveys of *hibakusha* conducted after the war, and by talking with physicians and scientists, gathering hospital records, and enlisting the help of local police. Although the ABCC was not officially under occupation authority, in Nagasaki's postwar climate, some *hibakusha* felt forced to participate because they perceived the ABCC as a function of the occupation and thereby an extension of the U.S. military. At Shinkōzen, they underwent physical examinations and were asked a series of questions about their location at the time of the bombing, distance from the hypocenter, direction they were facing, and physical symptoms they had experienced since then. In keeping with the Japanese social custom of reciprocity, ABCC staff sometimes gave survivors small gifts and offered them a taxi ride home.

"We went inside the building," Dō-oh remembered. "I was told to put on a white hospital gown. There was not much of an interview—I think they just looked at my injuries and took photographs of them. There were foreign doctors there, too." Dō-oh had thought she would be given medical treatment—at least to help with her pain—but ABCC staff provided no treatment and no emotional support. "I went home hugely disappointed," she explained. "As a young girl, I had been seen naked from the waist up and had taken the black cloth off my head in front of men. I felt something like rage."

Dō-oh was not alone. Although public opposition to the ABCC was suppressed by occupation censorship, within the highly sensitive medical, political, and economic climate in Nagasaki and Hiroshima, *hibakusha* anger toward the ABCC intensified. At a time when *hibakusha* were just beginning to come to terms with their identities as the only victims of atomic warfare in human history, the Americans who dropped the bombs imposed on them a disturbing new identity as research specimens for the U.S. government. Many survivors hated being studied by doctors from the country that had irradiated them. The ABCC also transgressed cultural boundaries with invasive and intimidating procedures, by examining young people like Dō-oh in the nude, collecting blood and semen samples, and taking photographs of survivors' atomic bomb injuries. Other social and economic oversights alienated survivors: Polished waiting room floors were slippery for women wearing *geta*; English-only magazines were placed in the waiting rooms; and the ABCC insisted that examinations take place during the day, resulting in loss of pay for those who worked. Even the word "examination" seemed objectifying to many.

The largest complaint, however, was that the ABCC conducted medical examinations without also offering medical care. What Dō-oh and other *hibakusha* didn't know was that the ABCC's mission to conduct detailed studies of survivors' radiation-related illnesses included a strict mandate to provide them no medical treatment. As *hibakusha* became aware of this directive, many felt even more dehumanized, and they experienced powerful feelings of being used by the United States as guinea pigs in a military experiment. Some also resented the ABCC's no-treatment policy in light of the shortage of medicine and medical equipment available in Japan after the war, contrasted with the millions of dollars that poured into the ABCC. In the United States, activist Norman Cousins praised the ABCC's work as both excellent and important, but he openly criticized the agency for what he saw as a "strange spectacle of a man suffering from [radiation] sickness getting thousands of dollars' worth of analysis but not one cent of treatment from the Commission."

The United States offered numerous reasons for its no-treatment policy. Early on, officials said that American physicians could not pass Japanese medical licensure exams because of the language barrier—but by 1951, 70 percent of doctors on ABCC staff were Japanese physicians who could have provided medical care. The United States also asserted that occupation policy did not allow American physicians to render aid to Japanese citizens, giving an inaccurate impression that the ABCC was under the occupation's authority. Other arguments included that medical care was not a relevant activity within the scope of the ABCC's scholarly scientific research, that the cost of providing care would be prohibitive, and that the ABCC's provision of care to survivors would have a negative impact on local physicians by depriving them of the opportunity to administer these services to their own community (a position many Japanese physicians disputed). As late as 1961, U.S. authorities overseeing the ABCC maintained that offering medical care to atomic bomb survivors would oblige the United States to deliver care to every Japanese citizen injured during the war, which in return would require Japan to provide treatment to every American injured in battles with Japanese soldiers, including those wounded at Pearl Harbor. In putting forth each of these reasons, the United States failed to distinguish between other Japanese war casualties and *hibakusha* who were subjects of the ABCC's long-term scientific study for U.S. military purposes.

Underlying every explanation was the highly charged concern that providing medical care to *hibakusha*—even while conducting studies on their medical conditions—could be interpreted as an act of atonement by the United States for using the atomic bombs, a position that was unequivocally rejected at every level of the U.S. government. The United States held tightly to this position despite the fact that in postwar Europe, the U.S. military provided medical care to former enemies under Allied occupation without any suggestion of responsibility for their injuries. So sensitive was this issue that ABCC directors rejected a hiring proposal to prioritize *hibakusha* as employees so as not to be perceived as atoning for the bombs by giving them preferential treatment.

Japanese scientists and early *hibakusha* activists also equated treatment to U.S. atonement, and *hibakusha* were caught between the polarized stances of the two governments, each wanting the other to claim moral, financial, and medical responsibility for the atomic bombings. As this fierce international tug-of-war dragged on, *hibakusha* continued to suffer and often die from illnesses related to their radiation exposure, and neither the barely solvent Japanese government nor the U.S.-directed ABCC provided financial or medical support. Out of compassion for their patients, some of the ABCC's Japanese doctors occasionally broke policy and provided medical care—including chemotherapy and other protocols—both at the ABCC's clinic and during house calls, where they could treat simple cases without notice or with the silent acceptance of their American supervisors.

The ABCC further inflamed survivors' ill feelings by conducting autopsies on *hibakusha* who died while participating in its studies, which inadvertently reinforced the survivors' perception that they were being used like laboratory animals for scientific purposes. *Hibakusha* sensitivities were exacerbated by the fact that autopsies were both foreign and invasive to Japanese family and community rituals, and because ABCC staff were dissecting their family members' bodies for U.S. military and civil defense research, without any apparent benefit to other atomic bomb survivors. The ABCC's Mortality Detection Network paid cash fees to Japanese medical providers in Nagasaki and Hiroshima to report *hibakusha* deaths as quickly as possible so that ABCC staff (called "vultures" by dissenters) could hurry to a deceased survivor's bedside to request permission to perform the autopsy. Some families refused, but despite their discomfort, others consented, perhaps because of direct pressure by ABCC staff, because they felt they had no choice, or because they hoped for better understanding of their loved ones' conditions.

In both cities combined, by the late 1950s, an estimated five hundred autopsies were conducted each year. Autopsy specimens of infants were stored in Nagasaki, but the tissues, slides, and body parts of older children and adults were extracted, examined, and quickly dispatched to the United States. Under the auspices of the U.S. Atomic Energy Commission (AEC), the new governmental agency established to oversee research, production, and control over nuclear weapons and atomic energy applications, these specimens were classified as state secrets and cross-categorized by various divisions of the Armed Forces Institute of Pathology (AFIP), where they were studied to understand the impact of high-dose radiation on the human body. After examination and data recording, the body parts and related records were stored in AFIP Quonset huts outside Washington, D.C., for ongoing research and later warehoused in a new building constructed to protect the materials from a potential atomic bomb attack.

Within this highly charged atmosphere, *hibakusha* found an advocate in thirty-three-year-old pediatrician James Yamazaki, the city's third ABCC director. A second-generation Japanese American, Yamazaki had served as a U.S. Army combat surgeon in northern Europe while his family was interned in a War Relocation Authority camp in Jerome, Arkansas. He later spent six months in a German prisoner-of-war camp. After the war, he continued his medical training in the United States before being asked to serve in Nagasaki.

Dr. Yamazaki had been briefed on his assignment before leaving for Japan, but it was only when he arrived in Nagasaki in late 1949 that the magnitude of destruction and human suffering became real. He wandered through the wreckage of a Mitsubishi torpedo factory and saw the still-razed hypocenter area and the ruins of Urakami Church. "There was, of course, a missing dimension," he later wrote. "The dead, the dying, the blistered survivors, and the victims in frantic flight were long since gone."

Dr. Yamazaki saw how pervasive the distrust had become between

Dr. James N. Yamazaki before leaving for battle in northern Europe, ca. 1944. (*Courtesy of Children of the Atomic Bomb, UCLA Asian American Studies Center*)

the ABCC and Nagasaki's medical professionals and survivors. As the only American doctor at the Nagasaki facility, and with limited Japanese language skills, he determined that one of his first goals would be to gain the confidence of both *hibakusha* and the Nagasaki medical community. To this end, after finding a new location for the ABCC's clinic, laboratory, and offices, Yamazaki developed a strong collaborative working relationship with Dr. Shirabe Raisuke, now the director of Nagasaki

Medical College Hospital. This relationship resulted in a mutually cooperative affiliation between the ABCC and the Medical College, which included the participation of Nagasaki medical students in the ABCC's studies as part of their training and weekly lectures by Dr. Yamazaki on current practices in American medicine. Dr. Yamazaki held Dr. Shirabe in great esteem. "I was most struck by his eyes," he remembered, ". . . that crinkled engagingly when he smiled or laughed. His geniality concealed the trauma of his bomb experience, the tragedy of his family."

In his capacity as liaison between the ABCC and Nagasaki Medical College, Dr. Shirabe guided Dr. Yamazaki through the ruins of the Medical College, still mostly unrestored from four years earlier. As they walked, Shirabe quietly identified each building, described how it was affected by the bomb, and told Yamazaki the numbers of faculty, nurses, staff, and students, including one of his sons, who had been killed instantly. Inside a demolished laboratory, the two doctors stood on piles of rubble and peered out of a broken window into the valley below, where the hypocenter was located a half mile away.

On another occasion, Shirabe arranged what Yamazaki called an "extraordinary briefing" for him and American physicians from Hiroshima's ABCC offices to hear from medical professionals who had experienced the Nagasaki bombing. In a small, partially demolished classroom, fifteen doctors, nurses, and support staff from Nagasaki Medical College Hospital told their stories of survival and their struggles to provide care to hibakusha after the bombing. Dr. Shirabe stood before charts and maps of Nagasaki, pointing out different locations and clarifying the range and scope of destruction throughout the city.

Several weeks later, Shirabe delivered to his new colleague the still-censored research study of the acute effects on eight thousand survivors that Shirabe had conducted four years earlier with the help of medical school faculty and students. It was difficult for Dr. Yamazaki to comprehend the extent, rationale, and impact of the occupation's censorship of Japanese research on the medical aftereffects of the bombs. "They completed the study in 1946," he explained, referring to Shirabe's team. "Four years later, he was handing it to me—the first medical report our team was to receive covering that critically important population."

Still, Dr. Yamazaki was barred access to numerous other studies carried out by Japanese research teams in the four years after the atomic
bomb attacks, and later he discovered that even he—an American serving American purposes who had security clearance from the Atomic
Energy Commission—had not been given access to early U.S. studies on
the short-term effects of the atomic bombs. In fact, he knew nothing of
their existence until shortly before he left Japan two years later. These
reports, Yamazaki remembered, "would have been immensely helpful . . . as we groped our way toward establishing our research on the
effects of the radiation."

During his tenure in Nagasaki, Dr. Yamazaki directed a staff of 250
and supervised numerous studies of adults and children on topics including cancers, reduced vigor, changes in vision, abnormal pigmentation,
hair loss, epidemiological changes, sterility, and shortened life span. As
a pediatrician, he gave particular focus to two comprehensive studies
involving Nagasaki infants and children—whom researchers expected to
be the most vulnerable to radiation exposure. The first study tracked
statistics on children who had been exposed to radiation inside their
mother's wombs, including fetal deaths and mortality rates for those
who died while a part of the study.

Dr. Yamazaki felt compassion for these families' losses, and he was
attuned to their sensitivities about the ABCC's conducting autopsies on
their children. Under his direction, a new policy was implemented: In
order to prevent grief-stricken parents from receiving a direct request
from the ABCC, a Nagasaki midwife with a relationship with the family
helped negotiate this difficult conversation. "With the quiet guidance of
the midwives," Yamazaki remembered, "the parents came to understand
the potential importance of autopsies to all of them. The great majority
gave their permission."

This study also recorded the health and development of children who
were exposed to radiation in utero and survived. One by one, mothers
accompanied their five- and six-year-old sons and daughters to the ABCC's
clinic and recounted vivid memories of the bombing, the deaths of their
family members, and their children's premature and difficult births.
They told ABCC staff about their confusion and anxiety over their babies' physical and mental development and the discrimination and

bullying their children had experienced—particularly after reaching school age, when their differences came into greater public view.

Dr. Yamazaki and his staff examined these children and diagnosed microcephaly, cardiac disease, incontinence, and severe mental and developmental disabilities, but they remained guarded in ascribing the children's disorders to radiation exposure until their studies could definitively document cause and effect. Yamazaki recalled that even five years after the bombing, many mothers knew little about the potential effects of radiation on their children and had also been told by their family doctors that their children's physical and mental challenges were "most likely caused by the malnutrition, trauma, and stress related to the bombing." Years later, when they realized that radiation from the bomb may have caused their children's conditions, they demanded to know why they hadn't been told earlier. One mother, scared for her young son, said, "To think that the bomb reached into my womb and hurt him leaves me bitter."

By the 1960s, long after Dr. Yamazaki had left, the in utero study cohort in Nagasaki and Hiroshima grew to 3,600 children, including their control groups. As these children grew older, the ABCC's outcomes confirmed radiation exposure as the cause of most of the children's health conditions, including high incidences of microcephaly and neurological impairments. The studies revealed the particular vulnerabilities of timing as it related to in utero radiation exposure. Children who had been exposed at eight to fifteen weeks after conception demonstrated significantly greater risk of developmental disabilities because fetal brain cells are more susceptible to radiation damage in this stage of pregnancy. In a Nagasaki substudy published in 1972, eight of nine children (89 percent) exposed before the eighteenth week of pregnancy were diagnosed with microcephaly—compared to two of nine children (22 percent) exposed to the same levels of radiation later in their gestational development. The ABCC periodically observed the children in this cohort through age nineteen and beyond. As young adults, these *hibakusha* continued to demonstrate reduced height, weight, and head and chest circumferences in addition to mental disabilities and decreased scores on intelligence tests compared with control groups.

Dr. Yamazaki's second major study searched for potential genetic effects on children conceived *after* the bombing, critical to understanding the generational impact of radiation exposure. Begun in Hiroshima before Yamazaki's arrival in Japan, the first step of this study had been to identify newborns whose parents were *hibakusha*. To do so, the ABCC had linked its study to Japan's postwar food-rationing system, which provided extra rations to women in the last twenty weeks of pregnancy; that is, when expectant mothers arrived at city offices to enroll in the rationing program, they were directed to register their pregnancies with the ABCC. This arrangement was so successful that over 90 percent of women at least five months pregnant signed up for the ABCC study.

During the pregnancy enrollment process, the ABCC was able to collect personal information and medical data on the mother, father, and baby without providing information about the potential genetic risks from radiation exposure that the ABCC believed might exist for these children. In a questionnaire and in on-the-spot interviews at the time of registration, for example, each woman was asked to provide details of her reproductive history, including abortions, stillbirths, and miscarriages, as well as the baby's due date and the name of the midwife who would attend the delivery. The ABCC also asked for information on both the mother's and her husband's atomic bomb experiences, including location, potential shielding, and symptoms of radiation illness they may have endured. How this information would be used—including the fact that the families' data would go to the United States for military evaluation—was not revealed. Instead, each woman received a pamphlet that described the ABCC's postbirth examination and stressed that mothers would be able to know their babies' "true physical condition" and at the same time make "an important contribution to medical science."

In what ABCC historian M. Susan Lindee calls "the largest epidemiological project of its kind up to that time," over the six years from 1948 to 1954, the first phase of this genetics study comprised nearly seventy-seven thousand infants conceived after the atomic bombings in Nagasaki and Hiroshima. In order to examine infants immediately after their birth, the ABCC established strong relationships with Nagasaki's approximately 125 midwives and paid them to report each birth they attended, including a bonus for immediate notification of newborns with potential medical problems. Upon news of a birth, the ABCC sent a Japanese pediatrician and a nurse to the family's home, where, with the midwife's support, they conducted a physical exam of the baby and asked a series of questions relating to specific problems during late pregnancy and birth, including prematurity, birth defects, or neonatal death. When they left, the ABCC staff gave the mother a bar of mild face soap to use on the infant.

Between five hundred and eight hundred babies were examined in Nagasaki each month under Yamazaki's supervision—an average of twenty-one per day. Within the first year of life, about 20 percent of the babies in the study were also selected randomly for follow-up examinations at the ABCC's clinic to check for cardiac problems and developmental delays that might not have been evident immediately after birth. The enormous amounts of data from these examinations were carefully collected, verified, and transferred to punch cards for processing.

Mothers and fathers may have appreciated that their babies received a comprehensive medical examination and at least initial diagnoses of any serious health conditions, but Dr. Yamazaki observed that the ABCC's home visits and follow-up examinations also stirred confusion and deep concern for the parents. "There was nothing any of us could do to alleviate the fear generated by our research," he remembered. "The routine examination of each newborn child brought home to many families for the first time the fact that the survivors were still at risk. We had no answers with which to reassure them." When Yamazaki returned to the United States in 1951, he understood the urgent need for further research in order to fully comprehend both the short- and long-term impacts of instant, whole-body radiation on the human body. "Some consequences," he wrote, "might not be known until we had completed careful observations of the survivors over their entire lifetimes."

To meet the need for in-depth knowledge of radiation's long-term impact on *hibakusha,* the ABCC designed and implemented numerous additional studies, many of which continue today. Outcomes of these studies—which would not be published for many years—revealed, in most cases, direct correlations between the levels of radiation exposure *hibakusha* received and the severity of their illnesses and risk levels for cancer throughout their lives. The ABCC's Life Span Study, established in 1958, has explored cancer occurrences throughout participants' lives and documented their causes of death in order to evaluate excess cancer risk compared with nonexposed people. Ultimately, the study's cohort increased to 120,000 subjects from both cities, and substudies have explored the effects of radiation on the immune system, gene analysis, and the underlying biological effects of radiation exposure that cause human illness and death. For survivors who were children at the time of the bombings, already statistically smaller in weight and stature, outcomes showed a higher risk than other adults for nearly every illness studied. In addition to the in utero study population, the ABCC has continued its lifelong investigation of potential genetic effects on children conceived and born after the bombings to one or both parents who were survivors. Studies have shown no observable effects on these children to date, but scientists will not draw conclusions until after they have studied these adults as they age.

All of this research has been possible because of the participation of tens of thousands of Nagasaki and Hiroshima survivors. Despite their political, cultural, and deeply personal concerns about the agency's methods, they have chosen to take part in the ABCC's studies for numerous reasons, including the provision of free medical exams and diagnoses even without medical care, a sense of admiration for the American facilities and scientific methodologies, and, over time, improved relationships between the ABCC and Japanese academic and medical institutions. Wada joined the ABCC's Life Span Study as a way to support important medical advancements. Others found some meaning in their survival through their contribution to scientific knowledge of radiation exposure, which they hoped could help abolish nuclear weapons development throughout the world.

Like Dō-oh, however, many *hibakusha* remained adamantly opposed to the ABCC. After her first and only visit to the ABCC clinic, Dō-oh decided never to go again, choosing to forgo potential diagnoses or postmortem analyses of her conditions rather than offer her body, and her suffering, to U.S. data collection. For the next twenty years, the ABCC called and sent letters asking how she was, but she never responded. Only years later did she speak to her family about her reasons. "I refused to cooperate because of the way I was treated," she explained. "I felt like an object being kept alive for research—and my pride wouldn't allow this to happen." She was also troubled by the agonizing and unbearable fear that her participation might in some way contribute to the development of an even more powerful nuclear weapon.

———

The ten-year state of war between Japan and the Allied nations that was declared after Japan attacked Pearl Harbor formally came to an end in September 1951, when representatives of Japan, the United States, and forty-six other Allied nations assembled in San Francisco to sign the Treaty of Peace with Japan. When the peace treaty went into effect in April 1952, the United States' occupation of Japan drew to a close. In Nagasaki, over three thousand people gathered at Urakami Church for a special High Mass to commemorate this historic transition for their nation.

Japan was barely recognizable as the country whose relentless military aggression had ended only seven years earlier. The nation's new constitution prohibited the government from arming itself except for purposes of self-defense. Seven Class A Japanese war criminals had been executed at the conclusion of the international Tokyo War Crimes Trials in 1948, including General Tōjō Hideki, Japan's prime minister who ordered the attack on Pearl Harbor. Almost 6,000 lower-level war criminals were also indicted, out of whom 920 were executed and more than 3,000 were given prison terms. As a means to preserve stability in postwar Japan, occupation authorities had exculpated the emperor of all responsibility for the war, but the emperor was no longer a divine leader, and the people of Japan were no longer his subjects. Many Japanese, including *hibakusha,* disavowed their nation's militaristic past and their own former indoctrination as the world's superior race. They were now citizens of a democratic state, free from direct military control for the first time in two decades.

After more than six years of nearly total disconnection from the world, Japan now had access to international news, and both Japanese citizens and foreign visitors could freely travel into and out of the country. The national economy was growing, and in many parts of the country, food and clothing were now accessible and affordable. The Japanese flag with its symbol of the rising sun again flew over the country. As it reclaimed its sovereignty, Japan entered a new stage in its history as a Westernized capitalist nation.

The occupation had ended, but few U.S. troops left Japan. Because Japan's new constitution mandated a perpetual state of disarmament, Japan and the United States signed a second agreement by which the United States became Japan's official military guardian. In exchange, the United States was allowed to maintain bases in Japan during and after the 1950–1953 Korean War, thereby keeping a large military presence in the Far East to monitor and suppress, if needed, Communist expansion by the Soviet Union, China, and Korea. In an ironic twist of history, Japan's national protection now lay solely in the hands of the U.S. military.

All censorship restrictions were now lifted, allowing non-ABCC Japanese scientists, research institutes, and governmental agencies to finally publish their studies on postbomb damages and medical conditions. The most significant scientific studies released after the occupation were the summary report (1951) and the sixteen-hundred-page full report (1953) of the Science Council of Japan's Special Committee on the Investigation of Atomic Bomb Casualties. For the first time, Japanese scientific and medical communities gained access to the detailed 1945 surveys, studies, and analyses conducted by Japanese physicists, engineers, and physicians. For *hibakusha*, however, any potential help these long-awaited reports may have provided had long expired.

Further, the Japanese public finally learned more about the damages, death, and suffering in Hiroshima and Nagasaki at the time of the bombings and in the years that followed. Between 1952 and 1955, more than sixty articles and books were published on the atomic bombings. They included striking images of the atomic aftermath that Japanese photographers and filmmakers had illegally concealed during the occupation—eliminating any vague impressions the Japanese people may have had about the bombings and bringing them face-to-face with the terrorizing realities of the nuclear attacks. Yamahata Yōsuke published *Atomized Nagasaki,* a selection of his photographs taken the day after the bombing. The Japanese Red Cross Society held an exhibit of atomic bomb materials at its headquarters in Tokyo. A Japanese media company released two Nippon Eiga-sha newsreels taken by filmmakers in the fall of 1945. A special edition of *Asahi Graph,* a *Life* magazine–style journal, was published on the seventh anniversary of the Hiroshima bombing, devoting almost its entire issue to information about the development of the bombs, including graphic images of mangled buildings and burned and irradiated *hibakusha* in both cities. The edition sold out immediately and required four additional printings, for a total of seven hundred thousand issues read by millions in Japan and throughout the world. This coverage, along with other atomic bomb–related books and publications released during the same period, elicited compassion for *hibakusha* by Japanese across the country and gave birth to a sense of collective national trauma relating to the nuclear attacks on Nagasaki and Hiroshima.

In the United States, too, more information on the bombings was released. In the early 1950s, the Atomic Energy Commission published *Medical Effects of Atomic Bombs*, a six-volume report comprising the studies conducted collaboratively by Japanese and American physicians in the months following the bombings, including acute radiation effects on thousands of survivors. Few people beyond the AEC and related agencies had access to these findings, however—even Dr. Yamazaki did not see them until 1956. After seven years of knowing almost nothing about the bombings, the American public finally gained a better, albeit still limited, grasp of the bombs' impact when *Life* magazine published photographs of *hibakusha* in its September 1952 issue. The seven-page feature story included ten of Yamahata's photographs, one of which revealed images of bodies that had been hurled from a streetcar into a ditch at the time of impact. The Nagasaki section of the story also included writer Higashi Jun's recollection of stepping on a scorched body in the predawn light and hearing a voice calling out to him for help.

The release of these images in the United States was historic, but in Tokyo, Dr. Shiotsuki Masao was outraged at the ignorance and utter foolishness of the U.S. media and the obliviousness of the American people regarding both their safety in the event of a nuclear attack and the medical support they would receive in its aftermath. "The other day while leafing through a popular U.S. magazine," Shiotsuki wrote in 1952, "I came across a picture of a patient lying on a bed under clean white sheets being injected with some sort of fluid while a doctor and nurse in spotless uniforms stood by." Under the headline, "Medical Attention Given to Victims of the Atom Bomb," Shiotsuki remembered, the article described how "the finest medical facilities" were well prepared to provide care for bomb victims. "What kind of impractical, theoretical nonsense is this?" he railed.

"Where in such a devastated city could one find a bed with such a soft downy mattress, such a healthy doctor ready and able to work, such a kindhearted and beautiful nurse? Where would medicine, bandages, or even a single sterilized needle be left preserved in good condition?"

The photo itself and Shiotsuki's response to it illuminated the fact that even with John Hersey's *Hiroshima* and the *Life* story depicting horrific devastation and death, U.S. policies of censorship and denial had succeeded in keeping Americans uninformed of the unimaginable power of atomic bombs and the ghastly consequences of whole-body exposure to high levels of radiation. In the meantime, the USSR had broken the United States' monopoly on nuclear weapons, and as the Cold War was escalating between the United States and the Soviet Union, the United States pushed for international control of atomic energy to ensure its use by other countries for peaceful purposes only—while simultaneously appropriating $3 billion to increase its capacity to produce nuclear weapons. Production and testing of atomic bombs burgeoned worldwide: By the end of 1955, the United States had stockpiled 3,057 nuclear weapons and tested 66, the Soviet Union had built 200 weapons and tested 24, and Britain had developed 10 nuclear warheads and tested 3. On average, these weapons were forty-eight times more powerful than the bomb used on Nagasaki.

Even after stories of *hibakusha* suffering emerged in the United States, President Truman never publicly acknowledged the human impact of whole-body, large-dose radiation exposure or expressed regret for using the atomic bombs on civilians. He came close, however, at a November 30, 1950, press conference, when he took a question about the possibility of using a nuclear weapon in Korea to end the deadly international conflict there. "There has always been active consideration of its use," Truman responded. "I don't want to see it used. It is a terrible weapon, and it should not be used on innocent men, women, and children who have nothing whatever to do with this military aggression. That happens when it is used."

———

"In the blink of an eye," one Nagasaki survivor wrote, "a decade had passed." The city and its people had outlived the long war; an atomic bomb; instantaneous and continuous losses of family, friends, and community; lack of adequate food and basic needs; isolation and censorship during the U.S. occupation; and years of severe medical conditions resulting from injury and radiation exposure. By 1955, the city's postwar economy had grown, in large part due to contracts from the United States for Mitsubishi and other companies to produce ships, military supplies, and other products for the Korean War, played out just 168 miles from Nagasaki across the Tsushima and Korea straits. Increased numbers of nonvictims had moved into Nagasaki, returning the city's population to prebomb levels.

In the older parts of the city less impacted by the bomb, commerce and daily life had somewhat normalized. Three movie houses exclusively showed Hollywood films, particularly Westerns and adventure movies. Even in the Urakami Valley, rows and rows of relief housing lined newly paved streets, and shops were now open to serve their local communities. The rebuilt and newly named Nagasaki University School of Medicine and its affiliated hospital had finally opened on their former sites. The hospital's state-of-the-art medical equipment and care allowed the temporary hospital at Shinkōzen Elementary School to close at last. Streetcars operated through most of the city. Hunger and deprivation had eased, and most people no longer scoured for food to survive.

But *hibakusha* still closed their eyes and remembered people's skin peeling off, their whispered cries for help, the bodies of the dead burning atop cremation pyres that filled the city with the stench of death. While most remained alone and silent in their grief, some formed small groups to honor Nagasaki's deceased and ensure their future remembrance. At the municipal level, the Nagasaki City Atomic Bomb Records Preservation Committee gathered artifacts and information as the first step toward the opening of an atomic bomb museum, and the annual commemorations of the atomic bombing in Nagasaki were unified into a single ceremony entitled the Memorial Service for the Atomic Bomb Victims and Ceremony to Pray for Peace. Every year since 1954, Nagasaki's mayor has read a "peace declaration" on behalf of the city.

At the hypocenter site, the small cylindrical marker posted in the rubble in 1945 was replaced by a tall wooden pillar rising from a large mound of dirt, framed from behind by young trees. Down the side of the post, large, hand-painted kanji identified the marker as the hypocenter. Visitors

Nagasaki harbor and environs, after the bombing (1945) and after reconstruction (1954). In the foreground is the Nishinaka-machi Catholic Church, and in the upper right across the bay is the Mitsubishi Nagasaki Shipyard. In the top photo, at center left, is Shinkōzen Elementary School. In the lower photo, the large building at center left is Nagasaki City Hall. (*Photographs by Ogawa Torahiko/Courtesy of Nagasaki Atomic Bomb Museum*)

could sit on a bench in front of the monument; to one side stood a large wooden sign in Japanese and English detailing the atomic bomb damages.

Nagano, her mother, and her older brother built a small family gravesite near the hypocenter where they placed Seiji's, Kuniko's, and her father's ashes. Wada found purpose in beginning to plan a monument for the twelve mobilized students and more than a hundred streetcar drivers and conductors who died in the bombing—"to comfort the souls," he said. To that end, he and his friends made a list of everyone who had died and where they had lived. If anyone in their families had survived, Wada tracked down their current addresses and visited them on weekends when he wasn't working. "I went as far as Osaka, Kansai, and Okinawa to ask them how they were doing after they had lost their daughters and sons." About a third of the families turned him away, unwilling to talk about the atomic bomb and the loss of their loved one. Others, however, invited Wada into their homes and asked him to tell them anything he knew about their son or daughter on the day of the bombing. It took Wada more than ten years to complete all the visits and organize the detailed notes he kept on each conversation.

The people of Nagasaki commemorated the tenth anniversary of the atomic bombing with new memorials, dedications, and acts of remembrance. The new six-story Nagasaki International Culture Hall opened on the hillside five hundred feet above the hypocenter, and its entire fifth floor became a small museum displaying materials and personal items relating to the bombing. More than 220,000 visitors saw the exhibit that year. The Nagasaki Peace Statue was dedicated at one end of a large area of elevated land just north of the hypocenter—though some *hibakusha* objected to this use of donated funds, believing the money could have been better spent on survivors' medical care. Created by Kitamura Seibō, a renowned sculptor and Nagasaki native, the thirty-two-foot-high statue situated atop a thirteen-foot-high stone base is a seated man facing the hypocenter. His raised right arm points toward the sky where the atomic bomb exploded, his left arm extends horizontally to symbolize peace, and his eyes are closed to symbolize prayer for those who died.

On the morning of August 9, large crowds assembled in front of the Peace Statue for the city's formal commemoration ceremony. The mayor of Nagasaki and other dignitaries appealed for remembrance and peace, offering flowers at the base of the memorial. A plane flew overhead, releasing flowers to remember the dead. A group of *hibakusha* orphans stood in front of the Peace Statue, and at 11:02 a.m.—the moment the atomic bomb had exploded a decade earlier—each child released a dove into the sky. That night, fireworks lit up the sky as a procession of children carrying paper lanterns moved toward the Urakami River. They attached the lanterns to thin wooden boards, placed them in small boats, and used string to pull the boats down the river like a train, creating a trail of flickering light.

At a time when much of the city's destruction had disappeared from public view, visual evidence of the bombing lingered silently in the night. On the knoll above the hypocenter near the new Peace Statue, the stone foundation of Urakami Prison protruded aboveground to outline the shape of each demolished building. Damaged stone pillars of the former Urakami Church stood upright in the far northeastern corner of the Urakami Valley. In the hills just south of the hypocenter, a single-legged *torii* archway balanced eerily at the top of a stone staircase, ten years after one of its immense cement support columns was blown away, still directing people to the intimate, tree-covered Sanno Shrine.

———

At the periphery of her city's recovery and remembrance, Dō-oh emerged from hiding. Year after year, she had sat alone in her room, asking herself over and over again what she should do with the life she had been given. Eight years after the bombing, she finally knew that it was time to transcend her atomic bomb experience and somehow create a new life for herself.

But while her injuries had healed and the immediate pain of the glass shards embedded in her body had eased, Dō-oh's hair had still not grown back. Desperate to overcome her shame and reclaim her life, she wore the black kerchief her mother had made for her and stepped outside her house. Like Yoshida, she stayed close to home at first, taking short walks only in her immediate neighborhood. Later she heard that people called her "the girl with the triangle cloth."

Dō-oh's father decided that she should go to dressmaking school so she could eventually support herself and have a good life. The commute to the school required Dō-oh to venture farther from home. One day on her way home, she saw a fatigued, middle-aged woman sitting on a straw mat on the ground with a young child strapped to her back. "Could you give me something?" the woman begged. "Anything is fine."

Dō-oh dropped some coins into her box and was overwhelmed by the sad and lonely sound they made. *What kind of life had this woman had?* she wondered. *Did she lose her husband in the war or the atomic bomb?* On her way home, she imagined what it would be like to live like this woman and was awakened to the crucial necessity of her own independence. She quickly found a part-time job as a kitchen worker making *takoyaki*—grilled dumplings with octopus. Some months later, she was hired as a Nagasaki representative for a cosmetics company.

For the first time since before the bombing, Dō-oh felt alive again and began envisioning a future for herself. She decided that she wanted to live an authentic and full life—for herself and for her friends who had died. Reconnecting to her love of fashion, Dō-oh focused her vision on cosmetics as a way to help young *hibakusha* women whose faces were scarred and burned.

She wanted to push herself and test her potential. She wanted to leave her hometown and move to a bigger city. Making a rare choice for a single Japanese woman, Dō-oh requested a transfer to her company's head office in Tokyo—"the place for fashion," she said, "the place for *anything*." Her application was accepted, but Dō-oh's parents adamantly objected to her leaving. "Your body is injured," they said. "At some point, you might become ill again. We can easily foresee your experiencing hardships there." Dō-oh was furious, and in another act of social defiance, she told her parents that she was going to Tokyo despite their wishes. Before she left, she rented a room in Nagasaki to practice living on her own, and she worked at the cosmetics company's local shop and took odd jobs to save money. In 1955, her hair finally grew back enough for her to remove the black kerchief from her head.

She was free. On the day of her departure, Dō-oh, now twenty-six, wrapped her clothes in two *furoshiki,* said good-bye to her family, and boarded a train for Tokyo. The trip took a day and a half. Her goal was to try to use the life she had been given. "I felt like I'd already died once, so if it didn't work out, I wouldn't have lost anything." From inside the slow, coal-burning train, Dō-oh watched the city, her childhood, and her atomic bomb experiences disappear in the distance. "Going to Tokyo was the true starting line of my life," she said. "I bet against myself that I would win."

CHAPTER 7

AFTERLIFE

Twenty-one-year-old Mizuta Hisako had studied hard to complete her training as a Nagasaki tour bus guide—and out of a pool of twenty applicants, she was thrilled to be one of only seven to be hired. Japan's economic boom of the late 1950s had begun to propel the nation out of its postwar collapse, and in Nagasaki, increased foreign trade and the thriving shipbuilding industry had helped the local economy surge. International hotels and restaurants crowded the downtown area, many with signage in both Japanese and English. Television towers rose high above Mount Inasa, and simple eight- and nine-story apartment and office buildings dotted the cityscape. In winter, remembered one of the ABCC's leading geneticists, William J. Schull, "Nagasaki's major shopping area rang with the sounds of Christmas carols, and images of Santa and his elfin helpers were to be found in both of the department stores."

As Nagasaki emerged as a modern metropolis, tourists began to discover the city. At Nagasaki Peace Park, just north of the hypocenter area, peace monuments donated by nations throughout the world began arriving and were placed around the park's perimeter, and visitors were often greeted by a brass band. Near the giant Peace Statue, survivors who otherwise could not work due to paralysis, crippling injuries, or illness operated the popular "*hibakusha* store," selling atomic bomb souvenirs, handmade Mother Mary dolls, Japanese noodles, and drinks.

Hisako's uniform was ready, and she was just about to start her new job when one of her superiors at the city transportation office approached her. He suggested that she meet a man named Wada who worked for the same agency in the streetcar division. He had also approached Wada. "Mr. Wada," the man had said, "Mizuta-san is a nice girl. Why don't you marry her?" Hisako told the man that she was working and had no desire to get married yet, but he insisted that she at least allow the introduction.

In Japan, marriage and children were societal expectations, key milestones in a young man's or woman's successful transition to adulthood. Most marriages were arranged through *omiai*—formal interviews between the potential bride and groom, often accompanied by their parents. These meetings were arranged by an older relative, a senior employee at work, or an elder in the families' social networks who could vouch for both parties and praise their virtues as good marital candidates. Families accepted or rejected prospective marriage partners based on various criteria, including social standing, appearance, economic stability, health, and the ability to bear healthy children.

Hibakusha—even those with economic and social status and with no visible injuries or illness—were routinely rejected as marriage partners because of widespread fears about radiation-related illnesses and possible genetic effects on children. "A lot of rumors circulated back then that *hibakusha* were carriers of serious diseases," Wada recalled, "or that if two survivors got married, they would have disabled children." Consequently, countless survivors hid their survivor status prior to marriage; some also made sure their spouses never found out. One woman kept her past a secret over the course of her entire marriage, destroying government notices related to her *hibakusha* status as soon as they arrived in the mail. Another was forced to abort her child and leave her marriage when her husband and his family discovered she was a *hibakusha*.

Wada and Hisako knew each other's faces, but they had barely spoken before they met at a Chinese restaurant. Neither spoke of their identities as *hibakusha*. Since 1946, Wada had never spoken to anyone about his atomic bomb experiences, and he did not want to risk doing so now; at age thirty, he wanted to find a wife and marry quickly so that his grandparents could know their great-grandchildren.

Hisako balked at the potential arrangement. She didn't have anything against Wada, but it was customary for young women to stop working

Wada Kōichi, age thirty, on his wedding day in 1957, wearing a
traditional male wedding kimono. (*Courtesy of Wada Kōichi*)

after they married, and Hisako wasn't ready to quit her new job before
she'd even started. Her aunt, however, insisted that she accept Wada and
marry him. "Women need to marry someone at some point anyway," she
told Hisako, implying that it was best for a woman to marry when asked.
The aunt had cared for Hisako's family after the bombing, so her words
carried particular weight. "Since it was my aunt's order," Hisako explained, "I had to do it."

Although they might have guessed, it was only after their wedding
that Wada and Hisako learned for certain that each was a *hibakusha*.
The third of five children, Hisako had been a third grader at Zenza

Elementary School in 1945. Her father was away at war. In one of the conventional bombing attacks on Nagasaki, her mother and older brother had been seriously injured, and the entire family had moved from their Urakami Valley home to her aunt's house on the outskirts of the city. A week later, the atomic blast destroyed Hisako's home. She had been at school only a mile from the hypocenter but was protected inside a bomb shelter. Her older sister, however, had been walking toward the city and suffered whole-body burns. For ten days, Hisako and her family lived in a bomb shelter and cared for her sister, who was wrapped in cotton gauze bandages, before leaving Nagasaki to live with relatives in northern Kyushu. When her father came home from the war in September, the family returned to Nagasaki to rebuild, but they were so poor that for a long time their house had no roof.

After Wada and Hisako's wedding in 1957, Hisako got pregnant immediately—"a honeymoon baby," she called her first child. By this time, *hibakusha* were terrified by widespread rumors and media coverage about potential genetic effects and infant malformation caused by parental exposure to radiation. No matter how explicitly the ABCC tried to reassure survivors that their radiation exposure would have no measurable genetic effects on their children, young married couples and their families never stopped worrying. When Hisako went to her first prenatal doctor's visit, a staff member told her that because she and Wada were *hibakusha,* it would be better that they didn't have children. The misinformed doctor warned them that there was some medical probability that their baby would be deformed. "These words," Wada remembered, "stabbed at my wife's heart."

They turned to a different doctor—a physician at Nagasaki University Hospital who conducted research on the medical effects of the atomic bomb. Although he did not deny his colleague's comments, the second doctor reassured them that even if their children were born with medical problems, they would be able to take care of them and raise them well. Grateful but still worried, Wada and Hisako waited for their baby's birth and were immensely relieved when their daughter was born without any of the rumored conditions. Two more healthy daughters followed over the next few years.

Wada and Hisako, along with Wada's aging, authoritarian grandmother, moved into a new house at the base of a hill in a northwest

Urakami Valley neighborhood. Wada drove a streetcar for several years, then worked in his company's administrative office, where, over time, he was promoted to manager, section chief, then department chief. He spent many weekends planning the details of a memorial for his lost colleagues.

But he rarely spoke about the atomic bomb. "When you talk about it, it brings back memories," he said. "I didn't talk about it even to my children."

"I'm sure they knew," Hisako added, "although we didn't tell them directly."

"It's not just that I didn't talk about the bombing," Wada explained. "I did not *want* to talk about it. I *didn't* talk about it because I didn't *want* to."

———

By the time of Wada's wedding, Nagano had already been married for seven years. She had begun thinking about marriage in 1949 after she turned twenty, but every time she brought a man she liked home to meet her mother, her mother rejected him. "She intensely opposed anyone I dated," Nagano recalled. "Eventually I learned that she would never accept someone I liked." Under the strain of unrelenting guilt, Nagano thought she should do whatever her mother said, regardless of her own feelings. What her mother wanted was for Nagano to marry a cousin who was also a *hibakusha*.

"He was my cousin by adoption, not by blood," Nagano explained. "My mother told me I should marry him because we felt sorry for him since he had lost his family in the bombing. I *really* didn't want to, and I rebelled—I left home and went to a friend's house in Isahaya and stayed there overnight without telling my mother where I was. There were no cell phones back then, or even any telephones, and my mother went to all my friends' houses and searched for me all night long." When Nagano returned home and realized how much her mother had worried, she decided never to do anything like that again.

Nagano married her cousin in 1950. She was twenty-one. Despite having no romantic feelings toward her husband, she persuaded herself to find a way to like him because she knew they would have children. After their wedding, Nagano's new husband moved into Nagano and her mother's tiny residence in Shiroyama-machi, originally built as relief housing. Nagano's mother now owned the unit after the city transferred ownership of these dwellings to the *hibakusha* occupying them. Eventually, Nagano and her husband moved to their own single-room, 150-square-foot accommodation on the same street.

Nagano stopped working after she married. Her first child, a son, was born in 1951, and over the next ten years she gave birth to two daughters as well. "We were fortunate," she said, "that all three of them were fine." As rumors persisted about serious health issues for children of *hibakusha,* however, Nagano took her children for frequent medical checkups and was hypervigilant to every cold, fever, or other illness they experienced. To accommodate their growing family, Nagano and her husband added rooms to the bottom floor of their house and built a second level. They lived there for eighteen years until their son took his college entrance exams.

For nearly their entire married lives, Nagano and her husband never spoke about what they had suffered. "It was too overwhelming," she explained. "We didn't want to talk about it because if we did, we would start to cry." In 1972, after twenty-two years of marriage, her husband finally broke his silence. At Nagano's older brother's *isshūki*—the ceremony commemorating the first anniversary of his death—her husband told Nagano that on the morning of the bombing, his father had finished his night shift at the Mitsubishi Ōhashi weapons factory and returned to their home—across the street from Shiroyama Elementary School and a third of a mile from the hypocenter. He had eaten breakfast and rested with his wife and younger son. That morning, Nagano's husband was working inside the Mitsubishi torpedo factory where his father had worked the night before—the same factory where Dō-oh was at the time of the bombing. Out of twenty-six laborers in his area, he was the only one to survive, possibly because he had crawled under a desk.

"My husband told me that he found the ashes of his father, mother, and younger brother lined up on the floor of their house where they were sleeping," Nagano remembered. He never found his sister's remains because he didn't know where she was in the city when she died. After he told Nagano his story, the two never spoke about the bombing again. Like countless other *hibakusha,* they lived a split life: On the outside, they worked, got married, and had children. On the inside, their self-imposed silence helped contain their grief, guilt, and devastating memories of the bombing. Living this divided life allowed them to move on.

———

Taniguchi could not accept the duality of his life as a *hibakusha*. He was a good-looking, hardworking young man, but beneath whatever clothes he wore, the physical scars from the bombing caused him constant pain, and his anger—toward both Japan and the United States—brewed just beneath the surface of his silence. In the early 1950s, as Taniguchi tried to create a normal life, he found himself at the edge of a nascent activist movement that would give him a way to integrate his atomic bomb experiences into his everyday life.

He started gently, talking with his friends at work about his memories of the bombing, his three-and-a-half-year hospitalization, and his current medical conditions. Still, Taniguchi always kept his injuries hidden from their sight. Even in the hot summer, he wore long-sleeved shirts to cover the scars on his arms, and a shirt when he went swimming in the sea—not only to protect his damaged skin from the sun, but also to avoid unwanted stares. "I didn't want people to see my scars," he remembered. "I didn't want them to gawk at me with weird expressions on their faces."

One day, however, at a company-sponsored swimming outing, a younger coworker urged Taniguchi to take off his shirt—not to worry about what people thought because everyone there already knew about his burns. In an early moment of public activism, Taniguchi decided to remove his shirt and allow his peers and their families to see the raised, reddened scars covering his back and arms, and the long, deep indentations in his misshapen chest. "I felt a little embarrassed, so I covered myself a bit with a towel. I was hoping people would understand why my body was like this. I wanted them to know about the war and the atomic bomb."

Taniguchi could not have known how quickly his desire for public awareness would be granted: Within a year, the United States would test the world's first deliverable hydrogen bomb—an event that would ignite international outrage, give birth to Japan's first nationwide campaign for the elimination of nuclear weapons, and bring national attention to the haunting realities of high-dose radiation exposure on *hibakusha*.

The nuclear test took place just before dawn on March 1, 1954, at the United States' Pacific Proving Grounds, located at the northern edge of the Marshall Islands, a 750,000-square-mile region in the South Pacific dotted with more than 1,200 tiny islands with a total combined landmass of only 70 square miles. The hydrogen bomb exploded on Bikini Atoll, a narrow, 3-square-mile crescent-shaped series of minute coral islands around a large lagoon. The bomb's force equaled fifteen million tons of TNT—almost seven hundred times more powerful than the bomb dropped on Nagasaki.

The blast instantly gouged a crater in the island a mile wide and two hundred feet deep. All vegetation on the atoll was destroyed. Within seconds, a fireball nearly 3 miles across rose 8 miles above the ocean, filled with tons of extracted sand, crushed coral, and water. Within ten minutes, the mushroom cloud's diameter spanned 65 miles. U.S. forces had cleared a 60,000-square-mile danger zone around the test site, and residents of Bikini Atoll had already been evacuated years earlier for a 1946 U.S. nuclear test there. The bomb's blast, however, was twice as powerful as scientists had anticipated, and along with an unpredicted shift in wind direction, radioactive fallout ultimately spread more than 7,000 square miles outside the danger zone. Two hundred and thirty-nine islanders, including children, elderly adults, and pregnant mothers, were exposed to radiation on four atolls more than eighty miles east of Bikini. Many developed symptoms of radiation illness. Twenty-eight American meteorological staff were also exposed as they observed the test from an island 155 miles east of the blast.

For Japan, the impact of what nonproliferation advocates call "the worst radiological disaster in the United States' testing history" began on March 14, when a Japanese fishing vessel called the *Daigo Fukuryu Maru* (*Lucky Dragon No. 5*) pulled into its home port at Yaizu, 90 miles south of Tokyo. Two weeks earlier, on the morning of the hydrogen bomb test, the boat had been trawling for tuna about a hundred miles east of Bikini Atoll, outside the authorized exclusion zone. Most of the twenty-three-man crew were on deck and saw the bomb's flash, followed by a huge explosion. Afraid of what they couldn't understand, they quickly reeled in their nets to escape the area. Within three hours, a white radioactive powder—what the Japanese later called *shi no hai* (ashes of death)—began falling from the sky. Within two hours, the white ash covered the boat and the men on board. The deck, they remembered, was covered "thickly enough to show footprints."

When the *Lucky Dragon* arrived at Yaizu after a two-week, 2,500-mile journey, all twenty-three crew members were severely ill with radiation-related symptoms. Two were in such serious condition that they were taken immediately to Tokyo University Hospital, while the other twenty-one were first hospitalized in Yaizu, then transferred to Tokyo. Japan was outraged at the victimization of their citizens by a third U.S. nuclear weapon and infuriated that the Atomic Energy Commission (AEC) denied Japan's request for details about the weapon tested there and the nature of radiation released—information Japanese scientists felt was critical for treating the victims. Contradicting years of refusal to provide medical care to survivors of Hiroshima and Nagasaki, both the ABCC and the AEC offered to treat the *Lucky Dragon* victims. Japanese scientists, however, rejected the offer, not wanting the fishermen to become subjects of another postbomb U.S. military study. American officials were allowed only limited examinations of the victims. Over the next months, many of the *Lucky Dragon* fishermen developed jaundice and other liver disorders, which doctors suspected but could not definitively link to the men's radiation exposure.

The *Lucky Dragon*'s tuna load tested positive for contamination, and although it was destroyed, a radiation panic spread throughout the country. For the first time, Japanese people outside of Nagasaki and Hiroshima feared the human effects of radiation toxicity that had haunted *hibakusha* for nine years. As weeks passed, other fish coming from the South Pacific—contaminated or not—were deemed too risky to consume and were discarded. Fears intensified when higher-than-normal levels of radiation were detected in ground and rain samples at various locations across Japan, presumed to have been caused by some combination of the Bikini test and five other U.S. hydrogen bomb tests conducted in the Marshall Islands within the next two months. In September, the national scare heightened further when the *Lucky Dragon*'s radio operator, Kuboyama Aikichi, died from infectious hepatitis believed to have resulted from blood transfusions he received to treat his radiation exposure.

The remaining *Lucky Dragon* crew members were released from To-kyo hospitals in 1955. Public alarm faded, and examinations of tuna and fishing boats ceased. By that time, anti-American sentiments and citizen opposition to nuclear weapons and testing had escalated into a full-scale national movement. Polls showed that over 75 percent of Japanese people opposed all nuclear weapons testing "under any circumstances." The National Diet adopted resolutions for international control of atomic energy and the abolition of nuclear weapons, and the governing bodies of nearly every city and rural community in the country passed local antinuclear resolutions. Government and private science councils were established to further study the human and environmental effects of radiation exposure and explore potential methods for reducing atomic bomb injuries in the future. A group of housewives in Tokyo began a neighborhood signature drive that quickly developed into a national nonpartisan coalition of school and youth groups, medical associations, trade unions, and businesses that held rallies across the country and gathered thirty-two million signatures—approximately one-third of Ja-pan's population at the time—for a petition against hydrogen bombs.

Stirred by these impassioned protests and Japan's new pacifist iden-tity, the city of Hiroshima organized the First World Conference Against Atomic and Hydrogen Bombs in 1955 to coincide with the tenth anni-versary of the atomic bombings. After an opening-night event that drew 30,000 people to Hiroshima Peace Memorial Park, approximately 1,900 people—including 54 citizen delegates from other nations—participated in the conference inside Hiroshima Peace Memorial Hall. Due to seating limitations, another 1,100 conference participants listened to the speeches through loudspeakers outside the building.

For the first time since the August 1945 bombings, a national spot-light shone on the conditions of the survivors of Hiroshima and Naga-saki. Some *hibakusha* did not appreciate that it had taken ten years and the irradiation of Japanese fishermen in the South Pacific for their country to turn its attention on them. Others, however—exhausted af-ter dealing with persistent illnesses, discrimination, arduous care of sick family members, and the slow and silent struggle to rebuild their lives—welcomed the opportunity to be seen, at least briefly, and to be included in a national movement to ban nuclear weapons. A small number of *hibakusha* from both cities used this national stage to tell their personal stories and fervently appeal for the abolition of nuclear weapons.

Momentum swelled, leading to the Second World Conference Against Atomic and Hydrogen Bombs in Nagasaki in 1956. "It was a powerful and determined movement," recalled Hirose Masahito, a high school teacher who served on the Nagasaki conference's steering committee. "Shop owners donated their money, goods, and services for the conference," another *hibakusha* remembered. Women's groups led the White Rose Campaign, making cloth roses, selling them for a small sum, and donating the proceeds to the conference. Throughout the city, people pinned roses to their shirts and blouses. "Ban the Bomb" signs could be seen at every turn.

On August 9, 1956, the Nagasaki conference convened in the gymnasium of East Nagasaki Senior High School, the largest venue in the city. Three thousand people participated, including thirty-seven representatives of other nations and international organizations. One of the most celebrated moments came when twenty-seven-year-old Watanabe Chieko, paralyzed in the bombing by a falling steel beam that crushed her spine, was carried to the podium by her mother. Held in her mother's arms, Watanabe appealed for *hibakusha* to transcend their suffering and shame to fight for the abolition of atomic and hydrogen bombs. "I called up my anger toward the atomic bomb," she remembered, "anger which had been bottled up inside me for eleven years. I was filled with joy, and all the distorted thoughts, the emptiness and despair hidden inside me were gone." Conference participants applauded vigorously, many of them in tears. For the first time, Watanabe reflected, "I discovered a purpose in my life."

Survivors and citizen activists from across Japan also gathered during the conference to establish local and national antinuclear and *hibakusha* support groups, including the Japan Confederation of A- and H-Bomb Sufferers Organizations (Nihon Hidankyō), Japan's first unified national *hibakusha* membership organization. In its founding declaration, Nihon Hidankyō proclaimed: "Now, eleven long years after the atomic bombing . . . we who were not killed at that moment are finally rising up. . . . Until now, we have remained silent, hidden our faces, and remained separate from one another. But now, no longer able to keep our silence, we join hands at this conference in order to take action." Members set visionary goals to support bans on nuclear weapons, advocate for national health care support, and establish vocational training, educational programs, and financial support programs for *hibakusha* living throughout Japan.

National press coverage of the conference allowed the Japanese people to finally hear the voices of Nagasaki *hibakusha,* and international conference participants spread the word abroad about survivors and their conditions. A Japanese antinuclear activist expressed his shock over the many adversities *hibakusha* had endured for more than ten years without government support. An American pastor who had attended the event told conference organizer Hirose Masahito that he had thought that everyone in Hiroshima and Nagasaki had died from burns and radiation exposure—so he was surprised to find out that *hibakusha* even existed.

Revelations like these emboldened small numbers of survivors in the newly born *hibakusha* movement to speak out and let their stories be heard. Like Watanabe, they felt a new and transcendent purpose for their lives: From now on, they would share their memories as a means to help people affected by the bombs and to fight for the total elimination of nuclear weapons. Yamaguchi Senji was one of these early activists. Fourteen years old at the time of the bombing, Yamaguchi was digging a ditch outside the Mitsubishi Ōhashi weapons factory and sustained extensive burns across the right side of his arms, chest, neck, and face. When the city of Nagano invited *hibakusha* representatives to speak to local antinuclear activists, Yamaguchi stood at a lectern inside the city library. In front of a standing-room-only crowd, he told his story in public for the first time. "There was dead silence as I spoke," he remembered. "Everyone listened attentively to my story. . . . Sometimes I heard people sobbing." Overcome with emotion that people finally understood what he had suffered for so long in silence, Yamaguchi began crying, too—then he spontaneously took off his shirt to fully expose the keloid scars spread across his upper body.

Taniguchi's work schedule had prevented him from attending the Nagasaki conference, but buoyed by accounts of young *hibakusha* speaking out, he, too, decided to venture beyond his friends at work and tell his story to people he didn't know. His first public speaking engagement was at the invitation of the Japan Telecommunication Workers' Union, an experience that inspired him to speak again whenever he could. During this period in his life, he continued to suffer intense pain and fatigue. At one particularly desperate moment, when Taniguchi contemplated ending his life, a critical shift in his perspective occurred. He sensed a significance to his survival even as it came with great suffering. "At that moment," he remembered, "I realized that I must live on behalf of those who died unwillingly."

Taniguchi joined a small group of young men, including Yamaguchi and later Yoshida, who had begun gathering informally in the early 1950s to share their experiences. All of them had been children or teenagers at the time of the bombing and had suffered severe injuries, burns, radiation-related illness, and loss of family members. The group provided the support and camaraderie the men needed to speak at a deeply personal level about their medical conditions, ongoing physical pain, discrimination, and jobs. They shared with one another bits of information they heard from their individual doctors about how radiation exposure was affecting their bodies. A similar group of young *hibakusha* women, including Watanabe, had also been meeting to discuss their postbomb challenges. Together they knit and made *zōka* (artificial flowers) as a way for their physically disabled members to earn money from home.

The two groups merged in 1956 to become the Nagasaki Atomic Bomb Youth Association. As nonnuclear nations across the globe raced to produce their first nuclear weapons, and as the United States, the Soviet Union, and Britain tested increasingly more powerful weapons aboveground, in the oceans, and hundreds of miles above the earth, this small group of survivors forged deep friendships and determined that they had no choice but to stand up individually and collectively to inform all who would listen about the horrendous realities of nuclear weapons. Taniguchi's commitment to this group and the larger antinuclear movement grew. "Unless we bomb victims ourselves tell what really happened," he thought, "how can others know the suffering engendered by war and the horrors of the atomic bomb? It is our responsibility to gather our courage and bear witness to what we experienced."

Taniguchi Sumiteru and Yoshida Katsuji at a meeting with Hiroshima activists, ca. 1961. (*Courtesy of Yoshida Naoji*)

As his political awareness intensified, Taniguchi turned twenty-six and began thinking about marriage. His grandmother, too, now ill and confined to bed, was anxious to see him married and well cared for before she died. For Taniguchi, however, the same *hibakusha* identity that empowered him as an activist minimized his chances for marriage, especially because of his extensive injuries and scars.

Taniguchi's grandfather prepared a list of prospects. One by one, his family and marriage brokers told the truth about his *hibakusha* status and

injuries to prospective wives and their families. Taniguchi was rejected
again and again. Some women were kind in their refusals; others were
harsh. "How can you imagine that I would marry someone with your
injuries?" they said. "You can't even look forward to a long life!" Taniguchi was disheartened. Unbeknownst to him, his family decided to minimize his conditions in their next discussion with a potential wife.

Taniguchi's aunt (surname Osa), had a friend with an unmarried daughter named Eiko, whom Osa was convinced would be a fine and caring wife
for her nephew. In her midtwenties, Eiko lived in the small fishing village
of Togitsu, north of Nagasaki. When she was a child, her father had taken
their family to live in Japanese-occupied Korea. Her two older brothers
were killed in action in the Pacific War, and as a teenager Eiko had contributed to Japan's war efforts by repairing soldiers' uniforms. After the war,
she and her family returned to Togitsu and were stunned to see the extent
of Nagasaki's destruction. Eiko finished school and helped farm her family's quarter-acre plot, which provided them food and a small income.

Osa paid a visit to Eiko's farm, where she promoted Taniguchi's
strengths. She told Eiko and her mother that the scars on Taniguchi's
arms and legs were barely visible and that he had undergone restorative
surgery on his face to repair scar tissue. She did not mention that his facial scars had been caused by long-term bedsores, that his arm was permanently injured, or that his back was a large mass of scar tissue and his
chest was covered with deep indentations. To follow up on her visit, Osa
took Taniguchi to the small restaurant where Eiko worked part-time as a
cook. They first observed Eiko in the kitchen without making their presence known, then Osa called Eiko to their table to meet her nephew. To
Eiko, the fully dressed Taniguchi looked no different from any other man.
In time, she declined the proposal without giving a reason. Osa was persistent, however, and finally persuaded Eiko to change her mind.

Taniguchi and Eiko were married on March 19, 1956, at his grandparents' house, where they met each other's families for the first time;
Taniguchi's father, older brother, and sister had traveled from Osaka
for the occasion. After the ceremony, Taniguchi and Eiko drove together to City Hall to register their marriage, then returned to the house
where Taniguchi's friends joined them for a celebration. From her bedside that night, Taniguchi's grandmother thanked Eiko for marrying
her grandson and taking good care of him. Her words piqued Eiko's

curiosity because they echoed similar statements of concern and gratitude she had heard from Taniguchi's family and friends throughout the day.

Taniguchi had suspected that Eiko had not been told about the burns on his back, and his anxiety grew as the time she would learn the truth drew closer. The couple spent their first night at his grandmother's house, where they slept in separate beds. The next day, however, they traveled by bus to a rural mountain inn in Unzen, about thirty-five miles east of Nagasaki, for a short honeymoon. That evening in the Japanese *ofuro* (bath), Taniguchi and Eiko sat on stools opposite each other to wash their bodies before entering the deep tub to soak. Taniguchi quietly asked Eiko to wash his back. Then he turned around. "She had thought that I was like other people," he said. From behind him, Eiko began to weep, and she didn't stop crying through most of the night and the following day. Taniguchi was afraid that she would leave him.

On the morning of the third day, the two departed for home. Taniguchi's family was waiting anxiously, doubting that he and Eiko would return as a couple. To everyone's amazement, however, Eiko stayed with her new husband, putting aside her initial anger at his aunt for holding back the truth of his injuries. She later told Taniguchi that she had realized that if she left, he would have no one else to take care of him.

His grandmother died less than two weeks later. Taniguchi and his grandfather wheeled her tiny body on a cart to the city crematorium, and later the family carried her urn to a Buddhist temple in Nagayo, just north over the mountains from Nagasaki, to store her ashes at their family's gravesite. Taniguchi and Eiko lived with his grandfather in the house in which Taniguchi was raised. The damaged tissue across his back remained a source of constant pain.

Within three years, he and Eiko became parents to a son and a daughter. Taniguchi continued to tell his story in public, but he never spoke with his children about the bombing and how he survived. As was typical in Japanese family life, though, he often bathed with his young children, so at an early age they, like their mother, became accustomed to his patchy, scar-covered back and arms, and the deep hollows in his chest.

———

Potential marriage partners were right to worry about survivors' long-term health conditions. Even ten years after the bombings, *hibakusha* were experiencing excessive occurrences of numerous medical conditions, including blood, cardiovascular, liver, and endocrinological disorders; low blood cell counts; severe anemia; thyroid disorders; internal organ damage; cataracts; and premature aging. Many survivors suffered multiple illnesses at the same time. Countless others experienced a generalized, unexplainable malaise—later nicknamed *bura-bura* (aimless) disease—with symptoms including overall poor health, constant fatigue, and, according to survivors' physicians, "insufficient mental energy to carry on their work."

Cancer rates rose again. Childhood leukemia rates had peaked between 1950 and 1953, but since then, adult leukemia cases had increased beyond normal levels, a situation that would not change for decades. By 1955, other cancers had also begun to occur at rates far higher than for non-*hibakusha*. Thyroid cancer incidences rose in the 1960s, and within the next five years, stomach and lung cancer rates escalated. Incidences of liver, colon, bladder, ovary, and skin cancers, among others, also increased. Women exposed within three-quarters of a mile from the hypocenter were 3.3 times more likely to develop breast cancer than the general population; those who had been exposed as children were at highest risk. Without a reliable means to assess their own risk, survivors remained constantly watchful of every physical symptom they developed, dreading the insidious effects that the bomb's invisible and omnipresent radiation might inflict on their bodies.

Riding the swell of antinuclear protests and world conferences, *hibakusha* activists turned to this critical issue of the atomic bombings' unique and ongoing medical effects. Most of their conditions were not covered by Japan's national health insurance plan. Further, a clause in the San Francisco Peace Treaty barred Japan from suing the United States for damages. Taniguchi, Yamaguchi, and others began a long and contentious fight for domestic health care laws to provide financial support for *hibakusha* medical expenses.

They had no shortage of data to support their petitions. Tens of thousands had died from their injuries and radiation exposure after the official fatality count for the end of 1945. Thousands more remained ill. In the late 1950s and 1960s, physicians and scientists at the rebuilt Nagasaki University School of Medicine and other local and national institutions had continued comprehensive studies of many *hibakusha* medical conditions. The city of Nagasaki established a municipal tumor registry to store thousands of radiation-related specimens from surviving and deceased *hibakusha* for ongoing research. Between 1959 and 1967, Dr. Shirabe alone authored or coauthored six studies on the characteristics and treatment of thermal burn scars, thyroid and breast tumors, thyroid cancers, and keloid scars. The ABCC in both cities amassed immense quantities of *hibakusha* medical data from its population-based studies. Combined, the Japanese and ABCC studies clearly demonstrated a correlation between survivors' estimated radiation dosages and their risk for various cancers—conclusions that would be confirmed by decades of continued studies. Verifying what survivors already knew, the data provided evidence of the overwhelming need for ongoing, specialized *hibakusha* medical care.

At the local level, the city of Nagasaki coordinated with the Japanese Red Cross Society to construct the 81-bed Nagasaki Atomic Bomb Hospital, which began operations in 1958 with specialized departments including internal medicine, surgery, pediatrics, gynecology, and ophthalmology. In its first seven years of operation, the hospital served 2,646 inpatient and 41,858 outpatient survivors; by 1977, it had expanded to 360 beds. Other facilities, too, opened to provide *hibakusha* medical support as well as job training, housing, and senior care.

Still, medical facilities and social service organizations had not yet caught up with the continuing health risks of whole-body radiation exposure—and even if they had, most *hibakusha* could not have afforded the care they required. To address these concerns, as early as 1952, groups of Nagasaki citizens had established *hibakusha* support groups and initiated widespread fund-raising campaigns to provide physical checkups and treatment at no cost or for a prorated fee for survivors experiencing financial hardship. The mayors of Nagasaki and Hiroshima also sent a petition to the National Diet appealing for medical care for survivors. In response, the Japanese government allocated modest funds from its 1954–1956 budgets to various medical institutions to cover *hibakusha* surveys, medical research, and publication of study outcomes.

In 1956, Nagasaki's small group of activists, including Taniguchi and Yamaguchi, established the city's largest peer-run *hibakusha* organization, the Nagasaki Atomic Bomb Survivors Council (Hisaikyō). In addition to advocating for the elimination of nuclear weapons, Hisaikyō members fought for recognition of *hibakusha* medical conditions, national aid to cover their health care costs, and services to support survivors' self-reliance. A similar organization was founded in Hiroshima. Survivor activists in both cities went door-to-door to collect donations for *hibakusha* health care relief and traveled to Tokyo to meet with Diet members and the prime minister to tell their stories and impress on them the need for a universal *hibakusha* health care law. "At last, an organization to voice our demands had been created," Yamaguchi remembered. "We proposed that since the Japanese government started the war, it should take responsibility for the victims of the bombings. That's what we wanted."

Their first victory came within a year. In 1957, the Japanese government passed the Atomic Bomb Victims Medical Care Law, providing funding for semiannual medical examinations for officially designated *hibakusha*—defined as anyone who had been within city limits at the time of the bombings, those in areas where black rain fell, children affected by in utero radiation exposure, and rescue workers and others who came into the city within the first two weeks. The law also provided treatment for a few sanctioned radiation-related illnesses such as leukemia.

But the government's stringent requirements for official *hibakusha* designation were discouraging to many *hibakusha*. In addition to a written application, survivors were required to submit either a certified statement by a public official or a photograph proving their specific location at the time of the bombing—both of which were immensely difficult to obtain. Alternatively, but equally challenging, applicants could submit written certification from two different people "excluding blood relatives to the third degree" swearing to their location at the time of the bomb. If no other proof was available, survivors were allowed, under oath, to submit written statements of their locations at the time of the bombing—but they still needed to find someone "who actually met the applicant somewhere in the city, or saw him or her at a relief station inside or outside the city, or fled with him or her to a safer place immediately after the bombing" *and* was willing to testify in writing to these facts. Despite these daunting requirements, by the end of the first year, 200,984 Nagasaki and Hiroshima *hibakusha* were issued a passport-size *techo,* a booklet that identified them as eligible for benefits. "One little handbook," Yamaguchi remembered. "But how much suffering we had had to go through before we could get it. . . . I gripped that A-Bomb Victims Health Book firmly in my hand."

For Taniguchi and others, however, Japan's early *hibakusha* health care law was profoundly inadequate, leaving thousands without support. Even after completing the problematic application process, *hibakusha* had to request consideration for claims relating to a condition on the government's list of sanctioned diseases. Their personal accounts and backup documentation—including medical records and estimated radiation doses (if available)—were reviewed by a government panel of experts who applied a strict formula to determine the "probability of causation" that radiation was the likely cause of their conditions. Few were approved. Activists contended that many more diseases than authorized by the medical care law could be linked to radiation exposure, including psychological conditions and an overall weakening of the body from damage to the blood, bone marrow, or organ tissues that caused secondary diseases and disorders. Delayed recuperation from disease or illness also resulted in increased medical costs and loss of wages.

Government officials resisted activists' efforts to expand benefits, fearing potentially huge expenditures to cover *hibakusha* medical care and potential implications of Japan's war responsibility. *Hibakusha* activists also believed that Japan evaded increasing survivors' benefits in order to avoid alienating the United States as a key economic and military ally. All Japanese citizens should endure the sacrifices of the war equally, officials argued, and the provision of compensation to *hibakusha* for conditions other than those directly proved to be radiation-related would require similar compensation to victims of incendiary bombings across the nation. These assertions contradicted the government's own 1965 survey of *techo* holders, which statistically confirmed higher occurrence rates for *hibakusha* medical conditions and disabilities compared with victims of traditional bombings. Families with a member suffering an atomic bomb–related physical disability incurred medical costs 3.5 times higher than the national average.

Four key issues complicated the government's deliberations to increase *hibakusha* health care benefits. The first was the need to determine accurate radiation doses for survivors in order to define parameters for eligibility and show that any current or future health conditions were the likely result of radiation exposure. Technologies to accurately measure radiation doses in the human body, however, did not exist; instead, U.S. and Japanese scientists developed tentative dosimetry systems to estimate what an individual survivor's radiation dose might have been. For the first system, introduced in 1957, scientists used complex calculations from the ABCC—in consultation with the Oak Ridge National Laboratory and data from the Nevada atomic bomb test site—to analyze survivors' locations and distances from the hypocenter at the time of the blast, their positions relative to neighboring structures, and the direction they were facing. For those who had been indoors at the time of the bombings, scientists evaluated the size and location of the houses or buildings they had been in, their orientation to the hypocenter, and the individual's distance from any windows. Based on further studies, an updated measurement tool was introduced in 1965.

These dosimetry systems were far from perfect in determining individual *hibakusha* radiation doses. Rather than being able to rely on controlled experiments, scientists had to use information provided by survivors' memories twelve years after experiencing an extreme traumatic event. Dosage assessments for survivors who had been in locations outside the scope of the ABCC's various studies could not be determined. Even with the best estimates available, scientists could not assess how each organ in each individual survivor may have been affected differently, the degree to which high levels of radiation attenuated over time within the body, or when or what kind of long-term effects would appear for any single individual. "Consequently," Taniguchi explained, "there are no complete conclusions about the side effects from the atomic bomb. No matter what anyone says, I don't know if sometime in the future my body will develop symptoms linked to my exposure to radiation."

Another challenge to the government's determination of eligibility for benefits related to *residual* radiation exposure—a possibility for Nagasaki residents who had been in Nishiyama-machi, where black rain fell, or who had entered the hypocenter area in the hours and days after the bombing to carry corpses, assist with medical relief, or search for family members. Studies in Nishiyama-machi, for example, showed residents' leukocyte levels were higher than normal, and at least two cases of leukemia were documented by 1970. No further adverse medical effects appeared after the mid-1970s, but some researchers remain cautious, believing that such effects could still surface at a future time. Innumerable adults and children who had come into the city after the bombing had reported immediate symptoms, including high fevers, diarrhea, and hair loss, similar to *hibakusha* who had been in the city at the time of the blasts—and countless experienced various medical conditions in the months and years that followed—including tumors, liver disorders, miscarriages, various cancers, and other illnesses with no identifiable causes. Many died at early ages from conditions their families attributed to radiation exposure.

Scientific studies have been unable to provide firm estimates of these survivors' residual radiation absorption because calculations require the evaluation of many complex factors that are difficult to accurately assess based solely on a survivor's memory—including the person's age, date of entry, length of time spent near the hypocenter, and the nature of their activities. Recent studies, however, indicate potential "significant exposure" for those in the hypocenter area within a week's time, findings that scientists are working to replicate and verify. Even without scientific proof of their radiation exposure, activists were able to negotiate agreement from the Japanese government to increase health care coverage for people who entered areas within 1.25 miles of the hypocenter of either city within two weeks of the bombings. The United States maintains its early postwar assessment that induced radioactivity near the hypocenters was minimal and did not cause harm.

The third complicating factor in the government's ability to address survivors' health care demands related to *hibakusha* living overseas. This included both Japanese and Korean, Chinese, and other non-Japanese *hibakusha* who had returned to their home nations or immigrated to other countries, all of whom had suffered from cancers and illnesses at the same rate as *hibakusha* in Japan. From the early years of the health care law, Japanese *hibakusha* living abroad were eligible for benefits, but only if they came back to Japan for treatment. In far greater numbers, thousands of foreign nationals who had survived the bombings and returned home after the war did not become eligible for health care support until 1978— and even then they were required to travel to Japan for treatments covered by the law, an impossible endeavor for all but a few. *Hibakusha* in East Asia often lived—and died—in impoverished rural areas totally isolated from doctors with any knowledge of the atomic bomb or its radiation effects. Many were discriminated against for their visible injuries, lack of skill in their native languages, or for being perceived as "pro-Japanese" by virtue of their having lived in Japan during the war. Their suffering was often ignored because their compatriots approved of the atomic bombings as events that had led to their liberation from Japanese rule. Some Korean *hibakusha* returned to Japan illegally to seek medical care or to search for two witnesses to support their eligibility for health care coverage, only to be deported without consideration of their atomic bomb–related conditions. *Hibakusha* activists in other nations, including the United States, worked for years with advocates in Nagasaki and Hiroshima to address, with incremental success, their atomic bomb–related medical needs.

Finally, the Japanese government had to determine health care eligibility for the tens of thousands of foreign (primarily Korean) *hibakusha* who had remained in Japan after the war. After years of wartime abuses followed by the atomic bombings, these *hibakusha* faced widespread anti-Korean sentiment in Japan and were legally barred from Japanese citizenship—even those who had fought for Japan during the war or had been born in Japan after their parents were forcefully relocated there. Like other *hibakusha*, they experienced employment and marriage discrimination. A 1965 treaty between South Korea and Japan barred Korean *hibakusha* from pressing for reparations against the Japanese government. Many became destitute due to their high medical costs and the absence of extended families to turn to for support. In the words of Kim Masako, a Korean survivor who was twenty-four years old at the time of the bombing, "It is not good we have two home countries."

Korean *hibakusha* organized in 1967 to fight for recognition, medical care, and compensation. After eleven years of petitions and court battles, Japan amended its *hibakusha* health care law to allow foreign-born survivors living in Japan to apply for the same health care benefits as Japanese survivors. By this time, however, hospital records and other required documentation from the 1940s were impossible to obtain. The new law also required that at least one of their witnesses be Japanese, a further barrier for Korean *hibakusha* because in 1945 most Koreans had lived and worked separately from the mainstream communities in Nagasaki and Hiroshima. Ryong Pak Su, one of an estimated ten thousand to twelve thousand Korean survivors of the Nagasaki bombing, explained, "All my neighbors died of the bomb. How could you bring them? Bring a ghost?"

Exasperated but undeterred, Taniguchi, Yamaguchi, and a small number of other young Japanese and foreign *hibakusha* activists continued to file petitions and lawsuits, lead sit-ins, meet with parliament members, and conduct nationwide campaigns to solicit citizen support for comprehensive surveys on *hibakusha* medical and economic conditions. Even as they struggled with their own medical challenges, they fought for complete health care support for all *hibakusha*—no matter what their nationality, health status, or distance from the hypocenter. They believed that full health care coverage and monetary compensation would signify the Japanese government's resounding acknowledgment of the terrifying, invisible, and long-term realities of atomic bombs. They often linked their health care efforts with their fight to eradicate nuclear weapons within their lifetimes. In a speech at a 1980 rally, Yamaguchi declared, "Our demand for the immediate enactment of a law for relief of all *Hibakusha* is not only a *Hibakusha* demand, but also the demand of all people in Japan, and of the whole world, for 'No More *Hibakusha*!'"

Over time, their activism resulted in multiple expansions of health care coverage to include previously denied *hibakusha*. Microcephaly was officially recognized as an atomic bomb–related disease, and later, compensation was granted to support microcephalic survivors' nonmedical living expenses. The distance from the hypocenter was increased for special cases based on physical examinations. New diseases were approved for coverage, and limited support was provided for nursing care, burials, and health maintenance and living allowances for survivors with particularly severe radiation-related illnesses. Still, both within and beyond Japan's borders, government support came too late for many survivors, including those who died before their cancers or other illnesses were designated as radiation-related conditions, and those who found it impossible to find two people to verify their location at the time of the bombing. Many survivors—in some cases even those with cancer—never applied out of continuing fear that self-identifying as *hibakusha* would result in discrimination for themselves or their children.

For his part, Taniguchi spent his days off from work helping *hibakusha* understand the law, assemble the required documentation, and complete their applications for health care handbooks. He did this even though he didn't need coverage for himself. His now-privatized company, Dendenkousha (Nippon Telegraph and Telephone Public Corporation), provided medical benefits to employees who were injured while working at the time of the bombing. To receive his company benefits, however, Taniguchi had to prove that his injuries had resulted from the bomb, so he returned to Ōmura National Hospital to try to find his medical records. After a long search with the help of hospital staff, Taniguchi entered a storage area and found a single file containing his records—more than forty pages of notes by his Ōmura doctors and nurses, all in German (the language used in Japan at the time for medical terminology). Each entry detailed his medical condition, test results, and treatments. Scattered line drawings of his body showed the locations of his burns and the holes in his chest.

Taniguchi's was the only *hibakusha* medical record there. Rumors had circulated that other *hibakusha* records had been burned or relocated somewhere in Japan, but no one could say for sure what had actually happened to them. Taniguchi is convinced that the U.S. government took them either to the ABCC or back to the United States, and that his record was left behind only because he had still been in the hospital at the time. Taniguchi took photographs of his wounds, attached them to a photocopy of his Ōmura medical record, and submitted them to Dendenkousha. He was approved for benefits, which meant that all of his examinations, surgeries, and treatment for atomic bomb–related injuries and illnesses were paid for by his company until his retirement.

Taniguchi was fortunate to have coverage, because his medical needs persisted, requiring regular trips to the hospital for blood tests and multiple surgeries. In 1960, doctors extracted an intensely painful skin cancer growth on his back, and for a while his pain diminished. A year later, at the invitation of East Germany, he traveled to Berlin for surgery on his left elbow to increase mobility of his arm. While he was there, Taniguchi spoke publicly about his experiences and showed his audience a collection of postbomb photographs. After three months, he was diagnosed with a chronic blood disorder and surgery was deemed impossible. Taniguchi returned home, his condition unchanged.

A new, much tougher and larger growth appeared on his back in 1965, and Taniguchi began losing strength. "It always felt like I was lying on a soft futon that had a rock in it," he remembered. "It was so hard that when a surgical knife was put to it, it dulled the blade to the point that it couldn't cut anymore." After numerous surgeries, the tumor was finally removed, but Taniguchi was unable to sustain his job delivering telegrams, so he was transferred to an office job within the company. Every summer, he felt a constant dull pain in his back, "a terrible heaviness," he said. Every winter he was perpetually cold because his body could not retain warmth. He remained extremely thin because he could eat only small amounts of food; anything more triggered a painful whole-body sensation—the feeling that the thin, tight skin covering his wounds was going to split open.

When Dō-oh left Nagasaki in 1956, she had willed herself a new life, far removed from her home, her family, and her city's nuclear devastation. In order to succeed, the twenty-six-year-old chose to conceal her *hibakusha* status. She was again in hiding, but this time, Dō-oh drew on her sense of purpose to construct a new and powerful identity that allowed her to overcome, at least in part, the harsh memories of her adolescence.

After a thirty-six-hour train trip, Dō-oh had arrived in Tokyo and proceeded to a tiny, two-hundred-square-foot apartment with no kitchen that her company, Utena, had located for her. She purchased a rice cooker, a bowl, and chopsticks—and to store her food, she carried home two apple crates from a neighborhood vendor. Her apartment was close enough to Utena's offices that she could walk to work—and on her first day, Dō-oh had passed through the company's large main gate, straightened her posture, and directed herself to her assigned division of six hundred low-level workers. She felt she had to work twice as hard as others to overcome her handicap. "Then I could be like other people," she thought. "I worked like crazy. . . . I asked them to give me all the work no one else wanted to do."

At home, Dō-oh made her own clothing—sophisticated and chic. She wrote letters to her family, and once a year, she made the long trip home to see them. Her father often teased her, saying that he'd always wished she had been a boy—meaning, perhaps, that she had a strong personality and he would have liked to banter with her about things he wouldn't otherwise have talked about with women. When he died in 1961, Dō-oh paused beside his coffin. "I felt that life is very fragile," she recalled. "People are born alone and die alone."

She returned to Tokyo and continued to take on hard tasks, living out an internal crusade to demonstrate what she could achieve. Her efforts were rewarded with promotions. When she was transferred into the public relations department, Dō-oh's campaign region included nearly all of the main island of Honshu north of Tokyo, requiring that she travel by train and bus to villages so remote that she was surprised any cosmetics store would even exist there.

Every August, national media coverage of atomic bomb commemorations that often focused on *hibakusha* disabilities and radiation-related diseases reinforced Dō-oh's vow of secrecy about her past. She always wore long sleeves in public to hide her scarred arms. To avoid any questions about her health, she tried never to miss work, even when she was ill—a choice that resulted in her collapsing from exhaustion and high fever nearly every New Year holiday. Sometimes she wanted to give up. "When I wavered in my determination to succeed, or when I had a hard time," she remembered, "I reproached myself for this weakness. . . . I could not afford to spoil myself. These were battles against myself. I felt no regret afterwards because they helped me cultivate courage."

Dō-oh was in her midthirties—well past a Japanese woman's typical marriageable age—when she was invited in 1965 to meet a potential husband, a man who worked for a stock market company. Until then, she had turned away from the idea of marriage, but at that moment, she was feeling tired and uneasy about her future. She agreed to the meeting.

At first glance, Dō-oh liked how the man looked. He made a strong initial impression. He asked her where she was from.

"Nagasaki," she answered, knowing what his next question would be.

"Did you experience the bomb?"

Dō-oh paused. She did not want to marry someone by lying. "Yes," she answered, "*hibaku shimashita* [I experienced the bomb]."

A tension rose between them, and Dō-oh sensed that this man did not want to marry a *hibakusha*. To preempt what she anticipated as his rejection, Dō-oh turned down further discussions with him and quietly resolved never to marry. As she grew older, she reflected on the unconscious influences that guided her to this significant decision: She had feared having a deformed child, she explained—and at a very personal level, her haunting memories, sense of interior contamination, and pressing guilt for stepping over people's bodies in the Mitsubishi factory had diminished her sense of confidence with people outside of work.

Letting go of the possibility of marriage and children, Dō-oh adjusted to what she called her "good life." She worked long hours—and in a workplace filled with beautiful women, she established a strong personal image of elegance and style. She searched for her own life mission that could fill the void of never becoming a mother and found renewed

Dō-oh Mineko, age sixty-four, ca. 1994. (*Courtesy of Okada Ikuyo*)

purpose in striving to fulfill her maximum potential. "If I was a flower that couldn't bloom," she thought, "then at least I wanted to bloom in my mind. At least I wanted to have a brilliant mind."

After seventeen years at Utena, in 1973, forty-three-year-old Dō-oh became the first woman executive in the company's sixty-year history—a remarkable feat by any account, but particularly in a culture of male dominance in which only an estimated 8 percent of the entire female workforce in Japan held professional or managerial positions. Within the huge Japanese cosmetics industry, there were only three women executives: one at Shiseido, one at Kanebo, and Dō-oh at Utena. The story of her promotion appeared in national newspapers and magazines, and she was interviewed for television newscasts. In her new position directing a staff of 350 and supervising the training of new employees, Dō-oh was able to purchase a small house in an area beyond central Tokyo, near a station that allowed her to take a limited express train to and from work each day. "It was my small castle," she remembered, "proof of my life and the results of my efforts. . . . I was thankful for this reward."

In private, Dō-oh composed haiku and tanka, developing a practice of reflection that allowed her to dwell on the world around her with a sense of wonder. One evening, on her way home from a business meeting in Hokkaido, she peered out the window of the plane. The sky was dull and overcast—"a field of black clouds," Dō-oh called it. When she looked up, however, the sky above her was clear and blue, with scattered white clouds tinged with red and orange as they reflected the setting sun. "It was so beautiful that I cried," she remembered. "That glorious world moved me." Although she did not believe in God, she imagined that perhaps there did exist "a refuge or heaven beyond my view." In that moment, Dō-oh relaxed, temporarily, from the constant strain of proving herself to the world.

———

By the early 1960s, many of the Urakami Valley's obvious signs of atomic destruction had faded. The mountains to the east and west that were stripped of vegetation and houses nearly twenty years earlier were green and lush, with new residences scattered all around. Students filled the restored classrooms at Shiroyama and Yamazato elementary schools, and new, wider roads accommodated increased automobile traffic. Hypocenter Park was enlarged and lined with Japanese cedars, and in one corner stood the last remaining sections of the crushed brick wall and original bell tower of Urakami Church. Against the protests of Catholic and other *hibakusha* organizations that sought to preserve the church ruins as a symbol of the destroyed city, Nagasaki officials had ordered the wreckage to be torn down. In its place northeast of the hypocenter stood a new reinforced concrete church with two ninety-five-foot-high bell towers—sixteen feet higher than the former structure—paid for by donations from Japanese and U.S. Catholic groups. In 1962, the church was consecrated as a cathedral and became the seat of the bishop for the Archdiocese of Nagasaki—although due to a shortage of funds, the cathedral's stained-glass windows were not yet installed, and the walls and ceilings remained unfinished.

Unlike those of his city, Yoshida's visible atomic bomb injuries did not fade with time. He had undergone multiple surgeries on his mouth intended to increase his ability to eat, but he still could not open it wide enough for anything but tiny pieces of food. He had held buckets of sand for thirteen years to straighten his curled fingers, but his hands still cramped frequently and he couldn't control his fingers curling back into fists. The flesh on the tops of his hands bulged and cracked each winter, causing extreme pain. His facial disfigurement elicited constant stares.

After years of anguish and constant reminders of his *hibakusha* identity, in the early 1960s, Yoshida made a choice to be happy. He realized that no matter how much he worried and fretted, he could never erase the experience of nuclear war or get back the face and body he used to have. "I resolved to make the best of the situation," he explained. Turning away from the deep sense of gloom that had pervaded his thoughts since the bombing, he began identifying positive aspects to his life, starting with the many people who had helped him over the years even as they, too, had suffered.

Every morning, Yoshida applied medical ointment to the transplanted skin on his face and headed to work at the wholesale food company. Over time, he began stepping out of the safety of the warehouse and visiting small shops to take their orders. He played on his company's early morning baseball team and gained a reputation as a fast runner and a strong hitter; at one point—even with the limitations of his swing because of his rib injuries—Yoshida had the highest batting average on the team. At his company's family sports days, he ran three-legged races with his coworkers. In early acts of public activism, he served as secretary-general of the Nagasaki Atomic Bomb Youth Association and was one of thirty-seven *hibakusha* who contributed to its testimony collection, *Mou, iya da!* [We've Had Enough!]. People thought of him as very *akarui* (bright).

Yoshida Katsuji, age thirty-one, ca. early 1960s. (*Courtesy of Yoshida Naoji*)

Yoshida gradually became comfortable talking with everyone around him, and he was known for his congeniality and lifelong friendships. He was stubborn, judgmental, and bossy—he hated arrogance, unions, and *hibakusha* who talked about their political views—and his vocal criticism of others often challenged or embarrassed his family and friends. But at parties, he drank beer and sake and entertained people with bad puns and imitations of famous singers. Photographs show a dapper young man looking straight into the camera—very cool—and in a radical change from earlier years when girls had cried at the sight of him, Yoshida became extremely popular among many young women, none of whom seemed at all concerned by his scarred face and black ear patch.

Even with his great popularity, Yoshida's disfigurement impeded his chances to marry. When he was thirty, his mother made a call on his behalf to a distant village outside of Nagasaki to discuss his possible

Yoshida Katsuji, with Sachiko, wedding photo, 1962. (*Courtesy of Yoshida Naoji*)

marriage to her sister-in-law's daughter, Sachiko. Yoshida was delighted, especially because Sachiko had already seen a photo of him, so he knew that she wouldn't be shocked when they met. They went on one date—to a movie—but Yoshida had already made up his mind: "I asked her if she wanted to marry me and she said she would. I was pretty lucky!"

They married in 1962. In their early years together, they lived with Yoshida's mother, who often criticized Sachiko, causing strain in their marriage because Yoshida often took his mother's side—perhaps out of filial loyalty, and also because he felt he owed his mother his life.

In the months and years that followed, Yoshida and Sachiko spoke only once about his experiences on the day of the bombing. Many years later, she told him that though they had been sleeping in the same bed every night, in those early days of their marriage she hadn't been able to look at his face because of his injuries. "I cried," Yoshida remembered. "I had a face that my own wife couldn't look at." Eventually, though, he learned to shrug it off. "No matter what I do, even if I cry or scream, my face won't get better," he said. "And compared to back then, I think I became a really good-looking guy! I think whoever tries to laugh at himself first will win the game. Yes. That's why I'm always smiling."

When his two sons, Naoji and Tomoji, were young, Yoshida spent as much time as he could with them, playing catch, going swimming, and taking them everywhere he went on his days off. Contrary to the choices of many *hibakusha* parents, he told his sons about his atomic bomb experiences as soon as he thought they were old enough to understand. Over and over, he taught them not to hide from the truth if anyone asked what had happened to him.

But the boys didn't oblige. Every time they brought friends home, one child or another would look at Yoshida and blurt out, "Your father has a black face!"—and Naoji and Tomoji would fall silent.

"My sons didn't say *anything*," Yoshida said. "So I would explain to the children what had happened to me. I showed them a photograph of myself from elementary school, before I was injured, to help them understand."

One day at Tomoji's school, everything changed. During a break in the all-school sports day, the children in Tomoji's class were sitting with their parents in a circle on the ground eating lunch together, when some of the children began staring at Yoshida. One boy called out to Tomoji, "Tomo-chan! Your father has an awful face, huh!"

Oh, my God! Yoshida thought. *It would have been better if I hadn't come!*

But this time, Tomoji spoke up for his father. "My daddy was hurt by the atomic bomb," he told his friend. "It's nothing scary!"

"I felt so grateful to my son," Yoshida recalled, recounting every detail of that day and every word his son uttered on his behalf.

"I was saved," he said. "I was saved by my son's words."

CHAPTER 8

AGAINST FORGETTING

Forty-one-year-old Taniguchi was glancing through the pages of a summer 1970 *Asahi Graph* when suddenly he stopped and fixated on a two-page color photograph of himself from 1946. This was the magazine's special edition commemorating the twenty-fifth anniversary of the atomic bombings, and there he was, lying facedown on a bed inside Ōmura National Hospital, his back and arms raw and infected, his shorn head resting against crumpled bedsheets, and the lower half of his face darkened in shadow. He leaned in closer to read the tiny print of the photo's caption. It described where the boy in the photo had been at the time of the bombing and informed readers that despite the severity of his injuries, he had not only survived but was also now married with two children. Visceral anguish coursed through Taniguchi's body. For months, he could not shake the impact of seeing that amplified photo or the memories it brought back of unrelenting pain every moment of every day for more than three years.

Remarkably, this and other color photos featured in *Asahi Graph*'s 1970 special edition were the first color photographs of postbomb Hiroshima and Nagasaki ever seen in Japan. *Asahi Graph* had gained access to them as the result of one of several rigorous new campaigns by a small number of *hibakusha* activists to reclaim postbomb film footage, photographs, autopsy specimens, and medical records still held in the United States. Over the next two decades, as the Shōwa era came to a close and the twentieth century neared its end, the number of Nagasaki *hibakusha* who began writing their stories and speaking about their experiences surged. At the same time, a new battle erupted in the United States over how the atomic bombings would be remembered and how—or if—the experiences of *hibakusha* would become part of the United States' historical narrative. It was during this time that Wada, Yoshida, Dō-oh, and Nagano would find their public voices and begin speaking out.

——

In their first act of reclaiming their histories, *hibakusha* activists petitioned the United States for the return of black-and-white 35 mm film footage of Hiroshima and Nagasaki after the bombings. These films— nineteen reels shot and edited by Japanese filmmakers—had been shipped to the United States and warehoused at military facilities for more than twenty years. After numerous Japanese appeals to the United Nations, the National Academy of Sciences, and the U.S. ambassador to Japan, in 1967, the United States finally sent copies of the footage back to Japan.

The earliest moving images of the aftermath of the atomic bombings had at last come home. Ten of the nineteen reels of edited film (approximately eighty-five minutes in total) contained grainy but powerful footage of Nagasaki in late 1945 and early 1946, including twisted steel girders of collapsed factories, bent smokestacks, the ruins of Urakami Church, and demolished bridges, schools, and homes. Human death, injury, and radiation-related illness were only hinted at in images of human skulls and bones in the ruins, adults and young children lying on mats inside Shinkōzen Elementary School being treated for burns across their bodies and faces, a woman with the patterns of her kimono fabric burned into the skin on her shoulders and back.

Much of the reclaimed footage aired on Japanese television in 1968, but prior to the broadcast, the Japanese government removed all evidence of human suffering. Officials claimed to have made this choice out of respect for the survivors and their families, but outraged activists believed the cuts were made to minimize the potential negative impact on Japan's economic and military relationship with the United States. In either case, this erasure of graphic images triggered memories of postwar censorship and sparked demands for the film to be rebroadcast in its entirety. The government refused, even after the twelve surviving *hibakusha* whose images appeared in the film gave written permission for their images to be aired.

Ironically, black-and-white footage showing human suffering was seen in the United States before it finally aired in Japan. Erik Barnouw, a film professor at Columbia University, had heard about the controversy from a Japanese colleague and decided to obtain a copy of the original silent footage from the National Archives. He was so moved by what he saw and distressed at the secrecy and censorship surrounding the film that he produced a sixteen-minute English-language documentary titled *Hiroshima-Nagasaki, August 1945*. The film premiered in early 1970 at the Museum of Modern Art in New York City, followed by a national broadcast on public television in August and airings in Canada and Europe. Later that year, Japanese public television bought the rights and aired the film in Japan, eliciting a huge public response—though Watanabe Chieko noted that "without the sounds of screaming voices," the terror of the bombing was greatly diminished.

As far as the Japanese knew, all U.S.-held postbomb footage was now back in Japan, including the short clips of color footage from which *Asahi Graph* created the still photographs of Taniguchi and others for its twenty-fifth anniversary edition. Eight years later, however, Taniguchi's photo and a series of serendipitous events led to the discovery of an additional ninety thousand feet of USSBS color footage of postbomb Hiroshima and Nagasaki.

A group of Japanese antinuclear activists led by Iwakura Tsutomu had spent years amassing thousands of photographs of the postbomb cities from individuals and collections across Japan, and in 1978, they selected several hundred for publication in *Hiroshima-Nagasaki: A Pictorial Record of the Atomic Destruction*. The first color photo to appear in the book was an image of Taniguchi's burned back, again enlarged and spread across two pages. Later that year, Iwakura and his group mounted a selection of the book's photos, including Taniguchi's, and took them to New York City for an outdoor exhibit several blocks from the United Nations headquarters. American passersby frequently admonished the Japanese team to "remember Pearl Harbor." Former lieutenant Herbert Sussan, who had filmed Taniguchi in 1945 as part of the USSBS team, saw the exhibit. Astounded to set eyes on the photograph of young Taniguchi at Ōmura National Hospital, Sussan quickly turned to Iwakura—and as he told the story of his connection to the photo, Sussan unwittingly revealed the existence of the full USSBS color footage.

The original film was now declassified and stored at the U.S. National Archives and Records Administration, and Iwakura's team was able to obtain permission to purchase a copy. Due to the film's length, however, the cost was exorbitant, so they returned to Japan and launched a nationwide fund-raising campaign. After an estimated three hundred thousand individual Japanese donors contributed small amounts totaling over $100,000, the team was able to purchase the film. In 1981, thirty-six years after the bombings, eighty-one reels of postwar color footage taken by American USSBS filmmakers were shipped back to Japan. At least eighteen reels included color footage of postbomb Nagasaki, far more intense and evocative than their black-and-white counterparts.

Another emotional controversy for *hibakusha* activists was the United States' postwar seizure and control of *hibakusha* autopsy specimens. It was commonly known by Japanese scientists that both in the fall of 1945 and for more than twenty years after 1948, U.S. researchers and ABCC scientists had surgically removed the body parts of deceased adults, children, infants, and miscarried fetuses. The specimens had been stored in five-gallon jars of formaldehyde solution or cut into smaller segments for preservation in blocks of paraffin wax. These, along with postmortem records, photographs, and diseased tissue slides, had been shipped to the United States, where they were cataloged and warehoused in an atomic bomb–proof archive outside Washington, D.C., for sole use by the U.S. military.

Impassioned negotiations for their return took place in two parts: Starting in the early 1960s, activists campaigned for the return of ABCC specimens that had been collected and shipped to the United States after 1948. The ABCC quickly ordered the repatriation of these materials to quell negative public relations generated by the controversy and also to alleviate the agency's ongoing budget pressures by eliminating the need to store the materials in the United States. By 1969, the Armed Forces Institute of Pathology had dispatched fifty-six shipments containing a total of twenty-two thousand specimens, including whole or partial brains, hearts, lungs, kidneys, livers, eyes, and other organs. In Nagasaki, the specimens were stored at Nagasaki University School of Medicine.

Claiming they were still classified materials, the United States refused to return the other collection of body parts and specimens, amassed in the fall of 1945 by U.S. and Japanese teams studying the effects of the atomic bombings. These specimens became a bargaining tool in an early 1970s negotiation between Japan and the United States that provided for their repatriation in exchange for Japan taking over majority leadership of and greater financial responsibility for the ABCC. The final agreement, overseen by Japanese prime minister Tanaka Kakuei and U.S. president Richard Nixon, allowed both nations to achieve their goals: For the United States, the ABCC became a new private, nonprofit foundation under Japanese law, renamed the Radiation Effects Research Foundation (RERF). Equally funded by both countries, the RERF carried forward all studies initiated by the ABCC. In turn, the Japanese won the right to elect a Japanese physician as the first chairman of the RERF's new binational board, and Japanese scientists would now share in the design and implementation of the agency's research. Twenty-eight years after the bombing, Japan had gained significant control of the medical research conducted on survivors' bodies, allowing the RERF the opportunity to shed much of its negative reputation among survivors. Once the agreement was finalized in 1973, all remaining *hibakusha* body parts held in the United States were sent back to Japan. Combined with the earlier shipments, a total of more than forty-five thousand pathology specimens, slides, medical reports, and related photographs were repatriated to the cities where the men, women, and children from whom they were seized had died. For *hibakusha,* this meant that the body parts and records of their deceased family members were finally where they belonged.

In 1970—the same year Taniguchi's photo appeared in *Asahi Graph*—forty-one-year-old Uchida Tsukasa walked through Hypocenter Park, now hidden from the main thoroughfare by a row of trees. A short distance away was the site of his childhood home, where Uchida's father and three siblings had been incinerated in the nuclear blast. Uchida was sixteen then; after the war, he and his mother had lived in the ashes and rubble of their former home, where he had collected shards of burned roof tiles and kept them in a box that he still had twenty-five years later.

Uchida stood in front of the hypocenter memorial, haunted by the invisibility of his former life. The hard-fought repatriation of postbomb film footage, color photographs, and *hibakusha* body parts provided critical documentation of the bomb's physical destruction and internal decimation to people's bodies. But what about his neighborhood—Matsuyama-machi—in the heart of the Urakami Valley, directly below the bomb's blast point? What about the estimated three hundred households and 1,865 people here who had been in their homes and workplaces, approximately 90 percent of whom died? Who were they, what kinds of lives had they led, and who would memorialize them and the parts of the city that had been instantly annihilated when the bomb detonated in the sky above them?

Fueled by persistent sadness and outrage, Uchida launched a "restoration" project that called on survivors' memories to re-create the former layout of Matsuyama-machi and collect data on the people who had died. It was Uchida's hope that instead of disappearing "into the darkness of history," each individual adult and child could be known and remembered. His plan captured the community's attention, and within months, the Association for the Restoration of the Atomic-Bombed Matsuyama-machi Neighborhood was formally organized. Chaired by Uchida and supported by Dr. Akizuki, Dr. Shirabe, and others, the group set out to create a map of every street, building, family, and individual who had lived in the area prior to the bombing.

Neighborhood members scoured cemeteries and examined gravestones to record the names of those who died on the day of the bombing and immediately after. Teams of volunteers interviewed or sent out letters to every survivor they knew and every survivor those survivors knew, asking them to draw detailed maps of their former streets, list the names and causes of deaths of their family members, and document everything they knew about the fates of anyone else in the area. With the support of local and national media coverage, responses poured in from thousands of survivors and family members of deceased *hibakusha* in Nagasaki and across the nation. Uchida and his colleagues collected and cross-checked the data. One house, family, shop, and ration station at a time, they filled in a comprehensive map of Matsuyama-machi, rendering back into historical existence the immediate hypocenter area and nearly all of the people who had lived and worked there.

The project quickly expanded to include all neighborhoods within two kilometers (1.25 miles) of the hypocenter—and in 1971, the city of Nagasaki established a municipal office to promote and oversee survey activities throughout the Urakami Valley. Dr. Akizuki cofounded the Yamazato-machi Recollection Committee where his hospital stood, an area particularly difficult to document because of the Korean laborers and medical school students who had lived in temporary housing there. Despite added challenges, including destroyed school registrations and employment records and a lack of accurate data on certain buildings and families, by 1975, the average completion rate for each neighborhood was 88 percent. In total, nearly ten thousand households were added to the prebomb maps, and 37,512 men, women, and children who had lived in them were reliably verified. Dr. Shirabe, now retired, helped collect, edit, and publish final reports on several of the neighborhoods' efforts. Fukahori Yoshitoshi, a medical administrator at Dr. Akizuki's St. Francis Hospital, collected families' personal photos of their pre- and postbomb neighborhoods to be included in the public records. By the project's conclusion in 1976, Uchida and his teams had fulfilled a strong sense of duty to both the deceased and the living by restoring the memory of their neighborhoods. Uchida fervently hoped that the efforts of so many people would help clarify "the true extent of the atomic bomb experience."

While the mapping project was under way, Dr. Akizuki came to believe that the *hibakusha* reclamation movement would remain unfinished until as many survivors as possible shared their individual stories and people throughout the world were able to grasp the human experience of nuclear war. He had already written significant segments of his own story, prompted by a visit in 1961 from a Japanese novelist who asked Akizuki what the bombing had been like. "Sixteen years after the bombing," Akizuki remembered, "this was the first time someone had asked me about the details of my experience." Instead of showing the writer his notes on the bombing and its aftermath, Akizuki described what it was like to be an atomic bomb physician who remained physically and mentally depleted—"like a living fossil who can't forget the past . . . who had never been able to mentally recover from witnessing hell."

From that day forward, Akizuki felt responsible for writing about his experiences and the people who died at his hospital and neighboring districts. Due to poor health and his daily work as a physician and hospital director, it took him three years to complete his first memoir, *Nagasaki genbaku ki: Hibaku ishi no shōgen* [The Nagasaki Bombing: A Surviving Doctor's Testimony], detailing the first two months of his postbomb life.

But Akizuki knew that this book and those by other *hibakusha* told only a tiny portion of what had happened on the day of the bombing and in the years that followed. Standing at a window of St. Francis Hospital, he would stare out at the Urakami Valley and see what he described as "a double image"—the rebuilt, modernized quadrant of his city, overlaid by images of blackened bodies scattered everywhere. So many people had died. No one knew their stories. As time and Japan's economic advances erased all signs of the war, *hibakusha* stories were disappearing—forgotten as if they didn't matter. By this time, most people in Japan spoke about the atomic bomb only around the anniversaries of the bombings—a phenomenon one *hibakusha* likened to goldfish sellers who by tradition peddled their fish only during the summer. Many Japanese misperceived the effects of the atomic bombings to be no different from conventional bombings. At a 1968 atomic bomb exhibit in Tokyo, Dr. Akizuki was further dismayed when he observed that Hiroshima had become such a singular symbol of the atomic bombings that few people were familiar with Nagasaki's story. Compared with the numerous books about Hiroshima, not one about Nagasaki was displayed. Back home, his wife, Sugako, remembered him repeatedly saying, "It's not good. It's not good."

To generate an expanded written record of the Nagasaki *hibakusha* experience, Akizuki and several of his colleagues established the Nagasaki Testimonial Society in 1969. By this time, many *hibakusha* had felt discouraged and left Japan's antinuclear movement due to political infighting between activist groups that had split over ideological differences as Japan's political parties had aligned themselves with Soviet or U.S. interests. Other *hibakusha* had withdrawn from the movement because they felt some groups were manipulating their experiences for political gain. In his desire to create a new organization with a united and inclusive stance, Dr. Akizuki invited all *hibakusha* to tell their stories, regardless of their political affiliations or engagement with the antinuclear movement. Akizuki envisioned that the collective voices of a hundred thousand survivors could lead to the worldwide abolition of nuclear weapons, and he entreated Nagasaki survivors to "speak out about the realities of being a *hibakusha*" on behalf of all humanity.

Hundreds of *hibakusha* responded to his initial call. They scribed their memories to honor their loved ones, articulate their fears about their own futures, promote their hopes for peace, or simply because they were aging and wanted the next generation to know the truths that only they could tell. Some revealed their *hibakusha* status for the first time in order to augment the government's incomplete surveys of survivors' conditions. Others wrote as a personal protest against Japan's reluctance, as a U.S. ally, to condemn the atomic bombings. For others, writing their stories was a way to counteract a gradual renewal of militaristic nationalism in Japan, exemplified by incidents of textbook censorship that minimized information or images of the negative impact of war, including the horrors of the atomic bombings. Akizuki's colleague Yamada Kan, an outspoken critic of Dr. Nagai—whom he called the "uninvited representative" of the Nagasaki survivor community—supported the testimony movement in part to collect enough non-Catholic survivors' stories to outweigh Nagai's pervasive message that Nagasaki *hibakusha* were spiritual martyrs.

In 1969, as the Vietnam War raged in Southeast Asia, the Nagasaki Testimonial Society published its first annual volume of *Nagasaki no shōgen* [Testimonies of Nagasaki]. For the twenty-fifth anniversary of the bombing the following year, the journal featured Taniguchi's color photo on its cover. By 1971, *Testimonies of Nagasaki* had more than tripled in size. Sugako often prepared dinner for Akizuki and the editorial team as they worked late into the night at the Akizukis' home. Over a thousand radio and television broadcasts of *hibakusha* stories followed, as did numerous other testimony collections, including those by members of the Nagasaki Atomic Bomb Youth Association, Nagasaki *hibakusha* teachers' associations, and the Nagasaki Women's Society. Local factory workers circulated their own journals of testimonies, and Nagasaki poets published the magazine *Hobō* [Scorched People].

To further the reclamation of *hibakusha* materials still held in the United States, the physically weak Akizuki and his wife joined a small team of Hiroshima and Nagasaki officials traveling to the National

Archives in Washington, D.C., to search for USSBS and other U.S. post-war records on the atomic bombings. After ten days, the group carried home photocopies of the documents they had located; after translating them into Japanese, they were able to read the contents of some of the detailed USSBS reports for the first time and learn how the United States had documented the effects of its air attacks on Japan. Disturbed by the reports' cold, technical details of U.S. incendiary and atomic bomb strategies and their dearth of information relating to human suffering, Dr. Akizuki deepened his commitment to the testimony movement to support a more complete historical record. Over the next decade, the Nagasaki Testimonial Society published ten volumes of *Testimonies of Nagasaki,* including personal narratives by Korean survivors and former Allied prisoners of war. Akizuki published his second book, *Shi no dōshinen* [Concentric Circles of Death], as well as a third memoir in 1975. With the support of numerous individuals and organizations, the Nagasaki Testimonial Society had succeeded in creating a comprehensive written record of survivors' experiences. This, Dr. Akizuki felt, was why God had allowed him to live.

———

Akizuki's passionate yearning for visibility and greater public under-standing was a reflection of how invisible *hibakusha* still remained in the public eye, both domestically and overseas. Behind the veil of Japan's economic recovery, many *hibakusha* in the 1970s still lived in poverty and experienced multiple debilitating medical conditions. More than 10 percent of all survivors were unemployed, a rate 70 percent higher than non-*hibakusha.* Those with low or no incomes led particularly precari-ous lives, especially those who were ill and elderly survivors who lived alone and struggled to feed and bathe themselves. In utero–exposed chil-dren were now thirty years old; those with milder symptoms worked at odd jobs, but those unable to function independently lived in mental institutions, separated from their families. Thyroid, breast, and lung cancer rates had peaked, but stomach and colon cancer rates for *hibaku-sha* remained high, as did leukemia, with reported cases of multiple deaths within the same family. Unexplained illnesses or deaths of *hiba-kusha* and their children kept many *hibakusha* on edge about long-term radiation effects. Those with visible injuries and scars were often turned away from public baths. For younger survivors now in their forties, junior and senior high school class reunions were sad reminders of how many more friends died each year.

Hibakusha pressed forward with little psychological support; Japanese psychologists and social workers were not yet experienced in the diagnosis and treatment of post-traumatic stress disorder, and *hibakusha* health care benefits did not cover the atomic bombings' psychological effects. Many survivors still flinched at a sudden flash of light or when they heard the sounds of fireworks, sirens, or airplanes flying overhead. Others experienced recurring nightmares that triggered memories of the nuclear attack and its aftermath. One woman clung to the memory of her husband by keeping the blood- and oil-stained gloves he had worn at the time of the bombing on the family altar in her home. Aging parents of in utero–exposed children, often impoverished and struggling with their own illnesses, feared for their children's futures. In the words of one father, "I can't close my eyes as long as this child is alive."

But Japan was now a Westernized nation with enviable economic growth, intent on leaving its past behind. Even after Nagasaki's successful reclamation and testimony movements, and even after the city produced a documentary film using the returned black-and-white footage and over 1.2 million people visited the Nagasaki Atomic Bomb Museum in 1975 alone, survivors' current conditions remained at best at the periphery of public awareness. In other countries as well, few people appreciated the long-term consequences of the atomic bombings. A group of foreign mayors visiting Nagasaki for the thirtieth anniversary ceremonies revealed their lack of understanding when they visited a photo exhibition about the bombing: Stunned by the images before them, some of them asked the exhibition curators if the photographs were real.

In the United States, both ignorance of the effects of the bombings and celebration of the bombs' use remained common—and nuclear weapons, now far more powerful than those used on Hiroshima and Nagasaki, were generally perceived as an inevitable reality. Civil defense campaigns taught that with a combination of community preparedness and individual integrity, nuclear attacks were survivable—a message unsupported by *hibakusha* narratives, which were rarely heard. In 1976, a U.S. group called the Confederate Air Force (CAF) performed an air show in Texas before an audience of more than forty thousand people. In the finale, a tribute to those who brought the Pacific War to its close, Paul Tibbets—the lead pilot of the Hiroshima mission—flew a B-29 overhead. As the narrator's voice over loudspeakers proclaimed that the bomb had ended "some of the darkest days of America's history," a device detonated on the ground beneath the plane to generate a rising mushroom cloud. When news of the air show reached Japan, both *hibakusha* leaders and the Japanese government vehemently protested. U.S. officials formally apologized to Japan, and the CAF canceled this portion of the show at future sites. Neither U.S. newspaper accounts of the controversy nor Tibbets himself acknowledged that the simulated bombing omitted the mass destruction and grotesque deaths and injuries suffered by the men, women, and children beneath the atomic clouds.

Against this backdrop of inadvertent ignorance and intentional minimization, *hibakusha* activists pushed to find new ways to awaken the world to the true impact of nuclear weapons. Locally, the Nagasaki Atomic Bomb Museum expanded its outreach education programs, and the city published a comprehensive, five-volume *Nagasaki genbaku sensaishi* [Records of the Nagasaki Atomic Bombing and Wartime Damage], a detailed narrative of the immediate destruction, deaths, injuries, and long-term effects of survivors in their city. With the support of the Science Council of Japan and consultants including doctors Akizuki and Shirabe, a team of thirty-four Japanese scientists and scholars collaborated to create the meticulously researched 504-page *Hiroshima and Nagasaki: The Physical, Medical, and Social Effects of the Atomic Bombings,* including hundreds of figures, photographs, and tables. Published in 1981 in Tokyo, New York, and London, copies of the English edition were sent to the heads of state of every nuclear-armed country as well as to the secretary-general and executive members of the United Nations, representatives from each UN member nation, and leading health and antinuclear organizations around the world. Taniguchi, Yamaguchi, and other representatives of local and national *hibakusha* organizations spoke out across Japan for the abolition of nuclear weapons. They also published numerous essays and articles, were interviewed by the foreign press, and appeared in documentary films about the bombings. Taniguchi often took off his shirt to reveal his present-day scars, providing images that filmmakers juxtaposed with photographs and footage of his back in the first months after the bombing.

Activists pressed to magnify their antinuclear influence internationally. In 1977, more than four hundred Japanese and over seventy delegates from approximately twenty countries gathered in Hiroshima, Nagasaki, and Tokyo to unify and focus their efforts in advance of the first UN Special Session on Disarmament. One of their key strategies was to effectively illuminate the "irrationality" of atomic bomb development with survivors' personal stories, scientific evidence on how the bombs destroyed human life, and statements of support by political and military leaders throughout the world. They also drafted a resolution to make the word *hibakusha* an internationally recognized term. Taniguchi and *hibakusha* activist Watanabe Chieko flew to Geneva in 1978 to address the International NGO Conference on Disarmament—"the first time," Watanabe remembered, "that atomic bomb survivors had spoken in person on the international political stage." Later that year, five hundred members of the Japanese delegation flew to New York to formally petition the United Nations to lead the world in the abolition of nuclear weapons. The delegation's spirits were buoyed when they read the UN's official post-session declaration, which echoed their deepest wishes for international understanding of the dangers of nuclear weapons and appealed for their total elimination.

Despite his chronic medical problems—or perhaps because of them—Taniguchi always showed up wherever he was needed in the fight to abolish nuclear weapons and expand *hibakusha* health care eligibility and benefits. He had multiple surgeries on his back to cut out reappearing tumors, some of them precancerous, and to remove scar tissue in the middle of his spine in order to graft new skin in its place. Doctors recommended a complete replacement of the skin on his back, but Taniguchi hesitated, unsure he could survive such a radical procedure. "Scientific knowledge has progressed enough to develop highly sophisticated missiles," he reflected with some bitterness, "but there is no cure for my illness."

Between medical procedures, he traveled to antinuclear conferences across the world, chain-smoking his way to universities, churches, and local forums throughout Western Europe and in Poland, Romania, the

Soviet Union, China, and Korea. In North America, he traveled to Canada and nine U.S. cities, including San Francisco, New York, Chicago, Seattle, Atlanta, and Washington, D.C.—often appearing at numerous events in a single city. "Nuclear weapons do not protect mankind from danger," Taniguchi told his audiences, rarely making eye contact. "They can never safely coexist with humans." He acknowledged Japan's wartime aggressions and the absence of his nation's apology for initiating the war, then—with subdued but detectable anger—he condemned the atomic bombings as scientific experiments on tens of thousands of innocent people in residential areas for which Americans had not shown remorse. Taniguchi had long realized the power of his most famous photograph to communicate the impact of nuclear war, and despite his aversion to looking at it and reliving the suffering it held for him, he had the photo printed on his business cards, and he frequently projected it onto a screen above him or held an enlarged copy mounted on poster board as he spoke. "I am not a guinea pig," he insisted. "You who have seen my body, don't turn your face away. I want you to look again."

Taniguchi did not deceive himself about the practical, large-scale impact of his efforts. Throughout the world, he faced constant reminders of how little—if anything—people knew about the atomic bombings and survivors' ongoing conditions and how erroneous their limited knowledge often was. Despite numerous complex international treaties that limited certain kinds of nuclear tests and weapons development, reduced stockpiles, and defined the world's nuclear weapons states as the United States, the Soviet Union, China, France, and the United Kingdom, Cold War tensions persisted. In the 1970s alone, 550 nuclear tests were conducted worldwide, and nuclear stockpiles increased by nearly 40 percent, heightening the threat of nuclear war, if only by the sheer number of weapons that existed. By 1981, the world's stockpiles totaled 56,035 weapons, 98 percent of which belonged to the United States and the Soviet Union. Every time a nuclear weapons test occurred somewhere in the world, survivors in Nagasaki felt a rush of chilling memories mixed with anger and despair. "Clever and foolish people have not changed at all since that August 9," Dr. Akizuki remarked, disparaging the countries who conducted these tests. "What is sad is that they are still making the same mistake more than a quarter of a century later." What kept

Taniguchi Sumiteru, age fifty-five, at an antinuclear protest, ca. 1984. (*Photograph by Kurosaki Haruo*)

Taniguchi going, despite constant pain and the discouraging realities of nuclear weapons development, was his sense of responsibility to all those whose voices, unlike his, that had been silenced—"hundreds of thousands of people who wanted to say what I'm saying, but who died without being able to."

Pope John Paul II's 1981 visits to Hiroshima and Nagasaki raised international awareness of the two cities and invigorated Japan's antinuclear movement. "War is the work of man," the pope declared in Hiroshima, countering Dr. Nagai's view that atomic bombs were acts of God.

Men who wage war "can also successfully make peace." At Nagasaki's Urakami Cathedral, the pope ordained fifteen priests, including two Americans, and in an open-air stadium near the hypocenter, he conducted a public Mass for forty-five thousand people in the falling snow. He also spoke at Martyrs' Hill, where twenty-six Christians were executed in 1597. During his visit to the Megumi no Oka (Hill of Grace) Nagasaki A-Bomb Home, a nursing home facility for atomic bomb survivors, many elderly survivors who had never spoken about their experiences began telling their stories. The pope challenged the status quo among nuclear powers by calling on them to take responsibility for their role in the threat of nuclear annihilation, and he encouraged Japan's Catholic hierarchy to engage more actively in peace efforts. Although many Catholic *hibakusha* still hesitated to speak out, for others, the pope's message transformed their visions of themselves from sacrificial lambs quietly suffering the will of God to potential contributors to the cause of global peace. For these men and women, speaking out became a realization of God's wishes.

Inspired and bolstered by the pope's words, Akizuki and his wife traveled to the United States again in 1982, with a Japanese delegation carrying a second petition to the United Nations. The petition, signed by 28,862,935 Japanese citizens, demanded that the United Nations heighten the priority of international antinuclear measures and tell the world the truth about the destruction and human suffering caused by nuclear weapons. In a preliminary meeting with UN officials prior to the General Assembly, Akizuki spoke in nervous English to communicate his antinuclear message. He and the Japanese contingent then led an estimated 750,000 peaceful antinuclear protesters from forty nations in a march through midtown Manhattan, culminating in a massive Central Park event featuring speeches by U.S. and international disarmament leaders and performances by Bruce Springsteen, Joan Baez, James Taylor, and Linda Ronstadt.

Yamaguchi had fallen sick and was unable to participate in the rally. The following day at the United Nations, however, he stood on the podium before more than sixty heads of state, foreign ministers, and delegation leaders, and gave what he felt was the speech of his lifetime. "What I wanted to do in my speech was to reproduce the horror of August 9th,"

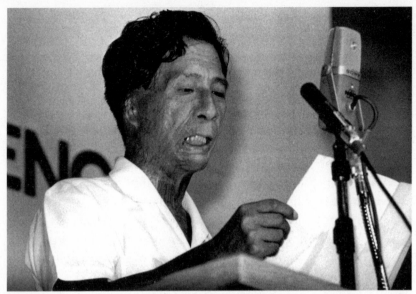

Yamaguchi Senji appealing for action on behalf of Nagasaki *hibakusha* at an anti-nuclear-weapons demonstration, 1978. (*Photograph by Kurosaki Haruo*)

he recalled. "I wanted everybody to understand the hell we lived. That was all I was thinking of." He held up a photograph of his keloid-scarred face. He asked listeners to look at it closely. He pleaded for the United Nations to lead the antinuclear effort to preserve the human race. "As long as I continue to live I will keep on appealing!" he boomed. "No more Hiroshima! No more Nagasaki! No more war! No more *hibakusha*!"

———

"When you talk about it," Wada would say, "it brings back memories. I couldn't see the usefulness of speaking about what happened." It was a sentiment in some part shared by Dō-oh, Nagano, and Yoshida. Having raised their children, retired, and mourned the death of parents, grandparents, and siblings, the four of them would find deeply personal reasons to break their silence. In the 1980s and 1990s, their choices to become visible and speak out, and the sense of meaning and purpose that ensued, came to represent a rebirth of sorts—the beginning of a third life.

Wada decided to speak out in 1983, when he held his first grandchild in his arms. "I saw her little clenched fists, and I suddenly remembered the tiny baby I'd seen two days after the bombing, lying burned and blackened on the ground along the streetcar tracks. That baby's fists were clenched in the same way. If an atomic bombing happened now, I thought, my granddaughter would end up like that baby. I *had* to start talking about it so that people don't use such a bomb again."

Wada sought out Dr. Akizuki, who, at sixty-seven, was retired as director of St. Francis Hospital in 1983 and had joined forces with Nagasaki's mayor to found and direct the new and visionary Nagasaki Foundation for the Promotion of Peace (NFPP). Established as a joint private and municipal organization, the NFPP's many antinuclear projects include a *hibakusha* speakers' bureau. Beyond survivors' written testimonies, Akizuki believed that their oral testimonies could powerfully communicate the impact of the bomb to the people of Nagasaki, Japan, and the world as a means to achieve their common goal: the abolition of nuclear weapons and the protection of future life on earth.

The NFPP's first cohort of speakers included Taniguchi and Uchida Tsukasa, the leader of the Urakami Valley mapping project. After Wada's meeting with Dr. Akizuki, he joined them. When he told his atomic bomb stories to schoolchildren, he tried to always begin by joking with them to help them laugh and relax. Gradually, he would begin speaking about the war and the atomic bombing. "I suffered less hardship than others," he explained, "so instead of talking about my personal experiences, I connect my stories to the photos the children have seen in the museum—and I insert jokes and puns when I see their faces are getting too serious. I do everything I can so the children will think about what is needed now for us not to repeat this horrible event."

Wada retired in 1987 after forty-three years with the Nagasaki Streetcar Company. He and Hisako built a home in the northwestern hills of the Urakami Valley, and Wada finally realized his dream to build a memorial to the fallen streetcar drivers and conductors. He and his colleagues from work solicited support from the streetcar company and many individuals, and the city gave its permission to use a small spot of land in Hypocenter Park. Wada helped oversee the memorial's design and construction using stones from a bombed-out station platform and actual

Wada Kōichi, age eighty, at the Nagasaki Streetcar Company Memorial, 2007. The plaque at right tells the story of the more than 110 boys and girls who died in their teens and early twenties, recalling that one female conductor was only twelve years old at the time of the bombing. (*Courtesy of Wada Kōichi*)

sharin (wheels) from Nagasaki's wartime streetcars. "When I stand here," Wada said in front of the memorial, "I remember those times and cannot laugh or smile."

In 1985, Yoshida was forced to retire early from the wholesale food company when he became ill with pancreatitis. His supervisor hadn't wanted him to leave permanently, so after a ninety-day hospitalization, Yoshida proudly returned to his company on two occasions to help the staff accurately determine gross and net prices of their products. His semiretirement took an abrupt turn when his wife, Sachiko, developed breast cancer that metastasized to her bones. After completion of her cancer treatments, she contracted pneumonia in the hospital and wasn't expected to survive. At her request, Yoshida brought Sachiko home, where he fed, bathed, and cared for her every day. "We thought she would be all right because she had the cancer removed," he said. "I wanted to take her to Hokkaido. I told her I would take her there when she got better. But we were too optimistic. She never got better and died six months later. She was fifty-one." Overwhelmed with grief, Yoshida nearly fainted at Sachiko's funeral. Previously, he had rarely gone to his family gravesite; after her death, he went often.

Yoshida had known Taniguchi and Yamaguchi from the 1950s, when he was a part of the Nagasaki Atomic Bomb Youth Association. Though he had admired them as pioneers in speaking publicly, he—like Wada—had remained silent. "I was shy to be in front of people, especially women. Everyone looked at me like this"—he grimaced—"I didn't like it." One day, however, Yamaguchi approached Yoshida to ask if he could take his place at a talk he was scheduled to give to junior high school students visiting Nagasaki. Yoshida agreed—but when he arrived at the site and saw all the students staring at him, he immediately regretted it. Unraveled by the students' fear of making eye contact with him and what he thought was their revulsion, Yoshida stood before them and told his story. Some students began crying, and when Yoshida looked up at them, he nearly burst into tears himself. Afterward, many of the children expressed their appreciation to him. Yoshida, however, was so shaken by the experience that he returned, momentarily, to silence.

But not for long. In his ongoing process of accepting his disfigurement, Yoshida again came to terms with the fact that he could not change what had happened to him or how he looked—and he decided no longer to let his shyness get in the way of speaking out for peace. In 1989, he joined the NFPP.

"This is what I say to children," he explained. "'Have you ever looked up *heiwa* [peace] in the dictionary?' They never have! They've never looked it up because we don't need to know what peace is during peacetime. 'Let's look it up together,' I say to them. 'Our greatest enemy is carelessness. We need to pay attention to peace.'"

Yoshida Katsuji, age seventy-four, speaking to children at Ikeshima Elementary School, 2005. (*Courtesy of Yoshida Naoji*)

"What will you do after your retirement?" Dō-oh's friend asked her in Tokyo, concerned that Dō-oh, unlike most Japanese women, had no children to rely on as she got older. As usual, Dō-oh saw things differently. "You are pessimistic about my life because you are seeing things in an ordinary pattern," she told her friend. "I have no regrets about my life. With a lot of effort and strong will, I've acted on my beliefs every step of the way. I did not trouble others and I took care of myself. I am very proud of myself."

After thirty years of arduous work and achievement, fifty-five-year-old Dō-oh retired from Utena and decided to take a break and rest for a while. But instead of feeling happy, she felt lonely, "like I was being pushed to the far corner of society." She worried that a radiation-related disease might be lying dormant in her body, ready to appear as she got weaker with age. Her sister suggested that she come back to live in Nagasaki, but Dō-oh was hesitant. "Nagasaki was where I was *allowed* to live," she remembered, "but Tokyo is where I *lived*."

Still, Dō-oh found herself walking alone through the stimulating streets of Shinjuku among "crowds of blank and silent people" she didn't know. One day on the train, a woman standing isolated and lonely mirrored Dō-oh's fears for her own future. It was then that she decided to move back to Nagasaki while she still had strength.

She prepared to sell her house in Tokyo and began designing her future home in Nagasaki with a Japanese-style room for her aging mother that looked out over a yard. Her plans were interrupted, however, when her mother became ill and was hospitalized. Dō-oh rushed to Nagasaki, where she helped care for her mother and encouraged her with the vision of their new life together. On a cold December day, Dō-oh noticed a rainbow outside the window—a rare sighting in winter—and propped up her mother to see it. "It's very beautiful," her mother replied, speaking her last words before she died the next day.

Returning to Tokyo, Dō-oh felt "empty, as if I had my heart taken away." Remembering her mother's appreciative and supportive letters, Dō-oh was tormented with guilt for doing so little for her mother during her life except to send money and gifts from Tokyo. Depleted of energy, she would leave her house and walk aimlessly through the streets. "I tried to listen to the faint voice of reason telling me to pull myself together, but I could not control my pain."

Dō-oh returned to Nagasaki in 1989, one year too late to fulfill her dream of living with her mother. Of her parents and six siblings, only she and her younger sister were still alive. Dō-oh built her new house and set up her family's Buddhist altar in the room she'd planned for her mother. Whenever she left the house, she spoke out loud to her mother's photo on the altar, saying that she was leaving and asking her to watch over the house while she was gone. Although her mother couldn't answer, Dō-oh's sadness was lifted by her mother's image smiling back at her.

Unlike the barely recovering city she had left thirty years earlier, Nagasaki was now modern, even prosperous. Most *hibakusha* still remained quiet about their experiences, but in ways Dō-oh could have never imagined in 1955, the number of *hibakusha* activist organizations and the amount of support for survivors' social, economic, and medical needs made it possible for her to reconsider her own silence. A *hibakusha* consultation center at the Nagasaki University School of Medicine offered medical examinations and counseling to more than sixty thousand survivors each year. The city regularly hosted antinuclear, peace, and atomic bomb–related medical conferences and symposia. A national controversy had ignited in 1988 when Nagasaki's outspoken mayor, Motoshima Hitoshi, broke a cultural taboo and publicly held Emperor Hirohito accountable for his role in the war. Right-wing militarists working to rearm Japan were irate, and in 1990, one of them attempted to assassinate Motoshima by shooting him in the back. The mayor survived, and crowds in Nagasaki rose up in protest over the violence against him.

In another news-grabbing event, Nagasaki *hibakusha* were outraged in 1989 when a U.S. warship docked at their port. For decades, people across Japan had vehemently protested the arrival of U.S. ships believed but not proven to be carrying nuclear weapons—which would have breached Japan's policies not to possess, produce, or allow nuclear weapons into the country. Protesters' suspicions about past ships had been confirmed earlier that year when newly uncovered reports revealed that in 1965, the USS *Ticonderoga* had lost a plane, its pilot, and a hydrogen bomb when the plane accidentally rolled off the ship en route to a Japanese port where it later docked. Consequently, when the USS *Rodney M. Davis* entered Nagasaki Bay purportedly carrying nuclear weapons, activists including Yamaguchi gathered in Peace Park holding photographs of their deceased family members and panoramic photos of the city after the bombing. When the ship's captain and some of his crew arrived to present a wreath before the giant Peace Statue, Yamaguchi felt his body shaking and experienced traumatic flashbacks of the bombing. After the captain laid the wreath at the base of the statue and left, a reporter accidentally knocked the wreath to the ground. Yamaguchi and other *hibakusha* spontaneously raced over to it and began trampling on it. The incident made national headlines, and Mayor Motoshima—who had refused to escort the ship's captain to the memorial—officially apologized to the U.S. ambassador to Japan for the protesters' actions. The ambassador reportedly adhered to U.S. policy by neither confirming nor denying the existence of nuclear weapons on the warship.

Dō-oh marveled at the survivors who so unabashedly revealed themselves in public—and for the first time in her adult life, she felt free to disclose her *hibakusha* identity. An escalation of nerve pain from the glass shards still embedded in her body motivated her to action: Dō-oh enrolled in a five-week community class at Nagasaki University called "The Nagasaki Atomic Bomb and Its Influences." Side by side with sixty other adult students, she finally learned about the immense power and the human effects of the atomic bomb.

For Dō-oh, it was Matsuzoe Hiroshi, a former classmate and longtime member of the NFPP, who encouraged her to speak out and tell her story. Unbeknownst to Dō-oh, Matsuzoe had been at Dr. Miyajima's house on the night of the bombing when Dō-oh's parents carried her into the yard. Years later, Matsuzoe—by then a famous Nagasaki artist and sculptor—painted a watercolor of that scene: In the foreground, dozens of people are sitting or lying on the ground, their bodies blistered and bleeding. A mother nurses her infant son. Another cradles a lifeless toddler in her arms. Young Matsuzoe himself appears in the painting, standing injured next to an adult who seems to be comforting him. On the veranda, Dō-oh is lying facedown on a table surrounded by six adults. Wearing a white lab coat, Dr. Miyajima is treating the injuries at the back of her head. Dō-oh's parents are standing at the other end of the table, their arms outstretched to hold down her legs and feet as she thrashes in pain. Matsuzoe called it a *jigokue* (a picture of hell).

He never imagined that Dō-oh had survived. One day in 1985, Matsuzoe was reading the newspaper when he came upon an article about

Dō-oh and her rise to executive leadership in Tokyo. Thrilled and in disbelief, Matsuzoe wrote to Dō-oh, describing his memories of that night. He enclosed a photocopy of the painting.

For Dō-oh, reading Matsuzoe's letter and seeing his artwork stirred deep memories of the bombing and years of physical anguish and hiding—and she felt an immediate sense of reconnection with a friend she hadn't seen in forty years. They reunited in Nagasaki, and when Matsuzoe learned about Dō-oh's professional experience speaking in front of large audiences, he persuaded her to join the NFPP and begin speaking about her atomic bomb survival.

In 1994, five years after she had returned to Nagasaki, doctors diagnosed Dō-oh with breast cancer. That year, a new cumulative study based on eighty thousand deceased *hibakusha* indicated their rate of leukemia deaths was thirty times higher than normal levels and showed elevated rates of breast, lung, colon, thyroid, stomach, and four other cancers. Other studies documented higher-than-average rates of multiple primary cancers in a single survivor and late-onset cardiovascular, circulatory, digestive, and respiratory diseases. RERF reports stated that all females and anyone exposed at a young age at the time of the bomb were at significantly higher risks of cancer in their lifetimes.

Dō-oh's heart pounded when she heard her diagnosis, but she quipped to her doctor, "So this means that now I won't be able to enjoy fashion?" Once alone, however, Dō-oh was consumed with anxiety. *It's finally come.* She looked back on the bombing, her injuries, her lost youth, her fear of marriage, and her thirty years in Tokyo. *And now, my breast,* she thought. *The ghost of the atomic bomb still haunts me.* She felt robbed of the ordinary life she had finally achieved in Nagasaki, and she feared the upcoming loss of her figure, in which she had always taken pride. As cancer "started building a nest" in her breast, she was overwhelmed that she could no longer live a life shaped by her own will.

But Dō-oh reawakened to her own power. Having smoked most of her life, she now quit. When tests revealed two tumors, she ranted at them, calling them greedy. After her mastectomy, she cried often and easily, even as she felt deep gratitude for the care of her nurses. She kept a journal, prayed for the elimination of nuclear weapons, and vowed, over and over, to become a more generous, loving, and self-reflective woman. When her treatment was complete, doctors declared Dō-oh cancer-free. "I was allowed to live," she would say, vowing to stay alive until she was seventy-five. That, she thought, would mean she had triumphed over the bomb.

Nagano did not speak out until after the fiftieth anniversary of the bombing in 1995. Six years earlier in 1989, her husband was injured in a car accident; he remained hospitalized for eleven years and never recovered. Nagano moved into a rental house near the hospital so she could be there every day—and when her mother, too, was hospitalized at a different facility for various health issues, Nagano eventually had her mother transferred to her husband's hospital where she could accommodate both of their needs.

All of her life, Nagano's mother had waited for the *tomuraiage,* the rite honoring the fiftieth anniversary of Seiji's and Kuniko's deaths—a significant event in Buddhist tradition when families gather at the gravesite for the ceremony to honor their deceased relatives. "We call it the fiftieth anniversary," Nagano explained, "but actually, we usually have the ceremony in the forty-ninth year, so for us that meant 1994. My mother felt she couldn't die until she participated in that commemoration for Kuniko and Seiji."

The day finally came, but Nagano's mother had been diagnosed with liver cancer and was too ill to attend. Nagano and her son oversaw the ceremony. "At family gravesites," Nagano explained, "the cabinet door where the ashes are stored typically remains closed. At this ceremony, though, the monk recites a special chant, and we open the door to let fresh air in, so that our deceased family members will be happy."

Nagano and her son opened the cabinet door and removed the lid from her older brother's urn. His *ikotsu* (cremated remains) were white and pinkish, as she had expected. Those of her father, who had died three years after the bombing, were a mixture of black and white. When they opened Seiji's and Kuniko's ashes, Nagano shivered. "They were *makkuro*—totally black! They were white when we cremated them, but when we opened them, they were *pitch-black*." The ashes of Nagano's husband's family who had died in the bombing were black, too. Her son felt sick. The monk told them that the ashes of twenty thousand

Nagano Etsuko, age eighty-one, speaking to students at Kakumei Girls' High School, Nagasaki, 2009. Nagano is using the map to indicate her locations and movements throughout the day on August 9, 1945; here she points to the neighborhood she walked through immediately after the bombing. (*Courtesy of Nagano Etsuko*)

unidentified *hibakusha* kept in a crate at the temple had also turned black. "Again—" Nagano remembered, her voice hushed. "Again, we grasped that nuclear weapons damage people's bodies all the way to the bone."

As the monk spoke at the service, Nagano reflected on her life. *It's been fifty years. What have I been doing, being sad for fifty years?* It was finally time to free herself from grief and guilt—not to forget her sad memories, but to change, to do something that could help others. Soon after that, Nagano read a newspaper article about *hibakusha* who spoke to schoolchildren about their experiences. Here was something she thought she could do.

Nagano submitted a brief summary of her experiences to the Nagasaki Foundation for the Promotion of Peace and was invited to join. By 1995, she was making her first speeches while her husband and mother were still hospitalized. Reading from a script, she recounted her memories but never mentioned the circumstances of her brother's and sister's deaths. "What I had done was so terrible, I could not bring myself to talk about it. It was too much for me to handle."

Nor could she have known what her decision to speak out would mean to her mother. One day, a nurse at the hospital spoke to Nagano's mother commending Nagano for speaking out. When Nagano arrived to visit later that day, her mother suddenly broke the fifty-year emotional silence that had separated them.

"I want you to do your best telling students how horrible the atomic bomb was," she told Nagano. "Take care of yourself, and do your best."

Nagano was stunned. It was the first time Nagano's mother had ever been happy for her, the first time in her life that she felt she had done right by her mother.

A few days later, her mother turned to Nagano again. *"E-chan,"* she said, using her nickname for Nagano. *"E-chan, gomen ne* [I'm sorry]."

Tears streamed down Nagano's face. *"I'm* sorry, Mother," she answered. "It should be *me* who apologizes to *you."*

Her mother reached out for her hand, and they cried together. Nagano stroked her mother's swollen, yellowish skin, apologizing again and again for breaking her promise and bringing Seiji and Kuniko back. The relief she felt was indescribable. "After fifty years, my mother had finally forgiven me."

Nagano's mother died a few days later, without suffering, as if she were going to sleep.

———

As Taniguchi, Wada, Yoshida, Dō-oh, and Nagano found deep purpose in speaking publicly about their experiences and illuminating the realities of nuclear war, a fierce debate erupted in the United States over the inclusion of *hibakusha* stories in a national exhibit commemorating the fiftieth anniversary of the end of World War II. In 1988, curators of the Smithsonian's National Air and Space Museum (NASM) in Washington, D.C., had begun planning an exhibit to spotlight the *Enola Gay* as an important historical artifact for its role as the plane that dropped the first atomic bomb on Hiroshima. Later titled "The Last Act: The Atomic Bomb and the End of World War Two," the exhibit was designed to honor the service, sacrifice, and memories of Pacific War veterans and also to inform the public about the effects of the bombings on the people of Hiroshima and Nagasaki and about their role in igniting the Cold War—which Smithsonian curators believed were important parts of the *Enola Gay* story.

The scope of the NASM's exhibit was based in part on research conducted by a new generation of U.S. scholars who, starting in the 1960s, had used newly declassified World War II documents to reassess the complex issues around the atomic bombings of Japan. Among numerous areas of study, these researchers had reexamined U.S. motives for using the bombs and their effectiveness in ending the war. Their inquiries often challenged the orthodox atomic bomb narrative put forth by Stimson, Truman, and others—that the bombs were a military necessity, had saved a million American lives, and had been used as the only reasonable means to end the war. "No one denies that these policy makers desired to hasten the war's end and to save American lives," historian John Dower concluded, "but no serious historian regards those as the sole considerations driving the use of the bombs on Japanese cities."

These investigations revitalized questions among scholars about the morality of dropping the bombs on Japanese civilians, but they had little impact on the American public. The government's official narrative, along with Americans' continued anger over Japan's attack on Pearl Harbor, mistreatment of Allied POWs, and atrocities in Asia, had long ago conjoined to create a powerful and multifaceted mythos about the atomic bombings that still pervaded the American consciousness. Inflated claims of the potential number of American lives saved by the bombings and the bombs' definitive role in ending the war were so ingrained in public thought and culture that many people still perceived the bombs as virtuous instruments of peace.

Even into the 1990s, most Americans had little knowledge of *hibakusha* experiences of nuclear war and its aftermath. In the 1960s, articles in *Time* and *U.S. News and World Report* led readers to believe that no increases in cancer rates had occurred in Nagasaki or Hiroshima. The U.S. government suppressed information about harm caused by nuclear fallout to those living and working in areas downwind of its nuclear weapons test sites, which eliminated an opportunity for heightened awareness of the human effects of large-dose radiation exposure. At the height of Cold War anxiety—when the controversial made-for-television movie *The Day After* (1983) portrayed a gruesome nuclear attack on a

U.S. city and the International Physicians for the Prevention of Nuclear War declared that U.S. civil defense procedures could not provide adequate protection from radiation exposure—most Americans still framed nuclear war as a terrifying potential event rather than a past actuality with historic and scientific value.

To create an exhibit that increased understanding and explored varying perspectives on the atomic bombings, curators at the National Air and Space Museum designed a series of connected galleries that would guide visitors through an abbreviated history of the Pacific War— including the bombing of Pearl Harbor, Japan's aggression throughout the Pacific theater, the making of the atomic bombs, attitudes and debates around the decisions of how and where to use them, and Japan's surrender position in the summer of 1945. The exhibit was to have concluded with information on the delivery of the bombs, their impact on the people of Hiroshima and Nagasaki, and their role in ushering in the nuclear age. The exhibit was intended to simultaneously celebrate the end of a horrific war and—while refraining from drawing conclusions about the morality of the bombs' use—remain compassionate to those who experienced the bombings.

NASM's director, Dr. Martin Harwit, visited Hiroshima and Nagasaki to meet with their mayors, museum curators, and RERF officials to discuss the exhibit and negotiate which artifacts and photographs might be included. Japanese officials were most concerned that the exhibit accurately document, and in no way minimize, the horrific effects of the bombs' heat, blast, and radiation, and the injuries, illnesses, and psychological impairments *hibakusha* suffered. Nagasaki artifacts proposed for the exhibit included a broken wall clock stopped at 11:02; the shadow of a clothesline imprinted on a fence; the head of an angel from a fallen statue at Urakami Church; melted ceramic roof tiles, coins, and bottles; and an infant's burned clothing. Several of Yamahata's early Nagasaki photographs were in negotiation, including one of an injured mother breastfeeding her child and another of a blackened corpse. Short statements from thirteen Nagasaki *hibakusha*—including Taniguchi and doctors Nagai and Akizuki—were also chosen for display.

But a commemorative exhibit attempting to span the stark differences between wartime memory and meaning on both sides of a conflict would prove impossible to achieve. Many U.S. veterans who had fought an enemy as vicious and tenacious as Japan believed that a national fiftieth anniversary exhibit should only celebrate their victory and commemorate their courage. The presence of historical analysis of the necessity of the bombs or evidence of *hibakusha* suffering would distort and even vilify their valor and sacrifice in the final months of the war, they claimed, and would also devalue the lives of soldiers who would have died in a U.S. invasion of Japan. Similar to how the ABCC's provision of medical treatment to survivors could have symbolized atonement, for World War II veterans, the inclusion of survivors' stories in the Smithsonian exhibit amounted to an undeserved apology for dropping the bombs to end a war that Japan had so brutally begun with its attack on Pearl Harbor.

The exhibit's initial design and narrative draft were released in early 1994, after which a committee of ten U.S. historians and scholars identified some imbalances and inaccuracies for the museum staff to address. Before revisions were made, however, the 180,000-member Air Force Association, which had close historical ties to the NASM, initiated a national protest; it was later joined by the 3.1-million-member American Legion. Fueled by media coverage supporting their views, these and other veterans' organizations accused the museum of "politically correct curating" and called the exhibit un-American. They declared a singular correct view of the bombings as having ended the war and saved lives, demanded the removal of *hibakusha* images and testimonies, called for more context about Japan's atrocities, and asserted that the exhibit should evoke American pride in its victory rather than shame for its use of the atomic bombs. Veterans also insisted on the elimination of any component of the exhibit that raised a moral question about the bombings. In a *Time* magazine interview, exhibit curator Tom Crouch reflected that the exhibit's critics had a "reluctance to really tell the whole story. They want to stop the story when the bomb leaves the bomb bay."

Nonetheless, curators revised the script four times to respond to many of the veterans' concerns over balance and accuracy. They removed historical documentation of several leading U.S. officials' opposition to or doubts about the bombs' use, including General Eisenhower's postwar claim that he had expressed his opposition to using the bomb to President Truman in July 1945. They also added more information and photographs about Pacific War conflicts, Allied casualties, and Japanese atrocities, and made subtle changes in language to reduce perceptions of sympathy toward the Japanese. The most explicit photos of dead and burned *hibakusha* selected for the exhibit were cut, including twelve of the grimmest images from Nagasaki. Nearly all *hibakusha* personal testimonies were deleted—including those by doctors Akizuki and Nagai—as was a majority of the planned final section of the exhibit on the Cold War and nuclear proliferation. Many historians believed the museum went too far in trying to accommodate veterans' views; their most serious concerns arose when curators seemed ready to acquiesce to veterans' demands to honor Secretary of War Stimson's claim that the bombs saved a million Americans lives despite documentary evidence to the contrary.

Ironically, Japan experienced similar controversies over its own fiftieth-anniversary commemoration of the war's end. New research in Japan had exposed details of the country's previously veiled wartime history—including Japanese soldiers' slaughter and rape of civilians during their invasion of China and other Asian countries, and their extreme brutality during the Pacific War. These revelations stirred passionate debates over Japan's own accountability, the emperor's culpability, and how the war would be remembered by future generations. Nagasaki itself became the center of a national controversy when it opened the newly rebuilt Nagasaki Atomic Bomb Museum in 1996. In response to Japanese critics' long-standing complaints that its exhibits had focused solely on *hibakusha* suffering without critical wartime context, the museum planned to expand its scope to include documentation of the Nanjing massacre, Japan's experiments with biological weapons on humans, and its seizure and sexual exploitation of women of other Asian nations as "comfort women" for the Japanese military. The proposed exhibit created a furor among conservative Japanese nationalists, however, who protested and made anonymous threats to museum curators and museum staff. The museum subsequently modified the exhibit, eliminating, among others, photographs of Chinese civilians brutally murdered by Japanese soldiers and of starving and beaten Allied POWs in the forced eighty-mile Bataan Death March.

At the National Air and Space Museum, the curators' revisions to the exhibit script did not satisfy critics' concerns. The veterans' opposition caught the attention of several U.S. congressmen, who also began to publicly denounce the planned exhibit. By September 1994, the U.S. Senate had passed a nonbinding resolution that called the script "revisionist and offensive to many World War II veterans," asserted the *Enola Gay*'s role in "helping to bring World War II to a merciful end," and resolved that the exhibit "should avoid impugning the memory of those who gave their lives for freedom." Four months later, in early 1995, the Smithsonian announced the cancellation of the planned exhibit and its accompanying catalog, to be replaced with a display of the *Enola Gay*'s enormous fuselage and brief explanations of the plane's role in dropping the first atomic bomb and Japan's surrender nine days later.

Reactions in the United States and Japan were expectedly mixed. U.S. veterans who had opposed the exhibit overwhelmingly approved its cancellation. Senator Ted Stevens (R-Ala.) concurred, condemning any reframing of the official narrative as "a constant erosion of the truth" and the exhibit as "a view of the events . . . that is contrary to the memory of those who lived through the war." At the same time, some veterans expressed reservations about the exhibit's closing. "Even if it is true that the atomic bombings saved thousands of Americans," veteran Dell Herndon wrote to the editor of the *Whittier Daily News* in California, "it is our patriotic duty to acknowledge the results of those bombs."

NASM director Harwit resigned in protest, and fifty U.S. historians signed a letter to Smithsonian secretary I. Michael Heyman decrying factual errors and omissions contained even in the final streamlined exhibit. Japanese prime minister Murayama Tomiichi made a short statement saying that the decision to close the exhibit was "regrettable." Nagasaki's mayor Motoshima, however, was outraged. He responded to the news by first apologizing to those who were killed and hurt in Japan's attack on Pearl Harbor and for Japan's invasion of numerous Asian nations. "But do you tell me," he went on, "that, because of this aggression and these atrocities committed by the Japanese, there is no need to reflect upon the fact that an unprecedented weapon of mass destruction was used on a community of noncombatants?"

Hibakusha experiences had again been excluded from the official atomic bomb narrative in the United States. Americans' ignorance about the atomic bombings and their human effects remained intact: A 1995 Gallup poll showed that one in four Americans did not know that the U.S. had dropped atomic bombs on Japan, and even fewer comprehended the scope of the destruction. In 1995, author Jon Krakauer took a step to fill this void by traveling to Nagasaki and writing a piece about the city's atomic bomb history. In "The Forgotten Ground Zero," distributed by Universal Press Syndicate to newspapers throughout the United States, Krakauer briefly chronicled Yoshida's experiences at the moment of the atomic blast and in the months and years that followed. Describing Yoshida, he wrote: "In left profile, he appears unmarked by the blast. From the other side, however, the story of the apocalypse is writ large on Yoshida's countenance: The entire right half of his face is a matrix of purplish scar tissue and disfigured flesh." Krakauer closed the article with a quote from Yoshida explaining his feelings toward Americans. "At first I hated Americans for what they did to me," Yoshida said. "I didn't understand how any nation could use such a cruel weapon on human beings. But in my old age, I have learned that holding a grudge does nobody any good. I no longer hate Americans. I only hate war."

In response, a letter to the editor of the *Seattle Times* from Olive V. McDaniel Nielsen, World War II veteran of the U.S. Coast Guard Women's Reserve, echoed veterans' earlier outcries over the Smithsonian exhibit: "Poor Nagasaki! Poor Hiroshima!" Nielsen wrote. "If there had been no Pearl Harbor, there would not have been a bombed-out Hiroshima and a bombed-out Nagasaki. . . . How nice that [Nagasaki survivor Katsuji] Yoshida no longer hates the U.S. for what the atom bomb did to him. Does he ever wonder how many Americans still remember what his country's planes did to Pearl Harbor?" Her letter captures the nearly insurmountable tensions between veterans' animosity toward a former enemy and historians' scrutiny of multilayered wartime events, particularly when the military of one country caused great harm to civilians of an enemy nation in the name of the greater good.

At a June 1995 press conference for the opening of the scaled-down NASM exhibit, Smithsonian secretary Heyman responded to a question about why he had omitted the realities of the atomic bombs' unprecedented destruction and human suffering. His answer: "I really decided to leave it more to the imagination."

———

For members of the Nagasaki Foundation for the Promotion of Peace, human imagination alone was incapable of grasping the true impact of the atomic bomb. Across Japan, a general antinuclear sentiment prevailed, but it was the *hibakusha* activists who believed that only by grounding the unimaginable in the specifics of human experience could people around the world comprehend the effects of nuclear war—a single bomb, instantaneously destroying a city and its population, and invisible, deadly radiation penetrating the bodies of those who survived. To fulfill their imperative, these men and women who chose to speak out persisted in openly claiming the *hibakusha* identities imposed on them as teenagers fifty years earlier. They chose to relive excruciating memories and opened themselves to alienation from family members, harsh judgment for publicly airing their anguish, and right-wing Japanese citizens' untrue labeling of them as liars or communists. Speaking candidly about their personal experiences provided each a unique opportunity to influence a world they saw as both obsessed with nuclear weapons and fundamentally ignorant about their real-life consequences. They were *kataribe*—storytellers in the centuries-long Japanese tradition by which selected individuals pass on historical information to their fellow citizens and future generations.

"We are now trembling at the thought of an all-out accidental nuclear war," Dr. Akizuki declared. "In my view the evil of nuclear weapons . . . has transcended all other issues." As the impassioned leader of the *kataribe* movement, Akizuki narrated one of the leading documentaries on the atomic bombings, published new *hibakusha* testimonies, and traveled to Europe and the Soviet Union to advocate, often before large crowds, for the elimination of nuclear weapons. In a personal meeting in Rome, Akizuki gave the pope documentary films about the atomic bombing and messages from the mayors of Nagasaki and Hiroshima. In his speeches, he had the rare quality of being able to express fully the truth of his own city's suffering while also profoundly apologizing for Japan's aggression and offering deeply felt sympathy for the immense harm his country had inflicted on others.

Still, no matter how much he advocated for *hibakusha* voices to be heard or how strongly he appealed to nuclear powers to stop their production of nuclear weapons, Akizuki could never shake the sadness and despair he had felt since the moment of the bombing. Into the early 1990s, the weakened, white-haired doctor clipped every newspaper article on the atomic bomb he could find and placed them in scrapbooks. "I think it's my duty to read them. I put them by my bedside, but often

I'm exhausted and fall asleep without looking at them. I know I'll do the same thing again, but still I continue clipping and pasting. Sadly, I'm an atomic bomb doctor."

One fall evening in 1992, Dr. Akizuki was returning home after presenting at an International Physicians for the Prevention of Nuclear War conference in Nagasaki, when the cold night air triggered a severe asthma attack. "My husband always carried his inhaler," Sugako remembered. "But he didn't have one that day. His mind was on the conference." An ambulance rushed Akizuki to the hospital, but his brain had been deprived of oxygen for too long. He lay unconscious in room 401 of St. Francis Hospital, the same room where he had treated patients after the bombing and in the decades since. Surrounded by gifts and flowers from family, friends, and colleagues across Japan, Sugako cared for him day and night for years, often placing her face next to his and talking softly to him as if he were conscious. When visitors came to pay their respects, Sugako brought in Akizuki's favorite seasonal meals and asked others to eat them for her husband. "Since he worked very hard," she said, "now God has told him to take a rest for a while."

The strength of Dr. Akizuki's vision and direction allowed the Nagasaki Foundation for the Promotion of Peace to thrive during his absence, both before and after Nagasaki's 1995 public commemoration of the fiftieth anniversary of the bombings. NFPP administrator Matsuo Ranko oversaw *kataribe* bookings and monitored their presentations to help them improve. Her work was not without the challenges of individual *hibakusha* personalities. Dō-oh and Yoshida, for example, wanted to tell their stories in their own way, without listening to her feedback. "I am a *hibakusha,* and you are not," Yoshida told Matsuo. "You cannot understand our suffering." Dō-oh felt the same way when Matsuo tried to advise her on how to better construct her speeches to help students not only *feel* the effects of nuclear war but also think about the *causes* of both the war and the atomic bombing.

"Dō-oh-san and Yoshida-san were very proud," Matsuo remembered. "They didn't like taking advice from someone like me who was younger and without firsthand experience of war or the atomic bombing. It took a long time to get there, but eventually they understood. When the children listened eagerly to their presentations and wrote them letters of thanks, both of them were so happy and moved. Many of the children said they would work hard to prevent another war."

In contrast to the vast majority of the more than two hundred thousand Nagasaki survivors who never spoke publicly about their experiences, forty *hibakusha*—including Yoshida, Dō-oh, Wada, and Nagano—made up the NFPP's core group of *kataribe*. Taniguchi joined them at times, while also working with several other activist organizations. Within the seemingly hopeless circumstances of thousands of nuclear warheads deployed across the globe, nuclear nations continuing to manufacture weapons, and new nations racing to develop them, this small group of *hibakusha* refused invisibility. Against cultural norms, they remained willing to tell their personal stories to adults and children at the Nagasaki Atomic Bomb Museum, in schools and universities across the country, and at local, national, and international conferences and events. Their mandate was to speak with neutrality, without promoting any political or religious agenda. With a sense of urgency as they approached the final years of their lives, they used their unique personalities and experiences to help audiences resist official narratives and vague impressions of the bombings and grasp the human cost of nuclear weapons. Their goal was clear: that Nagasaki remain the last nuclear-bombed city in history.

CHAPTER 9

GAMAN

Gaman: *Enduring the seemingly unbearable with patience and dignity*

Every morning at five a.m., Wada wakes up after six hours of sleep and pauses to look out his window at the expanse of the Urakami Valley that stretches all the way to the bay. After washing his face, he heads to the kitchen, waits for the newspaper delivery, and has breakfast—*misoshiru* (miso soup), rice, and various dishes Hisako prepares. On days when he has speaking engagements, he dresses in coordinated slacks, a dress shirt, a tie, and a wool or tweed jacket. Since he no longer drives, Wada walks everywhere, laughing with appreciation that at his age, his legs still work.

"In 1945, there were no cars or gas or oil—so everyone walked," he says. "You could see the mountains from everywhere." Now, from certain vantage points, tall buildings block his view of the mountains. Some things haven't changed, though: The Urakami and Nakashima rivers flow into Nagasaki Bay, centuries-old Buddhist temples and Shinto shrines still stand in the older sections of the city, and on early spring mornings, fog rolls in from the sea, blanketing the city. Nagasaki is still a Mitsubishi town, with factories rebuilt on two of the company's former sites and massive shipyards that produce some of the world's largest commercial ships and destroyers, the latter in defiance of Nagasaki's declaration as a city of peace.

Little else remains of the city Wada knew in 1945. He walks down narrow streets through his neighborhood crowded with Japanese-style homes, apartments, and condominium buildings. Following a path along the Urakami River, he passes schools, parks, and grocery stores filled with fresh produce, meats, fish, canned goods, and sweets. He crosses Ōhashi Bridge and strides past the former site of Dō-oh's Mitsubishi factory, near the streetcar stop where he would have died if another streetcar hadn't derailed that morning, resulting in a change in his route. Today, cars and trucks speed by him on the Urakami Valley's main thoroughfare, lined with storefronts, cafés, and offices. Wada passes a pachinko parlor just as someone exits, so he can hear the loud music and whirring of small metal pinballs racing through the machines inside. Color-coded streetcars still run along the same routes he drove before the bombing, their wires connected to cables overhead, though now an automated voice announces upcoming stops, and machines collect the fares. As the streetcars pass, Wada mentally calculates their speed.

Farther south, too, the city is barely recognizable from Wada's childhood. The circular observatory atop Mount Inasa provides an expansive view of the East China Sea and the islands off the coast of Kyushu. Below, large vessels, smaller boats, and city cruise liners dock at Nagasaki's port in view of waterfront shops and restaurants. The modern Nagasaki Station is surrounded by multistory office buildings, department stores, and hotels. Just north of the station on Nishizaka Hill is the Site of the Martyrdom of the Twenty-Six Saints of Japan, with a long wall of life-size bronze statues and a memorial hall with religious artifacts passed down through Nagasaki's complex Catholic history of freedom and forbidden practice. Approximately sixty-seven thousand Catholics now reside in Nagasaki Prefecture, attending services at Urakami Cathedral and other churches scattered throughout the city, prefecture, and surrounding islands. Chinatown in the old city thrives. At night, the central district of Shianbashi is filled with packed clubs. Along the main north-south street through the city, a small Ferris wheel on the roof of a department store lights up the skyline.

In the southernmost region of the city, tourists frequent Glover Garden, perched on a hill overlooking the bay—the nineteenth-century home and gardens of Thomas Glover, the Scottish merchant who established trade between Nagasaki and Britain. Dejima, the tiny fan-shaped residential and commercial island built in 1636 to segregate the Dutch East India Company traders from the rest of the city, has been restored to replicate its seventeenth-century design—a reminder that during Japan's two hundred years of national isolation, Nagasaki was the only Japanese port open to the West. Now foreigners are so common in Nagasaki that they are barely noticed except by schoolchildren, who frequently stare at them at bus stops or from across the aisle inside streetcars.

Veiled from view from the main road through the Urakami Valley, the bombing and its aftereffects are meticulously and elegantly remembered at Hypocenter Park, Peace Park, the Nagasaki Atomic Bomb Museum, and the Nagasaki National Peace Memorial Hall for the Atomic Bomb Victims. In Hypocenter Park, enclosed by lush green trees that block the sounds of traffic, a tall, black granite cenotaph points upward to the spot a third of a mile overhead where the bomb detonated. In front of the memorial, a large stone box holds a microfilm list of victims' names. Concrete concentric circles ring the monument. Scattered through the park are numerous smaller monuments, including one for the thousands of Korean slave laborers who died in the bombing. Against the banks of the small Shimonokawa River, which runs through the park, postbomb soil from the hypocenter area is encased in glass, revealing eerily preserved pieces of melted glass and fragments of tile, ceramic dishware, and bottles.

If you know where to look, lesser-known reminders of the atomic bomb are tucked away within the concentric circles of the bomb's reach. Behind the rebuilt Shiroyama Elementary School, atop a hill west of the hypocenter, the cherry trees planted in memory of students who died in the bombing have now matured. Bomb shelters dug into the hillsides around the perimeter of the school are now filled in with dirt or covered by boards or chain-link fencing. At the corner of the school closest to the hypocenter, a five-thousand-square-foot section of the original building now serves as a small gallery of atomic bomb artifacts and Hayashi Shigeo's 1945 photographs of the annihilated city.

Behind the enormous, U-shaped Yamazato Elementary School north of the hypocenter, three 1940s-era air raid shelters carved out of the hillside are preserved where countless teachers, children, and neighborhood residents fled and died. Down the hill is the tiny hut where Dr. Nagai lived during his final years; next door is a small gallery and library of the physician's books, photographs, and personal possessions. Scorched statues of Catholic saints stand in the front garden of Urakami

Urakami Valley, viewed from Mount Inasa, 2011. (*Photograph by Shirabe Hitomi*)

Cathedral, and one of its original fifty-ton domes still lies embedded in the hillside where it fell seconds after the blast.

At the base of Mount Kompira southeast of the hypocenter, Nagasaki University School of Medicine and its affiliated hospital host multiple organizations that serve *hibakusha* medical needs, document historical and current studies on radiation-related medical conditions, and provide the public with data on nuclear weapons stockpiles across the world. Nagasaki's famous one-legged stone *torii* gateway still perches, blackened and erect, at the hillside entrance to Sanno Shrine. Up the hill, two scarred camphor trees—once considered dead after the bomb's blast and heat had severed their trunks and branches and scorched them bare—are now more than twenty feet in circumference and rise fifty-five and sixty-nine feet high, their massive branches reaching out in all directions, creating a thick green canopy over the walkway leading to the shrine.

Except for those like Yoshida who cannot hide their disfigurement, most of the approximately fifty thousand aging *hibakusha* living in the Nagasaki area remain invisible to the public eye. Many avoid the hypocenter district altogether because of the terrifying feelings that still arise. Others agonize that their family members' bones lie beneath today's bustling roads, buildings, and memorial parks. Some bow their heads in silence as they pass by in their cars or by train.

The term "post-traumatic stress disorder" (PTSD) was introduced in Japan in the 1990s and came into public awareness as a psychological condition after the 1995 Hanshin-Awaji earthquake, but counseling remains culturally foreign and rarely available. Images of hideously burned people reaching out for help are permanently engraved in many survivors' memories. One woman feels like she's going insane because she can't forget the voices of small children and their mother buried beneath their collapsed house screaming for help. Another has never eaten a pomegranate since watching—and smelling—one of her family members being cremated on top of wood from a pomegranate tree. For many, silence has remained the only way to survive.

Dō-oh, Nagano, Taniguchi, Wada, and Yoshida remain among the select few who keep alive the public memory of the atomic bomb. Each year, the NFPP's forty *kataribe* make nearly 1,300 presentations in 137 Nagasaki schools, plus many more for students visiting Nagasaki on field trips. In addition to Taniguchi's U.S. travels, Wada, Nagano, and Yoshida have also traveled to American universities to tell their stories—Wada at Westmont College in California, Nagano at Oberlin College in Ohio, and Yoshida at DePaul University and Northwestern University in Chicago. Nagano was scheduled to depart Oberlin for a day of sightseeing in New York on the morning of the September 11, 2001, attacks in New York, Washington, D.C., and Pennsylvania. Unable to return home for nearly a week, she was terrorized by the images on television, not only because of their horrifying content but also because she initially misunderstood her interpreter and thought that Japan and United States were again at war.

This terrifying event notwithstanding, Nagano, Yoshida, and Wada are proud of the dialogues they were able to create with American students. They were frequently asked about Pearl Harbor and whether they, as atomic bomb survivors, hate Americans. In response, all three apologized for their country's attack on Pearl Harbor and told their audiences that the war had been between countries, not people. At the same time, they challenged students to think about the morality of the atomic bombings. "I don't blame the United States," Wada told his audience, "but I want people to understand what the nuclear bombs do. We can't have another atomic bomb experience."

Since 1995, numerous books, exhibits, and documentaries about the bombings have been released in the United States. Many are from Nagasaki, including Yamaguchi Senji's memoir *Burnt Yet Undaunted;* former ABCC physician James Yamazaki's book *Children of the Atomic Bomb;* an exhibit of Yamahata Yōsuke's photo collection with an accompanying book and film in English; and U.S. Marine Corps photographer Joe O'Donnell's *Japan 1945*—a collection with several photos of postbomb Nagasaki, including his gripping black-and-white image of Taniguchi's back. While speaking in the United States, however, Wada was shocked to discover how many American college students knew only about the Hiroshima bombing; they hadn't learned—or didn't remember—that Nagasaki had been bombed as well. "The voice of Nagasaki," he says, "has still not reached the world."

Back home, Wada speaks forty or fifty times a year, mostly in the fall and spring when most of Japan's school field trips are scheduled. Energized by talking with young people, he keeps changing his presentations to stay relevant to new generations of children. "When I was younger, I wanted to stand up for what was right, but I could not," he explains. "Now, if there's one thing I can do to protect our children, even if it's hard, I will do whatever I can to help."

Wada falls asleep easily each night, although a few times a year, his sleep is interrupted by nightmares of Hotarujaya Terminal crashing down on top of him. In the morning, he opens his window and looks out over Nagasaki, marveling that the city before him was built out of the atomic ruins. "One person can't do anything, but if many people gather together, they can accomplish unimaginable things," he says. "If it's possible to rebuild this city out of nothing, why isn't it possible for us to eliminate war and nuclear weapons, to create peace? We can't *not* do it!"

Wada Kōichi telling his story. (*Courtesy of Wada Kōichi*)

On a sunny April afternoon in 2011, Nagano arrives by taxi at a large hotel halfway up Mount Inasa to speak to a group of junior high school students from another part of Japan. They gather in a small meeting room, the students' chairs facing front—the boys seated on one side of the aisle, the girls on the other. Nagano sits at a table facing them, wearing a pale pink blazer and deep red lipstick. Her auburn hair is thinning.

She adjusts her mike. "*Konnichiwa* [hello]," she says to the students, slowly and clearly. "Thank you for taking the time today to listen to my story."

Three years after becoming a *kataribe*, Nagano was finally able to tell her audiences about Seiji's and Kuniko's deaths and her fifty-year isolation from her mother. At first, Nagano cried as she recounted these stories and spoke of her lifelong sadness and guilt; now her voice cracks only slightly. During busy school field trip seasons, Nagano often speaks two or three times a day, and she has traveled to cities all over Japan. "I never imagined I would do something like this," she says. "But I feel it is my responsibility to tell the truth. If people understand how terrifying the atomic bomb is, my survival and my witness to this experience will have had a purpose."

Speaking to the students at the Inasa hotel, Nagano begins with her life before the war—what it was like to be mobilized to work in the airplane parts factory, how lonely she was when her younger brother and sister were sent away for safety, and how determined she was to bring them back. She describes the moment of the flash—"*pikaaaaaaaaaaaaaah!*"— and her feeling of dread as she raced toward Nagasaki in near darkness to find her family. She recalls the scorched people wandering through the ruins with skin from their arms hanging down to the ground, and dead bodies everywhere she turned. The students listen intently as she describes seeing her father. "By *total* coincidence, I ran into him on that bridge!" she says, her voice rising to a high pitch. "I was *so* lucky!"

Nagano's eyes tear up and her voice shakes as she speaks about cremating Sei-chan in a scorched field. In Japan, most students would sit politely even if they weren't interested, but these boys and girls are just a few years younger than Nagano was at the time of the bombing, and they are riveted. "We gathered some wood scraps, laid Sei-chan on top of them, and burned his body," she says. "I watched it with my own eyes." She recounts Kuniko's death and cremation in the village of Obama. "*I* brought them back from Kagoshima. It was *my* fault that they died. I still think I should have died instead of them—and wonder why I have to live this long."

Nagano tells the students about her mother's icy silence and their ultimate reconciliation, about her shock at seeing about her brother's and sister's blackened ashes, and about being in the United States on 9/11. She leans forward and pulls them into her focus. *"Please* treasure your families and friends," she says. "You were born in an era of peace. *Please treasure it."*

"I was a young girl, healthy in both mind and body," Dō-oh writes in her opening to an autobiographical essay. "I was someone who talked with friends about our dreams and burning hopes. But in one instant the atomic bomb capsized my life." She directs her anger at the "stupidity of war . . . as a scream from the Shōwa era."

In the early 2000s, Dō-oh stands tall before a large group of students and teachers, dressed in an elegant black brocade jacket and skirt she made when she was in her thirties. A hand-painted gold blouse peeks through at the breastbone. She wears small diamond earrings, and her black hair is pulled back into a stylish twist. Dō-oh speaks directly, without hesitation, expressing her shame over Japan's atrocities in China and her government's silence about it. She describes the day of the bombing, her injuries, and her parents digging up young sweet potatoes, cooking them, and feeding them to Dō-oh as her final meal. She speaks with great feeling about her agonizing decade of isolation inside her house. Dō-oh presses the young people in her audience to think beyond economics and money and focus on deeper values. "We need to understand how to live with heart," she says. "The twenty-first century has got to be the century of sensitivity."

A few girls in the audience cry as Dō-oh draws them into her story. Dō-oh urges them not to waste their abilities and implores them to try to find their own independence and life purpose. "I want to be strong, like her," one girl comments afterward.

For a while, Dō-oh's speaking engagements were interrupted by health problems. After surviving breast cancer in the 1990s, Dō-oh suffered two strokes that left her face partially paralyzed and her body unable to feel hot or cold. Even as she recuperated in the hospital, however, she painted and composed a collection of tanka. "For the birds and for me," she wrote, "when the will to live rises up / even in the midst of turmoil / the unmovable mountain laughs." Once ambulatory, Dō-oh rejected her hospital gown and walked the hallways in an elegant navy cotton robe made from *yukata* (summer kimono) fabric. "'If you don't

Dō-oh Mineko recounting her story. (*Courtesy of Okada Ikuyo*)

become yourself, who will become you?'" Dō-oh declared, quoting a line from her favorite Japanese poet. "It's delightful, don't you think? This is what guides my life."

Extensive rehabilitation therapy gave Dō-oh the strength to continue serving as a *kataribe*. The small pieces of glass still lodged in her back remain sensitive to the touch and unpredictably painful when she moves in certain ways; her doctors want to remove them, but Dō-oh refuses, afraid that the shards are too close to the spine. She appears in dozens of television, radio, and print interviews, speaking on behalf of those whose bodies she had stepped over to escape the darkened, collapsed Mitsubishi factory—and for her two school friends who died. When Dō-oh gives presentations for school groups, students and teachers often gasp at her striking style—beautiful fabrics, bold colors, and eyeglasses to coordinate with whatever she is wearing—and her unique fashion sense frequently stirs negative comments by some of her *kataribe* peers. "Children who come to the Nagasaki Atomic Bomb Museum for presentations are very curious about what kind of people *hibakusha* are," NFPP *kataribe* coordinator Matsuo Ranko says. "Then Mrs. Dō-oh comes out in a bright red dress, long, manicured nails, and big earrings. Or a cheetah print. Jaw-dropping outfits. Other *kataribe* came to me and asked me to talk with Mrs. Dō-oh to get her to tone down what she wears."

Dō-oh was indignant. *"Why?"* she retorted when Matsuo broached the subject with her. *"Why* is this fashion inappropriate? There is no rule that says *hibakusha* should all dress the same! *I* am a *hibakusha*! I am *me!*'"

Matsuo agreed. She went back to those who were complaining and told them what Dō-oh said. "I'm not sure they were satisfied," Matsuo says, laughing, "but I thought it was truly wonderful."

———

In 2009, U.S. president Barack Obama gave a major speech in Prague addressing the state of nuclear weapons in the world and the United States' moral responsibility to lead disarmament efforts. "Today," Obama said, "I state clearly and with conviction America's commitment to seek the peace and security of a world without nuclear weapons." Taniguchi and thousands of *hibakusha* throughout Japan felt more optimistic than they had in decades. "I am counting on this new President Obama," Taniguchi said. "Although previous U.S. presidents never worked on reduction and elimination of nuclear weapons, President Obama actually presented a plan to approach nuclear weapons reduction. We have prayed for the day when we can say it was good for us to live this long."

Within two years, however, Taniguchi's hope for significant weapons reduction had deflated. He rails at Obama for continuing to modernize U.S. nuclear weapons for war readiness after receiving the 2009 Nobel Peace Prize for his antinuclear stance. "What happened to that speech in which he called for a world without nuclear weapons?" Taniguchi demands. "Just how long is he going to continue these nuclear tests that trample on the feelings of *hibakusha*?"

As of December 2014, more than 16,300 nuclear warheads were stockpiled at some 98 sites in 14 countries across the globe—94 percent of which were controlled by the United States and Russia. Still, Taniguchi keeps fighting for the complete elimination of nuclear weapons. He has protested against India's 1998 underground nuclear weapons tests and more recent subcritical tests in the United States. In his late seventies and now into his eighties, he has participated in the United Nations' Nuclear Non-Proliferation Treaty (NPT) Review Conferences, one of several focal points for his fight for the global reduction and eventual abolition of nuclear weapons.

Out of 193 United Nations member states, 190 have signed the NPT— only India, Israel, and Pakistan have not—making the NPT the most successful international disarmament agreement since the beginning of nuclear weapons development. The treaty, which came into force in 1970, binds signatory nations to an agreement that only the five current nuclear weapons states—the United States, Russia, China, France, and the United Kingdom— may possess nuclear weapons, and it mandates these nuclear nations' ongoing commitment to the long-term goal of complete disarmament. By signing the treaty, all other countries have agreed to renounce current or future development of nuclear weapons. Since 1995, the NPT has required a majority of signatory nations to gather every five years to review the treaty's technical aspects, report on compliance, and develop new strategies that all participating nations can agree upon to help achieve the treaty's goals.

Taniguchi joined the Nagasaki delegations to the 2005 and 2010 NPT Review Conferences at the United Nations in New York. Standing before more than 400 representatives from approximately 150 nations, he testified about his injuries, the long-term effects of nuclear weapons, and the critical need for faster action in international disarmament. He held up the 1946 USSBS color photo of his raw, exposed back—now one of Nagasaki's iconic images symbolizing the physical and emotional suffering caused by the atomic bombing—and he quietly implored his audience to take action. The 2005 Review Conference got bogged down in procedural disagreements, and no substantial action steps were agreed upon. The 2010 Review Conference, however, ended with the unanimous adoption of a plan to "speed progress on nuclear disarmament, advance non-proliferation, and work

Taniguchi Sumiteru, age eighty-one, speaking before the 2010 Review Conference of the Parties to the Treaty on the Non-Proliferation of Nuclear Weapons. He holds the 1946 photograph of his burned, raw back to give the audience a visual image of his injuries. Taniguchi spoke as a representative of Nihon Hidankyō. (*Courtesy of Taniguchi Sumiteru*)

towards a nuclear-weapon-free zone in the Middle East." A two-month exhibition of atomic bomb photographs and artifacts opened in the main lobby of the United Nations. Photographs of Taniguchi, Yamaguchi Senji, and others lined the wall.

Taniguchi contains his unabated rage toward the Japanese government for attacking Pearl Harbor and for never satisfactorily apologizing. He seethes over the United States' decision to use the bombs on Hiroshima and Nagasaki without understanding the extent of damage they would cause—especially to the human body—and the absence of official remorse. His anger is particularly triggered when he hears language that he believes distorts the truth about nuclear weapons. The phrase "peaceful use of nuclear weapons" for example, is often used by officials talking about how the atomic bombs ended the Pacific War or how, since then, nuclear weapons have deterred war. Taniguchi balks. "The word 'peaceful' is used to make everything acceptable," he says. For Taniguchi, always exhausted from the physical pain he endures each day, there is only one meaning for the word "peace," and it doesn't include nuclear weapons. "The atomic bomb," he says, "is the destroyer of peace."

––––––

"I'm as different now as clouds in the sky are to mud on the ground!" seventy-seven-year-old Yoshida declares in 2009, comparing himself to sixty years earlier. He zips through the hallways of the Nagasaki Atomic Bomb Museum, often taking the stairs instead of the elevator. "The stairs are better for you!" he says, laughing, racing up to the Nagasaki Foundation for the Promotion of Peace's third-floor offices for a meeting with staff. He carries snacks to give to his colleagues in case they missed lunch.

Always on a mission to promote peace, Yoshida meets with Japanese and foreign journalists or filmmakers reporting on survivors' lives. He escorts them through the Nagasaki Atomic Bomb Museum, where over six hundred thousand people visit each year, telling his guests about his own experiences as they walk.

The museum's first exhibit room captures life in Nagasaki before August 9, 1945. The next room, dark and cavernous, is filled with actual and re-created ruins of the city in the immediate aftermath of the bombing. Yoshida quickly guides his visitors into the next gallery, past a time line of the Manhattan Project, the development of the bombs, and events leading up to their delivery. On his left, they see a life-size model of Fat Man and scientific descriptions of the bomb's blast, heat, and radiation. Yoshida leads them through crowds of junior high school students to get to his destination: the long wall of photographs documenting survivors' injuries and the human effects of the bombing.

Taniguchi's famous color photo hangs here, as do the two photos of fifteen-year-old Yoshida's crusted, scorched face taken in 1946 before and after his skin graft surgeries. He touches the black patch covering the spot where his right ear used to be. "After a while," he says, "the swollen part here rotted and fell off. So there's no ear here. Nothing at all—just a hole, alone." He pauses, then grins slightly, changing the mood. "I'm okay now, but then I was completely messed up—such a handsome fellow that I was!" He happily points out that he often stands in front of these photos without anyone recognizing that he is the same person. "It's helped me realize that my face is much better than it used to be," he says, smiling broadly, no longer ashamed of the scars on his face and neck, the crookedness of his mouth and teeth, his shriveled left ear, or the black patch strapped to his head. "Every day I apply lotion on my skin," he says. "And now, after more than sixty years, my face has finally improved this much!"

He does not mention that on certain days, his right hand cramps so badly he can't open his fingers, and the skin still splits open sometimes, especially in winter, causing flesh to bulge out. Yoshida and his guests turn to walk through the final exhibits in the main hall, past Dr. Miyajima's examination table on which Dō-oh was treated on the night of the bombing. Glass cases are filled with melted coins and glass, blistered roof tiles, and a schoolgirl's melted metal lunch box filled with scorched rice. In the next room, they pass an exhibit about Dr. Nagai, a display of *hibakusha* paintings and poems, and three small television screens mounted on the wall show videotaped *hibakusha* testimonies, including those by Yoshida, Wada, and Taniguchi. "Mine is number twenty-one," Yoshida says without stopping. The museum's final exhibit hall documents Japan's war with China, the Pacific War prior to the atomic bombings, and the history of the nuclear age. Yoshida pushes on, ascending the spiral walkway to the museum lobby, seamlessly interrupting his conversation with his guests to bow slightly and say *ohayō gozaimasu* (good morning) to every person he passes, whether he knows them or not.

In the museum lobby, every wall is covered with artwork from schoolchildren across Japan and the world—most of them created with colorful origami cranes representing peace. Dozens more similar creations lean against the walls. A large bronzed map of the reconstructed prebomb neighborhoods in the hypocenter area, created with data collected by the Nagasaki restoration project volunteers in the 1970s, provides a visual of what instantaneously disappeared when the bomb exploded.

Off the main lobby of the museum is a corridor of meeting rooms where photo archivist Fukahori Yoshitoshi and his team of volunteers store a collection of more than three thousand pre- and post–atomic bomb photographs. Having gathered photographs for the Urakami Valley's reclamation movement in the 1970s, Fukahori came to understand the power of photographs to evoke profound sensory responses to the bombings. In order to support the Nagasaki Atomic Bomb Museum and ensure that still images would become and remain a vital part of the historic record, he and five colleagues established a special committee to collect, catalog, and caption photographs of the atomic bombing and its aftermath from *hibakusha* throughout the city. Over time, they also received significant contributions from Japanese photographers of the Nagasaki atomic bombing and acquired five hundred photographs taken by U.S. Army personnel during the occupation. Many from this collection are on display in the Nagasaki Atomic Bomb Museum. In 2014, at the age of eighty-five, Fukahori traveled to the National Archives in Washington, D.C., and brought back dozens of U.S. military photographs of postbomb Nagasaki that neither he nor anyone else back home had seen before.

Yoshida says good-bye to his guests and turns to the crowds of uniformed, talkative students lining up for tours and presentations in the museum lobby and on the sidewalks outside. He locates the group of students that is scheduled to hear his story that day, greets the head teacher, then races to the head of the line to hold the museum door open for the class, urging them inside until the last child has entered. "Now," he says, beaming, "9.5 out of 10 children don't cry when they see my face."

By the mid-2000s, Yoshida was one of only a few Nagasaki *kataribe* who could be easily identified as *hibakusha* on sight. His disfigurement gives him a unique voice in addressing bullying and prejudice. "Your face, your eyes, your hair . . . these are your treasures," he tells children. "Take good care of yourself."

Yoshida jokes with his students that he is "as good-looking as Kimutaku," a teen heartthrob in the 1990s. Now, however, Kimutaku—still a handsome actor in his forties—no longer evokes the humorous comparison Yoshida intends. The NFPP's Matsuo Ranko suggested that he update the actor he compares himself to, but Yoshida has never done so—except once in Chicago, when he likened his incredible good looks to those of Leonardo DiCaprio. In Nagasaki, however, even if children don't fully understand the reference, Yoshida's lighthearted twist on his appearance still gets children to smile. When children ask him for his autograph afterward, he signs it *Grandpa Yoshida* and adds in parentheses *Grandpa Kimutaku.*

———

Taniguchi, Nagano, Dō-oh, Yoshida, and Wada could have stayed silent. They could have buried their traumatic memories for the rest of their lives. And yet, even as the rest of the world has moved on, they chose to make sure their stories are heard. They have found purpose in communicating, in some small part, the extraordinary perils of nuclear war.

Although scientists have significantly refined their ability to accurately estimate radiation doses for individual *hibakusha,* they still don't fully understand the long-term medical effects of high-dose, whole-body radiation exposure. Successive revisions of the 1965 radiation dosimetry system include computer simulations and other new technologies to more closely measure survivors' gamma and neutron doses, allowing researchers to provide estimates of both an individual's overall radiation exposure and specific dose estimates for fifteen internal organs. Survivors' blood and tooth enamel (from teeth extracted for personal medical purposes) are now used to document radiation levels at a molecular level. Although challenges persist due to unknown survivor locations and shielding factors at the time of the bombings, the Radiation Effects Research Foundation has calculated dose estimates for over 90 percent of the one hundred thousand survivors in its study cohort. Using *hibakusha* autopsy specimens repatriated to Japan, a 2009 study at Nagasaki University's Atomic Bomb Disease Institute indicates that cells from *hibakusha* who died in 1945 are still radioactive; this suggests that not only were victims externally exposed to the bomb's radiation, but that the radioactive materials they ingested—such as dust or water—also irradiated their cells from the inside.

DNA mutations in living cells can take many years to result in detectable diseases, so researchers have not stopped investigating rates of *hibakusha* hypertension, diabetes, and other medical conditions possibly related to radiation exposure. In the meantime, outcomes of long-term studies indicate excess rates of and deaths from certain conditions in survivors even today, including chronic hepatitis and noncancerous heart, thyroid, respiratory, and digestive diseases. Above-normal incidences of leukemia and other cancers persist, including lung, breast, thyroid, stomach, colon, ovarian, thyroid, and liver. Double cancers— the emergence of a second cancer not linked to the spread of an earlier cancer—also occur at higher rates. Dr. Akahoshi Masazumi, cardiologist and director of the Department of Clinical Studies at the RERF in Nagasaki, explained that cancer risk for the youngest *hibakusha*—who were the most vulnerable to the effects of radiation exposure—will peak around 2015, when they have reached the age of seventy.

While genetic effects and increased cancer rates for children of *hibakusha* have not been observed to date, numerous Japanese institutions are continuing their studies using DNA and other emerging technologies. The reason for this, explains Dr. Tomonaga Masao, director of the Nagasaki Atomic Bomb Hospital, is that studies in the United States and Japan have shown concrete experimental evidence that the second generation of mice born to parents exposed to radiation experience higher rates of cellular malformation and higher incidences of cancer than the control groups. "We must be very careful about this," Dr. Tomonaga says, "because most survivors' children are passing the age of fifty and are moving into their cancer-prone age." In 2011, a new national study began on twenty thousand children of *hibakusha*, comparing them with the same number of children of non-*hibakusha* for incidence rates of cancer, diabetes, hypertension, and cardiovascular diseases. The RERF and other scientists are also concerned about potential recessive genetic mutations in future generations.

To continue their studies on the impact of radiation exposure on the immune system, medical conditions, and mortality, the RERF, the Atomic Bomb Disease Institute at Nagasaki University, and other research institutions continue to use immense cohorts of living *hibakusha* and the medical records of deceased survivors. The outcomes of their research have supported scientific-based responses to nuclear accidents such as the 1986 nuclear power plant meltdown in Chernobyl, Ukraine, and the 2011 Fukushima nuclear disaster in Japan following the massive earthquake and tsunami there, two events that traumatized many *hibakusha*. The Fukushima meltdown ignited a shift in Japan's antinuclear movement to include the gradual phasing out of nuclear power. Ironically, outcomes from *hibakusha* medical studies are also used to inform international standards for maximum tolerable radiation exposure.

The enormous number and size of studies conducted since 1945, and the need for their continuation, are further reminders of how little American scientists developing the bomb knew about the effects of momentary, high-dose radiation exposure on the human body.

———

After thirteen years in a coma with Sugako at his side, Dr. Akizuki died in 2005 at the age of eighty-nine. His biographer, Yamashita Akiko, recalled that in his coffin, Dr. Akizuki "was surrounded with white chrysanthemums and light pink roses and smiling peacefully, as if taking a nap." He was buried in a small neighborhood cemetery across the street from his hospital.

Dō-oh died on March 14, 2007, just as the buds on her beloved drooping cherry trees behind her house were ready to burst. Having surpassed by two years her goal to live until seventy-five, she had, by her own measure, defeated the atomic bomb. "What I mean is—I mean, they dropped the bombs thinking everyone will die, right? But not everyone was killed. I think it takes great emotional strength and force of will to triumph over nuclear weapons."

A year earlier, Dō-oh had been diagnosed with colon cancer—a second cancer unrelated to her earlier breast cancer—too far gone for any treatment. After her diagnosis, her younger sister, Okada Ikuyo, drove her to her last class reunion, where Dō-oh, in a wheelchair, posed with her childhood friends for a class photo. Her skin was pale and thin, her eyes red around the edges, and her hair completely white—a reflection of how weak she was; had she been able, she would have colored it. In early 2007, tests revealed that the cancer had spread to her lungs and brain. Okada cared for her sister day and night in the hospital. Dō-oh was both deeply grateful and constantly cranky to Okada and her care providers, leaving Okada scrambling to restore relationships with the hospital staff. Dō-oh had given up smoking after her first cancer diagnosis—but she still loved beer and was delighted when her friends and family sneaked small bottles into the hospital.

Her death came quickly, at home, where she had wanted to be in the end. Later, Okada found one of Dō-oh's last works of art in a drawer in Dō-oh's family altar. It was a *shikishi*—an elegant square of card stock used for hand-brushed poetry and short writings. On it, Dō-oh had watercolored a small purple iris with long green leaves shooting into the center of the board. From the top right corner downward, in clear, graceful strokes, she had brushed the words: *Thank you for a good life.*

Seventy-eight-year-old Yoshida died on April 1, 2010, only four months after a sudden illness. His family never told him that his diagnosis was terminal lung cancer, which quickly spread to his spine, nervous system, and bones. They guessed, though, that having cared for his wife with cancer before her death, Yoshida probably knew.

Near the end of his life, Yoshida lay in his hospital bed, always attended by one or more of his siblings, sons, daughter-in-law, or grandchildren. A bouquet of flowers sat on a small bedside table, IV equipment was positioned at the foot of his bed, and one of his caps hung on the bed's railing. As Yoshida drifted in and out of consciousness, at times his eyes remained slightly open—distant and mostly without recognition of his surroundings. His breathing was labored, and he could no longer talk. When someone spoke to him, his family could sometimes see energy surge through his body into his throat; his mouth would open wider and Yoshida would release a groaning sound—a clear intention to communicate, it seemed—though no understandable sounds emerged.

"It's going to be so lonely without him," his younger brother said prior to his death—and countless people felt the same way. Yoshida had overcome his disfigurement and won people over even when they were shocked or repulsed by his face. His legacy, for nearly everyone who ever met him or heard him speak, was determined joy.

Hibakusha are remembered in both typical and unique ways. In the Japanese Buddhist tradition, the deceased is represented on the family's *butsudan* (altar), a deep-set wooden cabinet with doors that serves as a place of prayer and remembrance and is passed on from one generation to the next. Inside, families place a bodhisattva statue or other symbolic icon, as well as candles, incense, an altar bell, and offerings for their deceased relatives such as special possessions or foods that she or he had loved in life. Here it is believed that the deceased are available for regular, direct communication, and close family members typically speak to them in the same way as when they were alive. For example, some people begin and end their day with greetings to their deceased family members. Others share their day's activities or pray to their relatives for help with personal struggles and decisions. Okada's large, multitiered *butsudan,* made primarily of black-and-red Japanese lacquer ware, has an elegant bronze Buddhist statue at the back surrounded by gilded Buddhist adornments. In the front, Okada has placed a framed photograph of Dō-oh and—to pay homage to one of her sister's favorite indulgences—freshly brewed coffee in a china cup and saucer. Okada speaks with Dō-oh regularly, joking, teasing, complaining, and showing her gifts that friends have brought for the altar to honor Dō-oh's life.

Another Buddhist tradition involves the deceased receiving a *kaimyō*— a posthumous name—by the monk in their family temple, conferred seven days after death to symbolize the transformation from the physical to the spiritual world. The *kaimyō* is usually inscribed on a small wooden name plate and given to the family for placement within the family altar. Yoshida's posthumous name is An-non-in-shaku-Katsuji, which means "Katsuji, who had an earnest wish that all the world would remain peaceful forever."

Families who wish may also register their deceased *hibakusha* loved ones at the architecturally stunning Nagasaki National Peace Memorial Hall for the Atomic Bomb Victims, which opened in 2003 to provide a place of beauty where *hibakusha* families, Nagasaki citizens, and visitors to the city can pay their respects to those who have died. In the mostly underground structure, narrow hallways with vaulted ceilings lead visitors into an anteroom lined with backlit photographs of *hibakusha,* young and old, who are remembered there. As their images slowly fade, others appear in their place. The largest room in the Peace Memorial Hall is Remembrance Hall, an expansive quiet space with cedar-paneled walls lined with benches on three sides. In the center of the enormous room, two rows of rectangular glass pillars, illuminated with soft light from within, form a walkway in the direction of the hypocenter. At the end of the walkway stands a thirty-foot tower, called the registry shelf. As of August 9, 2014, it holds more than 165 books with the hand-inscribed names of 165,409 deceased *hibakusha,* including a Chinese civilian and a British prisoner of war who died on the day of the bomb-ing. The lighted pillars rise through the ceiling and emerge aboveground into a voluminous, circular, shallow basin of clear water, representing the water that atomic bomb victims craved. At night, seventy thousand tiny lights on the floor of the basin are illuminated beneath the water to honor those who died in the first months after the bombing.

Dō-oh and Yoshida also live on through their stories. Dō-oh's child-hood classmate Matsuzoe Hiroshi and a group of Dō-oh's friends col-lected her essays and poems and published them posthumously in a single volume, *Ikasarete ikite* [Allowed to Live, I Live], named after the title of Dō-oh's most well-known essay. After Dō-oh's death, Matsuzoe also created eighteen more paintings of Dō-oh's life based on her writ-ings. Copies of these paintings have become Dō-oh's *kamishibai*— colorful illustrations of the key moments of her life that are presented to audiences while someone (first Matsuzoe and now others) tells her story—passing on her experiences and perspectives to those who can no longer hear her in person.

Yoshida's life is reflected in a *kamishibai* created by students at Na-gasaki's Sakurababa Municipal Junior High School before his death. Inspired by Yoshida's presentations at their school, the students first painted fifty original works representing Yoshida's atomic bomb experi-ences, simpler and more childlike than Matsuzoe's paintings of Dō-oh's life. Before his hospitalization, Yoshida selected sixteen of these paint-ings to become the *kamishibai* of his life story. The students combined their paintings and Yoshida's own words to present his story for students at nearby elementary schools. The Nagasaki Board of Education also printed and distributed five hundred copies of Yoshida's *kamishibai* and presentation scripts to schools throughout the city. With Yoshida's bless-ing, the Nagasaki Atomic Bomb Museum presents his *kamishibai* to interested groups.

Yoshida had planned to make his first trip to the United Nations' Nuclear Non-Proliferation Treaty Review Conference in 2010, but due to his illness, he could not go. In his place, Hayashida Mitsuhiro, an eighteen-year-old high school student, antinuclear activist, and grandson of a *hibakusha*, presented Yoshida's *kamishibai* at several New York City schools where Yoshida had been invited to speak. To prepare for his New

York trip, Hayashida watched videotapes of Yoshida's presentations, practiced Yoshida's tone, pacing, and expression, and rehearsed the English translation of his script. Yoshida died shortly before the young man's departure for New York. Yoshida's *kamishibai* provoked emotional responses from his American audiences. Hayashida closed every presentation with Yoshida's signature words, imploring students to remember: *The basis of peace is for people to understand the pain of others.*

———

Taniguchi, Nagano, Dō-oh, Yoshida, and Wada beat the odds of immediate death and life-threatening radiation-related diseases and lived to tell their stories. Despite years of denial, discrimination, hiding, and a sense of internal contamination, their drive and their willingness to reveal themselves allow us to understand what it took to survive *after* surviving. They insisted on being a part of deciding whose story is told, on becoming vocal rememberers of experiences they could not let be forgotten. They wanted to make sure the world sees the absurdity of perceiving nuclear weapons as peacekeepers in the context of the massive and lifelong trauma they cause.

The city of Nagasaki's peace education program strives for the same goals. All fifth-grade students in each of Nagasaki's more than fifty elementary schools visit the Nagasaki Atomic Bomb Museum. The NFPP lends films and a photographic panel exhibit about the bombing to the city's nearly thirty junior high schools. Shiroyama Elementary School takes its peace education even further: On the ninth of every month since August 1951, Shiroyama's students, teachers, and administrators have gathered in the school gymnasium for *hibakusha* presentations and discussions of war- and peace-related research in the context of the atomic bombing and Japan's wartime atrocities. When the assembly concludes, the student body stands together and bows to the east, in the direction of the atomic bomb hypocenter, to honor those who died and to hold the vision of a world without war or nuclear weapons. The students then file out to place flowers at different monuments and memorials across the school grounds. Ten times a year for the first six years of their school lives, the children at Shiroyama think about, study, and discuss peace.

In light of the increasing age of survivors and their decreasing numbers, the NFPP and other organizations feel a sense of urgency to find ways to support future generations' access to and understanding of *hibakusha* stories. They have launched legacy campaigns to create *kamishibai* and videotape as many *kataribe* presentations as they can. A large group of "Peace Guides" are being trained in Nagasaki's atomic bomb history to provide guided tours at the Atomic Bomb Museum, Peace Memorial Hall, and other atomic bomb sites.

Wada's nineteen-year-old granddaughter, Yukari, carried on her grandfather's story when she appeared in a play based on Wada's experiences of the bombing and its aftermath. "I was eighteen at the time of the bomb, right?" he says. "She was nineteen. She played me as I was back then." Wada sat in the audience, smartly dressed, bald on top, with thick white hair neatly cut above his ears. Visceral memories flooded his mind. He cried at times, and he felt deep appreciation for the actors, especially his granddaughter. "People who knew nothing about the times sixty-five years ago, or the war, or the atomic bomb, really tried to get what it was like back then." When the play ended, Wada stood on the stage next to Yukari dressed as him so long ago. Looking at his granddaughter, his face showed a depth of sadness and gratitude he rarely reveals.

At eighty-seven, Wada still takes visitors to the streetcar memorial, proudly explaining its design and his role in collecting the names of the mobilized students who died driving or collecting fares on the morning of the bombing. His guests speak loudly to accommodate his partial hearing loss. Every August, company employees gather here for a memorial service, though the number of survivors who worked there has significantly diminished. On the anniversary of the bombing, Wada comes to this spot in the early morning to pray.

He credits his wife for his good health and his happy life. Hisako beams as she pours him tea.

"I wanted to die first," Nagano says. "I wanted to die before my husband did because I didn't want to arrange for any more funerals. I did not want to see any more death. But in the year 2000, after eleven and a half years of being in the hospital, my husband died."

At eighty-three, Nagano lives with her eldest daughter and college-age grandson in Ōgi-machi, about a mile north of the hypocenter. After being hospitalized for a bleeding intestinal ulcer and seeing her children worry on her behalf, she strives every day to stay healthy. "I live peacefully," she says. "I get up whenever I want to. I go to speak as a *kataribe* when I am asked. I go out to eat with my friends. But I have a limited income. I can live well as long as I don't indulge in luxury." An avid karaoke singer, Nagano misses Yoshida, her frequent singing partner at social gatherings.

Less frequently now, Nagano takes a taxi to her family's cemetery just east of the hypocenter. From the top of the hill where the taxi stops, most of the Urakami Valley is spread before her: a metropolis of office buildings, residences, parks, and schools, edged by green mountains, with the Urakami River flowing southward into the bay. Nagano uses the railing to keep her balance and takes her time walking down a narrow paved walkway and turning into a long row of gravesites running horizontally across the hill. Her family's marble monument is second in the row, engraved on both sides with the names and dates of death of her husband's family members and her own, in order of their deaths. For Nagano's family, her older sister who died in infancy is listed first, then Seiji, Kuniko, her father, her older brother, and, last, her mother, Shina— June 5, 1995. Vases of bright yellow, purple, pink, and white *zōka* (artificial flowers) sit on smaller granite blocks in front of the main memorial. "Since I can't come often, real flowers would die," she says. "These stay beautiful." Stored in urns below are her family's ashes, though Nagano will never open them again.

She lights some incense and places it on the altar in a ceramic bowl filled with sand. "This," she says, "is because we imagine that our family members who have died like the scent." She steps back, claps her hands twice, bows her head, and stands in silence. When she is finished, she snuffs out the incense, gathers her things, and heads farther down the pathway to a steep stone staircase that leads to the street. "I used to be able to go down the stairs easily, *ton-ton-ton-ton*," she says, holding tightly to the iron handrail. At the bottom, she catches her breath, then hails a taxi to return home.

Her friends and the many students who write her letters after hearing her story remind Nagano that it would have been impossible to know of

Yoshida Katsuji and Nagano Etsuko singing karaoke at a New Year's Eve party, 2009. (*Courtesy of Nagano Etsuko*)

the imminent atomic bombing of her city when she brought Seiji and Kuniko back from Kagoshima. They urge her to release her self-blame and remorse. "But every night," Nagano says, "when I am in the bathtub alone, those memories just come back to me. It makes me sad and dreary. I wonder why only I survived to live happily in this time of peace. Even now, when I don't have to worry about anything because my children are grown, I can't erase my sorrow for what happened to my brother and sister."

"My children keep telling me to stop driving to my son's house, which is ten hours away," Taniguchi says. His hair is graying now, and deep vertical wrinkles ripple out from the corners of his mouth. "The truth is, since I turned seventy, they are constantly telling me what I shouldn't do because I am old!" What Taniguchi doesn't say, however, is that at eighty-five, he is in constant pain and suffers from many health problems. The post-bedsore indentations in his chest are still so deep that his heartbeat is visible. He has lost nearly all vision in one eye, and his memory is waning. After more than twenty-five surgeries, including at least ten skin transplants on his back and left arm, the middle of his back at the spine causes him the most pain—not on the surface, but deep inside. When he stands or walks, his arm—unable to straighten—remains bent, his hand hanging down from his wrist. More than half of his body is covered in scars. "My skin can't breathe," he says, "so the fatigue is terrible in the summer months." Taniguchi remains extremely thin, still eating only small amounts to avoid breaking the tightly stretched skin that covers his back, legs, and arms. The transplanted skin on his back often cracks. His wife, Eiko, applies cream to his back every day.

Fueled by determination, every morning since his retirement twenty-six years ago, Taniguchi has dressed in a suit and tie, combed back his hair, and driven from his home on Mount Inasa to the offices of Nagasaki Hisaikyō—the Nagasaki Atomic Bomb Survivors Council—on the second floor above a small souvenir shop in Peace Park. Tourists roam the seven-square-mile park that features the Peace Statue, the ruins of Urakami Prison destroyed in the bombing, and the Vault for the Unclaimed Remains of Victims containing shelves filled with urns holding the ashes of 8,962 unidentified *hibakusha*. On either side of tree-lined walkways, monuments from countries all over the world honor those who died. A large fountain at the south end of the park overlooks the Urakami Valley.

At Hisaikyō, Taniguchi supports survivors' successful applications for government health care benefits. A more comprehensive Hibakusha Relief Law went into effect in 1995, which greatly improved survivors'

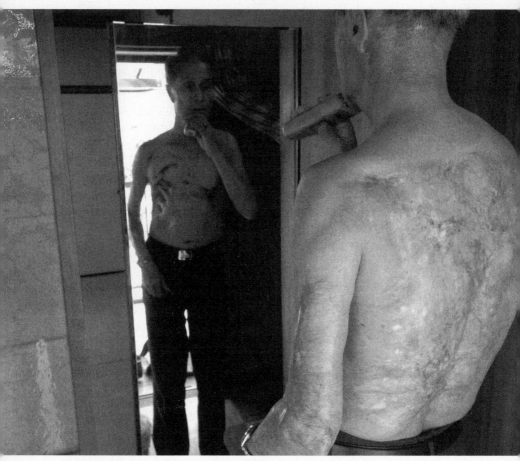

Taniguchi Sumiteru, age seventy-five, in 2004, revealing the injuries and scar tissue on his back, arms, and chest. (*Photograph by John Van Hasselt/Corbis Images*)

access to medical care and support. "However," Taniguchi says, "the law is very hard to understand, and the procedures for applying for and receiving support from the government are very complicated." Taniguchi helps survivors and their family members through this process. He also supports their efforts to sue the government for coverage of medical conditions not yet approved, claims that have sometimes resulted in the expansion and refinement of the definitions, boundaries, diseases, and disabilities covered by the *hibakusha* health care laws. Still, Taniguchi and other activists continue to argue that screening procedures and definitions are too restrictive, allowing the government to deny coverage to many who are still in need.

"It's strange that I am still alive," he says, almost in disbelief. In fact, all of the people Taniguchi worked with in 1955 to create Nagasaki Hisaikyō have died. "I am the only one left." As he ages, typical greetings from friends like "Please take care of yourself" bring him no consolation, and he falls silent when people wish him a long life. "That would mean many more years of pain," he says. "Either way, I'll have pain until I die."

From the windows of the Nagasaki Hisaikyō meeting room across the hall from his office, Taniguchi looks north toward Sumiyoshi-machi, the once-rural area where the bomb blasted him off his bike and melted the skin off his back and arms. "If you were to measure life with a ruler and an entire life were 30 centimeters long, 29.9 centimeters of my life were destroyed that day. That last millimeter . . . I found the strength to live within that one millimeter because I realized I had survived because of the support I received from so many people. So my life is not just for myself; I now have to live for other people. Even though it's excruciating, I feel that I have a responsibility to live my life to the very end."

Taniguchi stands up from the table to head to the balcony for a cigarette break. As he passes the young American girl videotaping the interview, he pauses for a moment and almost smiles.

"Erase the bad parts," he says, "okay?"

Nagasaki's first hypocenter marker, in Japanese and English, October 1945, designating the spot on the ground above which the atomic bomb detonated. (*Photograph by Hayashi Shigeo/ Courtesy of Nagasaki Atomic Bomb Museum*)

ACKNOWLEDGMENTS

I extend my deepest and most sincere gratitude to Dō-oh Mineko, Nagano Etsuko, Taniguchi Sumiteru, Wada Kōichi, and Yoshida Katsuji, the five *hibakusha* featured in *Nagasaki,* for their generosity of time, candor, and goodwill in telling me their atomic bomb experiences and key moments in their lives over the past seventy years. I also received openhearted assistance from their family members, who provided additional information about these survivors' lives and offered me access to their personal writings and photographs: Okada Ikuyo (Dō-oh's sister); Wada Hisako (Wada's wife); and Yoshida Naoji, Yoshida Tomoji, Yoshida Kenji, and Kanayama Kuniko (Yoshida's elder son, younger son, younger brother, and cousin, respectively).

My profound thanks to other Nagasaki *hibakusha* who offered me their time and insight into their personal experiences and perspectives: Akizuki Sugako (Dr. Akizuki's wife), Fukahori Yoshitoshi, Hamasaki Hitoshi, Hirose Masahito, Matsuzoe Hiroshi, Miyazaki Midori, Shimohira Sakue, Uchida Tsukasa, and one woman who asked that her name be withheld. I greatly appreciate Mitani Kazumi for introducing me to two *hibakusha* who had never told their stories outside of their personal circles of friends and family, and Nakamichi Keiko at St. Francis Hospital for arranging an inspiring meeting with Akizuki Sugako. Thank you to Sakato Toshihiro for guiding me through the campus of Shiroyama Elementary School, and to Sister Fusayo Tsutsumi at the Hill of Grace Nagasaki A-Bomb Home.

The written testimonies of hundreds of other Nagasaki *hibakusha* allowed me to expand my understanding of postnuclear survival. I deeply appreciate the commitment of editors, compilers, and English translators of these testimonies. Organizations that have spent decades gathering these testimonies and in many cases having them translated include the Nagasaki National Peace Memorial Hall for the Atomic Bomb Victims, the Nagasaki Foundation for the Promotion of Peace, the Nagasaki Testimonial Society, the Nagasaki International Culture Hall, the Nagasaki Association for Hibakushas' Medical Care, the Nagasaki Broadcasting Company, the *Asahi Shimbun,* and Nihon Hidankyō. Brian Burke-Gaffney and Geoff Neill provided superb translations of many of these testimonies. Brian Burke-Gaffney also gave me an insider's look into fascinating aspects of Nagasaki's history as we walked through the city.

In Nagasaki, I received many years of invaluable support from Matsuo Ranko, assistant section chief at the Nagasaki Foundation for the Promotion of Peace, who introduced me to Dō-oh, Wada, Nagano, and Yoshida; helped coordinate my interview schedule during my trips to Nagasaki; and connected me with numerous atomic bomb specialists. I am privileged to also call her my friend. The directors and entire staff at the Nagasaki Foundation for the Promotion of Peace, especially Taira Mitsuyoshi and Mizushita Ayumi, also offered assistance in numerous areas of research and coordination.

My most sincere thanks to Fukahori Yoshitoshi, chairperson of the Committee for Research of Photographs and Materials of the Atomic Bombing, for giving me access to his large archive of photographs and for his immense support in acquiring photograph permissions from aging *hibakusha* and other sources beyond my reach. His volunteer staff also provided valuable help, especially Shirabe Hitomi. At the Nagasaki Atomic Bomb Museum, Takagi Rumiko offered tireless research support in the early years of this project, followed by Shiraishi Hitomi. Special thanks to photo archivist Okuno Shōtarō for his valuable assistance in identifying and obtaining permissions for many of the photographs from the museum. Thank you, too, to Itō Sei at the *Asahi Shimbun* for his help in locating copies of 1945 editions of the newspaper and present-day feature articles on *hibakusha.*

Numerous atomic bomb physicians and specialists offered me their time and expertise, including Dr. Tomonaga Masao, director; Dr. Hideki Mori, vice president; and social worker Nakashima Seiji at the Japanese Red Cross Nagasaki Atomic Bomb Hospital. Dr. Kinoshita Hirohisa, in the Department of Neuropsychiatry at the Nagasaki University Hospital of Medicine and Dentistry, and Koshimoto Rika, clinical psychologist at Nagasaki University Graduate School of Biomedical Sciences, provided updated psychological research on *hibakusha* experiences. Dr. Akahoshi Masazumi, director of the Department of Clinical Studies at the Radiation Effects Research Foundation (RERF) in Nagasaki, provided both historical and current perspectives on RERF's research. Thank you to Fukushima Masako, master file section, Epidemiology Department at RERF, for her assistance.

In the United States, I offer my deep gratitude to my agent, Richard Balkin, and my editor at Viking, Melanie Tortoroli, for their vision and dedication in ushering *Nagasaki* to publication. I would also like to thank Wendy Wolf, vice president and associate publisher at Viking, and my first editor there, Kevin Doughten, for their faith in the project from the start. Huge appreciation to production editor Bruce Giffords and copy editor Lavina Lee for their remarkable work through numerous drafts, and to the entire team at Viking. Thank you.

For grants that supported the book, I am grateful to the Arizona Commission on the Arts, the Bill Desmond Writing Award, the Fund for Investigative Journalism, the Money for Women/Barbara Deming Memorial Fund, Inc., and the National Philanthropic Trust. Thank you to the Norman Mailer Center for providing me a month of writing time in Provincetown, Massachusetts, in the company of wonderful writers of nonfiction, fiction, and poetry. Heartfelt appreciation to Joan Kahn and to the following individuals who offered financial support for the completion of the book when I had run out of funds: Alison Arnold, Deborah Bauer, Andrea Beckham, Ken Blackburn, Mary Brown, Anne Canright, Wayne and Carol Daily, Bonnie Eckard, Debbie Elman, Amber E. Espar, Eloise Klein Healy, Homeopathy Care LLC, Saskia Jorda, Anne Kellor, James Lattin, Michele Lawson, Janet Linder, Christopher Mogil, Judy and Dan Peitzmeyer-Rollings, Ralph and Darcy Phillips, Marilyn Pursley, Khadijah Queen, Donna Ruby, Dick and Shirley Southard, Ry Southard, David Spielvogel, Judy Starr, Wendy White, Kim Scott Ziegler, and two anonymous donors.

A special thanks to historian John W. Dower for his time, historical insights, and encouragement; Rachelle Linner for our conversations about many aspects of our writing projects on the lives of *hibakusha;* Paul Morris and Christopher Burawa for their early encouragement; and Dr. James

Yamazaki for his kindness and engaging stories of Nagasaki in the late 1940s.

I have been fortunate to assemble a superb team to support my translation and research needs for *Nagasaki*. Immense thanks to the seven translators who spent thousands of hours helping me translate interviews, essays, articles, medical records, scientific studies, and correspondence. Led by the incomparable Mariko Sugawara Bragg, they are Yasuko Clark, Eiko Foster, Eriko Fujiyoshi, Sayako Fujii Head, Toshie Jones, and Akiko Wakao. Excellent administrative support was provided by Eva Black, Charlene Brown, Jeanne Callahan, Lorraine Ciavola, Shela Hidalgo, and Darcy Esch Phillips. Thank you to attorney Yuriko Kondo for her legal translations. For their reading and feedback on my book proposal and early drafts, I thank my former MFA mentor Valerie Boyd, Rebecca Godfrey, and fellow writers Anne Canright, Anne Liu Kellor, Khadijah Queen, and Christin Taylor. Many thanks, too, to Eva Black and Ken Blackburn for their careful reading and feedback on final drafts.

There are insufficient words to express my gratitude to project historian Robin LaVoie, M.A., who has worked side by side with me for eleven years. Robin located, analyzed, cross-referenced, and organized source materials; created detailed maps of Nagasaki to pinpoint locations significant to the survivors' stories; provided immense help in the acquisition of photographic rights and preparation of the chapter notes and bibliography; and offered superb editorial insights. All the while, she was the best colleague imaginable. It is no exaggeration to say that this book would not exist without Robin's immeasurable dedication and support.

To my sweet friends Charlene Brown and Judy Starr, thank you for your wisdom, constancy, strength, and love. To the Essential Theatre ensemble, past and present, my wholehearted appreciation for your ongoing exploration of listening and collaborative artistry in bringing our audiences' stories to life.

Finally, to my family, whose patience, cheerleading, practical support, and love have exceeded anything I could have imagined: Gary and Sue Southard; my brothers, Ry Southard and Jonathan Southard; and my daughter, Eva Black, who accompanied me on my first research trip to Nagasaki when she was ten years old and grew up with this book. This book is for you.

NOTES

Quoted passages of the five featured survivors are their own words, taken primarily from multiple personal interviews that I conducted in Japanese and translated with the help of a dedicated translation support team. I have edited the survivors' words for length, clarity, and to eliminate repetition and the off-topic threads of dialogue that naturally occurred in our conversations. These quotes are also drawn from their words in follow-up interviews, correspondence, and unpublished personal writings. To reconstruct the featured survivors' stories with accuracy, I also consulted hundreds of other sources related to their lives, including published and unpublished testimonies and biographies; newspaper and journal articles; transcripts of speeches; radio, television, and film interviews; photographs; and personal interviews and correspondence with their family members. Sources for quotations by the featured survivors other than my interviews are cited below, and a selected list of my primary and secondary sources, organized by featured survivor, is provided in the first section of the *Hibakusha* Sources.

As part of my research, I also read more than three hundred testimonies by other Nagasaki survivors that have been translated into English by the Nagasaki National Peace Memorial Hall for the Atomic Bomb Victims, the Nagasaki Foundation for the Promotion of Peace, and other survivor organizations. These testimonies provided extraordinarily valuable stories and images of the destruction and the physical and emotional pain survivors endured, expanding my understanding of atomic bomb survival beyond the experiences of Dō-oh, Nagano, Taniguchi, Wada, and Yoshida. Sources for these stories, including survivors' direct quotes, are cited below. A full list of the published, unpublished, and Internet sources for Nagasaki *hibakusha* testimonies in English is included in the second section of the *Hibakusha* Sources.

My primary source for the immediate and long-term medical, social, and psychological effects of the atomic bombings was *Hiroshima and Nagasaki: The Physical, Medical, and Social Effects of the Atomic Bombings,* edited by the Committee for the Compilation of Materials on Damage Caused by the Atomic Bombs in Hiroshima and Nagasaki and translated by Eisei Ishikawa and David L. Swain

(1981). I supplemented the information in this book with the most up-to-date findings in published studies of the Radiation Effects Research Foundation; interviews with medical providers, researchers, and atomic bomb specialists; and research provided by the Nagasaki Atomic Bomb Museum and the Atomic Bomb Disease Institute at Nagasaki University Graduate School of Biomedical Sciences.

For detailed information about the city of Nagasaki before, during, and after the nuclear attack, one of my most valuable resources was *Nagasaki genbaku sensaishi* [Records of the Nagasaki Atomic Bombing and Wartime Damage], originally compiled by the city of Nagasaki in five volumes between 1973 and 1984. In 2011, the Nagasaki National Peace Memorial Hall for the Atomic Bomb Victims released on its Web site a tentative English translation of the first volume, covering prewar and wartime Nagasaki. The full five-volume record is also available in English in a condensed form in *Nagasaki Speaks: A Record of the Atomic Bombing,* published in 1993 by the Nagasaki International Culture Hall, translated by Brian Burke-Gaffney. Additional sources include the hundreds of individual *hibakusha* testimonies mentioned above, and the exhibits and publications of the Nagasaki Atomic Bomb Museum, the city of Nagasaki, and the Nagasaki Foundation for the Promotion of Peace.

Numerous scholars and historians provided superbly researched information on Japanese history, the Pacific War, U.S. development of the first atomic bombs, the U.S. occupation of Japan, occupation censorship policies, U.S. denial of radiation effects, the Atomic Bomb Casualty Commission, and the 1995 Smithsonian exhibit. In particular, I would like to acknowledge John Toland's *The Rising Sun: The Decline and Fall of the Japanese Empire, 1936–1945;* John W. Dower's *War Without Mercy: Race and Power in the Pacific War* and *Embracing Defeat: Japan in the Wake of World War II;* Richard Rhodes's *The Making of the Atomic Bomb;* Monica Braw's *The Atomic Bomb Suppressed: American Censorship in Occupied Japan;* M. Susan Lindee's *Suffering Made Real: American Science and the Survivors at Hiroshima;* and *Hiroshima's Shadow: Writings on the Denial of History and the Smithsonian Controversy,* edited by Kai Bird and Lawrence Lifschultz.

Below are notes and citations for each chapter. As in the narrative, Japanese names are listed with the surname first, except when they appear in Western order (surname last) in their original publications.

For *Nagasaki* updates, photos, links, and other information, please visit http://www.susansouthard.com.

PREFACE

Taniguchi provided an unpublished copy of his 1986 speech, which was translated into English for the author's use.

The number of *hibakusha* living around the world as of March 2014 was reported on the sixty-ninth anniversary of the atomic bombings. See, for example, "Atomic Bomb Victims Stand Alone" by Norihiro Kato, *New York Times,* August 14, 2014.

Oyama Takami's poem: *Hiroshima/Nagasaki: After the Atomic Bomb—Volume V: Elegy for Nagasaki: 124 Tankas of Takami Oyama,* translated by Kemmoku Makato.

PROLOGUE

In addition to the translation of *Nagasaki genbaku sensaishi,* vol. 1, and *Nagasaki Speaks,* sources for Nagasaki history include *Nagasaki: The British Experience: 1854–1945* by Brian Burke-Gaffney; "The Atomic Bomb and the Citizens of Nagasaki" by Sadao Kamata and Stephen Salaff in *Bulletin of Concerned Asian Scholars* 14:2; "Historical Momentums at Nagasaki's Suwa Shrine" by John Nelson in *Crossroads* 2; *The Restoration of Urakami Cathedral: A Commemorative Album,* edited by Hisayuki Mizuura; "Religious Responses to the Atomic Bomb in Nagasaki" by Okuyama Michiaki in *Bulletin* 37; and numerous testimonies by Nagasaki *hibakusha.*

For wartime slogans and other personal remembrances of Japan during the war, see *Japan at War: An Oral History* by Haruko Taya Cook and Theodore F. Cook.

Key sources for prewar and wartime Japanese history include *Inventing Japan: 1853–1964* by Ian Buruma; *Japan: The Story of a Nation* by Edwin O. Reischauer; *Japan: A Documentary History, Vol. II: The Late Tokugawa Period to the Present,* edited by David J. Lu; *Embracing Defeat* by John W. Dower; *The Making of Modern Japan* by Marius Jansen; *Hirohito and the Making of Modern Japan* by Herbert P. Bix; and *Japan's Decision for War in 1941: Some Enduring Lessons* by Jeffrey Record.

The extent of Emperor Hirohito's active role in the direction of the war continues to be debated among historians, particularly because many Japanese government wartime documents were destroyed between Japan's surrender and the U.S. occupation a month later, and because of the likely pro-emperor bias in existing postwar Japanese sources, motivated by officials' desire to safeguard the emperor from prosecution for war crimes. See, for example, "Introducing the Interpretive Problems of Japan's 1945 Surrender" by Barton J. Bernstein in *The End of the Pacific War: Reappraisals,* edited by Tsuyoshi Hasegawa; and "Emperor Hirohito and Japan's Decision to Go to War with the United States: Reexamined" by Noriko Kawamura, *Diplomatic History* 31:1.

CHAPTER 1: CONVERGENCE

WARTIME JAPAN

Japanese national proclamations: "The Way of Subjects" and "Imperial Rescript on Education" in *Japan: A Documentary History, Vol. II: The Late Tokugawa Period to the Present,* edited by David J. Lu. For Tōjō's radio announcement following the attack on Pearl Harbor, nationalistic slogans, and Japanese citizens' remembrances of life during the war, see *Japan at War: An Oral History* by Haruko Taya Cook and Theodore F. Cook.

For an examination of the role of racism and nationalistic propaganda during the war, see *War Without Mercy: Race and Power in the Pacific War* by John W. Dower. The *Time* magazine quotation is from "The Enemy: Perhaps He Is Human," July 5, 1943, as quoted in "Hiroshima: Breaking the Silence" by Howard Zinn in *The Bomb.*

In addition to the sources listed in the prologue chapter notes, sources for war-time Japan include *Japan in War and Peace: Selected Essays* by John W. Dower; and *Japan's Struggle to End the War,* USSBS report no. 2. For exam-ples of Japanese resistance to the war, see "Evidences of Antimilitarism in Prewar and Wartime Japan" by Alvin D. Coox, *Pacific Affairs* 46:4; and *Leaves from an Autumn of Emergencies: Selections from the Wartime Dia-ries of Ordinary Japanese,* edited by Samuel Hideo Yamashita.

WARTIME NAGASAKI

Wada's quotation about his hunger during the war appeared in his testimony "There Was No 'War-End' in Nagasaki," English translation provided by the Nagasaki National Peace Memorial Hall.

Many Nagasaki *hibakusha* recalled mandated wartime service, neighborhood as-sociation activities, air raid preparations, rationing, militaristic indoctrina-tion, and the drafting of family members into the armed forces. Their stories supported and expanded on the information about life during the war in the translations of *Nagasaki genbaku sensaishi,* vol. 1. Mitsue Kubo, in *Hibaku: Recollections of A-Bomb Survivors,* remembered the wartime hunger that sparked her nickname, Senko (incense stick). See also *Nagasaki: The British Experience: 1854–1945* by Brian Burke-Gaffney.

Dō-oh's quotations about her father's strictness, the announcement of the attack on Pearl Harbor at her school, and her family's preparations in sending her brother off to war appeared in her essay "Ikasarete ikite" [Allowed to Live, I Live] in a collection by the same name, edited by Keishō bukai (Dō-oh Mineko ikō shuu) henshū iinkai [Legacy Group (Dō-oh Mineko Posthumous Collec-tion) Editorial Committee], translated into English for the author's use.

Additional details about Nagasaki's civil defense measures were recorded by U.S. Strategic Bombing Survey Civilian Defense Division investigators. See *Field Report Covering Air-Raid Protection and Allied Subjects in Nagasaki, Ja-pan,* USSBS report no. 5.

The connection between Nagasaki's Mitsubishi Ōhashi weapons factory and the air-launched torpedoes used in the attack on Pearl Harbor is noted in *Naga-saki genbaku sensaishi,* vol. 1. See also *At Dawn We Slept: The Untold Story of Pearl Harbor* by Gordon W. Prange, Donald M. Goldstein, and Katherine V. Dillon (New York: McGraw-Hill, 1981); and *Shinjuwan sakusen kaikoroku* by Genda Minoru (Tokyo: Yomiuri Shimbun, 1972).

For information about Nagasaki's first air raid in August 1944 as one of the early "test" raids of the USAAF's nighttime firebombing campaign, see *The Army Air Forces in WWII,* vol. 5, edited by Wesley Frank Craven and James Lea Cate; and *The Rise of American Air Power: The Creation of Armageddon* by Michael S. Sherry. See also the "Air Target Analysis" for the Nagasaki Region (Objective no. 90.36), produced by the U.S. Joint Target Group in June 1944, which outlined industrial and other targets within the Nagasaki area, includ-ing two key zones vulnerable to incendiary attack: the Nakashima and Urakami valleys, with "densely grouped houses" and limited rivers, canals, or streets to act as firebreaks. The Joint Target Group files are housed in the Records of the U.S. Strategic Bombing Survey, Record Group 243, National Archives at College Park, MD, Online Public Access catalog identifier 561744; digital copy available at http://www.fold3.com/page/2848_japanese _air_target_analyses/.

SPRING AND SUMMER 1945

The U.S. Joint Chiefs of Staff's directive that the air campaign against Japan should aim to impact the Japanese people's morale as well as the country's military infrastructure is noted in *The Army Air Forces in WWII,* vol. 5, edited by Wesley Frank Craven and James Lea Cate, chap. 23, p. 748. Due to the chaos of these air raids, evacuations of Japanese civilians before and after the attacks, and fires that destroyed city records, no one knows how many people died in these Allied air attacks. Some sources estimate 200,000 or more prior to Hiroshima and Nagasaki, with hundreds of thousands more wounded and missing. For an analysis of the various estimates of air raid casualties, see *War Without Mercy* by John W. Dower; and *The Rise of American Air Power: The Creation of Armageddon* by Michael S. Sherry, especially p. 413, fn. 43. For additional documents and testimonies related to the impact of the U.S. strategic bombing campaign against Japan, see http://www.japanairraids.org.

Air raid preparations at Nagasaki Medical College were noted by Takashi Nagai in *Testimonies of the Atomic Bomb Survivors.* Mori Sumi described the first-aid kits carried by mobilized students in *Footprints of Nagasaki,* edited by the Nagasaki Prefectural Girls' High School 42nd Alumnae. Hashimoto Yutaka remembered collecting pine sap for fuel in "Mom and Silver Rice" in *Crossroads* 4.

For the information Dr. Akizuki Tatsuichirō provided to USSBS medical team investigators about the city's wartime health conditions, including beriberi, see *Effects of the Atomic Bombs on Health and Medical Services in Hiroshima and Nagasaki,* USSBS report no. 13, pp. 74–75; and "Interrogation no. 417," November 8, 1945, Interrogations of Japanese Leaders and Responses to Questionnaires, 1945–1946 (Microfilm Publication M1654, roll 1, folder 42, 2.c.1–20), Records of the U.S. Strategic Bombing Survey, Record Group 243, National Archives at College Park, MD.

Tsunenari Masatoshi remembered infestations of fleas and lice in *Our Parents Were in Nagasaki on August 9, 1945.*

Japanese war weariness by the summer of 1945: *The Effects of Strategic Bombing on Japanese Morale,* USSBS report no. 14. For Fukahori Satoru's understanding, even as a child, that Japan was losing the war, see his interview in Steven Okazaki's film *White Light/Black Rain.*

For the state of Japan's war resources in the summer of 1945 and Japan's preparations for an Allied invasion, see *Japan's Struggle to End the War,* USSBS report no. 2; *Embracing Defeat* by John W. Dower; "Combined Chiefs of Staff: Estimate of the Enemy Situation" (document 28), in *The Atomic Bomb and the End of World War II,* edited by William Burr; and *Downfall: The End of the Imperial Japanese Empire* by Richard B. Frank.

For Japanese citizens' preparations to sacrifice themselves as "shattered jewels," see *Embracing Defeat* by John W. Dower and personal accounts of home front and military service in *Japan at War* by Haruko Taya Cook and Theodore F. Cook. Details about Nagasaki's civil defense activities and preparation for invasion, including first-aid training, volunteer brigades, land artillery stations, and suicide boats, are recounted in many survivors' testimonies as well as in *Nagasaki genbaku sensaishi,* vol. 1.

TARGET SELECTION

President Truman informed about the Manhattan Project: "Memorandum for the Secretary of War: Atomic Fission Bombs" by General Groves, April 23, 1945 (document 3a), and "Memorandum Discussed with the President" by Henry L. Stimson, April 25, 1945 (document 3b), in *The Atomic Bomb and the End of World War II,* edited by William Burr.

For target selection criteria for the atomic bombs, see "Defining the Targets" (documents 4–16) in *The Atomic Bomb and the End of World War II,* edited by William Burr, especially "Summary of Target Committee Meetings on 10 and 11 May 1945" (document 6). For General Spaatz's question regarding Nagasaki's POW camp, see *A World Destroyed* by Martin J. Sherwin. Evidence that U.S. officials gave only limited consideration to any alternatives to dropping the atomic bomb, including the use of a demonstration or warning, is noted by Barton J. Bernstein in "Truman and the A-Bomb: Targeting Noncombatants, Using the Bomb, and His Defending the 'Decision,'" *Journal of Military History* 62.

The report of the Trinity explosion as a "harmless accident" is described in *The Dragon's Tail: Radiation Safety in the Manhattan Project, 1942–1946* by Barton C. Hacker.

For Japanese leaders' prebomb surrender communications, the war cabinet's *mokusatsu* response to the Potsdam Declaration, and Tokyo's reaction to the Hiroshima bombing, see *Japan's Struggle to End the War,* USSBS report no. 2; *The Rising Sun* by John Toland; *Downfall* by Richard B. Frank; *Japan's Decision to Surrender* by Robert J. C. Butow; *Hiroshima and Nagasaki* by the Committee for the Compilation of Materials on Damage Caused by Atomic Bombs in Hiroshima and Nagasaki; "Why We Dropped the Bomb" by William Lanouette, *Civilization* 2:1; "*Mokusatsu:* One Word, Two Lessons," *National Security Agency Technical Journal* 13:4; and the various essays in *The End of the Pacific War: Reappraisals,* edited by Tsuyoshi Hasegawa.

The Potsdam Declaration: "Proclamation Defining Terms for Japanese Surrender, July 26, 1945" in *Japan: A Documentary History,* vol. 2, edited by David J. Lu. For the directive authorizing the use of the atomic bomb, see "Memo, Handy to Spaatz, 7-25-45" (document 41e), in *The Atomic Bomb and the End of World War II,* edited by William Burr.

President Truman's reaction to the news of the Hiroshima bombing was noted by White House correspondent A. Merriman Smith in *Thank You, Mr. President: A White House Notebook* (New York: Harper & Brothers, 1946), p. 257. For

Truman's post-Hiroshima statement, see "Statement by the President Announcing the Use of the A-Bomb at Hiroshima, 8-6-45," *Public Papers of the Presidents of the United States: Harry S. Truman, 1945–1953*.

CONVERGENCE (EVENING BEFORE AND MORNING OF THE NAGASAKI BOMBING)

The newspaper headline that told Nagasaki of "Considerable Damage" at Hiroshima appeared in the *Asahi Shimbun*, August 8, 1945. For reactions in Nagasaki to news of the Hiroshima bombing: Dr. Tsuno-o Susumu's report to the Nagasaki Medical College staff is quoted from *Nagasaki 1945* by Tatsuichirō Akizuki. Other responses: "Walking over Red-Hot Rubble" by Kazuo Nakagawa in *Testimonies of the Atomic Bomb Survivors*; and Governor Nagano Wakamatsu's testimony at the Nagasaki Broadcasting Company Web site, "Nagasaki and Peace," http://www2.nbc-nagasaki.co.jp/peace.

Sources for the Nagasaki bomb's preparation and delivery: *The 509th Remembered*, edited by Robert and Amelia Krauss, includes photographs of the signatures written on Fat Man and testimonies by *Bockscar* crew members. Other sources: *War's End: An Eyewitness Account of America's Last Atomic Mission* by Major General USAF (Ret.) Charles W. Sweeney with Marion K. and James A. Antonucci; "Memo, Commander F. L. Ashworth to Major General L. R. Groves, 2-24-45" (document 2) in *The Atomic Bomb and the End of World War II*, edited by William Burr; and *The Making of the Atomic Bomb* by Richard Rhodes. See also *We Dropped the A-Bomb* by Merle Miller and Abe Spitzer; and *Decision at Nagasaki: The Mission That Almost Failed* by Lt. Col. USAF (Ret.) Fred J. Olivi with William R. Watson Jr.

For the aiming point of the Nagasaki mission, see "Mission Planning Summary, Report No. 9, 509th Composite Group," GRO Entry (A1) 7530, Lt. General Leslie R. Groves Collection, General Correspondence, 1941–1970, National Archives at College Park, MD.

For the impact of the August 9 Soviet entry into the war on Japanese leaders, see the sources noted above for their early surrender debates. See also *The Soviet Strategic Offensive in Manchuria, 1945: "August Storm"* by David M. Glantz (London: Frank Cass, 2003); and "The Atomic Bombs and the Soviet Invasion: Which Was More Important in Japan's Decision to Surrender?" by Tsuyoshi Hasegawa in *The End of the Pacific War: Reappraisals*.

Yoshida remembered the "Japanese way" of following the emperor in Steven Okazaki's film *White Light/Black Rain*.

Activities throughout Nagasaki on the morning of August 9 are noted in various survivor accounts. Tsukasa Kikuchi in *Silent Thunder* surmised that drills with bamboo spears had been taking place on the Mitsubishi athletic field when he passed by the field strewn with corpses later that afternoon. Hirata Kenshi's story of returning home from Hiroshima carrying his wife's remains, and the story of eight other "double" atomic bomb survivors, appeared in *Nine Who Survived Hiroshima and Nagasaki* by Robert Trumbull. Dr. Akizuki Tatsuichirō reflected, *Im Westen nichts neues* in *Nagasaki 1945*. See also Tatsue Urata in *We of Nagasaki* by Takashi Nagai; and the

Mount Kompira antiaircraft battalion's instrumentation chief, Yoshimitsu Nakamura, in *Testimonies of the Atomic Bomb Survivors.*

Wada remembered sitting down with his friends to discuss that morning's derailment in his testimony "A Monument to 11:02 a.m.," at Nagasaki's "Peace and Atomic Bomb" Web site, http://www.city.nagasaki.lg.jp/peace/english/survivors/index.html.

CHAPTER 2: FLASHPOINT

FIRST SIXTY SECONDS

For technical information about the Nagasaki atomic bomb, see *Hiroshima and Nagasaki,* edited by the Committee for the Compilation of Materials on Damage Caused by the Atomic Bombs in Hiroshima and Nagasaki; *The Making of the Atomic Bomb* by Richard Rhodes; *The Effects of Nuclear Weapons,* 3rd ed., edited by Samuel Glasstone and Philip J. Dolan; *The Yields of the Hiroshima and Nagasaki Nuclear Explosions* by John Malik; and the Radiation Effects Research Foundation reports available at http://www.rerf.jp/library/archives_e/scids.html, including *U.S.-Japan Joint Reassessment of Atomic Bomb Dosimetry in Hiroshima and Nagasaki: Dosimetry System 1986,* edited by William C. Roesch; and *Reassessment of the Atomic Bomb Radiation Dosimetry for Hiroshima and Nagasaki: Dosimetry System 2002,* edited by Robert W. Young and George D. Kerr.

Physical damages caused by the blast force and heat: *Hiroshima and Nagasaki,* edited by the Committee for the Compilation of Materials on Damage Caused by the Atomic Bombs in Hiroshima and Nagasaki (especially chaps. 2–4); *Nagasaki Speaks;* "Medical Survey of Atomic Bomb Casualties" by Raisuke Shirabe, *The Military Surgeon* 113:4; *The Effects of Atomic Bombs on Hiroshima and Nagasaki,* USSBS report no. 3; *Effects of the Atomic Bomb on Nagasaki, Japan,* USSBS report no. 93; and *The Atomic Bombings of Hiroshima and Nagasaki* by the U.S. Army Corps of Engineers, Manhattan District. See also "What the Atomic Bomb Really Did" by Robert DeVore, *Collier's,* March 2, 1946.

Taniguchi described clinging to the shaking ground during the explosion in an unpublished 1986 speech, translated into English for the author's use. His memory of seeing a child tossed "like a fleck of dust" is quoted from his testimony in *The Light of Morning,* translated by Brian Burke-Gaffney.

UNDER THE MUSHROOM CLOUD

Views of the atomic cloud from *Bockscar:* Lieutenant Frederick Olivi and Captain Kermit Beahan, as quoted in "Defending the Indefensible: A Meditation on the Life of Hiroshima Pilot Paul Tibbets, Jr." by Peter J. Kuznick, *Asia-Pacific Journal: Japan Focus,* http://www.japanfocus.org/-Peter_J_-Kuznick/2642; and "Atomic Bombing of Nagasaki Told by Flight Member" by William L. Laurence, *New York Times,* August 9, 1945.

Descriptions of the cloud from outside the city: Yasumasa Iyonaga in *Doctor at Nagasaki* by Masao Shiotsuki; and Shogoro Matsumoto, as quoted in *Nagasaki*

Speaks. See also testimonies by others who were in neighboring towns on August 9, at "Memories of Hiroshima and Nagasaki: Messages from *Hibakusha*," http://www.asahi.com/hibakusha.

Hibakusha testimonies: Yoshie Yokoyama described how her sister jumped out of the third-story window at Shiroyama Elementary School in her testimony translated into English by the Nagasaki National Peace Memorial Hall. Michiko Hirata recalled the streetcar rails pulled like "taffy" in her testimony originally published in *Testimonies of Nagasaki,* vol. 5, edited by the Nagasaki Testimonial Society, English translation provided by the Nagasaki National Peace Memorial Hall. Other images of the first moments after the explosion came from the anonymous testimonies in *The Witness of Those Two Days,* vols. 1 and 2; and Setsuko Iwanaga in *Footprints of Nagasaki,* edited by the Nagasaki Prefectural Girls' High School 42nd Alumnae.

Records of instantaneous deaths: *Nagasaki Speaks; Hiroshima and Nagasaki,* edited by the Committee for the Compilation of Materials on Damage Caused by the Atomic Bombs in Hiroshima and Nagasaki; and "Prompt and Utter Destruction: The Nagasaki Disaster and the Initial Medical Relief" by Nobuko Margaret Kosuge, *International Review of the Red Cross* 89:866. For deaths of Allied POWs in Japan, see the information compiled by the POW Research Network Japan at http://www.powresearch.jp. While only eight deaths of Nagasaki POWs from the atomic bombing have been confirmed, some researchers have estimated higher fatalities at Fukuoka Camp 14, based on eyewitness testimonies and assuming a mortality rate similar to that of other sites at the same distance from the explosion. See *Hiroshima and Nagasaki,* edited by the Committee for the Compilation of Materials on Damage Caused by the Atomic Bombs in Hiroshima and Nagasaki, pp. 478–80.

Survivors near Yoshida within the second concentric circle: Susumu Yamamura in *Hand Them Down to the Next Generations!*; and Sano Fujita in *Voices of the A-Bomb Survivors: Nagasaki,* compiled by the Nagasaki Atomic Bomb Testimonial Society. Many *hibakusha* who had been trained as auxiliary police or volunteer aid workers reported being instructed not to give water to the injured—see, for example, Dr. Shigetsune Iikura's testimony at the Nagasaki Broadcasting Company Web site, "Nagasaki and Peace," http://www2.nbc-nagasaki.co.jp/peace.

Yoshida described bodies near the river "turned into charcoal" in an interview with Jerome McDonnell of Chicago Public Radio in 2005, translated by Geoff Neill.

Dō-oh recalled the silence in the destroyed factory immediately after the blast in her essay "Ikasarete ikite" [Allowed to Live, I Live], in a collection by the same name, edited by Keishō bukai (Dō-oh Mineko ikō shuu) henshū iinkai [Legacy Group (Dō-oh Mineko Posthumous Collection) Editorial Committee], translated into English for the author's use.

Images of the Mitsubishi Ōhashi weapons plant: Masatoshi Tsunenari described being thrown across the factory in *Our Parents Were in Nagasaki on August 9, 1945.* Kazue Abe found herself surrounded by "gray" figures in *Bearing a Small Cross.* Other stories of the chaos near the Ōhashi factory came from Senji Yamaguchi in *Burnt Yet Undaunted,* compiled by Shinji Fujisaki, and Ichiko Owatari's unpublished testimony, English translation provided by the Nagasaki National Peace Memorial Hall.

Dō-oh's memory of being frightened by a B-29 flying overhead not long after the bomb exploded is supported by numerous survivor accounts, including several who vividly recall planes spraying the ground with machine-gun fire that afternoon or evening. However, due to the anticipated level of radioactivity in the area, U.S. aircraft were officially prohibited from entering the air space within fifty miles of Nagasaki for six hours following the attack; see "Mission Planning Summary, Report no. 9, 509th Composite Group," GRO Entry (A1) 7530, Lt. General Leslie R. Groves Collection, General Correspondence, 1941–1970, National Archives at College Park, MD. Photographic planes were given clearance after four hours, and General Spaatz reported that these planes attempted to photograph the city (hindered by heavy smoke cover) after three and a half hours; see "Blast Seen 250 Miles Away," *New York Times*, August 11, 1945. Although no additional raids on Nagasaki were officially conducted following the atomic bombing, reports of "general hell raising" tactics and the strafing of civilians during the Pacific campaign have been recorded—see, for example, *The Army Air Forces in World War II*, vol. 5, edited by Wesley Frank Craven and James Lea Cate, p. 696—and further bombing raids and reconnaissance missions continued over Japan through August 15.

Taniguchi recalled that "there was not a single drop of blood," in his unpublished 1986 speech, translated into English for the author's use.

For Nagasaki's medical preparedness prior to the atomic bombing, see *Nagasaki genbaku sensaishi*, vol. 1; and *Field Report Covering Air-Raid Protection and Allied Subjects in Nagasaki, Japan*, USSBS report no. 5. In addition, the recollections of Nagasaki doctors and other survivors provided details about emergency medical care at makeshift relief stations on the day of the bombing.

Governor Nagano Wakamatsu's testimony is quoted in *Nagasaki Speaks*. See also his testimony at the Nagasaki Broadcasting Company Web site, "Nagasaki and Peace," http://www2.nbc-nagasaki.co.jp/peace. Translations of Governor Nagano's damage reports to the Air Defense General Headquarters in the days and weeks after the bombing, as well as other reports from various Nagasaki officials, can be found in *Effects of the Atomic Bomb on Nagasaki, Japan*, USSBS report no. 93:3, pp. 196–265.

AUGUST 9, AFTERNOON AND EVENING

Wada remembered the little girl he carried to the relief station in *Genbaku jū roku nen no koe* [Sixty Years of Voices: Stories of the A-Bomb Survivors], edited by Imaishi Motohisa and translated by Christopher Cruz; and in an informal 2008 interview, copy provided by Imaishi Motohisa and translated by the author.

Masayuki Yoshida recalled the citizens' firefighting efforts in *Voices of the A-Bomb Survivors: Nagasaki*, compiled by the Nagasaki Atomic Bomb Testimonial Society.

Nagano described encountering naked and injured people begging for water in her unpublished speech, "Watashi no hibaku taikenki" [My Atomic Bomb Memory], translated into English for the author's use. She remembered the "patches of torn clothing stuck to their wounds" in *The Light of Morning*, translated by Brian Burke-Gaffney.

For *hibakusha* memories of the afternoon and evening of August 9, see the anonymous testimonies in *The Witness of Those Two Days*, vols. 1 and 2. Mikiko Tanaka in *The Pain in Our Hearts: Recollections of Hiroshima, Nagasaki, and Okinawa* described the corpses like "potatoes" in the river.

Mieko Higuchi remembered how her mother was rebuked by military police for crying at her safe return, in *Footprints of Nagasaki*, edited by the Nagasaki Prefectural Girls' High School 42nd Alumnae.

Yoshida recalled the intense pain from the heat of the sun on his wounds in a History Channel interview (ca. 2009), copy provided by Yoshida Katsuji.

Dō-oh described her desire for "even muddy water" to quench her thirst, and the scene that evening at Dr. Miyajima's makeshift relief station, in her essay "Ikasarete ikite" [Allowed to Live, I Live], in a collection by the same name, edited by Keishō bukai (Dō-oh Mineko ikō shuu) henshō iinkai [Legacy Group (Dō-oh Mineko Posthumous Collection) Editorial Committee], translated into English for the author's use.

Leaflets warning Japan about the atomic bomb were printed after Hiroshima and scheduled to be dropped over Japanese cities of greater than 100,000 people beginning on August 9; see "Mission No: 'Special'; Flown: 20 July–14 August '45, 20th Air Force, 509th Composite Group Tactical Mission Report," Records of the Army Air Forces, Record Group 18, National Archives at College Park, MD. For Governor Nagano reporting that leaflets had been dropped on Nagasaki on the day of the atomic bombing, see "Air-Raid Damage Report no. 6, 8-10-45," in USSBS report no. 93:3, pp. 213–14. Nagasaki survivors' accounts vary—some report seeing leaflets being dropped on the night of August 9, while others remember that they were dropped early the following morning. Richard Rhodes, in *The Making of the Atomic Bomb*, cites a May 23, 1946, memo to General Groves that reported that, due to printing and distribution delays, leaflets were not dropped on Nagasaki until August 10; see pp. 736–37.

Taniguchi's memory of the fires "illuminating the sky like a midnight sun" appeared in *The Light of Morning*, translated by Brian Burke-Gaffney.

CHAPTER 3: EMBERS

SURRENDER NEGOTIATIONS, AUGUST 9–10

The evidence that the Nagasaki bombing had no impact on the surrender debate comes from the official history of the Japanese Imperial General Headquarters, Army Division (*Daihonei Rikugunbu*, vol. 10). As translated by Tsuyoshi Hasegawa, this volume notes that the Supreme Council for the Direction of the War received word of the Nagasaki bombing at about 11:30 a.m. on August 9, but that "there is no record in other materials that treated the effect [of the Nagasaki bomb] seriously." See "The Atomic Bombs and the Soviet Invasion: Which Was More Important in Japan's Decision to Surrender?" by Tsuyoshi Hasegawa in *The End of the Pacific War: Reappraisals*. In addition, decoded Japanese communications for August 9 include reports about Hiroshima and the Soviet invasion of Manchuria but make no mention of the Nagasaki bombing; see *Marching Orders: The Untold Story of World War II* by Bruce Lee (New York: Crown Publishers, 1995), p. 542; and *MacArthur's ULTRA: Codebreaking and the War Against Japan, 1942–1945* by Edward J. Drea (Lawrence, KS: University of Kansas Press, 1992), p. 224. The August 9 meeting included some debate about Japan's ability to defend itself against future atomic bomb attacks; see "'Hoshina Memorandum' on the Emperor's 'Sacred Decision [*Go-seidan*],' 9–10 August, 1945" (document 62), in *The Atomic Bomb and the End of World War II*, edited by William Burr. Although some analysts contend that the second atomic bomb provided additional leverage for the peace faction and the emperor to push for surrender (see, for example, *Truman and the Hiroshima Cult* by Robert P. Newman [East Lansing, MI: Michigan State University, 1995], chap. 5), there is no specific evidence of the Nagasaki bomb's direct impact on the decision makers.

Additional sources for Japanese leaders' surrender debates in Tokyo: *The Rising Sun* by John Toland; *Racing the Enemy: Stalin, Truman, and the Surrender of Japan* by Tsuyoshi Hasegawa; *Downfall* by Richard B. Frank; *Japan's Struggle to End the War*, USSBS report no. 2; "The Shock of the Atomic Bomb and Japan's Decision to Surrender: A Reconsideration" by Sadao Asada, *Pacific Historical Review* 67:4; and the various essays in *The End of the Pacific War: Reappraisals*, edited by Tsuyoshi Hasegawa.

Truman's radio address on the evening of August 9: "Radio Report to the American People on the Potsdam Conference, 8-9-45," *Public Papers of the Presidents of the United States: Harry S. Truman, 1945–1953.*

For U.S. leaders' responses to Japan's surrender communications, see *The Rising Sun* by John Toland; and "Diary Entries for August 10–11, Henry L. Stimson Diary" (document 66) and "Diary Entry, Friday, August 10, 1945, Henry Wallace Diary" (document 65) in *The Atomic Bomb and the End of World War II*, edited by William Burr.

NAGASAKI, AUGUST 10

Mayor Okada's experience is described by Governor Nagano in his testimony at the Nagasaki Broadcasting Company Web site, "Nagasaki and Peace," http://www2.nbc-nagasaki.co.jp/peace.

For photographer Yamahata Yōsuke, see the essays and interviews reprinted in *Nagasaki Journey: The Photographs of Yosuke Yamahata, August 10, 1945,* edited by Rupert Jenkins. Higashi Jun's recollections were quoted in *Nagasaki Speaks;* his memory of stepping on the corpse of a horse appeared in *Nagasaki Journey.*

Hibakusha memories of August 10: Shuzo Nishio remembered crying over his family's ashes in *Living Beneath the Atomic Cloud*, edited by Takashi Nagai. Other images came from Fukahori Yoshitoshi's testimony originally published in *Testimonies of Nagasaki 1970*, edited by the Nagasaki Testimonial Society, English translation provided by the Nagasaki National Peace Memorial Hall; Matsu Moriuchi in *We of Nagasaki* by Takashi Nagai; the collection of testimonies at "Memories of Hiroshima and Nagasaki: Messages from *Hibakusha*," http://www.asahi.com/hibakusha; an anonymous survivor in *The Deaths of Hibakusha*, vol. 1; and Hisae Aoki in *Testimonies of the Atomic*

Bomb Survivors. Sakue Shimohira was able to identify her mother's body by her gold tooth; see her interview in the film *The Last Atomic Bomb,* directed by Robert Richter.

Yoshida recalled the sun's brutal heat "like a slow execution" in his testimony "I Must Not Die," English translation provided by Nagasaki National Peace Memorial Hall for the Atomic Bomb Victims.

Governor Nagano's memory of the destruction in the Urakami Valley is quoted from his testimony at the Nagasaki Broadcasting Company Web site, "Nagasaki and Peace," http://www2.nbc-nagasaki.co.jp/peace.

Medical and food relief: *Hiroshima and Nagasaki,* edited by the Committee for the Compilation of Materials on Damage Caused by the Atomic Bombs in Hiroshima and Nagasaki; *Effects of the Atomic Bombs on Health and Medical Services in Hiroshima and Nagasaki,* USSBS report no. 13; "Prompt and Utter Destruction: The Nagasaki Disaster and the Initial Medical Relief" by Nobuko Margaret Kosuge in *International Review of the Red Cross* 89:866; and *Nagasaki Speaks.*

For Dr. Akizuki Tatsuichirō's experiences at First Urakami Hospital, see "A Week of Horror and Human Love" in *The Light of Morning.* His memory of feeling "depressed in spirit" by the night of August 10 is quoted from his memoir *Nagasaki 1945.*

Other *hibakusha* testimonies related to relief efforts: Tsuguyoshi Kitamura in *Voices of the A-Bomb Survivors: Nagasaki,* compiled by the Nagasaki Atomic Bomb Testimonial Society; Itonaga Yoshi in *Nagasaki August 9, 1945,* edited by Mary Wiesen and Elizabeth Cannon; and Fukahori Yoshitoshi, interview with the author in 2011.

NAGASAKI, AUGUST 11–14

Memories of searching for lost family members in the ruins: Chie Tayoshi in *Voices of the A-Bomb Survivors: Nagasaki,* compiled by the Nagasaki Atomic Bomb Testimonial Society; Motoko Moriguchi in *The Unforgettable Day,* edited by Miyuki Kamezawa; Hitoshi Hamasaki at *My Unforgettable Memory* at the Nagasaki Shimbun Peace Site, http://www.nagasaki-np.co.jp/peace/hibaku/english/07.html; and the testimonies of Tadao Nakazawa and Sumiko Sakamoto in *Testimonies of the Atomic Bomb Survivors.*

Family reunifications: An anonymous survivor described how she was left for dead in a pile of corpses in *War and Atomic Holocaust on Trial* by Shigeyuki Kobayashi. Hisako Kyuma was reunited with her father at a relief station; see *Voices of the A-Bomb Survivors: Nagasaki,* compiled by the Nagasaki Atomic Bomb Testimonial Society.

Wada's memory of cremating his friend Tanaka is quoted from *Genbaku jū roku nen no koe* [Sixty Years of Voices: Stories of the A-Bomb Survivors], edited by Imaishi Motohisa and translated by Christopher Cruz.

Allied POWs in Nagasaki: Charles Barkie and J. H. C. deGroot in *Voices of the A-Bomb Survivors: Nagasaki,* compiled by the Nagasaki Atomic Bomb Testimonial Society; *Nagasaki Speaks;* and *The Jack Ford Story: Newfoundland's POW in Nagasaki* by Jack Fitzgerald.

Living in the ruins: Kazue Abe's *Bearing a Small Cross;* Sano Fujita and Sachi
 Ogino in *Voices of the A-Bomb Survivors: Nagasaki,* compiled by the Nagasaki Atomic Bomb Testimonial Society; Matsu Moriuchi in *We of Nagasaki*
 by Takashi Nagai; and Wada Hisako, interview with the author. Ikuko Doira
 remembers how her family of eight slept in shifts on one *tatami* mat in *Living
 Beneath the Atomic Cloud,* edited by Takashi Nagai.
Fuji Urata Matsumoto remembered the "lonely funeral" she and her sister held for
 their mother in *We of Nagasaki* by Takashi Nagai.
Dr. Kenji Miake recalled the smell of "scorched chicken meat" and the dismal
 conditions at the Shinkōzen relief station in *Nagasaki Speaks.*
For relief personnel as of August 14, see Governor Nagano's "Report No. 8. Matters
 Concerning Air-Raid Damage and Emergency Counter Measures, 8-14-45" in
 Effects of the Atomic Bomb on Nagasaki, Japan, USSBS report no. 93:3, p. 215.
Dr. Akizuki described injured survivors comforting one another with Christian
 prayers in his testimony in *The Light of Morning.* His anger at the government and disbelief at the newspaper article claiming that protection against
 the "new-type bomb" was possible is quoted from *Nagasaki 1945.*

SURRENDER, AUGUST 15

The United States' reply to Japan's surrender offer was reported by the Associated
 Press; see "Text of U.S. Reply on Issue of Emperor," *Christian Science Mon-
 itor,* August 11, 1945.
The emperor's decision to surrender is quoted from *The Rising Sun* by John To-
 land. For the Japanese Cabinet's final debates, see also "'The Second Sacred
 Judgment' August 14, 1945" (document 74), in *The Atomic Bomb and the
 End of World War II,* edited by William Burr; and the sources listed above
 for the Tokyo meetings.
The last U.S. bombing attacks on Japan: *U.S. Army Air Forces in World War II:
 Combat Chronology 1941–1945,* compiled by Kit C. Carter and Robert Muel-
 ler; *The Making of the Atomic Bomb* by Richard Rhodes; and *The Army Air
 Forces in WWII,* vol. 5, edited by Wesley Frank Craven and James Lea Cate.
A translation of the emperor's "Imperial Rescript on Surrender, 1945" is in *Japan:
 A Documentary History,* vol. 2, edited by David J. Lu.
Reactions to the surrender by military and civilians: *The Rising Sun* by John Toland;
 Embracing Defeat by John W. Dower; and *Japan at War* by Haruko Taya Cook
 and Theodore F. Cook. For the execution of POWs in Fukuoka, see "'To Dispose
 of the Prisoners': The Japanese Executions of American Air-Crew at Fukuoka,
 Japan, During 1945" by Timothy Lang Francis, *Pacific Historical Review* 66:4.
Reactions to the surrender in Nagasaki: The emperor's radio address briefly inter-
 rupted Tsue Hayashi's search for her daughter; see *Hibaku: Recollections of
 A-Bomb Survivors,* edited by Mitsue Kubo. Atsuyuki Matsuo overheard the
 surrender announcement on the radio while cremating his wife's body; see
 Testimonies of the Atomic Bomb Survivors. Other testimonies: Kazue Abe in
 Bearing a Small Cross; Raisuke Shirabe in *The Light of Morning;* Tatsuichirō
 Akizuki in *Nagasaki 1945;* and numerous individual *hibakusha* accounts.

CHAPTER 4: EXPOSED

RADIATION EXPOSURE AND EARLY MEDICAL CARE

The initial stages of radiation illness and subsequent deaths in Hiroshima and
    Nagasaki are documented in *Hiroshima and Nagasaki,* particularly chap. 8,
    edited by the Committee for the Compilation of Materials on Damage Caused
    by the Atomic Bombs in Hiroshima and Nagasaki.
Sources for doctors quoted in this chapter: Dr. Shiotsuki Masao remembered the
    "pinprick"-sized purple spots that appeared on his patients and detailed his
    efforts to autopsy the deceased in his book *Doctor at Nagasaki: "My First
    Assignment Was Mercy Killing."* Dr. Akuzuki Tatsuichirō is quoted from his
    memoir, *Nagasaki 1945.* For Dr. Shirabe Raisuke, see "My Experience of the
    Atomic Bombing and an Outline of Atomic Bomb Disease" in *The Light of
    Morning;* "Medical Survey of Atomic Bomb Casualties," *The Military Sur-
    geon* 113:4; and *A Physician's Diary of Atomic Bombing and Its Aftermath*
    by Raisuke Shirabe, M.D., edited by Fidelius R. Kuo. Dr. Shirabe's original
    survey questionnaires and other materials are housed at the Division of Sci-
    entific Registry at the Atomic Bomb Disease Institute of Nagasaki University.
    See also *The Bells of Nagasaki* by Takashi Nagai for information on his
    Nagasaki Medical College relief team caring for victims who had fled to the
    countryside outside Nagasaki.
In *Death in Life,* Robert Jay Lifton traced the origins of the rumor that plants
    would not grow in the atomic-bombed cities for seventy years to a statement
    about the Hiroshima bombing by chemist Harold F. Jacobson, which was
    reported (and soon retracted) in U.S. newspapers on August 8, 1945.
Hibakusha testimonies: Hisae Aoki remembered walking with her sister through the
    ashes of her school's playground in *Testimonies of the Atomic Bomb Survivors.*
    An anonymous male, in *The Witness of Those Two Days,* vol. 2, described
    quenching his thirst with water from a gravesite memorial. Miyuki Fukahori
    recalled that corpses still floated in the river; see *Nagasaki Under the Atomic
    Bomb: Experiences of Young College Girls,* edited by Michiko Nakano.

U.S. RADIATION KNOWLEDGE AND DENIAL

Evidence of U.S. prebomb radiation effects knowledge: Dr. J. Robert Oppen-
    heimer's statement on the bomb's lethal radiation is quoted from "Memoran-
    dum from J. R. Oppenheimer to Brigadier General Farrell, May 11, 1945"
    (document 5) in *The Atomic Bomb and the End of World War II,* edited by
    William Burr. Dr. Stafford L. Warren noted the lack of scientific study on the
    potential radioactive aftereffects of the bombs in "The Role of Radiology in
    the Development of the Atomic Bomb" in *Radiology in World War II,* edited
    by Leonard D. Heaton et al. For other examples, see *The Making of the
    Atomic Bomb* by Richard Rhodes; *The Atomic Bomb and the End of World
    War II,* edited by William Burr, especially documents 6 and 12; *Permissible
    Dose: A History of Radiation Protection in the Twentieth Century* by J.
    Samuel Walker; and *The Road to Trinity* by Kenneth D. Nichols.

Several scholars have explored U.S. officials' postwar denial and minimization of radiation effects and the War Department's efforts to maintain control over the press reports related to the atomic bombs. See, for example, "Commemoration and Silence: Fifty Years of Remembering the Bomb in America and Japan" by Laura Hein and Mark Selden in their essay collection *Living with the Bomb: American and Japanese Cultural Conflicts in the Nuclear Age;* "Censorship and Reportage of Atomic Damage and Casualties in Hiroshima and Nagasaki" by Glenn D. Hook, *Bulletin of Concerned Asian Scholars* 23:1; "Covering the Bomb: Press and State in the Shadow of Nuclear War" by Robert Karl Manoff, in *War, Peace and the News Media, Proceedings, March 18 and 19, 1983,* edited by David M. Rubin and Marie Cunningham; and *Hiroshima in America: Fifty Years of Denial* by Robert Jay Lifton and Greg Mitchell.

An excellent resource on the impact of occupation censorship on the world's understanding of the effects of the atomic bombs is *The Atomic Bomb Suppressed: American Censorship in Occupied Japan* by Monica Braw. For the press code, censorship instructions, and other Japanese media restrictions during the U.S. occupation, see *Conquered Press: The MacArthur Era in Japanese Journalism* by William J. Coughlin; *User's Guide to the Gordon W. Prange Collection: Part I: Microform Edition of Censored Periodicals, 1945–1949,* edited by Eizaburō Okuizumi; and "Revised Basic Plan for Civil Censorship in Japan, September 30, 1945," Records of Allied Operational and Occupation Headquarters, World War II, Record Group 331, SCAP GHQ, box 8552 folder 8, National Archives at College Park, MD.

For General Groves's denials of radiation effects, see "Japanese Reports Doubted," *New York Times,* August 31, 1945, and "U.S. Atom Bomb Site Belies Tokyo Tales" by William L. Laurence, *New York Times,* September 12, 1945. *The Atomic Bomb and the End of World War II,* edited by William Burr, includes the transcript of Groves's conversation with Lt. Col. Rea at Oak Ridge (document 76) as well as General Farrell's September 1945 reports from Hiroshima and Nagasaki (documents 77a and 77b). Groves's belief that troops could enter an atomic-bombed area thirty minutes after an explosion is noted by Barton J. Bernstein in "An Analysis of 'Two Cultures': Writing About the Making and the Using of the Atomic Bombs," *Public Historian* 12:2. For Groves's characterization of radiation deaths as "pleasant," see his testimony before the U.S. Senate in "Atomic Energy, Part 1, Hearings Before the United States Senate Special Committee on Atomic Energy, 79th Congress, 1st Session, Nov. 27–30, December 3, 1945" (Washington, DC: U.S. Government Printing Office, 1945). Despite postwar assurances by Groves and others that the first atomic test at Alamogordo, New Mexico, had no detrimental radioactive impact, high levels of radioactivity from fallout were recorded several miles east of the testing site, and cattle in the area lost hair and developed skin lesions. Recently, U.S. health officials acknowledged that ingestion of contaminated food and water near the site has not been sufficiently studied and may have contributed to the overall level of radiation exposure for area residents. In 2014, the National Cancer Institute launched a follow-up investigation of the possible connection between reports of unusually high cancer rates in the area and residents' radiation exposure following the Trinity test;

see "Decades After Nuclear Test, U.S. Studies Cancer Fallout" by Dan Frosch, *Wall Street Journal*, September 15, 2014.

U.S. correspondent George Weller's reports from early postwar Nagasaki were rediscovered by his son, Anthony Weller, in 2002 and subsequently published in *First into Nagasaki: The Censored Eyewitness Dispatches on Post-Atomic Japan and Its Prisoners of War.*

For a reprint of Australian reporter Wilfred Burchett's first dispatch from Hiroshima and his confrontation with General Farrell, see his book *Shadows of Hiroshima.*

Japanese officials' concerns about the potential impact of residual radiation on those living in the hypocenter area, in contradiction to U.S. teams' assessments, are noted in "Report on Damage in the City of Nagasaki Resulting from the Atomic Air Raid, 10-3-45, Commander in Chief, Sasebo Naval District" in *Effects of the Atomic Bomb on Nagasaki, Japan,* USSBS report no. 93:3.

For the findings of the various U.S. military and scientific research teams in Nagasaki in the fall of 1945, see *The Atomic Bombings of Hiroshima and Nagasaki* by the U.S. Army Corps of Engineers, Manhattan District; *Medical Effects of the Atomic Bomb in Japan,* edited by Ashley W. Oughterson and Shields Warren, a condensed version of the six-volume report of the Joint Commission for the Investigation of the Effects of the Atomic Bomb in Japan; and the reports of the United States Strategic Bombing Survey (Pacific Survey).

USSBS film crew director Daniel A. McGovern argued for the value of the Nippon Eiga-sha film in "Memo, Lt. Daniel A. McGovern to Lt. Commander William P. Woodward, December 29, 1945," Production Materials from *The Effects of the Atomic Bomb on Hiroshima and Nagasaki,* edited by Abé Mark Nornes, University of Michigan Center for Japanese Studies Publications, accessed 2013, https://www.cjspubs.lsa.umich.edu/electronic/facultyseries/list/series/production.php. For other details on the appropriation of this film, see "Suddenly There Was Emptiness" in *Japanese Documentary Film* by Abé Mark Nornes; "Iwasaki and the Occupied Screen" by Erik Barnouw, *Film History* 2:4; and *Atomic Cover-up* by Greg Mitchell.

OCCUPIED NAGASAKI, FALL AND WINTER 1945

For Allied prisoner of war Syd Barber's memory of his first view of the destruction in Nagasaki, see *Twilight Liberation* by Hugh V. Clarke. Other details about Allied POWs released through Nagasaki: *Voices of the A-Bomb Survivors: Nagasaki,* compiled by the Nagasaki Atomic Bomb Testimonial Society; *The Jack Ford Story* by Jack Fitzgerald; *Surviving the Sword* by Brian MacArthur; *Prisoners of the Japanese* by Gavan Daws; and "Experiences at Nagasaki, Japan" by Benedict R. Harris and Marvin A. Stevens, *The Connecticut State Medical Journal* 9:12.

Quotations by occupation troops: Rudi Bohlmann, interview with Curt Nickisch on *All Things Considered,* NPR, August 9, 2007; and Keith B. Lynch in *World War II Letters,* edited by Bill Adler. Lt. George L. Cooper recalled how "everybody and his brother" quickly made their way to the hypocenter area in "Securing the Surrender: Marines in the Occupation of Japan" by Charles R.

Smith, Marine Corps Historical Center. The film *Nagasaki Journey,* produced by Judy Irving and Chris Beaver, contains footage of occupation troops arriving by ship into Nagasaki harbor.

An excellent source for the overall Japanese experience during the occupation is *Embracing Defeat: Japan in the Wake of WWII* by John W. Dower. For additional information about the occupation of Nagasaki, see "Securing the Surrender" by Charles R. Smith, Marine Corps Historical Center; *Reports of General MacArthur,* vol. 1 supp., by the U.S. Department of the Army; and *Nagasaki: The British Experience: 1854–1945* by Brian Burke-Gaffney.

Key details for Nagasaki troop movements and activities can be found in reports created by the U.S. Nuclear Test Personnel Review (NTPR) program of the Defense Threat Reduction Agency (formerly the Defense Nuclear Agency). In response to U.S. veterans' concerns over potential health risks resulting from exposure to ionizing radiation, the NTPR was established in 1977 to provide estimates of radiation exposure for military personnel engaged in "radiation-risk activities," including those who served in Hiroshima or Nagasaki during the occupation, prisoners of war held in or processed through the two cities, and personnel who participated in U.S. atmospheric nuclear testing through the early 1960s. For occupation veterans, these reports outline the movements, locations, and activities of personnel assigned to Hiroshima and Nagasaki, data that was then correlated with the measurements taken by U.S. scientists in the fall of 1945 to determine the "worst-case scenario" for their potential radiation exposure. While the NTPR's analysis concludes that residual radiation levels were not high enough to cause adverse health effects, no follow-up studies on the veterans themselves have ever been conducted, and many continue to press for injury claims through the U.S. Department of Veterans Affairs. See "Fact Sheet: Hiroshima and Nagasaki Occupation Forces" by the U.S. Defense Threat Reduction Agency; and *Radiation Dose Reconstruction: U.S. Occupation Forces in Hiroshima and Nagasaki, Japan, 1945–1946* by W. McRaney and J. McGahan. For the veterans' perspectives, see *Killing Our Own: The Disaster of America's Experience with Atomic Radiation* by Harvey Wasserman et al. (New York: Dell Publishing Co., 1982); and *Invisible Enemies of Atomic Veterans* by John D. Bankston (Victoria, B.C.: Trafford Publishing, 2003).

Atom Bowl: "Atom Bowl Game Listed," *New York Times,* December 29, 1945; "Omanski Tops Bertelli in 1st Atom Bowl," *Washington Post,* January 3, 1946; and "Nagasaki, 1946: Football Amid the Ruins" by John D. Lukas, *New York Times,* December 25, 2005.

For Hayashi Shigeo's experiences when photographing the city, see his testimony at the Nagasaki Broadcasting Company Web site, "Nagasaki and Peace," http://www2.nbc-nagasaki.co.jp/peace.

U.S. occupation medical support: "Impressions of Japanese Medicine at the End of World War II" by Richard B. Berlin, *Scientific Monthly* 64:1; "Radiation Effects of the Atomic Bomb Among the Natives of Nagasaki, Kyushu" by J. S. P. Beck and W. A. Meissner, *American Journal of Clinical Pathology* 6; *Effects of the Atomic Bombs on Health and Medical Services in Hiroshima and Nagasaki,* USSBS report no. 13; "Experiences at Nagasaki, Japan" by Benedict R. Harris and Marvin A. Stevens, *The Connecticut State Medical Journal* 9:12.

Joe O'Donnell's photographs and personal narrative can be found in his book *Japan 1945: A U.S. Marine's Photographs from Ground Zero* and essay "A Straight Path Through Hell," *American Heritage Magazine* 56:3.

Nagasaki survivors' memories of the early occupation: Hashimoto Yutaka in "Mom and Silver Rice," *Crossroads* 4, and Tsukasa Kikuchi in *Silent Thunder*, remembered the kindness of occupation soldiers; Michie Hattori Bernstein is quoted from "Eyewitness to the Nagasaki Atomic Bomb Blast," *WWII Magazine;* Uchida Tsukasa described the occupation bulldozers in *The Atomic Bomb Suppressed* by Monica Braw; and Chiyoko Egashira recalled schoolchildren "cheering one another up" in *Testimonies of the Atomic Bomb Survivors*. See also "Resurrecting Nagasaki" by Chad R. Diehl, Ph.D. dissertation, Columbia University.

For *hibakusha* commemorations, see Nagai Kayano in *We of Nagasaki* by Takashi Nagai; Takashi Nagai's *The Bells of Nagasaki;* Sakue Shimohira in *The Last Atomic Bomb*, directed by Robert Richter; and Itonaga Yoshi's "The Sun Dropped Out of the Sky" in *Nagasaki August 9, 1945*, edited by Mary Wiesen and Elizabeth Cannon. Itsuko Okubo is the mother who collected remnants of a school uniform in remembrance of her son, interviewed in the film *Nagasaki Journey*, produced by Judy Irving and Chris Beaver. According to Dr. Nagai Takashi and others, the November 1945 memorial at Urakami Church honored eight thousand Catholic deaths; other sources indicate the number of Catholics killed in Nagasaki may be closer to ten thousand. See "Religious Responses to the Atomic Bombing in Nagasaki" by Okuyama Michiaki, *Bulletin* (Nanzan Institute for Religion and Culture) 37; and *Hiroshima and Nagasaki*, edited by the Committee for the Compilation of Materials on Damage Caused by the Atomic Bombs in Hiroshima and Nagasaki, p. 382.

CHAPTER 5: TIME SUSPENDED

NAGASAKI, EARLY 1946

The U.S. Strategic Bombing Survey (USSBS) generated more than one hundred individual reports on their investigations of the impact of Allied air attacks against Japan during the war, including civilian defense, medical, economic, and military studies. The survey's aim to support "future development" of the U.S. military is quoted from *Summary Report: Pacific War*, USSBS report no. 1; additional reports specific to Nagasaki are listed in the Selected Bibliography.

For background on the USSBS film crew in Nagasaki, including interviews with Army Air Forces 2nd Lt. Herbert Sussan and Army Air Forces 1st Lt. Daniel McGovern, see *Atomic Cover-up* by Greg Mitchell, which includes Sussan's quotations, "Nothing and no one had prepared me for the devastation" and "I shuddered when the lights were turned on to film him." Sussan's observation that Nagasaki seemed "like an enormous graveyard" is from "38 Years After Nagasaki, A Chronicler of the Horror Returns to an Unfaded Past" by Dave Yuzo Spector, *Chicago Tribune*, January 5, 1984.

For the USSBS footage of Taniguchi at Ōmura National Hospital, see Video No. 342-USAF-11002, "Medical Aspect, 11/19/1945–02/04/1946," Records of

U.S. Air Force Commands, Activities, and Organizations, Record Group 342, Moving Images Relating to Military Aviation Activities, National Archives at College Park, MD. Digital copy available through the Online Public Access catalog (identifier 64449) at www.archives.gov/research/search. Taniguchi appears at marker 18:30.

Taniguchi reflected that "doctors were clueless" about his treatment in his interview in Steven Okazaki's documentary film *White Light/Black Rain.*

For details about postwar Japan's struggling economy and food shortages and Nagasaki's population changes and occupation troop movements, see the occupation-related sources listed in the notes for chapter 4, especially *Embracing Defeat* by John W. Dower.

Uchida Tsukasa's memory of the old woman who inadvertently carried in human bones when gathering firewood appears in his testimony "A Dark Spot on the Hill of the Atomic Bomb Hypocenter," originally published in *Atomic Bomb Testimonials by Nagasaki City Employees,* edited by the Nagasaki Testimonial Society, English translation provided by the Nagasaki National Peace Memorial Hall.

For stories of births following in utero radiation exposure, see Masahito Hirose's "The Parents of Children with Microcephaly Due to Atomic Bomb Radiation" and *Nagasaki Shimbun*'s "Atomic Bomb Survivors Today" in *Testimonies of the Atomic Bomb Survivors;* and *Children of the Atomic Bomb* by Dr. James N. Yamazaki.

Stories of postwar hardships: Fukahori Yoshitoshi, interviewed by the author in 2011, remembered being treated for tuberculosis with only vitamins and bed rest; Miyazaki Midori, interviewed in 2009, recalled sharing one pair of shoes with her siblings. See also *The Deaths of Hibakusha,* vol. 1; and Mihoko Mukai's "Recalling Hellish Memories of My Childhood" in *Voices of the A-Bomb Survivors: Nagasaki,* compiled by the Nagasaki Atomic Bomb Testimonial Society.

For the reopening of Nagasaki schools, see testimonies by teachers: Chiyoko Egashira's "The Day Shiroyama Primary School Was Destroyed" and Hideo Arakawa's "A Record of the Atomic Bombing" in *Testimonies of the Atomic Bomb Survivors;* Teruko Araki's "The Children and I" in *Living Beneath the Atomic Cloud,* edited by Takashi Nagai; and Hideyuki Hayashi's "From the Ruins of Yamazato Primary School" in *The Light of Morning.*

U.S. SILENCING

Sources for Japan's transformation during the occupation include *Embracing Defeat* by John W. Dower; *Inventing Japan: 1853–1964* by Ian Buruma; *A Modern History of Japan: From Tokugawa to the Present* by Andrew Gordon; *The Making of Modern Japan* by Marius Jansen; *Hirohito and the Making of Modern Japan* by Herbert P. Bix; and *Japan: The Story of a Nation* by Edwin O. Reischauer.

For Japan's postwar constitution, see the Japanese National Diet Library's online exhibition "The Birth of the Constitution of Japan," http://www.ndl.go.jp/constitution/e/.

For the rules and activities of the occupation's Civil Censorship Detachment (CCD), see *The Atomic Bomb Suppressed* by Monica Braw. See also *Reports of General MacArthur*, vol. 1 supp., chap. 8. For film restrictions, see *Screening Enlightenment: Hollywood and the Cultural Reconstruction of Defeated Japan* by Hiroshi Kitamura.

Nagasaki's anniversary ceremony: Domei News Agency journalist Hideo Matsuno describes the naming of the anniversary ceremony as the "Memorial Day for the Restoration of Peace" and other occupation censorship restrictions in his video testimony at the Global Network of the National Peace Memorial Halls for the Atomic Bomb Victims in Hiroshima and Nagasaki at http://www .global-peace.go.jp/. Occupation authorities noted their opposition to atomic bomb commemoration ceremonies, "for the reason that they are being used as a means of propagandizing 'atonement,' which in turn has an adverse effect on the war-guilt program," in "Memo: 'Nagasaki Ceremony,' H.G.S. to SCAP-GHQ, August 2, 1948," Record Group 5, MacArthur Memorial Library and Archives, Norfolk, VA.

For the CCD censor's concern that Ishida Masako's memoir would "tear open war scars," see *The Atomic Bomb Suppressed* by Monica Braw.

Nagai Takashi's view of Nagasaki as chosen "to expiate the sins" of the war is quoted from *The Bells of Nagasaki*. For details about the "Sack of Manila" appendix of the 1949 publication of Nagai's *Nagasaki no kane*, see *The Atomic Bomb Suppressed* by Monica Braw; and "Nagasaki Writers: The Mission" by Kamata Sadao in *Literature Under the Nuclear Cloud*, compiled by Ito Narihiko et al.

Censorship of medical studies: "Medical Censorship in Occupied Japan, 1945–1948" by Sey Nishimura, *Pacific Historical Review* 58:1; "Promoting Health in American-Occupied Japan" by Sey Nishimura, *American Journal of Public Health* 99:8; and "The Repatriation of Atomic Bomb Victim Body Parts to Japan: Natural Objects and Diplomacy" by M. Susan Lindee, *Osiris* 13. Dr. Shiotsuki Masao described the warning he received at a presentation about his Nagasaki experience in his book *Doctor at Nagasaki*.

For the U.S. public's reactions to the atomic bombings, see "The American People and the Use of Atomic Bombs on Japan: The 1940s" by Michael J. Yavenditti, *Historian* 36:2; *Hiroshima in America* by Robert Jay Lifton and Greg Mitchell; and "Commemoration and Silence: Fifty Years of Remembering the Bomb in America and Japan" by Laura Hein and Mark Selden in their essay collection *Living with the Bomb*.

The postwar U.S. media's emphasis on American scientific achievement when reporting about the atomic bombs was exemplified by the writings of *New York Times* science reporter William L. Laurence, hired by the Manhattan Project, while still on the *Times* staff, to draft exclusive press releases about the bomb's development. Laurence won the Pulitzer Prize in 1946 for his glorified account of the Nagasaki atomic bombing (from his vantage point aboard the companion plane *The Great Artiste*) and his ten-part series on the atomic bomb. For Laurence's role as the War Department's mouthpiece, see *Hiroshima in America* by Robert Jay Lifton and Greg Mitchell; "Covering the Bomb: Press and State in the Shadow of Nuclear War" by Robert Karl Manoff, in *War, Peace and the News Media, Proceedings, March 18 and 19, 1983,* edited by David M. Rubin and Marie Cunningham; and "Hiroshima Cover-up: How the War Department's Timesman Won a Pulitzer Prize" by Amy and David Goodman at commondreams.org, August 10, 2004.

Quotations related to U.S. opposition to the bombs: "Has It Come to This" by A. J. Muste, and "The Literacy of Survival" by Norman Cousins, reprinted in *Hiroshima's Shadow,* edited by Kai Bird and Lawrence Lifschultz. Admiral Halsey's doubts about the bombs' necessity were reported in an Associated Press dispatch; see, for example, the "Atom Tests" editorial in the *Washington Post,* September 11, 1946. Other concerns about the use of atomic weapons voiced in the U.S. press include "Gentlemen: Are You Mad!" by Lewis Mumford in the *Saturday Review of Literature,* March 2, 1946; and "Atomic Warfare and the Christian Faith" by the Federal Council of Churches. For reprints of these articles, and others, see *Hiroshima's Shadow,* edited by Kai Bird and Lawrence Lifschultz. See also "From Hiroshima: A Report and a Question" by Father John A. Siemes, *Time,* February 11, 1946; "What the Bomb Really Did" by Robert DeVore, *Collier's,* March 2, 1946; and commentary by former Los Alamos scientists, including "Beyond Imagination" by physicist Phillip Morrison, *New Republic,* February 1946, and "Atomic Bomb Damage—Japan and USA" by R. E. Marshak et al., *Bulletin of the Atomic Scientists,* May 1, 1946.

The USSBS summary reports released in June 1946 may have also contributed to the mounting concerns of U.S. leaders that public support for the bombs' use was in jeopardy. Although the conclusion was later determined to be unsupported by the survey's own data at the time, the USSBS claimed that, due to the depleted state of Japan's military and economy by 1945, Japan would have likely surrendered prior to the end of the year "even if atomic bombs had not been dropped." For analysis of this USSBS conclusion, see "Compelling Japan's Surrender Without the A-Bomb, Soviet Entry, or Invasion: Reconsidering the US Bombing Survey's Early-Surrender Conclusions" by Barton J. Bernstein, *Journal of Strategic Studies* 18:2.

John Hersey's *Hiroshima* appeared in the *New Yorker* on August 31, 1946. Book-of-the-Month Club president Harry Scherman's praise for Hersey's work was quoted in "'The Most Spectacular Explosion in the Time of Man'" by Charles Poore, *New York Times,* November 10, 1946; and Monica Braw describes the reaction of occupation censors to *Hiroshima* in *The Atomic Bomb Suppressed.* For more regarding the impact of Hersey's *Hiroshima,* see "John Hersey and the American Conscience: The Reception of 'Hiroshima'" by Michael J. Yavenditti, *Pacific Historical Review* 43:1 (February 1974).

For the official story of the atomic bomb decision, see "If the Atomic Bomb Had Not Been Used" by Karl T. Compton, *Atlantic Monthly* 178:6 (December 1946), and "The Decision to Use the Atomic Bomb" by Henry L. Stimson, *Harper's Magazine* 194:1161 (February 1947). President Truman approved Compton's appraisal of the situation in a letter printed in the *Atlantic Monthly* 179:1 (February 1947).

The creation of the official U.S. narrative is thoroughly explored in "Seizing the Contested Terrain of Early Nuclear History" by Barton J. Bernstein in

Hiroshima's Shadow, edited by Kai Bird and Lawrence Lifschultz. For an excellent overview of scholars' attempts to reconstruct the bomb decision, see "Historiographical Essay: Recent Literature on Truman's Atomic Bomb Decision: A Search for Middle Ground" by J. Samuel Walker, *Diplomatic History* 29:2. Bernstein offers expert analysis of U.S. leaders' misleading postwar claims of high casualty estimates for the planned invasion of Japan in "Reconsidering Truman's Claim of 'Half a Million American Lives' Saved by the Atomic Bomb: The Construction and Deconstruction of a Myth," *Journal of Strategic Studies* 22:1.

Quotations by U.S. leaders in defense of the bombing: Harvard president and Interim Committee member James B. Conant expressed his concern about bomb opponents causing a "distortion of history" in a letter to Harvey Bundy, September 23, 1946 (Records of President James B. Conant, Harvard University Archives). Additional quotations related to Stimson's 1947 article appear in the microfilm edition of the Henry L. Stimson Papers at the Yale University Library Manuscripts and Archives; see Felix Frankfurter to Stimson, 12-16-46 (reel 116); James Byrnes to Stimson, 1-28-47 (reel 116); and McGeorge Bundy to Stimson, 2-18-47 (reel 117). As noted by Barton J. Bernstein and others, McGeorge Bundy in *Danger and Survival* (New York: Random House, 1988) later regretted the purposeful half-truths and omissions in the "Decision" article that allowed the U.S. public to believe that the atomic bombs were given adequate forethought by Truman and his advisers.

NAGASAKI, LATE 1946–1948

Taniguchi's descriptions of his intense pain while lying facedown "on the verge of death" are quoted from his unpublished speeches from 1986 and 2010. Taniguchi provided copies of his speeches and his Ōmura National Hospital medical records.

Dr. Shiotsuki Masao recalled the "molten lava" of survivors' stubborn keloid scars in his book *Doctor at Nagasaki.*

For the psychological impact of the bombing, see *Hiroshima and Nagasaki,* edited by the Committee for the Compilation of Materials on Damage Caused by the Atomic Bombs in Hiroshima and Nagasaki, chap. 12; and *Death in Life* by Robert Jay Lifton. Numerous *hibakusha* testimonies provided personal perspectives on psychological trauma; the father who questioned his own survival daily while kneeling before his daughter's ashes described his experience anonymously in response to a 1985 Nihon Hidankyō survey; see *The Deaths of Hibakusha,* vol. 1, p. 130.

For Lt. Colonel Victor Delnore, see "Victor's Justice: Colonel Victor Delnore and the U.S. Occupation of Nagasaki" by Lane R. Earns, *Crossroads* 3. Delnore reflected on his aim to "wake the people up" in "Gentle Warrior Saw Beyond Bombs/Brought Compassion to Nagasaki Job" by Mary Frain, *Telegram and Gazette* (Worcester, MA), August 13, 1995. He described the Buddhist ceremony for unidentified survivors in a letter to his family; see *Victor's War: The World War II Letters of Lt. Col. Victor Delnore,* edited by his daughter, Patricia Delnore Magee. Delnore's memo to the Civil Censorship Detachment in support of the publication of Ishida Masako's book is in *The Atomic Bomb Suppressed* by Monica Braw.

Winfield Niblo and square dancing: "'Dancing People Are Happy People': Square Dancing and Democracy in Occupied Japan" by Lane R. Earns, *Crossroads* 2. See also "Yank Teaches Square Dance to 20,000 Japs in Nagasaki," *Reading Eagle* (Reading, PA), September 7, 1947; and "Japs Adopting Our Democratic Square Dances," *Milwaukee Journal*, April 14, 1949.

For *hibakusha* stories about suicides: Catholic *hibakusha* Fukahori Satoru described his resolve to "suck it up" in Steven Okazaki's film *White Light/Black Rain*. Toyomi Hashimoto remembered her husband's suicide attempt in "Hellish Years After Hellish Days" in *Cries for Peace*, edited by Soka Gakkai, Youth Division. Other sources include Senji Yamaguchi in *Burnt Yet Undaunted*, compiled by Shinji Fujisaki; Hisako Kyuma's "Engulfed in Light and Fire" and Kazuko Nagase's "The Twenty-nine Years I Have Lived Through" in *Voices of the A-Bomb Survivors: Nagasaki*, compiled by the Nagasaki Atomic Bomb Testimonial Society; Komine Hidetaka's "A Message to the World from Hiroshima and Nagasaki" exhibit panel at the United Nations Headquarters in New York, May 2010; multiple testimonies at "Memories of Hiroshima and Nagasaki: Messages from *Hibakusha*," http://www.asahi.com/hibakusha; and Shimohira Sakue in "In the Words of an Atomic Bomb Survivor" by Brian Burke-Gaffney in *Crossroads* 3.

Dō-oh's memories of her despair during the long days hidden inside her house are quoted from the title essay of her collection *Ikasarete ikite* [Allowed to Live, I Live], edited by Keishō bukai (Dō-oh Mineko ikō shuu) henshū iinkai [Legacy Group (Dō-oh Mineko Posthumous Collection) Editorial Committee], translated into English for the author's use.

Survivors' ways of remembering: School memorials are described in Chiyoko Egashira's "From Memories of Darkness and Hardship: Up Until the Day Shiroyama Primary School Was Closed" in *The Light of Morning*; and Itonaga Yoshi's "The Sun Dropped Out of the Sky" in *Nagasaki August 9, 1945*, edited by Mary Wiesen and Elizabeth Cannon. Tsue Hayashi planted cherry trees in honor of her daughter at Shiroyama Elementary School; see "Kayoko Zakura" in *Hibaku: Recollections of A-Bomb Survivors*, edited by Mitsue Kubo; and "Tsue Hayashi" in *At Work in the Fields of the Bomb* by Robert Del Tradici.

Tsujimoto Fujio and other student testimonies from Yamazato Elementary School appear in *Living Beneath the Atomic Cloud: Testimonies of the Children of Nagasaki*, edited by Takashi Nagai. A reprint of this collection is available from the Nagasaki National Peace Memorial Hall for the Atomic Bomb Victims. For an alternate translation of Tsujimoto's testimony, see also *The Atomic Bomb: Voices from Hiroshima and Nagasaki*, edited by Kyoko and Mark Selden.

CHAPTER 6: EMERGENCE
NAGASAKI'S RECOVERY, 1948–1949

Quotations by Taniguchi Sumiteru: His joy when he was finally able to walk again is quoted from *Give Me Water: Testimonies of Hiroshima and Nagasaki,* translated by Rinjiro Sodei. His feeling of being "resurrected" appeared in "Bomb Victims' Stories Reach into the Heart" by Imada Lee, *Maui News,* September 20, 1987, reprinted in *Beijin kisha no mita Hiroshima Nagasaki* [Hiroshima and Nagasaki Through the Eyes of American Reporters], Akiba Project 1987 (Hiroshima: Hiroshima International Cultural Foundation, 1988). Taniguchi's fears upon being discharged from the hospital are quoted from *The Light of Morning,* translated by Brian Burke-Gaffney.

Signs of Nagasaki's postwar recovery: *Hiroshima and Nagasaki,* edited by the Committee for the Compilation of Materials on Damage Caused by the Atomic Bombs in Hiroshima and Nagasaki, especially chap. 11. See also *Embracing Defeat* by John W. Dower; *A Modern History of Japan* by Andrew Gordon; and "Beyond the Black Market: Neighborhood Associations and Food Rationing in Postwar Japan" by Katarzyna Cwiertka in *Japan Since 1945: From Postwar to Post-Bubble,* edited by Christopher Gerteis and Timothy S. George.

Relaxation of occupation controls: *The Reports of General MacArthur,* vol. 1 supp.; "Japanese to Get Added Authority" by Lindesay Parrott, *New York Times,* August 16, 1949; and *The Atomic Bomb Suppressed* by Monica Braw.

For the four hundredth anniversary of St. Francis Xavier ceremonies: "A Monument Was Built at the Hypocenter of the Explosion" by Tomiomi Koda in *Living Beneath the Atomic Cloud,* edited by Takashi Nagai; "Nagasaki Plans Fete," *New York Times,* March 6, 1949; "Over 100,000 Japanese in Atom-Bombed City Honour Francis Xavier," *Catholic Herald,* June 3, 1949; and "The Arm of St. Francis Xavier," *Life,* June 27, 1949.

Nagasaki teacher Teruko Araki remembered the scent of "new wood" in the rebuilt classrooms and described her experiences teaching orphaned children in *Living Beneath the Atomic Cloud,* edited by Takashi Nagai. This collection also includes the testimony of another Nagasaki teacher, Tatsuo Oi.

Quotations by Dr. Nagai Takashi: "as we walk in hunger . . ." is quoted from *The Bells of Nagasaki;* Nagai blamed the "rhythm of military marches" in his work *Hanasaku oka* [Hill in Bloom], translated excerpts of which were provided by the Nagai Takashi Memorial Museum; and he described the atomic bombs as "anti-war vaccinations" in *We of Nagasaki.* For additional information on Nagai's impact as the "saint of Nagasaki," see *Embracing Defeat* by John W. Dower; *City of Silence: Listening to Hiroshima* by Rachelle Linner; "Resurrecting Nagasaki" by Chad R. Diehl, Ph.D. dissertation, Columbia University; and "The Atomic Bomb and the Citizens of Nagasaki" by Sadao Kamata and Stephen Salaff, *Bulletin of Concerned Asian Scholars* 14:2. For the editing and censorship of the film version of *The Bells of Nagasaki,* see *Screening Enlightenment* by Hiroshi Kitamura.

Survivors' reactions to Nagai's message: Masako Imamura defined the atomic bomb as God's "test of love and forgiveness" in *Living Beneath the Atomic Cloud,* edited by Takashi Nagai; an unnamed survivor expressed that "people without faith . . . could not have borne the burden" in "Through Survivors' Tales, Nagasaki Joins Japan's Timeless Folklore" by Nicholas D. Kristof, *New York Times,* August 9, 1995; and Fr. Paul Glynn, in *A Song for Nagasaki,* described his encounter with a *hibakusha* who converted to Christianity due to Nagai's message.

Dr. Akizuki Tatsuichirō's frustration with the Catholic sisters' beliefs and his anger at the governments who "willfully perpetuated this senseless war" are quoted from his memoir *Nagasaki 1945.* His decision to shed his "victim of war" mentality and his experiences in Yue are detailed in *Natsugumo no oka* [Hill Under the Summer Cloud] by Yamashita Akiko, translated into English for the author's use.

Later-occurring medical conditions: *Hiroshima and Nagasaki,* edited by the Committee for the Compilation of Materials on Damage Caused by the Atomic Bombs in Hiroshima and Nagasaki, chap. 9. See also *Radiation Effects Research Foundation: A Brief Description; Children of the Atomic Bomb* by Dr. James N. Yamazaki; and "Long-Term Radiation-Related Health Effects in a Unique Human Population: Lessons Learned from the Atomic Bomb Survivors of Hiroshima and Nagasaki" by Evan B. Douple et al., *Disaster Medicine and Public Health Preparedness* 5:S1.

An anonymous *hibakusha* recalled the results of her brother's autopsy following his death from leukemia in *The Deaths of Hibakusha,* vol. 2.

Many survivors hold memories of taunts and discrimination; examples in this chapter include Komine Hidetaka's "A Message to the World from Hiroshima and Nagasaki" exhibit panel at the United Nations Headquarters in New York, May 2010; and Toyomi Hashimoto and Masako Okawa in *Cries for Peace,* edited by Soka Gakkai, Youth Division. See also *The Impact of the A-Bomb: Hiroshima and Nagasaki, 1945–85,* edited by the Committee for the Compilation of Materials on Damage Caused by the Atomic Bombs in Hiroshima and Nagasaki.

For work discrimination and difficulties in employment, see *Hiroshima and Nagasaki,* edited by the Committee for the Compilation of Materials on Damage Caused by the Atomic Bombs in Hiroshima and Nagasaki, chap. 11; "The Hibakusha: The Atomic Bomb Survivors and Their Appeals" in *Appeals from Nagasaki: On the Occasion of SSD-II and Related Events,* edited by Shinji Takahashi; and "Hiroshima and Nagasaki: The Voluntary Silence" by Monica Braw in *Living with the Bomb,* edited by Laura Hein and Mark Selden.

THE ATOMIC BOMB CASUALTY COMMISSION (ABCC)

Dō-oh recalled her experience at the ABCC in her essay "Ikasarete ikite" [Allowed to Live, I Live] in a collection by the same name, edited by Keishō bukai (Dō-oh Mineko ikō shuu) henshū iinkai [Legacy Group (Dō-oh Mineko Posthumous Collection) Editorial Committee], translated into English for the author's use.

For an excellent study of the survivors' relationship with the ABCC and the agency's no-treatment policy, see the works of M. Susan Lindee: *Suffering Made Real: American Science and the Survivors at Hiroshima;* "Atonement: Understanding the No-Treatment Policy of the Atomic Bomb Casualty Commission," *Bulletin of the History of Medicine* 68:3; and "The Repatriation of Atomic Bomb Victim Body Parts to Japan: Natural Objects and Diplomacy," *Osiris* 13. In *Suffering Made Real,* Lindee acknowledges that Dr. James V. Neel, head of the ABCC's genetics program, Dr. William J. Schull, and other ABCC personnel whom she interviewed did not agree with her characterization of the ABCC, saying that she, in her words, had "overemphasized the impact of political and social concerns on the science of the ABCC." Lindee responded, "I do think that Neel and his colleagues struggled heroically to conduct their science in that neutral zone in which language, culture, and history do not exist, that is, in the realm of the idealized Science that they learned in the course of their formal education. My text operates from the assumption that such a neutral zone does not exist, for anyone, at any time." My effort here is to capture some of the Nagasaki survivors' most serious concerns related to their participation in the ABCC studies.

For the establishment of the ABCC, see Colonel Ashley W. Oughterson's August 1945 memo in *Medical Effects of Atomic Bombs,* vol. I, app. 1 (1), by Oughterson et al. See also "The Atomic Bomb Casualty Commission in Retrospect" by Frank W. Putnam, *Proceedings of the National Academy of Sciences, USA* 95:10, which includes a copy of Truman's presidential directive that established the agency in 1946; and the historical and scientific materials available from the Radiation Effects Research Foundation at http://www.rerf.jp.

Fears over the "free unrestrained use" of ABCC material by Japanese scientists: Memo from James K. Scott to Charles L. Dunham, October 14, 1954, Series 2, AEC Correspondence: 1951–1961, ABCC collection, National Academy of Sciences Archives, Washington, DC.

Nagasaki physician Nishimori Issei is quoted in "Hiroshima and Nagasaki: The Voluntary Silence" by Monica Braw in *Living with the Bomb,* edited by Laura Hein and Mark Selden.

Norman Cousins's critique: "Hiroshima Four Years Later," the *Saturday Review of Literature* 32.

For ABCC operations and studies in Nagasaki, see *Children of the Atomic Bomb* by Dr. James N. Yamazaki; and *Song Among the Ruins: A Lyrical Account of an American Scientist's Sojourn in Japan After the Atomic Bomb* by William J. Schull. The ABCC pamphlets and exam questions for new mothers are reprinted, along with the genetic program's original 1956 report, in *The Children of Atomic Bomb Survivors: A Genetic Study,* edited by James V. Neel and William J. Schull.

Further information about Dr. Yamazaki's experiences in Nagasaki and his lifelong contribution to the health of children, as well as photographs, survivors' paintings, testimonies, and lesson plans, can be found at the "Children of the Atomic Bomb" Web site, developed by Dr. Yamazaki in collaboration

with UCLA's Asian American Studies Center at http://www.aasc.ucla
.edu/cab.

For Dō-oh's refusal to participate with the ABCC: With her family's permission,
I was able to locate medical records completed by the ABCC at the Atomic
Bomb Materials collection of the Otis Historical Archives, U.S. National
Museum of Health and Medicine. These records indicate that Dō-oh visited
the ABCC at least three times. However, Dō-oh consistently describes only
one visit before her decision not to participate in any further ABCC studies,
perhaps collapsing her multiple visits into one. The Atomic Bomb Materials
collection also includes medical documentation on Taniguchi and Yoshida.

NAGASAKI, 1952–1955: END OF U.S. OCCUPATION AND THE FIRST DECADE OF POSTBOMB SURVIVAL

For Nagasaki's celebration of the end of the occupation, see "Two Atom-Bomb
Cities Hail Peace Treaty," *New York Times,* September 10, 1951.

For the Tokyo War Crimes Trials and Japan at the end of the U.S. occupation:
Embracing Defeat by John W. Dower; *Inventing Japan: 1853–1964* by Ian
Buruma; and *A Modern History of Japan: From Tokugawa to the Present* by
Andrew Gordon.

Release of scientific studies and other atomic bomb publications in Japan: *Hiroshima and Nagasaki,* edited by the Committee for the Compilation of Materials on Damage Caused by the Atomic Bombs in Hiroshima and Nagasaki,
chap. 13; *Nagasaki Journey: The Photographs of Yosuke Yamahata, August
10, 1945,* edited by Rupert Jenkins; and *Japanese Documentary Film* by Abé
Mark Nornes. The *Asahi Graph* reprinted the 1952 "atomic bomb" special
edition in full on its thirtieth anniversary in 1982. See also "Nuclear Images
and National Self-Portraits: Japanese Illustrated Magazine *Asahi Graph,*
1945–1965" by Utsumi Hirofumi, *Kansei gakuin daigaku sentan shakai
kenkyūjo kiyō* [Annual Review of the Institute for Advanced Social Research,
Kwansei Gakuin University] 5.

Hibakusha photographs in the U.S. press: "When Atom Bomb Struck—
Uncensored," *Life,* September 29, 1952. See also Dr. Shiotsuki Masao's
recollection of the popular U.S. magazine article in *Doctor at Nagasaki.*

For nuclear arsenals by the end of 1955, see "A History of the Atomic Energy
Commission" by Alice L. Buck; "Global Nuclear Weapons Stockpiles, 1945–
2002" by the National Resources Defense Council; "Fact Sheet: The Nuclear
Testing Tally" by the Arms Control Association.

For President Truman's remarks about the use of nuclear weapons during the
Korean War, see "The President's News Conference," November 30, 1950,
in *Public Papers of the Presidents of the United States: Harry S. Truman,
1945–1953.* For information about U.S. nuclear strategy during the Korean
War, see "American Atomic Strategy and the Hydrogen Bomb Decision" by
David Alan Rosenberg, *Journal of American History* 66:1 (1979): 62–87;
and "American Airpower and Nuclear Strategy in Northeast Asia Since

1945" by Bruce Cumings in *War and State Terrorism: The United States, Japan, and the Asia-Pacific in the Long Twentieth Century*, edited by Mark Selden and Alvin Y. So (Lanham, MD: Rowman & Littlefield, 2004), pp. 63–90.

The passing of the first decade and the city's tenth anniversary ceremony was remembered by Chie Setoguchi in "The Human Dam" in *Testimonies of the Atomic Bomb Survivors*. See also "Nagasaki Marks 1945 Atom Blast" by Robert Trumbull, *New York Times*, August 10, 1955.

Nagasaki in 1955: *Hiroshima and Nagasaki*, edited by the Committee for the Compilation of Materials on Damage Caused by the Atomic Bombs in Hiroshima and Nagasaki; *Nagasaki Speaks; Burnt Yet Undaunted*, compiled by Shinji Fujisaki; and *Screening Enlightenment* by Hiroshi Kitamura. Photographs of the hypocenter marker, taken in 1954 by Dave Patrykus and other U.S. servicemen serving aboard the USS *Wisconsin*, can be found at http://www.usswisconsin.org.

Dō-oh's reputation as the "girl with the triangle cloth" and her decision to move to Tokyo despite her parents' objections are quoted from her essay "Ikasarete ikite" [Allowed to Live, I Live] in a collection by the same name, edited by Keishō bukai (Dō-oh Mineko ikō shuu) henshū iinkai [Legacy Group (Dō-oh Mineko Posthumous Collection) Editorial Committee], translated into English for the author's use.

CHAPTER 7: AFTERLIFE

NAGASAKI, 1960s

Descriptions of Nagasaki: *Song Among the Ruins* by William J. Schull; *Burnt Yet Undaunted*, compiled by Shinji Fujisaki; *Nagasaki: The Forgotten Bomb* by Frank Chinnock; "Letter from Nagasaki" by E. J. Kahn Jr., *New Yorker*, July 29, 1961; and various survivor accounts.

For the clearing of the Urakami Church ruins and its reconstruction, see "The Atomic Bomb and the Citizens of Nagasaki" by Sadao Kamata and Stephen Salaff in *Bulletin of Concerned Asian Scholars* 14:2; and *The Restoration of Urakami Cathedral: A Commemorative Album*, edited by Hisayuki Mizuura.

MARRIAGE AND CHILDREN

Japanese marriage traditions and discrimination faced by *hibakusha*: "Marriage with the Proper Stranger: Arranged Marriage in Metropolitan Japan" by Kalman D. Applbaum, *Ethnology* 34:1; *Death in Life* by Robert Jay Lifton; and "Hiroshima and Nagasaki: The Voluntary Silence" by Monica Braw in *Living with the Bomb*, edited by Laura Hein and Mark Selden.

Many *hibakusha* described fears regarding marriage and children, including Tsutae Takai in "A-Bomb Victim Moved to Talk About Past by Earthquake Disasters," *Mainichi*, August 11, 2012; and the testimonies at "Memories of Hiroshima and Nagasaki: Messages from *Hibakusha*," http://www.asahi.com/hibakusha.

Wada remembered how his pregnant wife felt "stabbed" by their doctor's warnings of potential birth defects in "There Was No 'War-End' in Nagasaki,"
English translation provided by Nagasaki National Peace Memorial Hall.

Taniguchi described how he was rejected by potential marriage partners who
feared he could not "look forward to a long life" in *Hibakusha: Survivors of
Hiroshima and Nagasaki,* translated by Gaynor Sekimori. His marriage and
honeymoon with Eiko are detailed in *The Postman of Nagasaki: The Story
of a Survivor* by Peter Townsend.

Dō-oh reflected on her personal determination and her work life in the title essay
of her collection *Ikasarete ikite* [Allowed to Live, I Live], edited by Keishō
bukai (Dō-oh Mineko ikō shuu) henshū iinkai [Legacy Group (Dō-oh Mineko
Posthumous Collection) Editorial Committee], translated into English for the
author's use.

ANTINUCLEAR ACTIVISM

Sources for the "Castle Bravo" hydrogen bomb test on March 1, 1954, include
Castle Series 1954 by Edwin J. Martin and Richard H. Rowland; *Radiation:
What It Is and How It Affects You* by Jack Schubert and Ralph E. Lapp; and
The Struggle Against the Bomb, Vol. 2: Resisting the Bomb by Lawrence S.
Wittner.

The Preparatory Commission for the Comprehensive Nuclear Test Ban Treaty
Organization (CTBTO) has deemed the 1954 test on Bikini Atoll the "worst
radiological disaster in the United States' testing history"; see http://www
.ctbto.org/nuclear-testing.

The Marshall Islanders' radiation illnesses, including nausea, skin lesions, loss of
hair, and hemorrhaging beneath the skin, were documented by U.S. researchers from Brookhaven National Laboratory; see, for example, *A Twenty-Year
Review of Medical Findings in a Marshallese Population Accidentally Exposed to Radioactive Fallout* by Robert A. Conard et al. (Upton, NY:
Brookhaven National Laboratory, 1975). The U.S. Department of Energy continues to monitor the atolls of the former Pacific Proving Grounds for radiological damage and provide medical screenings for residents who were
exposed; see "Marshall Islands Dose Assessment and Radioecology Program," Lawrence Livermore National Laboratory, updated August 2014,
https://marshallislands.llnl.gov; and "Nuclear Issues" at the Embassy of the
Republic of the Marshall Islands, accessed August 2014, http://www.rmiem
bassyus.org/Nuclear Issues.htm.

The effect of the test's fallout on the *Lucky Dragon* crew, and the U.S. response,
is detailed in the sources above, as well as in *Suffering Made Real* by M.
Susan Lindee; *The Voyage of the Lucky Dragon* by Ralph E. Lapp; *Elements
of Controversy: The AEC and Radiation Safety in Nuclear Weapons Testing,
1947–1974* by Barton C. Hacker; and "Aide-Memoire Given to the U.S. Ambassador Allison by the Vice-Minister of Foreign Affairs, Okumura, March
27, 1954" in *Castle Series 1954* by Edwin J. Martin and Richard H. Rowland, p. 465.

Eizo Tajima recalled the fishermens' description of the white ash that coated their boat and the ensuing panic in Japan over radioactive contamination in "The Dawn of Radiation Effects Research," *RERF Update* 5:3. For more on the outcomes and experiences of the *Lucky Dragon* crew, the Marshall Islanders, and others impacted by radiation around the world, see *Exposure: Victims of Radiation Speak Out,* available at the Hiroshima Peace Media Center, http://www.hiroshimapeacemedia.jp.

The Japanese public's opposition to nuclear testing was noted in "Resisting Nuclear Terror: Japanese and American Anti-Nuclear Movements Since 1945" by Lawrence S. Wittner in *War and State Terrorism,* edited by Mark Selden and Alvin Y. So. See also Wittner's three-volume history of the international nuclear disarmament movement, *The Struggle Against the Bomb,* which includes a discussion of earlier antinuclear activism, dampened by occupation policies, that had begun in postwar Japan prior to the Bikini test; *Hiroshima and Nagasaki,* edited by the Committee for the Compilation of Materials on Damage Caused by the Atomic Bombs in Hiroshima and Nagasaki, chap. 14; and reports by the Nuclear Coverage Team of the *Asahi Shimbun,* collected in *The Road to the Abolition of Nuclear Weapons.*

Hirose Masahito remembered the "powerful and determined" beginnings of the antinuclear movement in Nagasaki in his 2009 interview with the author.

Yamaguchi Senji's recollections of the White Rose Campaign, the first conferences against atomic and hydrogen bombs in Hiroshima and Nagasaki, and his own emerging activism are detailed in *Burnt Yet Undaunted,* compiled by Shinji Fujisaki. Yamaguchi and other *hibakusha* also became involved in protests against the U.S.-Japan Security Treaty renewal in 1960, a precursor to the still-continuing national effort by activists to safeguard the principles of peace in Japan's constitution.

Watanabe Chieko's testimony appeared in *Voices of the A-Bomb Survivors: Nagasaki,* compiled by the Nagasaki Atomic Bomb Testimonial Society.

For Nihon Hidankyō's founding declaration, see http://www.ne.jp/asahi/hidankyo/nihon/about/about2-01.html, translated by the author.

Taniguchi recalled his determination to "live on behalf of those who died unwillingly" during his interview on the PBS program *People's Century: Fallout (1945),* broadcast June 15, 1999. His call to "bear witness" is quoted from his testimony in *Hibakusha: Survivors of Hiroshima and Nagasaki,* translated by Gaynor Sekimori.

ACTIVISM FOR *HIBAKUSHA* MEDICAL CARE

Ongoing health effects for *hibakusha,* including "insufficient mental energy," were described in the first published guidelines for the medical treatment of atomic bomb illnesses by the A-Bomb Aftereffects Research Council in 1954, as quoted in *Hiroshima and Nagasaki,* edited by the Committee for the Compilation of Materials on Damage Caused by the Atomic Bombs in Hiroshima and Nagasaki, chap. 13. See also *Radiation Effects Research Foundation: A Brief Description;* and "Cancer Takes Many Forms Among the *Hibakusha,*"

Anniston Star (Alabama), September 13, 1981, reprinted in *Beijin kisha no mita Hiroshima Nagasaki* [Hiroshima and Nagasaki Through the Eyes of American Reporters], Akiba Project 1981 (Hiroshima: Hiroshima International Cultural Foundation, 1982).

Quotations by Yamaguchi Senji: For Nagasaki Hisaikyō as "an organization to voice our demands" and the health care law's "little handbook," see *Burnt Yet Undaunted,* compiled by Shinji Fujisaki. His call for the Japanese government to take responsibility for *hibakusha* care is quoted from his interview in Steven Okazaki's film *White Light/Black Rain.* Yamaguchi's 1980 speech appealing for "No More *Hibakusha*" is quoted in "The Atomic Bomb and the Citizens of Nagasaki" by Sadao Kamata and Stephen Salaff, *Bulletin of Concerned Asian Scholars* 14:2.

The Atomic Bomb Victims Medical Care Law: Application requirements are quoted from *Hiroshima and Nagasaki,* edited by the Committee for the Compilation of Materials on Damage Caused by the Atomic Bombs in Hiroshima and Nagasaki, chap. 11. For the issue of "probability of causation," see "Certification of Sufferers of Atomic Bomb–Related Diseases," *Nuke Info Tokyo* 131, http://cnic.jp/english/newsletter/nit131/nit131articles/abombdisease.html. Additional sources for *hibakusha* medical care and health care activism include *Report on the Problem of the Hibakusha* by the Japan Federation of Bar Associations; "The Atomic Bomb and the Citizens of Nagasaki" by Sadao Kamata and Stephen Salaff, *Bulletin of Concerned Asian Scholars* 14:2; and "The *Hibakusha*: The Atomic Bomb Survivors and Their Appeals" by Shinji Takahashi in *Appeals from Nagasaki: On the Occasion of SSD-II and Related Events.*

For the development of atomic bomb radiation dosimetry for Hiroshima and Nagasaki survivors, see "Historical Review" by George D. Kerr, Tadashi Hashizume, and Charles W. Edington in *U.S.-Japan Joint Reassessment of Atomic Bomb Dosimetry in Hiroshima and Nagasaki: Dosimetry System 1986,* edited by William C. Roesch; and *Ichiban: The Dosimetry Program for Nuclear Bomb Survivors of Hiroshima and Nagasaki—A Status Report as of April 1, 1964* by J. A. Auxier. See also *Permissible Dose: A History of Radiation Protection in the Twentieth Century* by J. Samuel Walker.

For a recent study suggesting "significant exposure" for early entrants, see "Gamma-Ray Exposure from Neutron-Induced Radionuclides in Soil in Hiroshima and Nagasaki Based on DS02 Calculations" by Tetsuji Imanaka et al., in *Radiation and Environmental Biophysics* 47:3. For a review of current research on the impact of residual radiation, see "Workshop Report on Atomic Bomb Dosimetry—Residual Radiation Exposure: Recent Research and Suggestions for Future Studies" by George D. Kerr et al., *Health Physics* 105:2. doi: 10.1097/HP.0b013e31828ca73a.

Claims of injuries, deaths, and lingering medical conditions from residual radiation exposure appear in multiple survivor accounts. See especially "Memories of Hiroshima and Nagasaki: Messages from *Hibakusha,*" http://www.asahi.com/hibakusha and the anonymous testimonies collected by a 1985 Nihon Hidankyō survey, published in *The Deaths of Hibakusha,* vols. 1 and 2.

The city of Nagasaki has provided support for overseas *hibakusha.* See *Devotion of Nagasaki to the Cause of Peace* by the city of Nagasaki; and the Nagasaki

Association for Hibakushas' Medical Care (NASHIM), established in 1992 to offer travel assistance to survivors seeking to return to Japan for medical care, at http://www.nashim.org/en/index.html.

Hibakusha living in the United States have also struggled for recognition and health care. See "Medical Care for the Atomic Bomb Victims in the United States" by Stephen Salaff, *Bulletin of Concerned Asian Scholars* 12:1; *Were We the Enemy? American Survivors of Hiroshima* by Rinjiro Sodei; *City of Silence* by Rachelle Linner; and Steven Okazaki's documentary film *Survivors*.

Korean *hibakusha*: "Korea's Forgotten Atomic Bomb Victims" by Kurt W. Tong, *Bulletin of Concerned Asian Scholars* 23:1; and "Three-Fold Hardships of the Korean *Hibakusha*" by Korean Atomic Bomb Casualty Association president Choi Il Chul, available at https://afsc.org/resource/hibakusha-h-bomb-survivors. Quotations from Korean survivors: Masako Kim in *Voices of the A-Bomb Survivors: Nagasaki,* compiled by the Nagasaki Atomic Bomb Testimonial Society; and Pak Su Ryong in *Give Me Water: Testimonies of Hiroshima and Nagasaki*.

Taniguchi remembered the hard scar on his back that "dulled the blade" of the surgical knife in his testimony at the Nagasaki Broadcasting Company Web site, "Nagasaki and Peace," http://www2.nbc-nagasaki.co.jp/peace. The "terrible heaviness" he felt is quoted from *Voices of the A-Bomb Survivors: Nagasaki,* compiled by the Nagasaki Atomic Bomb Testimonial Society.

CHAPTER 8: AGAINST FORGETTING

RECLAIMING ATOMIC BOMB MATERIALS

The *Asahi Graph* published its commemorative issue about the twenty-fifth anniversary of the atomic bombings on July 10, 1970. A preview of the issue appeared in the *Asahi Shimbun* on June 21, 1970. Copies provided by Taniguchi Sumiteru and the Nagasaki Atomic Bomb Museum library.

Nippon Eiga-sha film footage: "Iwasaki and the Occupied Screen" by Erik Barnouw, *Film History* 2:4; and "Suddenly There Was Emptiness" in *Japanese Documentary Film* by Abé Mark Nornes. For the edited film with sound track, "Effect of Atomic Bomb on Hiroshima and Nagasaki, 9/21/45–10/45," and a descriptive shot list of all nineteen reels, see Video No. 342-USAF-17679, Records of U.S. Air Force Commands, Activities, and Organizations, 1900–2003, Record Group 342, Moving Images Relating to Military Aviation Activities, 1947–1984, National Archives at College Park, MD; digital copy available through the Online Public Access catalog (identifier 65518) at www .archives.gov/research/search.

Watanabe Chieko described her reaction to the silent film footage of postbomb Nagasaki in her testimony at "Nagasaki and Peace," http://www2.nbc-naga saki.co.jp/peace.

Toshiro Ochiai described the "remember Pearl Harbor" reaction to the photo exhibition near the UN headquarters in "Participation in the First Special Session of the United Nations General Assembly on Disarmament: Recollections of a Student Representative," available at http://ir.lib.hiroshima -u.ac.jp/en/00025548.

For the recovery of the USSBS film footage, see *Atomic Cover-up* by Greg Mitchell; and "38 Years After Nagasaki" by Dave Yuzo Spector, *Chicago Tribune*, January 5, 1984. Most of the films in the *Hibakusha* Sources feature either the early Nippon Eiga-sha or USSBS footage from Hiroshima and Nagasaki.

The return of scientific materials and autopsy specimens is detailed by M. Susan Lindee in "The Repatriation of Atomic Bomb Victim Body Parts to Japan: Natural Objects and Diplomacy," *Osiris* 13, and in her book *Suffering Made Real*. See also the materials available through the Division of Scientific Data Registry at the Atomic Bomb Disease Institute of Nagasaki University at http://www-sdc.med.nagasaki-u.ac.jp/abcenter/index_e.html; and in the Atomic Bomb Material collection of the Otis Historical Archives, National Museum of Health and Medicine.

Uchida Tsukasa's concern about the victims of the bombing disappearing "into the darkness of history" is quoted from his testimony originally published in *Atomic Bomb Testimonials by Nagasaki City Employees,* edited by the Nagasaki Testimonial Society, English translation provided by the Nagasaki National Peace Memorial Hall. His vision of recording the "true extent" of their experiences appears in *Testimonies of the Atomic Bomb Survivors.* See also "Survivor Keeps Reminder of Destruction," *Tri-City Herald* (Washington), August 6, 1995.

The efforts by Uchida, Akizuki, and others to complete the mapping of the prebomb hypocenter area were detailed in the film *Hiroshima and Nagasaki: Harvest of Nuclear War* by Iwanami Productions; and in materials provided by the Nagasaki Atomic Bomb Museum. Fukahori Yoshitoshi provided access to his photographic collection and described his contributions to the movement in multiple interviews.

NAGASAKI *HIBAKUSHA* SPEAKING OUT

Akizuki Tatsuichirō's motivations to write his first memoir, his establishment of the Nagasaki Testimonial Society, and his call to *hibakusha* to "speak out about the realities" appeared in *Natsugumo no oka* [Hill Under the Summer Cloud] by Yamashita Akiko, translated into English for the author's use. Akizuki recalled seeing an overlaid "double image" of the atomic destruction outside his modernized hospital in his testimony at "Nagasaki and Peace," http://www2.nbc-nagasaki.co.jp/peace.

Additional sources on the collection of Nagasaki survivor testimonies include "Nagasaki Writers: The Mission" by Kamata Sadao in *Literature Under the Nuclear Cloud,* edited by Ito Narihiko et al.; "The Atomic Bomb and the Citizens of Nagasaki" by Sadao Kamata and Stephen Salaff, *Bulletin of Concerned Asian Scholars* 14:2; and *Hiroshima and Nagasaki,* edited by the Committee for the Compilation of Materials on Damage Caused by the Atomic Bombs in Hiroshima and Nagasaki, chap. 14. Yamada Kan's comment on Dr. Nagai was quoted in "Resurrecting Nagasaki" by Chad R. Diehl, Ph.D. dissertation, Columbia University.

Ongoing medical and psychological issues for survivors were recorded in multiple *hibakusha* accounts, as well as in RERF-published studies and *Hiroshima and Nagasaki,* edited by the Committee for the Compilation of Materials on Damage Caused by the Atomic Bombs in Hiroshima and Nagasaki. For the experiences of elderly parents of in utero–exposed children, see "Atomic Bomb Survivors Today" in *Testimonies of the Atomic Bomb Survivors.*

Fukahori Yoshitoshi, in an interview with the author, described the foreign mayors' shocked reactions to a Nagasaki photographic exhibit.

For a discussion of U.S. civil defense programs that neglected the stories of the only survivors of nuclear war, see "'There Are No Civilians; We Are All at War': Nuclear War Shelter and Survival Narratives During the Early Cold War" by Robert A. Jacobs, *Journal of American Culture* 30:4.

The Confederate Air Force's "reenactment" of the Hiroshima bombing is described in *Sacred Ground: Americans and Their Battlefields* by Edward Linenthal. For Japan's reaction, see "The Mushroom Cloud and National Psyches: Japanese and American Perceptions of the Atomic Bomb Decision—A Reconsideration, 1945–2006" by Sadao Asada in his *Culture Shock and Japanese-American Relations: Historical Essays.* In 2013, CBS News reported a more recent protest that forced the cancellation of a similar show; see http://www.cbsnews.com/news/world-war-ii-atomic-bomb-re-enactment -dropped-from-ohio-air-show-after-outcry.

For international efforts by *hibakusha*, see the 1977 declaration, working documents, and other materials in *A Call from Hibakusha of Hiroshima and Nagasaki: Proceedings of the International Symposium on the Damage and Aftereffects of the Atomic Bombing of Hiroshima and Nagasaki, July 21–August 9, 1977: Tokyo, Hiroshima and Nagasaki,* compiled by the Japan National Preparatory Committee. Watanabe Chieko is quoted from her testimony at the Nagasaki Broadcasting Company Web site, "Nagasaki and Peace," http://www2.nbc-nagasaki.co.jp/peace. See also *The Struggle Against the Bomb, Vol. 3: Towards Nuclear Abolition—A History of the World Nuclear Disarmament Movement, 1971 to the Present* by Lawrence S. Wittner.

Survivors' stories also received limited international attention through the Hibakusha Travel Grant Program. Established in 1979 by Akiba Tadatoshi, a non-*hibakusha* teaching at Tufts University who would later become Hiroshima's mayor, this program provided funds for three foreign journalists to travel to Nagasaki and Hiroshima each year for research and reporting, resulting in dozens of articles about *hibakusha* in local newspapers in the United States and elsewhere. These articles were reissued in a series of yearly compilations as *Beijin kisha no mita Hiroshima Nagasaki* [Hiroshima and Nagasaki Through the Eyes of American Reporters] and were provided to the author by the Nagasaki Atomic Bomb Museum library.

Quotations by Taniguchi Sumiteru: Taniguchi's complaint against modern science for creating "highly sophisticated missiles" instead of cures is quoted from his testimony in *Testimonies of the Atomic Bomb Survivors.* His warning that nuclear weapons and humans cannot coexist and his appeal to audiences not to turn away from his scars are quoted from his speeches provided to the author. Taniguchi expressed his desire to speak out on behalf of the thousands who died as a result of the bombing in the film *Hiroshima and Nagasaki: Harvest of Nuclear War* by Iwanami Productions.

For the worldwide proliferation of atomic weapons, see the chapter 5 notes for nuclear arsenals and testing.

Akizuki admonished the "clever and foolish people" who still promote nuclear weapons development in *Natsugumo no oka* [Hill Under the Summer Cloud] by Yamashita Akiko, translated into English for the author's use.

Pope John Paul II's peace appeal at Hiroshima on February 25, 1981, is available at http://atomicbombmuseum.org/6_5.shtml. For his activities while visiting Nagasaki, see "Pope Winds Up Japan Visit in Nagasaki" by Lewis B. Fleming, *Los Angeles Times,* February 26, 1981; and "Excerpt from Pope Commemorates Nagasaki Martyrs" by Donald Kirk, *Globe and Mail* (Canada), February 27, 1981.

Yamaguchi Senji remembered his aim to "reproduce the horror" of the bombing in his 1982 speech before the United Nations in *Burnt Yet Undaunted,* compiled by Shinji Fujisaki; his speech is quoted from his testimony at the Nagasaki Broadcasting Company Web site, "Nagasaki and Peace," http://www2.nbc-nagasaki.co.jp/peace. For additional information about the demonstrations at the United Nations Second Special Session on Disarmament, see "Throngs Fill Manhattan to Protest Nuclear Weapons" by Paul L. Montgomery, *New York Times,* June 13, 1982.

For the Nagasaki Foundation for the Promotion of Peace (NFPP): *Devotion of Nagasaki to the Cause of Peace* by the city of Nagasaki; *Natsugumo no oka* [Hill Under the Summer Cloud] by Yamashita Akiko; newsletters and other materials provided by the NFPP; and the author's interview with Matsuo Ranko, assistant section chief, NFPP.

Dō-oh reflected on her retirement, her return to Nagasaki following her mother's death, and her cancer diagnosis and treatment in her essay "Ikasarete ikite" [Allowed to Live, I Live] in a collection by the same name, edited by Keishō bukai (Dō-oh Mineko ikō shuu) henshū iinkai [Legacy Group (Dō-oh Mineko Posthumous Collection) Editorial Committee], translated into English for the author's use. In his interview with the author, Matsuzoe Hiroshi described his reunion with Dō-oh and provided color photocopies of his paintings depicting her experience.

For more information on Mayor Motoshima's controversial comments about the emperor and the assassination attempt on the mayor, see *City of Silence* by Rachelle Linner; "Resurrecting Nagasaki" by Chad R. Diehl, Ph.D. dissertation, Columbia University; "Mayor Who Faulted Hirohito Is Shot" by David E. Sanger, *New York Times,* January 19, 1990; and "Japanese Responsibility for War Crimes" by Iwamatsu Shigetoshi, *Keiei to Keizai* 71:3.

Protests against nuclear ships: "Japan Under the U.S. Nuclear Umbrella" by Hans M. Kristensen for the Nautilus Institute; and Yamaguchi Senji's recollection of the *hibakusha* protest against the USS *Rodney M. Davis* in *Burnt Yet Undaunted,* compiled by Shinji Fujisaki; see also "Nuclear Foes Protest U.S. Ship in Nagasaki," *Times Daily* (Alabama), September 17, 1989.

Leukemia and other cancer incidences: *Children of the Atomic Bomb* by Dr. James N. Yamazaki; and the multiple reports on "Cancer Incidence in Atomic Bomb Survivors," *Radiation Research* 137:2s. See also "Long-term Radiation-Related Health Effects in a Unique Human Population," by Evan B. Douple et al., *Disaster Medicine and Public Health Preparedness* 5:S1.

COMMEMORATION AND CONTROVERSY

Historical scholarship and debate on the use of the atomic bomb are outlined in "The Struggle Over History: Defining the Hiroshima Narrative" by Barton J. Bernstein in *Judgment at the Smithsonian,* edited by Philip Nobile; and "Historiographical Essay: Recent Literature on Truman's Atomic Bomb Decision: A Search for Middle Ground" by J. Samuel Walker, *Diplomatic History* 29:2. For John W. Dower's comment on the complexities of telling atomic bomb history, see "Triumphal and Tragic Narratives for the War in Asia" in *Living with the Bomb,* edited by Laura Hein and Mark Selden.

Limited U.S. public awareness of *hibakusha* experiences: See *Suffering Made Real* by M. Susan Lindee. See also, for example, "A Tale of Two Cities," *Time,* May 18, 1962. For U.S. efforts to downplay radiation effects and atomic bomb survivor narratives in order to maintain public support for nuclear programs, especially during the Cold War, see *The Struggle Against the Bomb,* vols. 1–3, by Lawrence S. Wittner; and "Memory, Myth and History" by Martin J. Sherwin in *Hiroshima's Shadow,* edited by Kai Bird and Lawrence Lifschultz. The made-for-television movie *The Day After,* directed by Nicholas Meyer and starring Jason Robards, shocked viewers with graphic, fictional images of nuclear annihilation in the fall of 1983. Information on the International Physicians for the Prevention of Nuclear War, founded in 1980, is at http://www.ippnw.org.

The *Enola Gay* exhibit at the Smithsonian's National Air and Space Museum: *An Exhibit Denied: Lobbying the History of Enola Gay* by Martin Harwit; *Judgment at the Smithsonian,* edited by Philip Nobile; and "The Battle of the *Enola Gay*" by Mike Wallace, and other commentaries about the exhibit, in *Hiroshima's Shadow,* edited by Kai Bird and Lawrence Lifschultz. The initial and the final revised script drafts are available at http://www.nuclearfiles.org.

The disputes over the National Air and Space Museum exhibit occurred in the context of other controversies surrounding the fiftieth anniversary of the end of World War II. For example, the U.S. Postal Service planned to issue a commemorative stamp with the image of a mushroom cloud. After Japanese protests, the stamp was canceled; in opposition to that decision, veterans' groups printed their own version. See, for example, "The Legacy of Commemorative Disputes: What Our Children Won't Learn" by Lane R. Earns, *Crossroads* 3; "Patriotic Orthodoxy and U.S. Decline" by Michael S. Sherry, *Bulletin of Concerned Asian Scholars* 27:2; and "Apologizing for Atrocities: Commemorating the 50th Anniversary of World War II's End in the United States and Japan" by Kyoto Kishimoto, *American Studies International* 42:2/3.

The Smithsonian curators' negotiations with Japan for exhibit materials were detailed in *An Exhibit Denied* by Martin Harwit. See also "Artifacts Requested from the Hiroshima and Nagasaki Museums, September 30, 1993" and the letter from Motoshima to Harwit, December 7, 1993, in Correspondence with Japan, box 8, folder 7; and the letter from Ito to Crouch, April 26, 1994, in Unit 400-432, box 8, folder 5, all in accession number 96-140, NASM *Enola Gay* Exhibition Records, Smithsonian Institution Archives. The consideration of Yamahata Yōsuke photographs for the exhibit was noted in "Making Things

Visible: Learning from the Censors" by George H. Roeder Jr. in *Living with the Bomb,* edited by Laura Hein and Mark Selden; and "Notes on *Nagasaki Journey*" by Chris Beaver, *Positions: Asia Critique* 5:3. See also "Pictures eliminated, June Script, Unit 400," box 3, folder 7, in accession number 96-140, NASM *Enola Gay* Exhibition Records, Smithsonian Institution Archives.

For the Air Force Association's critiques of the planned exhibit, see John T. Correll's articles: "War Stories at Air & Space," *Air Force Magazine,* April 1994; "'The Last Act' at Air and Space," *Air Force Magazine,* September 1994; and *The Activists and the Enola Gay,* AFA Special Report, August 21, 1995, accessed 2012, http://airforcemag.com. For one historian's analysis of the imbalances within the initial exhibit plan, see "History and the Culture Wars: The Case of the Smithsonian Institution's *Enola Gay* Exhibition" by Richard H. Kohn, *Journal of American History* 82:3.

Curator Tom Crouch was quoted in "War and Remembrance" by Hugh Sidey and Jerry Hannifin, *Time,* May 23, 1994.

Controversies over war memory in Japan and Nagasaki: "Exhibiting World War II in Japan and the United States Since 1995" by Laura Hein and Akiko Takenaka, *Pacific Historical Review* 76:1; and "Commemoration Controversies: The War, the Peace, and Democracy in Japan" by Ellen H. Hammond in *Living with the Bomb,* edited by Laura Hein and Mark Selden. See also "Nagasaki Museum Exhibits Anger Japanese Extremists," *Vancouver Sun,* March 26, 1996; and "Today's History Lesson: What Rape of Nanjing?" by Nicholas D. Kristof, *New York Times,* July 4, 1996.

The U.S. Senate's September 19, 1994, resolution condemning the Smithsonian exhibit, and excerpts from the May 1995 hearings before the Senate Committee on Rules and Administration, including remarks by Senator Ted Stevens, are available in "History and the Public: What Can We Handle? A Round Table About History After the *Enola Gay* Controversy," *Journal of American History* 82:3.

Reactions to the NASM exhibit cancellation: The letter to the editor from veteran Dell Herndon was quoted in *An Exhibit Denied* by Martin Harwit, chap. 29. A copy of the protest letter sent by the Historians' Committee for Open Debate on Hiroshima to Smithsonian secretary I. Michael Heyman is available at http://www.doug-long.com/letter.htm. For Prime Minister Murayama's statement, see "Smithsonian Action Saddens Japanese: They Saw *Enola Gay* Display on A-Bomb as a Reminder," *Seattle Times,* January 31, 1995. Mayor Motoshima's comment on the exhibit's cancellation was quoted in "Introduction," *Crossroads* 3.

For the results of the 1995 Gallup poll that revealed Americans' overall ignorance about the atomic bombs, see a "Nation of Nitwits" by Bob Herbert, *New York Times,* March 1, 1995. The poll also found that over 20 percent of respondents "knew virtually nothing about an atomic bomb attack. They didn't know where—or, in some cases, even if—such an attack had occurred."

Yoshida interviewed by Jon Krakauer: "The Forgotten Ground Zero—Nagasaki, Reduced to Ashes by an Atomic Bomb, Rises Again in Beauty, Grace and Good Will," *Seattle Times,* March 5, 1995. Response to the article: "Japan— Forget the Sympathy for Hiroshima, Nagasaki," letter to the editor, *Seattle Times,* March 26, 1995.

Smithsonian secretary I. Michael Heyman's preference to leave the human impact of the bombs "to the imagination" was quoted in "The Battle of the *Enola Gay*" by Mike Wallace in *Hiroshima's Shadow,* edited by Kai Bird and Lawrence Lifschultz.

Akizuki Tatsuichirō: Dr. Akizuki's belief that the threat of nuclear weapons "transcended all other issues" is quoted from "Nagasaki: A Phoenix from the Holocaust" by Tony Wardle, *Catholic Herald,* December 17, 1982, reprinted in *Beijin kisha no mita Hiroshima Nagasaki* [Hiroshima and Nagasaki Through the Eyes of American Reporters], Akiba Project 1982 (Hiroshima: Hiroshima International Cultural Foundation, 1983). Akizuki expressed his sympathy for the victims of Japan's wartime atrocities in his speech "The Nagasaki Testimony Movement," printed in *Literature Under the Nuclear Cloud,* compiled by Ito Narihiko et al. He described his identity as "an atomic bomb doctor" and his wife, Sugako, recalled his 1992 asthma attack and hospitalization in *Natsugumo no oka* [Hill Under the Summer Cloud] by Yamashita Akiko, translated into English for the author's use.

CHAPTER 9: *GAMAN*

NAGASAKI AND THE *HIBAKUSHA* TODAY

For photographs and information about the memorials and atomic bomb sites throughout Nagasaki, see the city's "Peace & Atomic Bomb" site at http://www.city.nagasaki.lg.jp/peace/english/map/.

Estimates of the number of Koreans who died in the Nagasaki atomic bombing vary considerably due to incomplete wartime records of the Korean forced laborers in the city on August 9. The Committee for the Compilation of Materials on Damage Caused by the Atomic Bombs in Hiroshima and Nagasaki concluded that approximately fifteen hundred to two thousand Koreans were killed. See *Hiroshima and Nagasaki,* p. 474. In contrast, through its own thorough investigation, the Nagasaki Association for Protecting Human Rights of Korean Residents in Japan estimates ten thousand Korean victims; see "Hiroshima and Nagasaki at 65: A Reflection" by Satoko Norimatsu, *Asia-Pacific Journal: Japan Focus,* http://www.japanfocus.org/-Satoko-NORIMATSU2/3463.

Many survivors describe living with bouts of anxiety, stress, guilt, and fear related to their atomic bomb experiences. Miyazaki Midori revealed that she cannot forget the cries of children trapped beneath the rubble in "Nagasaki nōto [Nagasaki Notes]: Miyazaki Midori" by Itō Sei, *Asahi Shimbun,* February 23, 2010.

Dr. Kinoshita Hirohisa at the Department of Neuropsychiatry of Nagasaki University Hospital provided information about the lasting psychological impact of the bombing and the support services available for *hibakusha* today. For recent research on the psychological effects of the bombing, see "Psychological Effect of the Nagasaki Atomic Bombing on Survivors After Half a Century" by Yasuyuki Ohta et al., *Psychiatry and Clinical Neurosciences* 54; "Mental Health Conditions Among Atomic Bomb Survivors in Nagasaki" by Sumihisa Honda et al., *Psychiatry and Clinical Neurosciences* 56:5; "Resilience

Among Japanese Atomic Bomb Survivors" by A. Knowles, *International Nursing Review* 58; and "Persistent Distress After Psychological Exposure to the Nagasaki Atomic Bomb Explosion" by Yoshiharu Kim et al., *The British Journal of Psychiatry* 199.

Information about Nagasaki Foundation for the Promotion of Peace (NFPP) activities comes from NFPP newsletters and the author's interview with Matsuo Ranko, assistant section chief, NFPP.

Dō-oh's description of how the bombing "capsized" her life is quoted from her title essay in *Ikasarete ikite* [Allowed to Live, I Live], edited by Keishō bukai (Dō-oh Mineko ikō shuu) henshō iinkai [Legacy Group (Dō-oh Mineko Posthumous Collection) Editorial Committee], translated into English for the author's use. In the same volume, the young student's response to Dō-oh's presentation appears in "Reaction from Students and Teachers After a Presentation." Dō-oh's tanka poetry was provided by her sister Okada Ikuyo.

For President Barack Obama's remarks outlining his aims for a world without nuclear weapons in Prague on April 5, 2009, see the White House press release, "Remarks by President Barack Obama, Hradcany Square, Prague, Czech Republic, 4-5-09," at http://www.whitehouse.gov/the_press_office/Remarks-By-President-Barack-Obama-In-Prague-As-Delivered.

Taniguchi expressed his optimism about President Obama's nuclear stance in a letter to the author. His complaint about the Obama administration's continued nuclear testing is quoted from "Looking Directly at the Truth of Nuclear Suffering," *Mainichi*, October 30, 2012.

For worldwide nuclear stockpiles as of December 1, 2014, see the Federation of American Scientists' "Status of World Nuclear Forces," at http://fas.org/issues/nuclear-weapons/status-world-nuclear-forces/; and the more detailed report "Worldwide Deployments of Nuclear Weapons, 2014" by Hans M. Kristensen and Robert S. Norris, *Bulletin of the Atomic Scientists* 70:5.

For Nagasaki's protests against nuclear tests, see "Nagasaki Asks Communities to Protest India N-tests," *Chugoku Shimbun*, May 19, 1998; and "Nuclear Free Local Authorities in Japan Protest a New Type of Nuclear Weapons Testing by the U.S.," *Dispatches from Nagasaki*, no. 4, by the Research Center for Nuclear Weapons Abolition (RECNA) at Nagasaki University, at http://www.recna.nagasaki-u.ac.jp/en-dispatches/no4/.

Information on the Nuclear Non-Proliferation Treaty (NPT) is available through the United Nations Office for Disarmament Affairs; see http://www.un.org/disarmament/WMD/Nuclear/NPT.shtml. For the 2010 NPT Review Conference conclusions, see "Nuclear Non-Proliferation Treaty Review Adopts Outcome Document at Last Moment," United Nations Press Release, May 28, 2010, at http://www.un.org/press/en/2010/dc3243.doc.htm.

For a report on Fukahori Yoshitoshi's retrieval of Nagasaki photographs from the U.S. National Archives and Records Administration, see "Photos Found in U.S. Show Life, Activity in Nagasaki Soon After Atomic Bombing" by Shohei Okada, *Asahi Shimbun*, August 7, 2014, http://ajw.asahi.com/article/behind_news/social_affairs/AJ201408070003.

ENDURING EFFECTS

For an overview of the updated dosimetry system used to calculate radiation dose estimates for atomic bomb survivors, see *Radiation Effects Research Foundation: A Brief Description*. The full report, *Reassessment of the Atomic Bomb Radiation Dosimetry for Hiroshima and Nagasaki: Dosimetry System 2002*, edited by Robert W. Young and George D. Kerr, is available at http://www.rerf.jp/library/archives_e/scids.html.

Materials and information about the ongoing and anticipated medical concerns for aging atomic bomb survivors were provided by Dr. Akahoshi Masazumi, director of the Department of Clinical Studies at the Radiation Effects Research Foundation in Nagasaki, and Dr. Tomonaga Masao, director of the Nagasaki Atomic Bomb Hospital.

Recent studies on the long-term medical effects of the bombings: "Electron-Spin Resonance Measurements of Extracted Teeth Donated by Atomic-Bomb Survivors..." by Nakamura et al., at http://www.rerf.or.jp/library/update/rerfupda_e/dosbio/tooth.htm; "Radioactive Rays Photographed from Nagasaki Nuclear 'Death Ash,'" *Japan Times*, August 8, 2009; "Long-Term Radiation-Related Health Effects in a Unique Human Population: Lessons Learned from the Atomic Bomb Survivors of Hiroshima and Nagasaki" by Evan B. Douple et al., *Disaster Medicine and Public Health Preparedness* 5:S1; "Risk of Myelodysplastic Syndromes in People Exposed to Ionizing Radiation: A Retrospective Cohort Study of Nagasaki Atomic Bomb Survivors" by Masako Iwanaga et al., *Journal of Clinical Oncology* 29:4; "Longevity of Atomic-Bomb Survivors" by John B. Cologne and Dale L. Preston, *Lancet* 356; and "Genetic Effects of Radiation in Atomic-Bomb Survivors and Their Children: Past, Present and Future" by Nori Nakamura, *Journal of Radiation Research* 47:SB. For a 2014 study investigating fallout effects from the 1945 Trinity test, see the notes for chapter 4.

For ongoing research and activities at the Radiation Effects Research Foundation and the Atomic Bomb Disease Institute in Nagasaki, see the materials, overviews, and publications available at http://www.rerf.jp and http://www-sdc.med.nagasaki-u.ac.jp/abdi/index.html.

MEMORIALS AND LEGACIES

Journalist Yamashita Akiko described Dr. Akizuki's funeral in her biography of the atomic bomb doctor, *Natsugumo no oka* [Hill Under the Summer Cloud], translated into English for the author's use.

Dō-oh Mineko's sister Okada Ikuyo provided a copy of Dō-oh's final *shikishi*.

Yoshida Katsuji's posthumous name, and its meaning, was provided by his son Yoshida Naoji.

For the Nagasaki National Peace Memorial Hall for the Atomic Bomb Victims, see http://www.peace-nagasaki.go.jp/. The names of *hibakusha* who died in the previous year are dedicated each August 9, following the city's annual commemoration at Peace Park.

Yoshida's *kamishibai* can be viewed at the Nagasaki Atomic Bomb Museum's "Kids *Heiwa* [Peace] Nagasaki" Web site, http://www1.city.nagasaki.nagasaki.jp/ peace/english/kids/digital/index.html. The presentation of his *kamishibai* at the Nagasaki Atomic Bomb Museum was described in the article series "Nagasaki nōto [Nagasaki Notes]: Yoshida Katsuji" by Ōkuma Takashi, *Asahi Shimbun,* August 5, 2010, through August 24, 2010. For Hayashida Mitsuhiro's presentation on behalf of Yoshida at the United Nations NPT Review Conference, see "High School Student to Recite A-Bomb Survivor's Story in New York" by Takashi Ōkuma, *Asahi Shimbun,* May 1, 2010, http://www.asahi.com/english/ TKY201004300415.html; and "Sending Voices from Atomic-Bombed Areas to the World" (in Japanese), *Asahi Shimbun,* May 12, 2010.

Yoshida said that he borrowed the phrase "The basis of peace is for people to understand the pain of others" from a former Hiroshima Peace Memorial administrator. He felt the words captured the most important message he could convey out of his experience.

Information about the *hibakusha* legacy campaigns of the Nagasaki Foundation for the Promotion of Peace and the citywide peace education programs came from "All Elementary and Junior High School Students in Nagasaki Learn About Peace and the Atomic Bombing for Nine Years," *Dispatches from Nagasaki,* no. 2, RECNA, Nagasaki University, http://www.recna.nagasaki -u.ac.jp/en-dispatches/no2/; "New Generation of Youth Get Active in Campaign to Abolish Nukes" by Yosuke Watanabe, *Asahi Shimbun,* November 25, 2013; *Devotion of Nagasaki to the Cause of Peace,* printed by the city of Nagasaki; and materials provided by Sakata Toshihiro, vice principal, Shiroyama Elementary School.

Taniguchi described how his skin can't breathe during the summer in "My Back Won't Let Me Forget That Day," *Mainichi,* August 8, 2009.

HIBAKUSHA SOURCES AND SELECTED BIBLIOGRAPHY

I. FEATURED *HIBAKUSHA* SOURCES

Interviews

Dō-oh Mineko, 1 interview, 2003

Nagano Etsuko, 6 interviews, 2007–2011

Okada Ikuyo (Dō-oh Mineko's sister), 4 interviews, 2007–2011

Taniguchi Sumiteru, 6 interviews, 1986–2011

Wada Hisako (Wada Kōichi's wife), 2 interviews, 2007–2009

Wada Kōichi, 6 interviews, 2003–2011

Yoshida Katsuji, 3 interviews, 2007–2009

Yoshida Kenji (Yoshida Katsuji's brother), 2 interviews, 2010–2011

Yoshida Naoji (Yoshida Katsuji's son), 2 interviews, 2010–2011

Yoshida Tomoji (Yoshida Katsuji's son), 2 interviews, 2010–2011

Other Sources (Selected)

DŌ-OH MINEKO

Dō-oh, Mineko. "Hibaku taiken kōwa" [Lecture on Atomic Bomb Experience],'98 *Shūgaku ryokō, Asahikawa fuji joshi kōtō gakkō* [School Field Trip, Asahikawa Fuji Girls' High School]. Privately printed, October 18, 1998. Copy provided by Dō-oh Mineko.

———. Interview. *The Children of Nagasaki.* DVD. Produced by Nippon Eiga Shinsha, Ltd. City of Nagasaki, March 2005.

Itō, Sei. "Nagasaki nōto [Nagasaki Notes]: Dō-oh Mineko-san, 1930–2007." Pts. 1–10, *Asahi Shimbun,* April 24, 2009–May 3, 2009.

Keishō bukai (Dō-oh Mineko ikō shuu) henshū iinkai [Legacy Group (Dō-oh Mineko Posthumous Collection) Editorial Committee], ed. *Ikasarete ikite* [Allowed to Live, I Live]. Nagasaki: Nagasaki heiwa suishin kyōkai keishō bukai [Nagasaki Foundation for the Promotion of Peace Legacy Group], 2009.

"Ms. Mineko Douo." In "My Unforgettable Memory: Testimonies of the Atomic Bomb Survivors." *Nagasaki Shimbun,* March 14, 1996; updated October 19, 2005. Translated by Seiun High School. http://www.nagasaki -np.co.jp/peace/hibaku/english/05.html.

"Nyūsu Nagasaki Eye [Nagasaki Eye News] No. 610." DVD. NHK (Nippon Hōsō Kyōkai) broadcast, July 9, 2009.

NAGANO ETSUKO

Nagano, Etsuko. "Fifty Years from the End of World War II: My Experience of the Atomic Bombing." In *The Light of Morning: Memoirs of the Nagasaki Atomic Bomb Survivors,* 97–106. Nagasaki: Nagasaki National Peace Memorial Hall, 2005.

———. "Watashi no hibaku taikenki" [My Atomic Bomb Memory]. Unpublished speech, n.d. Copy provided by the Nagasaki Foundation for the Promotion of Peace.

———. Interview. *White Light/Black Rain: The Destruction of Hiroshima and Nagasaki.* DVD. Directed by Steven Okazaki. HBO Documentary Films, 2007.

Ōkuma, Takashi. "Nagasaki nōto [Nagasaki Notes]: Nagano Etsuko-san: born 1928." Pts. 1–13. *Asahi Shimbun,* June 29, 2010–July 11, 2010.

Roose, Diana Wickes. *Teach Us to Live: Stories from Hiroshima and Nagasaki.* Pasadena, CA: Intentional Productions, 2007. See especially pp. 77–87.

TANIGUCHI SUMITERU

"Kurushimi no bōkyaku osoreru/kaku, ningen to kyōzon dekinu: Taniguchi-san enzetsu zenbun" [Fear That the Suffering Will Be Forgotten/Nuclear and Humans Cannot Coexist: Mr. Taniguchi's speech in its entirety]. *Asahi Shimbun,* May 12, 2010.

"Genshi bakudan ketsuryō nisshi [Complete Daily Atomic Bomb Record for] Taniguchi Sumiteru. Ōmura National Hospital. November 1, 1945–March 20, 1949." Unpublished medical record. Translated (from German to Japanese) by Asao Manabu, March 2006. Copy provided by Taniguchi Sumiteru.

"Mr. Sumiteru Taniguchi." Testimony no. 2 and no. 3, *Nagasaki and Peace: Testimonies of the Atomic Bomb Survivors,* Nagasaki Broadcasting Company. Excerpts from interviews originally broadcast December 1968–October 1986. Translated by Geoff Neill. http://www2.nbc-nagasaki.co.jp/peace/.

Taniguchi, Sumiteru. Interview. *Hiroshima and Nagasaki: Harvest of Nuclear War.* VHS. Produced by Iwanami Productions. Tokyo, 1982.

———. Interview. *Nagasaki Journey.* DVD. Produced by Judy Irving and Chris Beaver. Oakland, CA: Independent Documentary Group, 1995.

———. Interview. *People's Century: Fallout (1945)*. Originally broadcast June 15, 1999. Public Broadcasting System. Transcript at http://www .pbs.org/wgbh/peoplescentury/episodes/fallout/taniguchitranscript .html.

———. Interview. *White Light/Black Rain: The Destruction of Hiroshima and Nagasaki*, DVD. Directed by Steven Okazaki. HBO Documentary Films, 2007.

———. "Eternal Scars." In *Testimonies of the Atomic Bomb Survivors: A Record of the Devastation of Nagasaki*, 46–48. Translated by Brian Burke-Gaffney. City of Nagasaki, 1985.

———. "Remembering for Twenty-Five Years: The Heat Rays That Burned a 16-Year-Old Back." In *The Light of Morning: Memoirs of the Nagasaki Atomic Bomb Survivors*, 89–96. Nagasaki: Nagasaki National Peace Memorial Hall, 2005.

———. "A Survivor's Responsibility." In *Hibakusha: Survivors of Hiroshima and Nagasaki*, 113–19. Translated by Gaynor Sekimori. Tokyo: Kohei Publishing Co., 1986.

———. "Twenty-Five Years Later: Memories and Evidence." In *Give Me Water: Testimonies of Hiroshima and Nagasaki*, 52–54. Translated by Rinjiro Sodei. Tokyo: A Citizens' Group to Convey Testimonies of Hiroshima and Nagasaki, 1972.

———. Unpublished speech. U.S. speaking tour representing Nihon Hidankyō (Japan Confederation of A- and H-Bomb Sufferers Organizations). Washington, DC, 1986.

———. "The Whole Surface of My Back Was Burnt." In *Voices of the A-Bomb Survivors: Nagasaki*, edited by the Nagasaki Atomic Bomb Testimonial Society, 86–91. Nagasaki: Shōwado Printing Co., 2009.

Townsend, Peter. *The Postman of Nagasaki: The Story of a Survivor*. London: Collins, 1984.

WADA KŌICHI

Nakamura, Keiko. "Hamaguchimachi Stop (Nagasaki): Streetcar Shows Spirit of Nagasaki." *Daily Yomiuri Online*, n.d., ca. 2005. Accessed August 2008. http://www.yomiuri.co.jp/.

Wada, Kōichi. Interview. *The Last Atomic Bomb*. Directed by Robert Richter. New Day Films, 2006. Online streaming: http://www.newdaydigital.com/ The-Last-Atomic-Bomb.html.

———. Interview. *The Children of Nagasaki*. DVD. Produced by Nippon Eiga Shinsha, Ltd. City of Nagasaki, March 2005.

———. "A Monument to 11:02 a.m." In "Peace and Atomic Bomb: Atomic Bomb Survivors, Narratives of A-Bomb Experience." Nagasaki City: Nagasaki Atomic Bomb Museum, 2009. http://www1.city.nagasaki .nagasaki.jp/peace/english/survivors/koichi_wada.html.

————. "Nagasaki." In *Genbaku jū roku nen no koe* [Sixty Years of Voices: Stories of the A-Bomb Survivors], edited by Imaishi Motohisa, translated by Christopher Cruz, 58–66. Hiroshima: Printed by author, 2005.

————. "There Was No 'War-End' in Nagasaki." Unpublished excerpt from "Testimonies of Hiroshima and Nagasaki, 1988," based on an interview conducted by the Nagasaki Testimony Seminar, group 3, n.d. Translated by the Nagasaki National Peace Memorial Hall for the Atomic Bomb Victims.

YOSHIDA KATSUJI

Krakauer, Jon. "The Forgotten Ground Zero—Nagasaki, Reduced to Ashes by an Atomic Bomb, Rises Again in Beauty, Grace and Good Will," *Seattle Times,* March 5, 1995. http://community.seattletimes.nwsource.com/archive/?date=19950305&slug=2108264.

"Nyūsu Nagasaki Eye [Nagasaki Eye News] No. 610." In *No More Hibakusha.* NHK (Nippon Hōsō Kyōkai [Japan Broadcasting Corporation]), n.d. Accessed 2011. http://www.nhk.or.jp/no-more-hibakusha/hibakukoe/nagasaki005.html.

Ōkuma, Takashi. "Nagasaki nōto [Nagasaki Notes]: Yoshida Katsuji." Pts. 1–19, *Asahi Shimbun,* August 5, 2010–August 24, 2010.

Yoshida, Katsuji. "I Must Not Die." Unpublished excerpt from *Mou, iya da!* [We've Had Enough!], vol. 1, n.d. Translated by the Nagasaki National Peace Memorial Hall for the Atomic Bomb Victims.

————. Interview. *White Light/Black Rain: The Destruction of Hiroshima and Nagasaki.* DVD. Directed by Steven Okazaki. HBO Documentary Films, 2007.

————. Interview with Jerome McDonnell. "Nagasaki: A Survivor's Story." In *Worldview.* Translated by Geoff Neill. Chicago Public Radio, May 31, 2005. http://www.wbez.org/.

————. Interview with Watanabe Kuniko and Ōmoto Akiko. Produced by *ANT-Hiroshima.* DVD. February 18, 2009.

————. Interview. "Zenshin yakedo de seishi no saki wo samayō" [Lost on the Border between Life and Death with Whole-Body Burns]. NHK News broadcast, 2007.

————. Interview. "Atomic Bomb Survivor." DVD. The History Channel, n.d. [2009?]. Copy provided by Yoshida Katsuji.

II. ADDITIONAL NAGASAKI *HIBAKUSHA* SOURCES

Hibakusha Interviews

Akizuki Sugako (Dr. Akizuki Tatsuichirō's wife)
Anonymous (name withheld by request)
Fukahori Yoshitoshi

Hamasaki Hitoshi
Hirose Masahito
Matsuzoe Hiroshi
Miyazaki Midori
Shimohira Sakue
Uchida Tsukasa

Interviews and Conversations with Nagasaki Atomic Bomb Specialists and Researchers

(Titles at time of interview)

Akahoshi Masazumi, M.D., cardiologist and director, Department of Clinical Studies, Radiation Effects Research Foundation, Nagasaki

Brian Burke-Gaffney, professor, Nagasaki Institute of Applied Science

Fukushima Masako, Master File Section, Epidemiology Department, Radiation Effects Research Foundation, Nagasaki

Hashimoto Fujiko, administrator, Nagasaki University Atomic Bomb Disease Institute

Kinoshita Hirohisa, M.D., Ph.D., Department of Neuropsychiatry, Nagasaki University Hospital of Medicine and Dentistry

Koshimoto Rika, M.A., psychologist, Nagasaki University Graduate School of Biomedical Sciences

Matsuo Ranko, assistant section chief, Nagasaki Foundation for the Promotion of Peace

Mori Hideki, M.D., Ph.D., vice president, Nagasaki Atomic Bomb Hospital

Nakashima Seiji, social worker, Nagasaki Atomic Bomb Hospital

Geoff Neill, translator, Nagasaki National Peace Memorial Hall for the Atomic Bomb Victims

Sakata Toshihiro, vice principal, Shiroyama Elementary School

Taira Mitsuyoshi, director, Nagasaki Atomic Bomb Museum

Takagi Rumiko, researcher, Nagasaki Atomic Bomb Museum

Tomonaga Masao, director, Nagasaki Atomic Bomb Hospital

Tsutsumi Fusayo, director, Megumi no Oka (Hill of Grace, Nagasaki A-Bomb Home)

Unpublished English Translations of *Hibakusha* Testimonies

The Nagasaki Foundation for the Promotion of Peace provided twenty-seven *hibakusha* testimonies and three testimony compilations, translated into English and printed by the Nagasaki National Peace Memorial Hall for the Atomic Bomb Victims.

Published Memoirs and Testimony Collections

Abe, Kazue. *Bearing a Small Cross*. Japan: Kazue Inoue, 1995.

Akizuki, Tatsuichirō. *Nagasaki 1945: The First Full-Length Eyewitness Account of the Atomic Bomb Attack on Nagasaki*. Translated by Keiichi Nagata. Edited by Gordon Honeycombe. London: Quartet Books, 1981.

Bernstein, Michie Hattori. "Eyewitness to the Nagasaki Atomic Bomb Blast." *WWII Magazine,* July/August 2005. Published on historynet.com, June 12, 2006. http://www.historynet.com/michie-hattori-eyewitness-to-the -nagasaki-atomic-bomb-blast.htm.

Burke-Gaffney, Brian. "In the Words of an Atomic Bomb Survivor." *Crossroads: A Journal of Nagasaki History and Culture* 3 (Summer 1995): 37–42. http://www.uwosh.edu/faculty_staff/earns/sakue.html.

The Deaths of Hibakusha, Vol. I: The Days of the Bombings to the End of 1945. Translated by the English Translation Group of "The Witness of Those Two Days." Tokyo: Nihon Hidankyō, 1991.

The Deaths of Hibakusha, Vol. II: Forty Years Since 1946. Translated by the English Translation Group of "The Witness of Those Two Days." Tokyo: Nihon Hidankyō, 1995.

Del Tredici, Robert. "Tsue Hayashi." In *At Work in the Fields of the Bomb*, 189–91. New York: Harper & Row, 1987.

Fujisaki, Shinji, compiler. *Burnt Yet Undaunted: Verbatim Account of Senji Yamaguchi*. Tokyo: Nihon Hidankyō, 2002.

Give Me Water: Testimonies of Hiroshima and Nagasaki. Translated by Rinjiro Sodei. Tokyo: A Citizens' Group to Convey Testimonies of Hiroshima and Nagasaki, 1972.

Hand Them Down to the Next Generations! Here Are Live Voices of Atomic Bomb Victims, Vol. I. Fukuoka, Japan: FCO-OP, 1995.

Hashimoto, Yutaka. "Mom and Silver Rice: Boyhood Reminiscences of the End of the War and Occupied Nagasaki." Translated by Brendon Hanna. *Crossroads: A Journal of Nagasaki History and Culture* 4 (Summer 1996): 53–68. http://www.uwosh.edu/home_pages/faculty_staff/earns/silver .html.

Hibakusha: Hiroshima/Nagasaki. Tokyo: Nihon Hidankyō, 1982.

Hibakusha: Survivors of Hiroshima and Nagasaki. Translated by Gaynor Sekimori. Tokyo: Kohei Publishing Co., 1986.

Hiroshima/Nagasaki: After the Atomic Bomb, Vol. IV: Selected Haikus. Translated by Kemmoku Makato and Christopher Cliplef. Kobe, Japan: Kinoshita Press, 2006.

Hiroshima/Nagasaki: After the Atomic Bomb, Vol. V: Elegy for Nagasaki: 124 Tankas of Takami Oyama. Translated by Kemmoku Makato. Kobe, Japan: Kinoshita Press, 2006.

Ishitani, Susumu. "Looking for Meaning." *Friends Journal: 1945–95 Remembering Hiroshima and Nagasaki* 41:8 (August 1995): 8–9.

Kamezawa, Miyuki, ed. *The Unforgettable Day: Cries of "Hibakusha" from Hiroshima and Nagasaki.* 3rd ed. Nagoya, Japan: Group for Spreading Out "The Unforgettable Day" Over the World, 1995.

Kido, Sueichi. "I Desire to Abolish Nuclear Weapons." Pamphlet. Nihon Hidankyō, May 2010.

Kobayashi, Shigeyuki, with Conan O'Harrow. *War and Atomic Holocaust on Trial: Seeking an Enactment of a Law to Give Support to the Victims of the Atomic Bombings.* Tokyo: Conference for the People of Setagaya, n.d. Copy provided by the Nagasaki Atomic Bomb Museum Library.

Kubo, Mitsue. *Hibaku: Recollections of A-Bomb Survivors.* Translated by Ryoji Inoue. Coquitlam, B.C., Canada: Nippon Printing, 1990.

The Light of Morning: Memoirs of the Nagasaki Atomic Bomb Survivors. Translated by Brian Burke-Gaffney. Nagasaki: Nagasaki National Peace Memorial Hall for the Atomic Bomb Victims, 2005.

"Messages from *Hibakusha* for the 2010 NPT Review Conference." Tokyo: Nihon Hidankyō, 2009.

Nagai, Takashi. *Atomic Bomb Rescue and Relief Report.* Edited by Fidelius R. Kuo. Translated by Aloysius F. Kuo. Nagasaki: Nagasaki Association for Hibakushas' Medical Care, 2000.

———. *The Bells of Nagasaki: A Message of Hope from a Witness, a Doctor.* Translated by William Johnston. Tokyo: Kodansha International, 1984.

———, ed. *Living Beneath the Atomic Cloud: Testimonies of the Children of Nagasaki.* Compiled by Frank Zenisek. Translated by the Nagasaki Appeal Committee Volunteer Group. Nagasaki: Nagasaki Appeal Committee, 1985.

———. *We of Nagasaki: The Story of Survivors in an Atomic Wasteland.* Translated by Ichiro Shirato and Herbert B. L. Silverman. New York: Duell, Sloan and Pearce, 1951.

Nagasaki Atomic Bomb Testimonial Society. *Voices of the A-Bomb Survivors: Nagasaki.* Foreword by Masahito Hirose. Nagasaki: Showado Printing Co., 2009.

Nagasaki Prefectural Girls' High School 42nd Alumnae, ed. *Footprints of Nagasaki: Excerpt from "Anohi Anotoki."* Translated by Yuriko Kitamura. Nagasaki: Seibonokishi-sha, 1995.

Nagatsu, Kōzaburō, Hisao Suzuki, and Toshio Yamamoto, eds. *Against Nuclear Weapons: A Collection of Poems by 181 Poets 1945–2007.* Translated by Naoshi Koriyama et al. Tokyo: Koru Sakkusha, 2007.

Nakano, Michiko, ed. *Nagasaki Under the Atomic Bomb: Experiences of Young College Girls.* Tokyo: Soeisha/Sanseido Bookstore Ltd., 2000.

Nobuko, Margaret Kosuge. "Prompt and Utter Destruction: The Nagasaki Disaster and the Initial Medical Relief." *International Review of the Red Cross* 89:866 (June 2007): 279–303.

Our Parents Were in Nagasaki on August 9, 1945. Nagasaki: Nagasaki Teachers' Association of Children of Atomic Bomb Survivors, 1988.

The Pain in Our Hearts: Recollections of Hiroshima, Nagasaki, and Okinawa. Tokyo: Soka Gakkai, Youth Division, 1975.

Roose, Diana Wickes. *Teach Us to Live: Stories from Hiroshima and Nagasaki.* Pasadena, CA: Intentional Productions, 2007.

Selden, Kyoko, and Mark Selden. *The Atomic Bomb: Voices from Hiroshima and Nagasaki.* London: East Gate Books, 1989.

Shiotsuki, Masao. *Doctor at Nagasaki: "My First Assignment Was Mercy Killing."* Translated by Simul International. Tokyo: Kosei Publishing Co., 1987.

Shirabe, Raisuke. "Medical Survey of Atomic Bomb Casualties." *The Military Surgeon* 113:4 (Oct. 1953): 251–263.

———. "My Experience of the Nagasaki Atomic Bombing and an Outline of the Damages Caused by the Explosion." 1986. Atomic Bomb Disease Institute, Nagasaki University, Graduate School of Biomedical Sciences. Accessed 2012. http://www-sdc.med.nagasaki-u.ac.jp/abcenter/shirabe/index_e.html.

———. *A Physician's Diary of Atomic Bombing and Its Aftermath.* Edited by Fidelius R. Kuo. Translated by Aloysius F. Kuo. Nagasaki: Nagasaki Association for Hibakushas' Medical Care, 2002.

Silent Thunder: From the Book "Te yo katare" (Let These Hands Speak). Translated by Brian Burke-Gaffney. Nagasaki: Nagasaki Prefectural Association for the Welfare of the Deaf and Dumb, Nagasaki Branch of the Japanese Study Group of Sign Language Problems, 1976.

Soka Gakkai, Youth Division, ed. *Cries for Peace: Experiences of Japanese Victims of World War II.* Tokyo: Japan Times, 1978.

Speaking of Peace I: Something We Want You to Know. Nagasaki: Nagasaki Foundation for the Promotion of Peace, 1990.

Testimonies from Hiroshima and Nagasaki, 3rd ed. Kanagawa, Japan: Zushi Atomic Bomb Sufferers Association, 1995.

Testimonies of the Atomic Bomb Survivors: A Record of the Devastation of Nagasaki. Translated by Brian Burke-Gaffney. City of Nagasaki, 1985.

Trumbull, Robert. *Nine Who Survived Hiroshima and Nagasaki: Personal Experiences of Nine Men Who Lived Through the Atomic Bombings.* Tokyo: Charles E. Tuttle Company, 1957.

Vance-Watkins, Lequita, and Mariko Aratani, eds. *White Flash/Black Rain: Women of Japan Relive the Bomb.* Minneapolis, MN: Milkweed Editions, 1995.

Wasurerarenai anohi: The Day Never to Be Forgotten: A Collection of Testimonies and Pictures. Yokohama, Japan: Kanagawa Atomic Bomb Sufferers Association, 2005.

Wiesen, Mary, and Elizabeth Cannon, eds. *Nagasaki August 9, 1945.* Translated by Junshin Junior College English Club. Nagasaki: Junshin Junior College English Club, 1983.

The Witness of Those Two Days: Hiroshima & Nagasaki, August 6 & 9, 1945. 2 vols. Translated by the English Translation Group of "The Witness of Those Two Days." Tokyo: Nihon Hidankyō, 1989.

Yamashita, Akiko. *Natsugumo no oka: Hibaku ishi Akizuki Tatsuichirō* [Hill Under the Summer Cloud: Atomic Bomb Physician Akizuki Tatsuichirō]. Nagasaki: Nagasaki Shimbunsha, 2006.

Yasuyama, Kodo. *Collection of Memoirs of the Atomic Bombardment of Nagasaki 1945–55.* Edited by Shunichi Yamashita. Nagasaki: Nagasaki Association for Hibakushas' Medical Care, 2005.

Internet Collections

"Global Network." The National Peace Memorial Halls for the Atomic Bomb Victims in Hiroshima and Nagasaki. February 2010. http://www.global -peace.go.jp/en/.

"*Hibakusha:* Atomic Bomb Survivors." United Nations Office for Disarmament Affairs. 2014. http://www.un.org/disarmament/content/slideshow/ hibakusha/.

"Memories of Hiroshima and Nagasaki: Messages from *Hibakusha.*" *Asahi Shimbun.* September 2011. http://www.asahi.com/hibakusha/english/nagasaki/.

"My Unforgettable Memory: Testimonies of the Atomic Bomb Survivors." *Nagasaki Shimbun.* Translated by Seiun High School. 2005. http://www .nagasaki-np.co.jp/peace/hibaku/english/index.html.

"Nagasaki and Peace: Testimonies of the Atomic Bomb Survivors." Nagasaki Broadcasting Company. Excerpts of the radio program "Speaking of the Atomic Bomb" aired since the fall of 1968. Accessed 2008. http://www2 .nbc-nagasaki.co.jp/peace/.

"Peace and Atomic Bomb—Atomic Bomb Survivors." Nagasaki City. 2009. http://www.city.nagasaki.lg.jp/peace/english/survivors/index.html.

Pictorial Works

Asahi Graph. Special Issue. *Asahi Shimbun,* July 10, 1970.

Goldstein, Donald M., Katherine V. Dillon, and J. Michael Wenger. *Rain of Ruin: A Photographic History of Hiroshima and Nagasaki.* Dulles, VA: Brassey's, 1999.

Hiroshima-Nagasaki: A Pictorial Record of the Atomic Destruction. Tokyo: Hiroshima-Nagasaki Publishing Committee, 1978.

Jenkins, Rupert, ed. *Nagasaki Journey: The Photographs of Yosuke Yamahata, August 10, 1945.* San Francisco, CA: Pomegranate Art Books, 1995.

Kazuo, Kuroko, and Shimizu Hiroyoshi, eds. *No More Hiroshima, Nagasaki.* Translated by James Dorsey. Japan: Nihon Tosho Center Co. Ltd., 2005.

O'Donnell, Joe. *Japan 1945: A U.S. Marine's Photographs from Ground Zero.* Nashville, TN: Vanderbilt University Press, 2005.

Rubinfien, Leo, Shōmei Tōmatsu, Sandra S. Phillips, and John W. Dower. *Shōmei Tōmatsu: Skin of the Nation.* San Francisco, CA: San Francisco Museum of Modern Art in association with Yale University Press, New Haven, 2004.

Kurosaki, Haruo. *Nagasaki shoukon ienumama-kunou no gojyuu nen wo ikite: shashin shuu* [Nagasaki: Scarred and Not Yet Healed After Fifty Years of Anguish: A Photo Collection]. Nagasaki: Shōwa do insatsu [Shōwa Do Printing], 1995.

Genbaku hibaku kiroku shashin shu [A Photographic Record of the Atomic Bombing]. Nagasaki: Fujiki hakuei sha [Fujiki Hakuei Co.], 2001.

Documentary Films

The Children of Nagasaki. DVD. Produced by Nippon Eiga Shinsha, Ltd. City of Nagasaki, March 2005.

Dark Circle. DVD. Produced and directed by Chris Beaver, Judy Irving, and Ruth Landy. New York: Independent Documentary Group, 2006.

Hiroshima and Nagasaki: Harvest of Nuclear War. VHS. Produced by Iwanami Productions. Tokyo, 1982.

Hiroshima-Nagasaki, August 1945. VHS. Produced by Kazuko Oshima, Paul Ronder, and Erik Barnouw. Oakland, CA: Center for Mass Communication, Columbia University Press, 1980.

The Last Atomic Bomb. Directed by Robert Richter. New Day Films, 2006. Online streaming. http://www.newdaydigital.com/The-Last-Atomic-Bomb.html.

Nagasaki Journey. VHS. Produced by Judy Irving and Chris Beaver. Oakland, CA: Independent Documentary Group, 1995.

Survivors. VHS. Directed by Steven Okazaki. San Francisco, CA, 1982.

"Victor's Plea for Peace: An American Officer in Occupied Nagasaki." Television documentary. Produced by NHK World, 2001. http://www3.nhk .or.jp/nhkworld/english/tv/featured/ac/lineup.html. Copy provided by Patricia Delnore Magee.

White Light/Black Rain: The Destruction of Hiroshima and Nagasaki. DVD. Directed by Steven Okazaki. HBO Documentary Films, 2007.

III. SELECTED BIBLIOGRAPHY

Adler, Bill, ed., with Tracy Quinn McLennan. *World War II Letters: A Glimpse into the Heart of the Second World War Through the Words of Those Who Were Fighting It.* New York: St. Martin's Press, 2002.

Akizuki, Tatsuichirō. "The Nagasaki Testimony Movement." In *Literature Under the Nuclear Cloud,* edited by Ito Narihiko, Komura Fujihiko, and Kamata Sadao, 41–46. Tokyo: Sanyusha Shuppan, 1984.

"All Elementary and Junior High School Students in Nagasaki Learn About Peace and the Atomic Bombing for Nine Years." *Dispatches from Nagasaki* no. 2. Research Center for Nuclear Weapons Abolition (RECNA), Nagasaki University, August 30, 2012. http://www.recna.nagasaki-u.ac.jp/en-dispatches/no2/.

Applbaum, Kalman D. "Marriage with the Proper Stranger: Arranged Marriage in Metropolitan Japan." *Ethnology* 34:1 (Winter 1995): 37–51.

Arms Control Association. "Fact Sheet: The Nuclear Testing Tally." February 2007. Updated February 2013. http://www.armscontrol.org/factsheets/nucleartesttally.

Asada, Sadao. "The Mushroom Cloud and National Psyches: Japanese and American Perceptions of the Atomic Bomb Decision—A Reconsideration, 1945–2006." In *Culture Shock and Japanese-American Relations: Historical Essays*, 207. Columbia, MO: University of Missouri Press, 2007.

———. "The Shock of the Atomic Bomb and Japan's Decision to Surrender: A Reconsideration." *Pacific Historical Review* 67:4 (November 1998): 477–512.

Ashworth, Fredrick L. "Dropping the Atomic Bomb on Nagasaki." *Proceedings of the U.S. Naval Institute* 84:1 (1958): 12–17.

Atomic Bomb Disease Institute, Nagasaki University, Graduate School of Biomedical Sciences. 6th ed. Nagasaki: Nagasaki University Graduate School of Biomedical Sciences, 2004.

Atomic Bomb Disease Institute. *The Medical Effects of the Nagasaki Atomic Bombing: 1945–2008.* Nagasaki: Nagasaki University Graduate School of Biomedical Sciences, 2008.

Auxier, J. A. *Ichiban: The Dosimetry Program for Nuclear Bomb Survivors of Hiroshima and Nagasaki—A Status Report as of April 1, 1964.* Civil Effects Test Operations, U.S. Atomic Energy Commission. Washington, DC: U.S. Technical Services, April 1964. http://digital.library.unt.edu/ark:/67531/metadc13058/.

Barnouw, Erik. "Iwasaki and the Occupied Screen." *Film History* 2:4 (November–December 1988): 337–57.

Beaver, Chris. "Notes on *Nagasaki Journey*." *Positions: Asia Critique* 5:3 (Winter 1997): 673–85.

Beck, J. S. P., and W. A. Meissner. "Radiation Effects of the Atomic Bomb Among the Natives of Nagasaki, Kyushu." *American Journal of Clinical Pathology* 6 (June 1946): 586.

Beijin kisha no mita Hiroshima Nagasaki [Hiroshima and Nagasaki Through the Eyes of American Reporters]. 7 vols. Akiba Project, 1981–1987. Collection of newspaper and journal articles in English, with Japanese translation. Hiroshima: Hiroshima International Cultural Foundation, 1982–1988.

Berlin, Richard B. "Impressions of Japanese Medicine at the End of World War II." *Scientific Monthly* 64:1 (1947): 41–49.

Bernstein, Barton J. "An Analysis of 'Two Cultures': Writing About the Making and the Using of the Atomic Bombs." *Public Historian* 12:2 (Spring 1990): 83–107.

———. "Compelling Japan's Surrender Without the A-Bomb, Soviet Entry, or Invasion: Reconsidering the U.S. Bombing Survey's Early-Surrender Conclusions." *Journal of Strategic Studies* 18:2 (1995): 101–48.

———. "Introducing the Interpretive Problems of Japan's 1945 Surrender: A Historiographical Essay on Recent Literature in the West." In *The End of the Pacific War: Reappraisals*, edited by Tsuyoshi Hasegawa, 9–64. Palo Alto, CA: Stanford University Press, 2007.

———. "Reconsidering Truman's Claim of 'Half a Million American Lives' Saved by the Atomic Bomb: The Construction and Deconstruction of a Myth." *Journal of Strategic Studies* 22:1 (1999): 54–95.

———. "Seizing the Contested Terrain of Early Nuclear History." In *Hiroshima's Shadow: Writings on the Denial of History and the Smithsonian Controversy*, edited by Kai Bird and Lawrence Lifschultz, 163–196. Stony Creek, CT: Pamphleteer's Press, 1998.

———. "The Struggle over History: Defining the Hiroshima Narrative." In *Judgment at the Smithsonian*, edited by Philip Nobile, 127–256. New York: Marlowe and Company, 1995.

———. "Truman and the A-Bomb: Targeting Noncombatants, Using the Bomb, and His Defending the 'Decision.'" *Journal of Military History* 62 (July 1998): 547–70.

Bird, Kai, and Lawrence Lifschultz, eds. *Hiroshima's Shadow: Writings on the Denial of History and the Smithsonian Controversy*. Stony Creek, CT: Pamphleteer's Press, 1998.

Bix, Herbert P. *Hirohito and the Making of Modern Japan*. New York: HarperCollins, 2000.

Bohlmann, Rudi. Interview with Curt Nickisch. "Nagasaki Aftermath Haunts U.S. Veteran." *All Things Considered*. National Public Radio, August 9, 2007. http://www.npr.org/templates/story/story.php?storyId=12638594.

Braw, Monica. *The Atomic Bomb Suppressed: American Censorship in Occupied Japan*. Armonk, NY: M. E. Sharpe, 1991.

———. "Hiroshima and Nagasaki: The Voluntary Silence." In *Living with the Bomb: American and Japanese Cultural Conflicts in the Nuclear Age*, edited by Laura Hein and Mark Selden, 155–72. New York: M. E. Sharpe, 1997.

Buck, Alice L. "A History of the Atomic Energy Commission." Washington, DC: U.S. Department of Energy, 1983. http://energy.gov/management/downloads/history-atomic-energy-commission.

Burchett, Wilfred. *Shadows of Hiroshima*. London: Verso, 1983,

Burke-Gaffney, Brian. *Nagasaki: The British Experience, 1854–1945*. Kent, UK: Global Oriental, Ltd., 2009.

Burr, William, ed. *The Atomic Bomb and the End of World War II: A Collection of Primary Sources*. National Security Archive Electronic

Briefing Book No. 162. Washington, DC: National Security Archive, 2005. Updated April 27, 2007. http://www2.gwu.edu/~nsarchiv/NSAEBB/NSAEBB162/index.htm.

Buruma, Ian. *Inventing Japan: 1853–1964*. New York: Modern Library, 2003.

Butow, Robert J. C. *Japan's Decision to Surrender*. Palo Alto, CA: Stanford University Press, 1954.

"Cancer Incidence in Atomic Bomb Survivors." Special Issue. *Radiation Research* 137:2s (February 1994). http://www.rrjournal.org/toc/rare/137/2s.

Carter, Kit C., and Robert Mueller, compilers. *U.S. Army Air Forces in World War II: Combat Chronology 1941–1945*. Washington, DC: Center for Air Force History, 1991. http://www.afhra.af.mil/shared/media/document/AFD-090529-036.pdf.

"Certification of Sufferers of Atomic Bomb-Related Diseases." *Nuke Info Tokyo* 131 (July/Aug. 2009). http://cnic.jp/english/newsletter/nit131/nit131articles/abombdisease.html.

Chinnock, Frank. *Nagasaki: The Forgotten Bomb*. New York: World Publishing Company, 1969.

Chul, Choi Il. "Three-Fold Hardships of the Korean *Hibakusha*." 1999. American Friends Services Committee. https://afsc.org/resource/hibakusha-h-bomb-survivors.

Clarke, Hugh V. *Twilight Liberation: Australian Prisoners of War Between Hiroshima and Home*. Boston: Allen & Unwin, 1985.

Cologne, John B., and Dale L. Preston. "Longevity of Atomic-Bomb Survivors." *Lancet* 356 (July 2000): 303–7.

Committee for the Compilation of Materials on Damage Caused by the Atomic Bombs in Hiroshima and Nagasaki, ed. *Hiroshima and Nagasaki: The Physical, Medical, and Social Effects of the Atomic Bombings*. Translated by Eisei Ishikawa and David L. Swain. New York: Basic Books, 1981.

——— *The Impact of the A-Bomb: Hiroshima and Nagasaki, 1945–85*. Translated by Eisei Ishikawa and David L. Swain. Tokyo: Iwanami Shoten, 1985.

Compton, Karl T. "If the Atomic Bomb Had Not Been Used." *Atlantic Monthly*, December 1946. Accessed 2011. http://www.theatlantic.com/past/docs/issues/46dec/compton.htm.

Cook, Haruko Taya, and Theodore F. Cook. *Japan at War: An Oral History*. New York: New Press, 1992.

Coox, Alvin D. "Evidences of Antimilitarism in Prewar and Wartime Japan." *Pacific Affairs* 46:4 (Winter 1973–74): 502–14.

Coughlin, William J. *Conquered Press: The MacArthur Era in Japanese Journalism*. Palo Alto, CA: Pacific Books, 1952.

Cousins, Norman. "Hiroshima Four Years Later." *Saturday Review of Literature* 32 (September 17, 1949): 5–10, 30.

———. "The Literacy of Survival." In *Hiroshima's Shadow: Writings on the Denial of History and the Smithsonian Controversy,* edited by Kai Bird and Lawrence Lifschultz, 305–6. Stony Creek, CT: Pamphleteer's Press, 1998. Originally published in *Saturday Review of Literature,* September 14, 1946.

Craven, Wesley Frank, and James Lea Cate, eds. *The Army Air Forces in WWII, Vol. 5: The Pacific: Matterhorn to Nagasaki, June 1944 to August 1945.* Washington, DC: Office of Air Force History, 1983. Originally published by University of Chicago Press, 1953.

Cwiertka, Katarzyna. "Beyond the Black Market: Neighborhood Associations and Food Rationing in Postwar Japan." In *Japan Since 1945: From Postwar to Post-Bubble,* edited by Christopher Gerteis and Timothy S. George, chap. 6. London: Bloomsbury Academic, 2013.

Daws, Gavan. *Prisoners of the Japanese: POWs of World War II in the Pacific.* New York: William Morrow, 1994.

Days to Remember: An Account of the Bombings of Hiroshima and Nagasaki. Tokyo: Hiroshima-Nagasaki Publishing Committee, 1981.

DeVore, Robert. "What the Atomic Bomb Really Did." *Collier's,* March 2, 1946: 19, 36–38.

Devotion of Nagasaki to the Cause of Peace. Nagasaki: City of Nagasaki, 1985.

Diehl, Chad R. "Resurrecting Nagasaki: Reconstruction, the Urakami Catholics, and Atomic Memory, 1945–1970." Ph.D. dissertation, Columbia University, 2011.

Douple, Evan B., Kiyohiko Mabuchi, Harry M. Cullings, Dale L. Preston, Kazunori Kodama, Yukiko Shimizu, Saeko Fujiwara, and Roy E. Shore. "Long-Term Radiation-Related Health Effects in a Unique Human Population: Lessons Learned from the Atomic Bomb Survivors of Hiroshima and Nagasaki." *Disaster Medicine and Public Health Preparedness* 5:S1 (2011): S122–33.

Dower, John W. "The Bombed: Hiroshimas and Nagasakis in Japanese Memory." *Diplomatic History* 19:2 (Spring 1995): 275–95.

———. *Embracing Defeat: Japan in the Wake of WWII.* New York: W. W. Norton & Co., 2000.

———. *Japan in War and Peace: Selected Essays.* New York: New Press, 1993.

———. "Triumphal and Tragic Narratives for the War in Asia." In *Living with the Bomb: American and Japanese Cultural Conflicts in the Nuclear Age,* edited by Laura Hein and Mark Selden, 37–51. New York: M. E. Sharpe, 1997.

———. *War Without Mercy: Race and Power in the Pacific War.* New York: Pantheon Books, 1986.

Earns, Lane R. "'Dancing People Are Happy People': Square Dancing and Democracy in Occupied Japan." *Crossroads: A Journal of Nagasaki History and Culture* 2 (Summer 1994): 91–102. http://www.uwosh.edu/home _pages/faculty_staff/earns/niblo.html.

———. "The Legacy of Commemorative Disputes: What Our Children Won't Learn." *Crossroads: A Journal of Nagasaki History and Culture* 3 (Summer 1995): 99–119. http://www.uwosh.edu/home_pages/faculty_staff/earns/legacy.html.

———. "Reflections from Above: An American Pilot's Perspective on the Mission Which Dropped the Atomic Bomb on Nagasaki." *Crossroads: A Journal of Nagasaki History and Culture* 3 (Summer 1995): 1–20. http://www.uwosh.edu/faculty_staff/earns/olivi.html.

———. "Victor's Justice: Colonel Victor Delnore and the U.S. Occupation of Nagasaki." *Crossroads: A Journal of Nagasaki History and Culture* 3 (Summer 1995): 75–98. http://www.uwosh.edu/faculty_staff/earns/delnore.html.

Federation of American Scientists. "Status of World Nuclear Forces." December 1, 2014. http://fas.org/issues/nuclear-weapons/status-world-nuclear-forces/.

Fitzgerald, Jack. *The Jack Ford Story: Newfoundland's POW in Nagasaki.* St. John's, Newfoundland and Labrador: Creative Publishers, 2007.

Frank, Richard B. *Downfall: The End of the Imperial Japanese Empire.* New York: Random House, 1999.

"Genbaku no kiroku: Soshuhen: 1945 Hiroshima, Nagasaki." *Asahi Graph.* Tokyo: Asahi Shimbun, 1982.

Glasstone, Samuel, and Philip J. Dolan, eds. *The Effects of Nuclear Weapons.* 3rd ed. Washington, DC: U.S. Government Printing Office, 1977.

Glynn, Paul, Fr. *A Song for Nagasaki: The Story of Takashi Nagai—Scientist, Convert, and Survivor of the Atomic Bomb.* San Francisco: Ignatius Press, 2009.

Gordon, Andrew. *A Modern History of Japan: From Tokugawa Times to the Present.* New York: Oxford University Press, 2003.

Hacker, Barton C. *The Dragon's Tail: Radiation Safety in the Manhattan Project, 1942–1946.* Berkeley: University of California Press, 1987.

———. *Elements of Controversy: The AEC and Radiation Safety in Nuclear Weapons Testing, 1947–1974.* Berkeley: University of California Press, 1994.

Hammond, Ellen H. "Commemoration Controversies: The War, the Peace, and Democracy in Japan." In *Living with the Bomb: American and Japanese Cultural Conflicts in the Nuclear Age,* edited by Laura Hein and Mark Selden, 100–21. New York: M. E. Sharpe, 1997.

Harris, Benedict R., and Marvin A. Stevens. "Experiences at Nagasaki, Japan." *The Connecticut State Medical Journal* 9:12 (Dec. 1945): 913–17.

Harwit, Martin. *An Exhibit Denied: Lobbying the History of Enola Gay.* New York: Copernicus, 1996.

Hasegawa, Tsuyoshi, ed. *The End of the Pacific War: Reappraisals.* Palo Alto, CA: Stanford University Press, 2007.

———. *Racing the Enemy: Stalin, Truman, and the Surrender of Japan.* Cambridge: Harvard University Press, 2005.

Hein, Laura, and Mark Selden. "Commemoration and Silence: Fifty Years of Remembering the Bomb in America and Japan." In *Living with the Bomb: American and Japanese Cultural Conflicts in the Nuclear Age,* 3–34. New York: M. E. Sharpe, 1997.

Hein, Laura, and Akiko Takenaka. "Exhibiting World War II in Japan and the United States Since 1995." *Pacific Historical Review* 76:1 (February 2007): 61–94.

Hersey, John. *Hiroshima.* New York: Vintage Books, 1989. Originally published as an article in the *New Yorker,* August 31, 1946, and in book form by Alfred A. Knopf, 1946.

"History and the Public: What Can We Handle? A Round Table About History After the *Enola Gay* Controversy." *Journal of American History* 82:3 (December 1995): 1029–144.

Honda, Sumihisa, Yoshisada Shibata, Mariko Mine, Yoshihiro Imamura, Masuko Tagawa, Yoshibumi Nakane, and Masao Tomonaga. "Mental Health Conditions Among Atomic Bomb Survivors in Nagasaki." *Psychiatry and Clinical Neurosciences* 56:5 (October 2002): 575–83.

Hook, Glenn D. "Censorship and Reportage of Atomic Damage and Casualties in Hiroshima and Nagasaki." *Bulletin of Concerned Asian Scholars* 23:1 (January–March 1991): 13–25.

Imanaka, Tetsuji, Satoru Endo, Kenichi Tanaka, and Kiyoshi Shizuma. "Gamma-Ray Exposure from Neutron-Induced Radionuclides in Soil in Hiroshima and Nagasaki Based on DS02 Calculations." *Radiation and Environmental Biophysics* 47:3 (July 2008): 331–36.

"Introduction." *Crossroads: A Journal of Nagasaki History and Culture* 3 (Summer 1995). http://www.uwosh.edu/home_pages/faculty_staff/earns/intro3.html.

Introduction to the Radiation Effects Research Foundation. Hiroshima: Radiation Effects Research Foundation, 2007.

Ito, Narihiko, Komura Fujihiko, and Kamata Sadao, eds. *Literature Under the Nuclear Cloud.* Tokyo: Sanyusha Shuppan, 1984.

Iwamatsu, Shigetoshi. "Japanese Responsibility for War Crimes." *Keiei to Keizai* 71:3 (December 1991): 55–92. http://hdl.handle.net/10069/28584.

Iwanaga, Masako, Wan-Ling Hsu, Midori Soda, Yumi Takasaki, Masayuki Tawara, Tatsuro Joh, Tatsuhiko Amenomori, et al. "Risk of Myelodysplastic Syndromes in People Exposed to Ionizing Radiation: A Retrospective Cohort Study of Nagasaki Atomic Bomb Survivors." *Journal of Clinical Oncology* 29:4 (2011): 428–34. doi: 10.1200/JCO.2010.31.3080.

Jacobs, Robert A. "'There Are No Civilians; We Are All at War': Nuclear War Shelter and Survival Narratives During the Early Cold War." *Journal of American Culture* 30:4 (December 2007): 401–16.

Jansen, Marius. *The Making of Modern Japan.* Cambridge, MA: Harvard University Press, 2000.

Japan National Preparatory Committee. *A Call from Hibakusha of Hiroshima and Nagasaki: Proceedings of the International Symposium on the Damage and Aftereffects of the Atomic Bombings of Hiroshima and Nagasaki, July*

21–August 9, 1977: Tokyo, Hiroshima and Nagasaki. Tokyo: Asahi Evening News [for the Editorial Committee of Japan National Preparatory Committee for ISDA], 1978.

A Journey to Nagasaki: A Peace Reader. Translated by Geoff Neill. Nagasaki: Nagasaki Atomic Bomb Testimonial Society, 2005.

Kamata, Sadao. "Nagasaki Writers: The Mission." In *Literature Under the Nuclear Cloud*, edited by Ito Narihiko, Komura Fujihiko, and Kamata Sadao, 47–53. Tokyo: Sanyusha Shuppan, 1984.

Kamata, Sadao, and Stephen Salaff. "The Atomic Bomb and the Citizens of Nagasaki." *Bulletin of Concerned Asian Scholars* 14:2 (1982): 38–50.

Kawamura, Noriko. "Emperor Hirohito and Japan's Decision to Go to War with the United States: Reexamined." *Diplomatic History* 31:1 (2007): 51–79.

Kim, Yoshiharu, Atsuro Tsutsumi, Takashi Izutsu, Noriyuki Kawamura, Takao Miyazaki, and Takehiko Kikkawa. "Persistent Distress After Psychological Exposure to the Nagasaki Atomic Bomb Explosion." *British Journal of Psychiatry* 199 (2011): 411–16.

Kishimoto, Kyoko. "Apologizing for Atrocities: Commemorating the 50th Anniversary of World War II's End in the United States and Japan." *American Studies International* 42:2/3 (June–October 2004): 17–50.

Kitamura, Hiroshi. *Screening Enlightenment: Hollywood and the Cultural Reconstruction of Defeated Japan*. Ithaca, NY: Cornell University Press, 2010.

Knowles, A. "Resilience Among Japanese Atomic Bomb Survivors." *International Nursing Review* 58 (2011): 54–60.

Kohn, Richard H. "History and the Culture Wars: The Case of the Smithsonian Institution's *Enola Gay* Exhibition." *Journal of American History* 82:3 (December 1995): 1036–63.

Krauss, Robert, and Amelia Krauss, eds. *The 509th Remembered: A History of the 509th Composite Group as Told by the Veterans That Dropped the Atomic Bombs on Japan*. Buchanan, MI: 509th Press, 2007.

Kristensen, Hans M. "Japan Under the U.S. Nuclear Umbrella." The Nautilus Institute, July 21, 1999. http://oldsite.nautilus.org/archives/nukepolicy/Nuclear-Umbrella/index.html.

Kristensen, Hans M., and Robert S. Norris. "Worldwide Deployments of Nuclear Weapons, 2014." *Bulletin of the Atomic Scientists* 70:5 (September/October 2014): 96–108. doi: 10.1177/0096340214547619.

Kuznick, Peter J. "Defending the Indefensible: A Meditation on the Life of Hiroshima Pilot Paul Tibbets, Jr." *Asia-Pacific Journal: Japan Focus*, January 22, 2008. http://www.japanfocus.org/-Peter_J_-Kuznick/2642.

Lanouette, William. "Why We Dropped the Bomb." *Civilization* 2:1 (January/February 1995): 28–39.

Lapp, Ralph E. *The Voyage of the Lucky Dragon*. New York: Harper & Brothers, 1958.

Lifton, Robert Jay. *Death in Life: The Survivors of Hiroshima*. New York: Random House, 1968.

Lifton, Robert Jay, and Greg Mitchell. *Hiroshima in America: Fifty Years of Denial.* New York: G. P. Putnam and Sons, 1995.

Lindee, M. Susan. "Atonement: Understanding the No-Treatment Policy of the Atomic Bomb Casualty Commission." *Bulletin of the History of Medicine* 68:3 (Fall 1994): 454–90.

———. "The Repatriation of Atomic Bomb Victim Body Parts to Japan: Natural Objects and Diplomacy." *Osiris* (The History of Science Society) 13 (1998): 376–409.

———. *Suffering Made Real: American Science and the Survivors at Hiroshima.* Chicago: University of Chicago Press, 1994.

Linenthal, Edward Tabor. *Sacred Ground: Americans and Their Battlefields.* 2nd ed. Urbana, IL: University of Illinois Press, 1993.

Linner, Rachelle. *City of Silence: Listening to Hiroshima.* Maryknoll, NY: Orbis Books, 1995.

Lu, David J., ed. *Japan: A Documentary History, Vol. II: The Late Tokugawa Period to the Present.* New York: M. E. Sharp, 1997.

MacArthur, Brian. *Surviving the Sword: Prisoners of the Japanese in the Far East, 1942–45.* New York: Random House, 2005.

Magee, Patricia Delnore, ed. *Victor's War: The World War II Letters of Lt. Col. Victor Delnore.* Paducah, KY: Turner Publishing Co., 2001.

Malik, John. *The Yields of the Hiroshima and Nagasaki Nuclear Explosions.* Los Alamos, NM: Los Alamos National Laboratory, 1985.

Manoff, Robert Karl. "Covering the Bomb: Press and State in the Shadow of Nuclear War." In *War, Peace and the News Media, Proceedings, March 18 and 19, 1983,* edited by David M. Rubin and Marie Cunningham, 197–207. New York: NYU Center for War, Peace and the News Media, 1987.

Martin, Edwin J., and Richard H. Rowland. *Castle Series 1954.* Technical Report DNA6035F. United States Defense Nuclear Agency, April 1982. http://www.dtra.mil/documents/ntpr/historical/T23748.pdf.

McRaney, W., and J. McGahan. *Radiation Dose Reconstruction: U.S. Occupation Forces in Hiroshima and Nagasaki, Japan 1945–1946.* United States Defense Nuclear Agency. August 6, 1980. http://www.dtra.mil/documents/ntpr/relatedpub/DNATR805512F.pdf.

Miller, Merle, and Abe Spitzer. *We Dropped the A-Bomb.* New York: Thomas Y. Crowell, Co., 1946.

Mitchell, Greg. *Atomic Cover-up: Two U.S. Soldiers, Hiroshima & Nagasaki, and the Greatest Movie Never Made.* New York: Sinclair Books, 2011.

Mizuura, Hisayuki, ed. *The Restoration of Urakami Cathedral: A Commemorative Album.* Translated by Edward Hattrick, O.S.A. Nagasaki: Urakami Catholic Church, 1981.

"*Mokusatsu*: One Word, Two Lessons." *National Security Agency Technical Journal* 13:4 (1968): 95–100. National Security Agency Public Information, last modified April 29, 2014. https://www.nsa.gov/public_info/declass/tech _journals.shtml.

Motoharu, Kimura, with John M. Carpenter. "Survey in Nagasaki." In *Living with Nuclei: 50 Years in the Nuclear Age: Memoirs of a Japanese Physicist*, 86–105. Sendai, Japan: Sasaki Printing and Publishing Co., 1993.

Muste, A. J. "Has It Come to This." In *Hiroshima's Shadow: Writings on the Denial of History and the Smithsonian Controversy*, edited by Kai Bird and Lawrence Lifschultz, 309–11. Stony Creek, CT: Pamphleteer's Press, 1998. Originally published in *Not by Might*, Harper & Brothers, 1947.

Nagasaki Peace Guidebook: Handbook of Peace Studies. Nagasaki: Nagasaki Foundation for the Promotion of Peace, 2004.

Nagasaki Speaks: A Record of the Atomic Bombing. Translated by Brian Burke-Gaffney. Nagasaki: Nagasaki International Culture Hall, 1993.

Nakamura, N., M. Iwasaki, C. Miyazawa, M. Akiyama, and A. A. Awa. "Electron-Spin Resonance Measurements of Extracted Teeth Donated by Atomic-Bomb Survivors Correlate Fairly Well with the Lymphocyte Chromosome-Aberration Frequencies for These Same Donors." Originally published in *RERF Update* 6:2 (1994): 6–7. http://www.rerf.or.jp/library/update/rerfupda_e/dosbio/tooth.htm.

Nakamura, Nori. "Genetic Effects of Radiation in Atomic-Bomb Survivors and Their Children: Past, Present and Future." *Journal of Radiation Research* 47:SB (2006): B67–73.

National Resources Defense Council. "Global Nuclear Weapons Stockpiles, 1945–2002." NDRC Archive of Nuclear Data, last revised November 25, 2002. http://www.nrdc.org/nuclear/nudb/datab19.asp.

Neel, James V., and William J. Schull, eds. *The Children of Atomic Bomb Survivors: A Genetic Study*. Washington, DC: National Academy Press, 1991.

Nelson, John. "Historical Momentums at Nagasaki's Suwa Shrine." *Crossroads: A Journal of Nagasaki History and Culture* 2 (Summer 1994): 27–40. http://www.uwosh.edu/home_pages/faculty_staff/earns/suwa.html.

Nichols, Kenneth D. *The Road to Trinity*. New York: William Morrow, 1987.

Nihon Hidankyō. "Message to the World." Proclamation at the Establishment Meeting of Hidankyō, August 10, 1956. Accessed 2013. http://www.ne.jp/asahi/hidankyo/nihon/about/about2-01.html.

Nishimura, Sey. "Medical Censorship in Occupied Japan, 1945–1948." *Pacific Historical Review* 58:1 (1989): 1–21.

———. "Promoting Health in American-Occupied Japan: Resistance to Allied Public Health Measures, 1945–1952." *American Journal of Public Health* 99:8 (August 2009): 1364–75.

Nobile, Philip, ed. *Judgment at the Smithsonian: The Bombing of Hiroshima and Nagasaki*. New York: Marlowe and Company, 1995.

Norimatsu, Satoko. "Hiroshima and Nagasaki at 65: A Reflection." *Asia-Pacific Journal: Japan Focus* (December 27, 2010). http://www.japanfocus.org/-Satoko-NORIMATSU2/3463.

Nornes, Abé Mark. "Suddenly There Was Emptiness." In *Japanese Documentary Film: The Meiji Era Through Hiroshima,* 191–219. Minneapolis, MN: University of Minnesota Press, 2003.

"Nuclear Free Local Authorities in Japan Protest a New Type of Nuclear Weapons Testing by the U.S." *Dispatches from Nagasaki* no. 4. Research Center for Nuclear Weapons Abolition, Nagasaki University, December 25, 2012. http://www.recna.nagasaki-u.ac.jp/en-dispatches/no4/.

Ochiai, Toshiro. "Participation in the First Special Session of the United Nations General Assembly on Disarmament: Recollections of a Student Representative." Presentation at the International Network of Universities (INU) Student Seminar on Global Citizenship: What Is a Global Citizen? Hiroshima University, August 8, 2008. http://ir.lib.hiroshima-u.ac.jp/en/00025548.

O'Donnell, Joe. "A Straight Path Through Hell." *American Heritage Magazine* 56:3 (June–July 2005): 48.

Ohta, Yasuyuki, Mariko Mine, Masako Wakasugi, Etsuko Yoshimine, Yachiyo Himuro, Megumi Yoneda, Sayuri Yamaguchi, Akemi Mikita, and Tomoko Morikawa. "Psychological Effect of the Nagasaki Atomic Bombing on Survivors After Half a Century." *Psychiatry and Clinical Neurosciences* 54 (2000): 97–103.

Okuizumi, Eizaburō, ed. *User's Guide to the Gordon W. Prange Collection: Part I: Microform Edition of Censored Periodicals, 1945–1949.* Tokyo: Yūshōdō Booksellers, 1982.

Okuyama, Michiaki. "Religious Responses to the Atomic Bomb in Nagasaki." *Bulletin* [Nanzan Institute for Religion and Culture] 37 (2013): 64–76.

Olivi, Fred J., with William R. Watson Jr. *Decision at Nagasaki: The Mission That Almost Failed.* Self-published, 1999.

Oughterson, Ashley W., George V. LeRoy, Averill A. Leibow, E. Cuyler Hammond, Henry L. Barnett, Jack D. Rosenbaum, and B. Aubrey Schneider. *Medical Effects of Atomic Bombs: The Report of the Joint Commission for the Investigation of the Effects of the Atomic Bomb in Japan.* 6 vols. Oak Ridge, TN: U.S. Atomic Energy Commission Technical Information Service, 1951. Volumes and supplemental material housed at the Otis Historical Archives, National Museum of Health and Medicine, Silver Spring, MD.

Oughterson, Ashley W., and Shields Warren, eds. *Medical Effects of the Atomic Bomb in Japan.* New York: McGraw-Hill, 1956.

Public Papers of the Presidents of the United States: Harry S. Truman, 1945–1953. Washington, DC: U.S. Government Printing Office, 1966. http://www.trumanlibrary.org/publicpapers/.

Putnam, Frank W. "The Atomic Bomb Casualty Commission in Retrospect." *Proceedings of the National Academy of Sciences, USA* 95:10 (May 1998): 5426–31.

Radiation Effects Research Foundation: A Brief Description. Hiroshima: Radiation Effects Research Foundation, 2008.

Record, Jeffrey. *Japan's Decision for War in 1941: Some Enduring Lessons.* Strategic Studies Institute, U.S. Army War College, February 2009. http://www.StrategicStudiesInstitute.army.mil/.

Records of the Nagasaki Atomic Bombing. Nagasaki: Nagasaki Foundation for the Promotion of Peace, 2004.

Records of the Nagasaki Atomic Bombing and Wartime Damage. Tentative publication of the English translation of *Nagasaki genbaku sensaishi,* vol. 1. Nagasaki: Nagasaki National Peace Memorial Hall for the Atomic Bomb Victims, March 2011. http://www.peace-nagasaki.go.jp/sensaishi/itibu.html.

Reischauer, Edwin O. *Japan: The Story of a Nation.* Tokyo: Charles E. Tuttle Company, 1981.

Report on the Problem of the Hibakusha. Japan Federation of Bar Associations. July 1977: 15–50. Copy provided by the Nagasaki Atomic Bomb Museum Library.

Rhodes, Richard. *The Making of the Atomic Bomb.* New York: Simon & Schuster, 1986.

The Road to the Abolition of Nuclear Weapons. Tokyo: Asahi Shimbun, 1999. http://www.asahi.com/hibakusha/english/shimen/book/.

Roeder, George H., Jr. "Making Things Visible: Learning from the Censors." In *Living with the Bomb: American and Japanese Cultural Conflicts in the Nuclear Age,* edited by Laura Hein and Mark Selden, 73–99. New York: M. E. Sharpe, 1997.

Roesch, William C., ed. *U.S.-Japan Joint Reassessment of Atomic Bomb Dosimetry in Hiroshima and Nagasaki: Dosimetry System 1986.* Hiroshima: Radiation Effects Research Foundation, 1987. http://www.rerf.jp/library/archives_e/scids.html.

Salaff, Stephen. "Medical Care for the Atomic Bomb Victims in the United States." *Bulletin of Concerned Asian Scholars* 12:1 (January–March 1980): 69–71.

Schubert, Jack, and Ralph E. Lapp. *Radiation: What It Is and How It Affects You.* New York: Viking Press, 1957.

Schull, William J. *Song Among the Ruins: A Lyrical Account of an American Scientist's Sojourn in Japan After the Atomic Bomb.* Cambridge: Harvard University Press, 1990.

Sherry, Michael S. "Patriotic Orthodoxy and U.S. Decline." *Bulletin of Concerned Asian Scholars* 27:2 (April–June 1995): 19–25.

———. *The Rise of American Air Power: The Creation of Armageddon.* New Haven, CT: Yale University Press, 1987.

Sherwin, Martin J. "Memory, Myth and History." In *Hiroshima's Shadow: Writings on the Denial of History and the Smithsonian Controversy,* edited by Kai Bird and Lawrence Lifschultz, 343–54. Stony Creek, CT: Pamphleteer's Press, 1998.

———. *A World Destroyed: Hiroshima and Its Legacies.* 3rd ed. Palo Alto, CA: Stanford University Press, 2003.

Silberner, Joanne. "Psychological A-Bomb Wounds." *Science News* 120 (November 7, 1981): 296–98.

Smith, Charles R. "Securing the Surrender: Marines in the Occupation of Japan." Marines in World War II Commemorative Series, 1997. National Park Service, Marine Corps Historical Center. http://www.nps.gov/ parkhistory/online_books/npswapa/extContent/usmc/pcn-190-003143-00/ index.htm.

Sodei, Rinjiro. *Were We the Enemy? American Survivors of Hiroshima.* Boulder, CO: Westview Press, 1998.

Stimson, Henry L. "The Decision to Use the Atomic Bomb." *Harper's Magazine* 194:1161 (February 1947): 96–107.

Sweeney, Charles W., James A. Antonucci, and Marion K. Antonucci. *War's End: An Eyewitness Account of America's Last Atomic Mission.* New York: Avon Books, 1997.

Tajima, Eizo. "The Dawn of Radiation Effects Research." *RERF Update* 5:3 (Autumn 1993): 7–8.

Takahashi, Shinji. "The *Hibakusha:* The Atomic Bomb Survivors and Their Appeals." In *Appeals from Nagasaki: On the Occasion of SSD-II and Related Events,* edited by Shinji Takahashi, 29–45. Nagasaki: Nagasaki Association for Research and Dissemination of Hibakushas' Problems, 1991.

———. "Listening to the Wishes of the Dead: In the Case of Dr. Nagai Takashi." Translated by Brian Burke-Gaffney. *Crossroads: A Journal of Nagasaki History and Culture* 5 (Autumn 1997): 23–32. http://www .uwosh.edu/home_pages/faculty_staff/earns/takahash.html.

Toland, John. *The Rising Sun: The Decline and Fall of the Japanese Empire, 1936–1945.* New York: Modern Library, 2003.

Tong, Kurt W. "Korea's Forgotten Atomic Bomb Victims." *Bulletin of Concerned Asian Scholars* 23:1 (1991): 31–37.

United States Army Corps of Engineers. Manhattan District. *The Atomic Bombings of Hiroshima and Nagasaki.* Washington, DC: U.S. Government Printing Office, 1946. Reprint, Booksurge Classics, Title No. 083, 2003.

United States Defense Threat Reduction Agency. "Fact Sheet: Hiroshima and Nagasaki Occupation Forces." Nuclear Test Personnel Review Program, September 2007. Updated 2014. http://www.dtra.mil/SpecialFocus/NTPR/ NTPRFactSheet.aspx.

United States Department of the Army. *Reports of General MacArthur: MacArthur in Japan: The Occupation: The Military Phase.* vol. 1 Supp. Washington, DC: U.S. Department of the Army, 1966. Reprinted by the U.S. Army Center for Military History, 1994. Last updated December 11, 2006. http://www.history.army.mil/books/wwii/MacArthur%20Reports/ MacArthurR.htm.

United States Strategic Bombing Survey. *Summary Report: Pacific War.* USSBS report no. 1, Office of the Chairman. Washington, DC: U.S. Government Printing Office, 1946.

———. *Japan's Struggle to End the War.* USSBS report no. 2, Office of the Chairman. Washington, DC: U.S. Government Printing Office, 1946.

———. *The Effects of Atomic Bombs on Hiroshima and Nagasaki.* USSBS report no. 3, Office of the Chairman. Washington, DC: U.S. Government Printing Office, 1946.

———. *Field Report Covering Air-Raid Protection and Allied Subjects in Nagasaki, Japan.* USSBS report no. 5, Civil Defense Division. Washington, DC: U.S. Government Printing Office, 1947.

———. *The Effects of Atomic Bombs on Health and Medical Services in Hiroshima and Nagasaki.* USSBS report no. 13, Medical Division. Washington, DC: U.S. Government Printing Office, 1947.

———. *The Effects of Strategic Bombing on Japanese Morale.* USSBS report no. 14, Morale Division. Washington, DC: U.S. Government Printing Office, 1947.

———. *Effects of Air Attack on the City of Nagasaki.* USSBS report no. 59, Urban Areas Division. Washington, DC: U.S. Government Printing Office, 1947.

———. *Effects of the Atomic Bomb on Nagasaki, Japan.* Vols. 1–3. USSBS report no. 93, Physical Damage Division. Washington DC: U.S. Government Printing Office, 1947.

Utsumi, Hirofumi. "Nuclear Images and National Self-Portraits: Japanese Illustrated Magazine *Asahi Graph*, 1945–1965." *Kansei gakuin daigaku sentan shakai kenkyūjo kiyō* [Annual Review of the Institute for Advanced Social Research, Kwansei Gakuin University] 5 (March 2011): 1–29. http://hdl.handle.net/10236/7245.

Walker, J. Samuel. "Historiographical Essay: Recent Literature on Truman's Atomic Bomb Decision: A Search for Middle Ground." *Diplomatic History* 29:2 (April 2005): 311–34.

———. *Permissible Dose: A History of Radiation Protection in the Twentieth Century.* Berkeley: University of California Press, 2000.

Wallace, Mike. "The Battle of the *Enola Gay*." In *Hiroshima's Shadow: Writings on the Denial of History and the Smithsonian Controversy,* edited by Kai Bird and Lawrence Lifschultz, 317–42. Stony Creek, CT: Pamphleteer's Press, 1998.

Warren, Stafford L. "The Role of Radiology in the Development of the Atomic Bomb." In *Radiology in World War II (Medical Department, United States Army),* edited by Leonard D. Heaton et al., 831–921. Washington DC: Office of the Surgeon General (Army), 1966. Accessed 2014. http://oai.dtic.mil/oai/oai?&verb=getRecord&metadataPrefix=html&identifier=ADA286759.

Weller, George. *First into Nagasaki: The Censored Eyewitness Dispatches on Post-Atomic Japan and Its Prisoners of War.* Edited by Anthony Weller. New York: Crown Publishers, 2006.

Wittner, Lawrence S. *The Struggle Against the Bomb.* 3 vols. Palo Alto, CA: Stanford University Press, 1993–2003.

———. "Resisting Nuclear Terror: Japanese and American Anti-nuclear Movements Since 1945." In *War and State Terrorism: The United States, Japan, and the Asia-Pacific in the Long Twentieth Century,* edited by Mark Selden and Alvin Y. So, 251–76. Lanham, MD: Rowman & Littlefield Publishers, 2004.

Yamashita, Samuel Hideo. *Leaves from an Autumn of Emergencies: Selections from the Wartime Diaries of Ordinary Japanese.* Honolulu: University of Hawaii Press, 2005.

Yamazaki, James N., with Louis B. Fleming. *Children of the Atomic Bomb: An American Physician's Memoir of Nagasaki, Hiroshima, and the Marshall Islands.* Durham, NC: Duke University Press, 1995.

Yavenditti, Michael J. "The American People and the Use of Atomic Bombs on Japan: The 1940s." *Historian* 36:2 (February 1974): 224–47.

———. "John Hersey and the American Conscience: The Reception of 'Hiroshima.'" *Pacific Historical Review* 43:1 (February 1974): 24–49.

Young, Robert W., and George D. Kerr, eds. *Reassessment of the Atomic Bomb Radiation Dosimetry for Hiroshima and Nagasaki: Dosimetry System 2002.* Hiroshima: Radiation Effects Research Foundation, 2005. http://www.rerf.jp/library/archives_e/scids.html.

Zinn, Howard. *The Bomb.* San Francisco, CA: City Light Books, 2010.

INDEX

Page numbers in *italics* indicate photographs and illustrations.